Governing Uganda

British Colonial Rule and its Legacy

Gardner Thompson

Fountain Publishers

Fountain Publishers Ltd
P.O. Box 488
Kampala
E-mail: fountain@starcom.co.ug
Website: www.fountainpublishers.co.ug

ISBN 9970 02 394 2

Cover photographs
Top, left to right: Governor Sir Walter Coutts with the Kabaka on the Governor's
last visit to Bulange in 1963; a warden receives the colonial service prison medal
(The New Vision); Sir John Hathorn Hall, Governor 1944 to 1952. *Below:* Victorious
supporters of the Uganda National Congress celebrate their 1959 election victory,
led by I.K. Musaazi and Dr Kununka. (Bailey's African Photo Archives).

Typesetting: Ruth Spriggs
Cover design: Tom Tibaijuka

To
Elizabeth
and
Edward

Contents

Acknowledgements

My interest in Africa's colonial history was first developed at Cambridge by Eric Stokes. As an undergraduate there, I gained much from the insights of Norman Stone. Later, as an MA student, at the School of Oriental and African Studies, London, I found the teaching of Richard Rathbone particularly stimulating. After registering thereafter at the Institute of Commonwealth Studies as a part-time PhD student, I benefited greatly from the guidance and encouragement of my supervisor, Michael Twaddle. My wife, Elizabeth, has supported both that project and subsequent research and writing unreservedly, and also applied her own expertise on the colonial period in Africa's history to a scrutiny of the draft text for this book. She has accepted dislocation to family life with great understanding and patience.

I would like to thank all who have given me assistance over these years: staff at Rhodes House in Oxford, at the public Record Office in Kew, and at the British Library in Colindale. Librarians at SOAS and the ICS, and in the libraries of the Foreign and Commonwealth Office and the Royal Commonwealth Society were also most helpful. I am grateful, more recently, to those who provided access to files – including those 'partially destroyed by termites' – in the Uganda National Archive in Entebbe. I must also acknowledge the support of the Governors of Dulwich College who have granted me two sabbaticals to enable me to pursue my research and writing, in England and in Uganda too.

I would also like to thank one generation of bright students at the Aga Khan Secondary School in Kampala and many generations more at Dulwich, for their part in sustaining my historical interests.

Finally, I am grateful to London University's Thornley Fund for its support.

I am indeed indebted to all the above, and more. Nonetheless, I alone am responsible for this study. It is my own work, so any shortcomings are mine alone.

Gardner Thompson
Dulwich, London, February 2003

Preface

History has two chief characteristics: continuity, rather than change, is its hallmark; and such changes as do take place are generally not the intended products of famous men but rather the work of human agents both innumerable and anonymous.

Returning to Uganda in 1998 – twenty-six years after teaching in Kampala, and eight years after completing a doctoral thesis on the limits of British rule in the protectorate during the Second World War – I was struck by how similar, how recognisable, were the issues facing Yoweri Museveni's government. From questions concerning external relations, even the long-term territorial definition of the country, through matters of economic viability, social cohesiveness and the future of representative government, to more specific problems like the status of Buganda (even, title to land within that region), there appeared to be a perennial quality, a durability, about the challenge of 'governing Uganda'. Many of these issues were not so much *caused* by colonial rule, in any crude sense, as confronted by Uganda's British rulers ... without being resolved. They thus represent continuities. Nor were the changes which the country underwent during those three generations – let alone the colonial legacy in 1962 – quite what anyone in London or Entebbe intended as the outcome of colonial rule.

What follows is a history which focuses on 'governing' and on the origins of issues such as those mentioned above. It is not essentially a tale of heroes and villains, though we do encounter individuals variously perceived as both: men for example like Governor Hall and, by contrast, Ignatius Musazi – irritant of colonial administrators in the middle of the twentieth century, yet a particular focus of veneration on Heroes Day at the end of it. This study is intended above all as a kind of treatise which reveals something of the reality, ignoble perhaps yet not irredeemable, of the colonial period, and which may interest any who hope to see Uganda governed well in the future.

Above: Administrative boundaries before and at independence, 1962.
Below: Uganda and its neighbouring countries today.

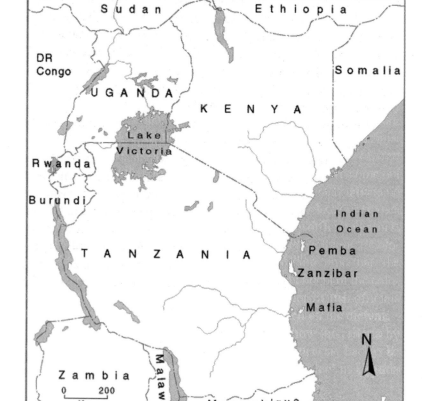

1
Introduction

Governing Uganda is an essay on British colonial rule; it is an investigation of probably the most revealing (if until now perhaps the most neglected) single decade in Uganda's colonial history; and it is a reappraisal of the long-term significance of the whole colonial period, for Uganda after 1962.

The study begins, in the next chapter, with a critical response to ways in which Uganda's experience of British colonial rule has frequently been represented – or rather, misrepresented – in recent years. It ends, in Chapter 15, with a re-examination of the flawed colonial legacy; and, in a postscript, with a consideration of some remarkable parallels between the late colonial period and, subsequently, Uganda at the start of the twenty-first century. In between, it offers, within a chronological framework, a fresh analysis of British power in the territory: the *exercise* of that power, and the *limits* of that power. It seeks to investigate the claim of a governor such as John Hall (1944-1952), who is quoted as saying 'one had a good deal of power really' (Gartrell 1979: 41). It attempts to reconsider, up to a point, the nature of power in *any* state – including, and perhaps especially, contemporary Uganda. It places governing Uganda, today, in its historical perspective.

There is no attempt here to be comprehensive in time and space: this is not a text which ranges evenly over every phase within the colonial period and every location within the British protectorate. Rather, it is a sustained exploration of central themes and essential characteristics in the colonial relationship between rulers and ruled – an understanding of which alone can make *sense* of this momentous

1

episode in Uganda's history. It does take as its overall scope the whole period of the protectorate (1894 to 1962); but in order to identify the eventual colonial legacy it deliberately focuses, in its central section, on 'governing Uganda' during the previously disregarded but critical decade of the 1940s.

Why are the 1940s of any distinct interest – or relevance – sixty years on? Uganda's involvement in the Second World War during the first half of that decade had disturbing consequences and, in the strategic heart of the protectorate at least, a turbulent aftermath – hence the greater attention given to Buganda than to some other provinces in parts of the text which follows. So critical indeed was that decade that one may propose a simplified periodisation of British colonial rule in Uganda: until 1939, British officials had only to administer; from 1940, they had also to try to exploit. The primary function of colonial government changed. A war which began (and in some respects remained) 'phoney' in Uganda nevertheless prompted the British to attempt something like the 'total' war being waged in Britain and elsewhere. Escalating tensions, in Buganda especially, and the widespread post-war disturbances of 1945 and 1949, illustrated the shortcomings of British officialdom in pursuit of that goal and in handling its unforeseen consequences; and they confirmed that henceforth the protectorate must react to a newly explicit and overwhelmingly African agenda. When we put the 1950s, too, under our spotlight, we will find a lame-duck colonialism – in all, a dozen years of ever accelerating transition towards political independence.

There was nothing new, however, about 'an African agenda'. From the arrival of the first foreign explorers, missionaries, soldiers, traders and officials, Africans and Europeans had *acted on each other*. Africans were never passive observers of their own fate: every dimension and detail in the emergent relationship between 'ruler' and 'ruled' had to be forged and crystallised, through the human agency of the colonised as well as the colonisers. Europeans had choices, which were often circumscribed; meanwhile Africans, too, often had choices to make – and there were innumerable points on the spectrum of considered response to the British presence, between outright opposition and wholehearted support. In what was at first a strange, uninvited, and alarming new context, African individuals and groups had goals of their own to pursue and found means of pursuing them. New, in the later 1940s and the 1950s, was the unmistakable visibility of this abiding truth and the primacy of African aspiration and demand over all other pressures on an increasingly perplexed colonial state.

After British colonial rule ended in 1962, the state in Uganda appeared to collapse: political power was seen to grow out of the barrel of a gun. But if we are to seek the origins of the notorious fragility of the state in Uganda in those years, we must look well beyond the regimes of Idi Amin and Milton Obote. We must return to the colonial period, and we must look beyond even the period of de-colonisation. Our subject is thus the British colonial state, not merely in terms of its transmission of responsibility at the end of empire, but during its heyday. Through this perspective we will observe not so much a change, the *collapse* of state power, as a continuity – the *limits* of state power in Uganda.

Karl Popper remarked that 'history is characterised by its interest in actual, singular, or specific events, rather than in laws or generalisations' (Popper 1957: 143). This is a study of one colonial state, largely concentrating on one period of its existence. And it seeks to ground its analysis in the marshalling and interpretation of *specific* evidence. Yet a study of Uganda during the Second World War and after – a study of colonialism in crisis – may contribute to a wider theoretical debate on the nature of British colonialism in Africa. Uganda perhaps has an advantage here precisely because, in the words of one historian of Uganda, its 'special characteristic is that it has no very special characteristic' (Wrigley 1959: v).

The central subject of this study is the colonial state. The argument at its centre is that the war period exposed the essential and abiding boundaries of British power. Before the end of the 1930s, these had been largely latent. But limitations were clearly exposed once a new global context made unprecedented demands. A valuable framework for a reappraisal of British colonial power in Uganda was provided by John Lonsdale and Bruce Berman when, in a study of neighbouring Kenya, they stressed the essentially 'dual character' of the colonial state (Lonsdale and Berman 1979: 487-505). In their terms, we may say that the British colonial state in Uganda proved ill equipped during the Second World War to serve either as a 'subordinate agent' of the metropolis or as a 'local factor of cohesion' within the protectorate itself.

What was the British colonial state in Uganda for? Its purpose and significance cannot be reduced to a single catch phrase. It was, first, the agency of a foreign power, Britain. As such it had first to secure the territory and then to incorporate it into the world economy and promote production, and consumption, to ensure the protectorate's own financial viability. It was, secondly, an instrument locally for the maintenance of a political order. It had administrative, judicial and, if needed, coercive power – although for the most part police and troops were a potential rather than a real presence and their actual use, rare indeed after the initial phase of acquisition and pacification, was regarded as an admission of administrative failure. Thirdly, here as in Kenya, the colonial state had to 'cope with the contradictions'– arising from its dual character, and from having to act as a referee in perennial competition between various groups defined by interest, class, or race. But the colonial state was more than an instrument in the service of imperial expectations or an arena for contestants in the processes of accumulation and control of resources. It was, fourthly, also itself an actor in the play, its official mind, deliberations and responses having their own significance.

The record of British rule in Uganda, at any stage, can only be evaluated by reference to the context in which it found itself. Very seldom indeed was it able to operate freely. It had to mediate between imperial expectations and local realities, in an internal context that was constantly in flux. Indeed its own impact induced change initially and it continued to do so: ironically, colonial rule was itself eventually to undermine some of the collaborative political relationships on which it was first established. There were dramatic changes in the external context too: world war, depression, world war. Each brought new problems which required choice and decision on the part of local British officials. Relationships between state and society, meanwhile, remained shallow-rooted. The colonial state was an agent but it was never a free agent; and colonial rule – governing Uganda – entailed a constant search for a lasting formula that was never found.

Before 1939, the colonial state was favoured by the modesty of its goals and by relatively co-operative African societies. The war changed all this. The wider world was in many respects transformed. Simultaneously, Uganda's immediate East African location assumed new significance, as the protectorate's dependence on its neighbours, Kenya and Ruanda-Urundi, was further highlighted and underlined. Yet limits to the extent of colonial exploitation and mobilisation of materials, money and men in Uganda from 1940 were primarily set by indigenous society. To a large extent, African farmers chose which crops to grow (and labourers chose whether and where to work); political constraints restricted the range of possible new taxation measures; and many who would not willingly join the army succeeded in avoiding military service. The administration's new, wartime, agenda could not be fully carried out.

The war period disclosed the nature of the British colonial power itself. Power is usually best understood as a *relationship* between parties or agents. And it is not one simply of master and servant, ruler and ruled, but a relationship of interdependence – in which appearances of initiative and authority can be deceptive. In Uganda, there existed a relationship between a British authority and a cluster of African peoples. It may have appeared that the governor in Entebbe and his officials possessed and dispensed absolute power over their subjects. Yet this was an illusion. The reality was that the colonial state was severely limited in what it could impose against the will of the territory's inhabitants. It had to have acquiescence, if not co-operation. Colonialism required consent.

The concept of 'collaboration' requires here an application far beyond that which historians have tended to employ. First, 'collaboration' does not have to be a pejorative term. It can be used (and here, is) to describe practical if calculating co-operation, the recognition and pooling of shared interests – free of any moral misgivings regarding any party involved. Secondly, and more specifically, it has been argued that the collaboration which was fundamental to the establishment and initial functioning of a colonial state was primarily *political*, hingeing on relationships between colonial officials and indigenous elites (Robinson 1972: 141). This analysis can still be applied to Uganda, and especially Buganda, its main province, at the start of the century and after. But it misleadingly omits peasant cultivators – let alone labourers in towns and on plantations and in mines – from the arrangements. Furthermore, the economic significance of peasant farmers has tended to be too narrowly defined. Thus Mahmood Mamdani, for example, has stressed that the primary function of Ugandan peasants was that of production (Mamdani 1976: 41). But we need to recognise that the peasant as consumer was just as important as the peasant as producer. For much of the colonial period, the peasant produced *in order to* consume the manufactured goods that were imported into Uganda. No consumption, no production: that was the principal character of collaborative *economic* relationships in Uganda by the time of the onset of the Second World War. Ultimately it was the peasant – as consumer –and not the British official as representative of the metropolitan bourgeoisie, on whose interests the colonial economy rested. It is symbolic that, during the Second World War, the Uganda Protectorate's finances would rely more on taxes levied on goods imported for Africans' consumption than on poll taxes paid from the proceeds of their production.

By the 1930s there was a general toleration, even positive acceptance, of British hegemony in Uganda, at two levels. Politically, British officials worked closely with indigenous African elites, notably in Buganda. Economically, the British colonial state gained far wider acceptance through its ability to introduce into the territory goods from outside which made the efforts of Ugandan farmers and labourers more worthwhile. Its role was no longer, as it had been earlier, to persuade if not coerce peasant farmers to produce, but to provide for them as consumers. It had itself become dependent on the continuation of numerous, anonymous Africans' calculating participation in this colonial economic relationship. These levels were of course not wholly distinct. Indeed, we may echo Berman's depiction of 'the complex but often shrouded underworld of collaboration, negotiation (and conflict) at local levels that intimately tied the colonial state to African society *and significantly constrained its power'* (Berman 1998: 314. My italics).

The Second World War forms a turning point in Uganda's history in the qualified sense that both these levels of collaboration – political and economic – stuttered and all but collapsed. A British protectorate administration seriously reduced in manpower proved unable to wage 'total war'. Specifically, it could not maintain the inward flow of goods in quantities and at prices which the mass of producers and consumers demanded. Africans in Uganda suffered the severe economic repercussions of world war, notably shortages and inflation. In this sense, the British protectorate could not 'protect'. In particular, British control of Buganda, the most central and important province, could no longer be guaranteed. Post-war disturbances in 1945 were succeeded by disturbances on an even larger scale in 1949. By the end of the decade, if not already by the end of the war in 1945, British colonial authority had lost much of its legitimacy and initiative. The colonial state before the Second World War had leaned towards the interests of expatriate Europeans and Indians. By the end of the war, it was Africans – those who had stayed at home as much as those who had gone away on war service – who were setting the pace and direction of change. They were not only making demands (notably for access to economic opportunities hitherto blocked by Indians) but threatening at times to make the territory, especially Buganda, ungovernable.

Their experience of the early 1940s thus demonstrates that the British struggled to mobilise resources or govern in any 'absolutist' sense: that they could *administer* far more easily than they could *exploit*. Though officials might delay the emergence of alternative political forces, they could not fully carry into effect widely unpopular measures of their own. Up until the Second World War, as in pre-revolutionary Russia, it may be said of the colonial state that 'like other autocracies its great strength was not that it governed harshly but that it governed less' (Stone 1975: 214). But during the war it had to try to govern more, in the course of mobilising men, money and materials in Uganda for the British war effort. Its efforts were not fruitless, but they were frustrated and inadequate. Inadequate, too, was its response to the disturbances of 1945. This was hardly absolute rule. No wonder that by then Hall was attracted to Stalinism, for Stalinism at that time appeared so much more capable of getting things done (Worthington 1946: Foreword).

The Second World War and its immediate aftermath laid bare the basic truth about the colonial state in Uganda, and revealed the conditions of African collaboration and acquiescence on which alone it could hope for a long-term future. British officials at the time however did not see things so clearly. Indeed, another limitation of British colonial power in Uganda was its poverty of imagination, knowledge and understanding. Lessons were not learned, and necessary adjustments were not made. In this particular sense, the Second World War changed little. When British governors up to and including John Hall claimed to be wielding 'a good deal of power' over their subjects, they were largely deluding themselves. At times, certainly, affairs proceeded as the governors wished – because there was a tolerance or willingness on the part of African society that they should so proceed. At other times, however, governors met frustration and failure – because tolerance and willingness were withdrawn. Hall himself presided over an historic loss of colonial authority in Uganda at the end of the Second World War.

The power which he claimed to have exercised evaporated just ten years after Hall left Uganda, for in 1962 the British Protectorate came to an end. Its legacy remains, and it remains intriguing. Forty years after independence, the colonial period no longer looks as fundamental a discontinuity in the history of Africa as it might once have done. How colonial rule affected African society has now to be weighed against *how African society affected colonial rule*. Moreover, a closer analysis of this British experience in 'governing Uganda' will help us in some measure to understand why and how subsequent African political leaders in the territory have found it so difficult to sustain an orderly civilian administration, enjoying 'a good deal of power', in the years since then.

2

The British Colonial State in Uganda: Myth and Reality

Overview

Having arrived in East Africa uninvited, the British defined a territory without regard for either history or rationality; and established a regime in Uganda without regard for the wishes of the Africans who lived there, largely against their will. Where they needed to, the British imposed their own will by force initially; and they subsequently used the coercive power of the state when they felt threatened by popular protest. British policies were designed from the outset to achieve their own, metropolitan, goals; and British colonial rule came to provide a new arena in which foreign agents of commerce could shape the economy of Uganda in their own interests. Unfree politically, and unequal participants in the local and global economies, even the most favoured Africans in Uganda found themselves forming the lowest (yet most numerous) tier of a racially stratified society, in which preferential treatment for Indian immigrants helped to sustain domination by Europeans. Meanwhile, ethnic diversities were reinforced rather than diminished; and religious rivalries arising from the earliest period of contact – part of a far wider imported, alien, cultural hegemony – further held back any growth of national cohesion. By the time they formally withdrew in 1962, for three generations the British had been wrenching 'Uganda' from its own organic African evolution, before leaving it ill-equipped to prosper in the political and economic world order of the late twentieth century.

So much is incontestable; and it does not cast British colonial rule in a favourable light. But such a truth is not the whole truth. It needs to be appropriately augmented and enriched; and this chapter

9

looks at ways in which we should proceed. We will consider – and reject – the way in which some recent writers have already proceeded by so exaggerating elements of the above overview that their representations have lost touch with its original credibility.[1] Their treatment of the subject – which we shall tackle shortly – has been so selectively, exclusively and insistently negative that what emerges from their work is more myth than history. The remorseless pursuit of a number of charges which together present British rule as nothing other than wickedly oppressive and cynically exploitative does little to enhance our understanding, and it must be challenged.

At the same time, and with such a distorted portrayal in mind, we ought to acknowledge that the British colonial state was probably far less capable and effective – in short, far less powerful – than either its critics, old and new, or its erstwhile admirers would have us believe. In accepting the limits of its competence – evidence of which pervades this study – we may better recognise that it simply could not have been the tyranny its current assailants claim that it was. All governments make demands, notably fiscal demands, of their subjects. But, having no alternative, the British governed Uganda relatively lightly for the most part; and governed in *conjunction* with, rather than in constant *conflict* with, numerous elements in the African societies over whom they ruled.

If we are properly to understand the colonial state – and perhaps thereby learn something of interest and value in relation to its post-colonial successor state today – it deserves to be investigated with a level head and an open mind, as free as possible of prejudice and partisanship. Such a study requires less devotion to theoretical baggage that should have been jettisoned – application of hand-me-down general theories of colonialism, class struggle, underdevelopment, or whatever, which can serve as a substitute for independent thought – and more diligent attention to, and evaluation of, detailed evidence of the particular case.

One of our tasks is to acknowledge – both intellectually and imaginatively – the intentions of the colonial administration and the workings of 'the official mind' of the British, as far as we can. In so doing we should seek no more to excuse than to blame. But like the

history of any subject, in any time and in any place, the British colonial state in Uganda must be studied in its own right and in its own
material and moral context, and not merely as the preparation for, or
the background to, what came afterwards (known to us now, but not
knowable then). After all, we are studying here not a crude and static
impersonal structure, but a complex human process over time. As
Jean-Francois Bayart has written, in a generalisation that serves us
well, 'although brief, colonization went through substantial changes
... and since they were clearly a result of history, the forms of subjection ... on the African continent were riddled with fractures' (Bayart
1993: 12,13). We must recognise both change and fracture; and the
range of *options* (albeit often narrow) facing both rulers and ruled.
Pre-determined selectivity and off-the-peg theorisation may simplify,
but they do not inform or enlighten. The past is so much more complicated than is sometimes acknowledged.

What made possible the exercise of British power?
In looking afresh at British colonial rule in Uganda we may ask at
the outset: what enabled the British colonial state to exercise such power
as it did? It clearly had some strengths. First among these was the availability of sufficient force. 'It is only by stressing the centrality of force
that we can evaluate the real drama of the state's origins' (Hoffman
1995: 5). *In extremis* the British could resort to coercion (as they did for
example in Buganda – its most favoured province, ironically – in 1945
and 1949, albeit to little effect). As it happened, however, the perennial
strength of the colonial state lay, as was well understood by its personnel, in its *not* doing so. That it in fact seldom had to resort to force can
be attributed to particular advantages which it enjoyed. Its limited ambition was one. Moreover, it did not need to be essentially a military
entity: its borders and territorial integrity were not threatened by its
neighbours (after all, other territories within the British Empire lay to
the north, the east and the south, while Belgian governments to the west
and south-west presented no menace); and once the protectorate was
established there was seldom if ever a significant internal challenge to
British rule from within.

This is largely because, secondly, the British set out from the start to seek collaboration – to win acquiescence if not consent – and they found the means to do so. The term 'collaboration' is used here, once again, not in the pejorative sense it has when applied to the relations of Vichy France with Nazi Germany, but in the value-free pragmatic sense already defined in this book.[2] The remarkable success of the British in this area owed much to two features of their administration: the opportunities for material advancement which they introduced and made available for many of their African subjects; and in turn, and concurrently, the relatively few demands which they made on them. In large measure, this state resembled Adam Smith's preferred model. He had written – without having European colonial expansion in mind – 'Little else is requisite to carry a state to the highest degree of opulence ... but peace, easy taxes and a tolerable administration of justice' (Hall and Ikenberry 1989: 4). This may not be a complete definition of British rule in Uganda – taxes were never less than perennially burdensome – but it is an approximation which in, say, the inter-war period still catches its essence. We have been reminded that this regime was an 'administration' rather than a 'government': policy-making 'government' resided in London (Kabwegyere 1974: 171). The point to be stressed, however, is that for several decades British officials in Uganda had such a limited ambition that they sought only to administer, and not (in anything like the fullest sense) to explore the colonial state's potential to exploit.

Thirdly, to some extent and for some time at least, being a foreign, alien, power gave the British a positive advantage. At the outset they enjoyed a certain mystique associated with a Western European culture and technology as confident and dominant in relation to that of equatorial Africa as the Roman culture had once been in relation to that of the British Isles, centuries before. Indeed, Roman imperialism was not as different in kind from British as their reputations in general would imply. And this mystique, allied to those minimal ambitions, enabled the British (to a degree) to become an acceptable suzerain by appearing disinterested, Olympian, above African politics – notwithstanding their usual prejudice in favour of the kingdom of Buganda. As Dan Mudoola wrote, 'the colonial power

... established sufficient legitimacy to enable it to act as arbiter among conflicting interest groups' (Mudoola 1993: 6). In some important respects the period of the Second World War provided an exception to this picture. Then the British had a new and different agenda: they did seek fully to mobilise resources, and the state did then assume a new kind of military purpose. But the fact remains that this was indeed the exception (however revealing of the limits of British power it proved to be, as we shall see) and moreover, in the military dimension at least, a temporary one.

What limited the exercise of British power?

Without advantages and qualities such as those identified above, the survival of the British colonial state in Uganda would have been called into question long before the 1950s. But these advantages were almost outweighed by inherent weaknesses and objective obstacles to effective government which combined to limit severely the competence and potential of British rule. This is a complex, even at times contradictory, picture, in which even some of the positive qualities we have referred to had reverse, perverse, implications for the colonial state. What were these weaknesses?

We may begin with Uganda's location: the geographical – and with it the social – soil in which British colonial rule was to be planted. It is not enough merely to repeat the observation that the Uganda Protectorate brought together into one territory a cluster of peoples of great ethnic diversity which, of course, did present difficulties over time. A preliminary consideration was Uganda's very location in the interior of East Africa. Not only was it thousands of miles from the metropolis in north-western Europe, it was hundreds of miles from the coast (and so, one might add, in the context of nineteenth-century British imperialism, from the nearest gunboat). The Uganda Protectorate was landlocked – yet immediately locked, also, into a global economy to which from the outset it would always be subservient, and within which it would prove incapable of significant development through its own autonomous industrialisation. Much of this land moreover was inhospitable and unattractive, if less so to Indians than to Europeans; and furthermore its territory was almost totally uncharted and its peoples were almost totally unknown. We cannot understand colonialism at the turn of the century without reference to this starting-point, this context and to the real (and imagined) problems it presented to contemporary European administrators.

This was indeed most unpromising, unfertile, ground for the export and implant of the apparatus of a late nineteenth century type of 'state' which was still a relatively new concept and enterprise, even in its own continent of origin. This was an underdeveloped state model, of limited competence and ambition. As A.J.P.Taylor observed in the striking opening sentence of his volume of *The Oxford History of England*: 'Until 1914, a sensible, law-abiding Englishman could pass through life and hardly notice the existence of the state, beyond the post-office and the policeman' (Taylor 1965: 1). The 'colonial' version of this state, exported to tropical Africa, was undermanned and under-funded. We may echo Bruce Berman when he writes that colonialism in Africa introduced 'partial and skewed' representations of Europe (Berman 1998: 313).

Whatever the precise specifications of the turn-of-the-century state, equatorial East Africa was ill prepared to accommodate it in its colonial form and extent. Indeed, if social conditions there had been favourable to the emergence of such an entity in 'Uganda', why had none materialised? Buganda, of course, was a local African state of some maturity and sophistication; but it remained the exception. Moreover it had to the north and east, especially, neighbours with whom it had little in common in terms of social organisation or culture. Nor had it fully asserted its pre-eminence over its neighbours independently – before the British helped it militarily against Bunyoro, and used its 'agents' to preside over other neighbours to the east. Thereafter Buganda was itself incorporated into a territory that was entirely new and arbitrary: so new that not even a concept of it existed, in Africa or outside, before the British stumbled and scrambled uncertainly onto the scene.

The 'ethnic diversity' which arose from this episode explains little on its own; and it should be seen only as part of a wider picture of social raw material that was unpromising for state-building. Bayart has recently written, of contemporary Africa, that 'none of the ... political phenomena which some have attempted to reduce to an ethnic dimension can be limited to this single explanation' (Bayart 1993: 53). This salutary observation may usefully be extended to cover the whole period of the establishment and subsequent record of colonialism, partly because 'ethnicity' itself changed over time. To an extent ethnic groups of the post-colonial independence era 'are the products of the colonial period – the precipitation of ethnic identities becomes incomprehensible if it is divorced from colonial rule' (Bayart 1993: 51).

More important still is what the nature of all this ethnic diversity implied. The African society – societies – over which the British came to rule in Uganda lacked the basic common characteristics and hence the social cohesion, that alone makes the establishment of effective government, of a functioning state, likely or even possible. Moreover, additional religious differences, and enduring competition between Protestants, Catholics, and Muslims, had arrived in the years preceding 1894, and these were to lay deeper roots than those of any alien patterns of government. In other respects, such as their absence of knowledge and understanding of the wider world and of the experiences and assumptions of the aliens, the character of Uganda's peoples at that moment of collision was hardly conducive to an emergent statehood. Reference to another, contrasting, case may be revealing here. Hall and Ikenberry have compared the experiences of Japan and Uganda. In the late nineteenth century, Japan was 'underdeveloped'– but it enjoyed 'pre-existing patterns of literacy, bureaucracy and authority on which to draw when reaching for the modern world' (Hall and Ikenberry 1989: 70). Within the 'geopolitical artifice' of Uganda, not even the Baganda could match that.

The British colonial state in Uganda was alien not only in origin but also in purpose. What was it for, but to satisfy metropolitan ambitions, however modest? Who was it for, *pace* Lugard and The Dual Mandate, but a body of foreign officials and, in their wake, foreign businesses? This state could never pretend to be an expression of a single national community. It had not grown organically out of such a community; indeed, that community did not even exist.

This state was not, and could not be, founded on the kind of social contract that was by then established in parts of Europe and America: the provision of some, still few, services by the state for the public good, in return for taxes approved by representatives of society. The protectorate's tax base was small and had to remain so. By 1915, the protectorate's books were balanced, but financial scope for the provision of services remained narrow. For many years, too, administrative capacity was inadequate. By the time that investment in economic development and social welfare could become much more than a rhetorical device, in the 1950s, the colonial state was taking its own first unsteady steps to departure. And even the belated arrival, only after the Second World War, of the first (albeit unelected) Africans in the corridors of central government in Uganda could not disguise the fact that this remained a government *over* the people: latterly perhaps *for* the people, but never *by* the people.

In distinguishing between 'despotic' and 'infrastructural' aspects of power, Michael Mann has contributed to our understanding of the state in general and the colonial state in particular. 'The sound and fury of command means little if orders do not translate into reality', he writes – though one might observe that in Uganda the British largely avoided frustrations of this kind, at any rate before the Second World War, by restricting their own ambitions and hence their commands. More illuminating for students of colonialism is Mann's further reminder that 'the strength of a state depends greatly upon its ability to penetrate and organize society: the pretensions of despotism must not be taken at face value' (quoted in Hall and Ikenberry 1989: 13). We search in vain for 'despotic power' in the Uganda Protectorate. And how could the British, through the agency of this particular colonial state, 'penetrate and organise' such a society as they found in Uganda? When they tried to – notably, in seeking to mobilise men and money and materials for the Second World War – they failed. Or rather they succeeded in part: but only to the extent that society was persuaded to acquiesce at a high political price. Was this despotism? Hardly. The price of unpopular intervention, of 'penetration and organization' beyond the consent and tolerance of society, was to be a popular rejection of African chiefly authorities employed as agents of the British, which threatened the collapse of the fragile concept of legitimacy and the fragile structure of political collaboration. However 'enlightened' and conscientious the colonial regime of the post-war period thereafter sought to be, it still held power *over* society. It could not build or re-build such a legitimacy as would enable it fruitfully to co-ordinate *with* society and so achieve that 'powering that can result when autonomous bodies ... contribute to a common good' (Hall and Ikenberry 1989: 14). Collaboration of that kind and degree was out of reach.

The point thus remains for the colonial period as a whole that the power held by the British was limited. If African *states* at the close of the nineteenth century were weak by comparison with European, by contrast African *society* was vigorous, adaptable and durable. Bayart is persuasive when he argues that on account of 'the vitality of these regional areas and the depth of their historical roots [they] could never have been the passive objects of a process of dependency' (Bayart 1993: 20). Colonialism represented 'a new development' for which they, Africans, had their own strategies for 'dynamic interaction'. Perhaps it is distorting to consider this simply as a 'weakness' of the state rather than as a further reminder of the truism that all states interact with their subjects in a dynamic interrelationship. African individuals, as well as African groups, had choices. There was no simple surrender to exploitation here. While some Baganda famously took advantage of their favoured position – at least for a limited period – innumerable individuals, across the protectorate, saw their route to material advancement and followed it. This is not surprising: after all, the colonial state, just as they did, put a high value on security, order and prosperity.

While state and society shared such goals, the protectorate enjoyed some success. But it eventually failed when called upon to resolve particular conflicts with and within African society in the post-war period – not least because it now suffered from a terminal weakness. In view of changes in the British Empire elsewhere – whether in India or in West Africa – the question of independence was, by the early 1950s at the latest, largely a matter of timing. This was indeed 'lame duck' colonialism – so lame that in this decade the

British in Uganda could do little more than concede to political pressure or postpone political conflict. Claims of European superiority, if understandable and even persuasive at the turn of the century, were difficult for the British to sustain after 1945. Moreover, political memories are not always long. Such benefits as had been introduced by colonialism were eventually taken for granted, and there was African impatience by the 1950s to satisfy new aspirations. The colonial state had visibly peaked. As elsewhere in British Africa, so for Uganda: the Second World War, appearing to mark a turning-point, served in fact to reveal the inherent weaknesses and hence the impermanence of such protectorates. Now, timing was all. As British rule accelerated towards its own eclipse in the 1950s, attempts to adapt and to reinforce the state in Uganda, as preparation for independence, were doomed. They lacked not only authority but time itself.

The representation of British colonial rule in the historiography of Uganda

Taking into account this assessment of the strengths and weaknesses, especially the latter, of British rule in Uganda, we may now find that some of what has been written about the subject, recently in particular, can look like distorting over-simplification, fuelled on occasion by misplaced moral outrage.

In his otherwise admirable *Uganda since Independence*, Phares Mutibwa makes sweeping observations on the preceding period, of British rule, which demand attention. He refers, at the outset, to the 'evils' of colonialism (Mutibwa 1992: ix). Alleged 'evils' are not identified, however – except perhaps in the relatively restrained subsequent observation that 'colonialism ... tended to emphasize the differences and rivalries between one region and another'. But how serious a charge is even this one? Mutibwa concedes that Buganda and Bunyoro 'had been arch-enemies throughout the nineteenth century' – but he does not go on to acknowledge the unmistakable political convenience, for a colonial administration devoted to whatever was minimal and cheap, in accepting and then using Buganda's existing pre-eminence in the region. One is entitled to ask, why would the British – how could they – rationally have behaved otherwise? If such questions cannot be answered, then the charge of 'evil' serves only to blame rather than to explain. Like others, Mutibwa also highlights the arbitrariness of Uganda's boundaries. One may agree that this was a 'negative legacy' indeed – though once again it is difficult to show it to have been the result of 'evil' intention. Mutibwa's only other specific criticism is that British policies 'also introduced new class formations ... and cleavages'. These, in turn, however, are not defined. Perhaps they would embrace the 'three main fragments' identified elsewhere as civil servants, cash-crop farmers and traders (Twaddle 1993: 229)? If so, one might reply, first, that it is a historical truism that social change accompanies economic change; and, secondly, that these particular classes can all be said to represent beneficiaries as much as victims – albeit frustrated beneficiaries – of economic change under colonial rule.

There is one more point where Mutibwa seems still to have the 'evils' of British colonial rule in mind. While explaining sympathetically why the National Resistance Movement went to the bush to engage in guerrilla warfare in the 1980s, he suggests that they had to fight 'the system'. What system? It was 'the system of Idi Amin, and the system Obote had used to rule Uganda back in the late 1960s ... *it was the colonial system*' (Mutibwa 1992: 155. My italics). Mutibwa then endorses the following definition: 'the system of institutionalized violence unleashed upon the people of Uganda; the system of government which allowed its soldiers and armed agents to go on rampage [*sic*] of looting ... killings ... rape ... road-blocks ... torture and death'. Is this dramatic comparison with British colonialism in general (as distinct from episodes in the initial phase of subjugation, perhaps) intended? Apparently so, for Mutibwa goes on to say that 'the system which had been created by the colonial power and then inherited at independence ... and perfected by Obote ... and matured under Amin's dictatorship ... was still there'. On reflection, is this not a somewhat capricious denunciation of British rule? Does the evidence truly reveal no difference in kind between half a century or so of the colonial period, on the one hand, and what Mutibwa powerfully terms 'the agony' of Uganda after independence, on the other?

More generally, a fashionable contemporary view of British colonial rule in Uganda tends to have three standard dimensions – not
always labelled 'evil' though invariably presented as negative. First,
critics ascribe 'absolute power' to the colonial state; they see its
essential purpose as having been, secondly, the 'exploitation' of Africans; and they discern, thirdly, at the heart of British colonialism, a
calculated policy of 'divide and rule'. It may be fruitful to review
each of these alleged attributes in turn; and to end with an examination of one further much favoured claim often cited as proof, as it
were, of all three of them. This is that the British deliberately promoted an 'uneven development' in the protectorate – to the relative
benefit of the Bantu, especially Baganda, southern peoples, and to
the detriment of northerners who thus (and with tragic consequences
for Uganda's subsequent experience) had little choice but to seek
employment in the colonial armed forces.

Absolute power

'The colonial regime controlled absolute power' (Gariyo 1993: 17).
'Absolute power' is an attractive concept because it is simple, but it
is questionable whether – or at least to what extent – it has ever been
exercised. In recent years, historians have reached a remarkable consensus in agreeing that 'absolutism' in Europe was clearly no such
thing, anywhere from 1648 to 1917, including the France of Louis
XIV and the Russia of Nicholas II. Recent study of even twentieth
century dictatorships, moreover, has severely qualified any casual
application of the label 'totalitarian' to the inter-war regimes of Hitler and Stalin. In these cases, history itself confirms the sceptical
view: the Thousand Year Reich collapsed under the strains of its
own unstoppable drive towards unwinnable international conflict;
and Stalin's successors found that inefficiencies and contradictions
within the Soviet system meant that *perestroika* was swiftly followed
by ignominious collapse, three generations after 1917. If this has
been the case in Europe, where 'the state' emerged and matured, it
seems unlikely that far-flung European colonial regimes established
in alien territory over alien peoples would have exercised any greater
degree of 'absolute' power.

In the case of British regimes in Africa, and in Uganda in particular, if the colonial state had absolute power then by definition African society must have had no power. This proposition is rendered absurd not only in the light of Bayart's provocative general analysis, already cited, but also specifically in view of the British administration's experience of governing Uganda during, say, the Second World War. Extensive evidence from that period, which lies at the core of this study, challenges Aidan Southall's judgement that during the war 'tight control was exercised over Uganda and little change occurred' (Southall 1988 : 56). Control will be shown to have been loose (and increasingly so), and change both serious and lasting – as this is the period in which collaboration at both political and economic levels all but broke down.

The evidence also challenges Tarsis Kabwegyere's representation of British colonial rule, which insistently stresses domination, oppression and violence. Drawn to Lenin's view of the state as 'the organ of oppression' he is thereby bound to see colonial rule not only in terms of class but also in terms of conflict. He asserts as a general rule that in the colonial state there is 'a fundamental difference between the ruling class and the ruled', which is perhaps an unexceptionable proposition in itself. But the deductions he draws from this 'difference' – that 'the gap between the two interests is unbridgeable' and 'overthrowal [*sic*] as a means of getting rid of the ruling class is inevitable' – stray from the evidence (1974: 8). In Uganda, the interests 'gap' was in fact bridged – to a considerable extent, for many people, for much of the time. And to describe the winding down of colonial rule in Uganda in the 1950s as 'overthrowal' is to approach the world of fiction.

Kabwegyere assumes moreover that because restrictive laws existed on the colonial statute book, they were actually applied, enforced, and hence used to legitimise oppression: but in the case of conscription during the Second World War, for example, he does not support this contention with evidence. The mere existence of the Compulsory Service Ordinance is allowed to serve as proof that 'the majority were forced ... to join the army' – a claim which is confronted and heavily qualified later in this work (Kabwegyere

1974:172). A similar technique is adopted by another student of the period who sees the colonial state as essentially oppressive. Zie Gariyo sees no contradiction in quoting at length a number of seemingly draconian laws restricting press freedom, yet subsequently saying (of the early years of African independence) that 'the period *after* 1962 ... saw the extinction of the dominant section of the African press which had shown its vibrancy and had caused the colonial regime a lot of headache' (Gariyo 1993: 26. My italics). Some vibrancy; some absolutism!

How, again, could there have been 'absolutism', given the actual inadequacies of the British colonial state and given, too, the favoured practice of 'indirect rule', adopted in various forms in the protectorate? While the latter may have maintained existing tribal distinctions, through the sustaining and use (or even fabrication) of local political institutions, it was not – as Chabal and Daloz have recently reminded us – consistent with effective state-building (Chabal and Daloz 1999: 12).

A more persuasive perception of British colonial rule in Uganda was that of Dan Mudoola when he described it as 'foreign, remote, authoritarian and paternalistic' (Mudoola 1993: 17). Co-existing with contemporary assumptions of a natural racial hierarchy – which certainly permeate official and unofficial British sources of the period – paternalism served to temper those assumptions. However objectionable, 'paternalistic' still implies condescension rather than oppression. 'Foreign' and 'authoritarian', to be sure: but perhaps it is 'remoteness' which deserves most emphasis here. Mudoola pointed out that, at the height of the initial conquest, there had been no more than five Britons in Uganda. The British presence remained thin on the ground thereafter – far too thin for their power to be 'absolute' (unless acquiescence itself is presented as proof of the efficacy of alternative and apolitical forms of oppression, as Kabwegyere seeks to maintain).

One illustration of persistent remoteness must suffice at this point. In 1955, the population of Lango District was 340,000. In his annual report, the District Commissioner pointed out that for most of the year his administrative staff numbered just three men (including himself), who had maintained a British presence only by touring each of the forty-two jagoates three times. This, 60 years after the establishment of the protectorate, does not appear to amount to sufficient manpower to sustain an essentially absolutist or exploitative regime. Jacobs went on to report that 'there are ... still far too many places in the district where the unexpected sight of an unescorted white face is still capable of causing alarm amongst women and children, and not infrequently among grown men'. Here he was surely illustrating the remoteness and slightness and recentness of British colonial rule in this area, rather than a well grounded fear of oppression.[3] And if a colonial army was a potential instrument of oppression – and like Mutibwa, Yoweri Museveni has recently implied as much in stating that previous armies in Uganda, those of the 1960s and 1970s under African command, 'were brutal because they came from the colonial system' (Museveni 1997: 175) – it may be worth observing that the army bequeathed to independent Uganda by the British in 1962 numbered just 700 soldiers (Omara-Otunnu 1987: 51).

Exploitation

The 'exploitation' school of critics of British colonialism has a distinguished pedigree. Tarsis Kabwegyere, for example, writes: '... that colonies were founded partly to provide markets for manufactured goods is a recognized fact' (Kabwegyere 1974: 175). Dani Nabudere continues the story for Uganda thus: 'This whole structure was erected upon the super-exploitation of the peasant producer and the worker who had emerged with the colonial economy.' (Nabudere 1988: 310) And then Phares Mutibwa adds, for the period as a whole: 'The extent to which Uganda's natural resources were pillaged will take years to compute. Ill-educated men who were failures in their own countries presided over the exploitation of Uganda's wealth...' (Mutibwa 1992: 8). This verdict is not only vague regarding the extent of 'exploitation' but also groundless regarding the educational background of the British colonial service. Ralph Furze's recollections, as the chief figure responsible for recruitment at the Colonial Office in London, bear constant references to the universities, medical schools and technical colleges (Furse 1962:

passim). Future governors and district officers may have received little specific training and have been selected primarily on grounds of perceived strength of character (as well as class) but to describe them as ill-educated is simply wrong.

Moreover, the evidence suggests that Uganda – contrary to Kabwegyere's claim – was not founded 'partly to provide markets for manufactured goods'. It was *founded* for other reasons.[4] After having been founded, of course it was expected to pay its way. This is not an insignificant point: economic development, if we may term it that,[5] was not the 'end' of British rule but only a 'means' to another end (essentially, possession – as we shall see in the next chapter). Hence the promotion of cotton cultivation. Tax-revenue needs lay at the heart of this simple policy. If subsequently there was purchasing power left over – and often there was, in the event – then these cash-crop producing farmers were as ready to buy manufactured goods as foreign manufacturers were to sell them. But was this 'super-exploitation'? Any relationship in which over time there are benefits accruing to both sides, albeit unequally, cannot adequately be described as exploitative. And which resources were being 'pillaged'? Neither cotton nor coffee – which provided a huge proportion of Uganda's export earnings under the British – was a resource native to Uganda that might be said to have been pillaged. Or is this a reference to Uganda's mineral wealth? The Second World War did indeed prompt a belated concentration on such resources. 'In respect of mineral production, attention is primarily directed to winning [*sic*] those metals which are of vital necessity to the war effort' – tin, wolfram, mica and tantalite ('War Effort' [6] November 1943). But in view of this policy shift, the figures for Uganda's exports in the Blue Book for 1944 are illuminating. Only two minerals make the table: £68,000 worth of tin ore was exported, and £20,000 of gold bullion. This was less than 2% of total exports in value; by contrast, cotton and coffee together accounted for 80%. Anyway, as we shall see later, workers in Uganda's mines declined to be exploited, let alone 'super-exploited': when paid inadequate war-time wages, they voted with their feet and abandoned the mines.

But there is far more to this discussion than statistics. The 'exploitation' school needs to be directly challenged on its use of language. The term 'exploitation' is ill suited to the degree of economic collaboration visible by the 1920s in Uganda's cotton-growing regions. Initially, indeed, potential cash-crop producers had been given little choice: they were directed into cotton production. But before long this incorporation into the global economy (and meeting of Protectorate government revenue needs) became in large measure self-driven – with much of the hard work, moreover, in Buganda at least left to immigrant workers from Ruanda-Urundi. If this form of cotton production is described as 'super-exploitation', language itself is being abused, for what words are left for us to describe, say, the slaves' position on the cotton plantations of the Southern states of America before the American Civil War?

This school also errs in conflating the colonial state, on the one hand, and capitalists, on the other. Dan Mudoola was rightly preoccupied with the different and competing 'interest groups' within *African* society in the colonial period. The same has to be done with *European* society. Berman and Lonsdale's ground-breaking article, with particular reference to Kenya and discussed in the previous chapter, is most eloquent on this point. More recently, Bayart has underlined this analysis, again in relation to Kenya, by stressing 'the contradictions between the key players of colonialism' such as administrators, settlers (who, themselves, 'did not make up a homogeneous community') and missionaries (Bayart 1993:12). This analysis looks far more persuasive than Kabwegyere's assertion that 'missionary activity' was 'an illustration of how the foreign agent of change ... inflicted violence on the colonised peoples' (Kabwegyere 1974: 11). For innumerable Africans over many decades, missionaries were valued as educators, not resented as oppressors.

While the colonial state in Uganda did provide an arena, opportunities, for capitalist enterprise, it was not established for that purpose; nor did it even actively promote it thereafter. Colonial officials certainly encouraged the production and sale of cash crops, but they did not advocate the wholesale import of capitalism into the protectorate. They welcomed some forms of economic development which had positive implications for government revenue. However, protective and paternalistic, and always mindful of their primary *adminis-*

trative responsibilities and particularly the challenging task of maintaining social and political stability and order, they did what they could to prevent any capitalist take-off (though in the 1950s they indulged in a form of state-capitalism under their own auspices). Any emergence of a de-tribalised proletariat would clearly not have been compatible with the normal administration of the districts, largely defined on ethnic lines; and the emergence of a middle class of independent entrepreneurs would have led to early and potent challenges to the exclusive political and economic, social and racial, pattern of colonial rule.

Christopher Wrigley has pointed out that it was precisely because the colonial state had been rather successful at putting the brakes on capitalism that, by 1962, the capitalist class, and proletariat, remained remarkably small. 'Society thus consisted effectively of a mass of peasant cultivators, living in communities that had not wholly lost their tribal character.... The development of an indigenous commercial bourgeoisie had been inhibited by colonial policy' (Wrigley 1988 : 28). This may have benefited the colonial state but it was not to be of much benefit to its successor, since it confirmed, as Wrigley continues, 'the belief that economic advance could most easily be achieved by favour of the government'. In a context in which the British had developed a number of parastatal bodies in the 1950s, it is not surprising that men of ambition sought state-funded employment in the early 1960s, nor that government payrolls in subsequent years of political independence grew to an unprecedented extent.

It is hard to maintain any longer a model of colonial rule wherein the state simply allowed capitalism to flourish (or, in the monolithic variant of the model, was itself in effect the agent of capitalism). Alien forms of economic activity were imposed; indigenous choices were limited; and producers were denied the full value of their produce. But the evidence does not go far to support that view of Uganda's colonial experience which isolates 'exploitation' and takes it out of context and out of scale. However, elsewhere a quite different verdict can be found. Taking the long perspective, James Katorobo concludes: 'The creation of the Uganda state was a positive development increasing the scale of opportunities of modern economy and governance' (Katorobo 1996: 154). Of course, the 'truth' is complex and lies elusively somewhere in between any bald generalisation from the extremes; but there is more to be said for this representation than for many others proposed in recent literature.

Divide and rule

For a concise introduction to the 'divide and rule' theme we may again turn to Kabwegyere. 'The differences among [Africans] were aggravated', he writes, 'by the colonial practice of "divide and rule", a practice that was imposed to reduce social interaction and the emergence of a collective consciousness among the oppressed' (Kabwegyere 1974: 218). This kind of representation has become a commonplace depiction of British colonialism. Recently Bruce Berman has echoed it, arguing that 'the colonial state's strategy of fragmentation and isolation of distinct tribal units promoted ethnic competition and conflict' (Berman 1998: 328). But such a perception, too, is in need of fresh critical analysis: both in the light of the options that actually confronted British administrators, and in the light of the evidence. Whatever the outcome, was there the intention to promote conflict? Was this British policy?

Dan Mudoola's identification of exclusive African 'interest groups' within colonial Uganda seems to offer us a promising way into this discussion. Various groups were in mutual competition, he suggested: so interest groups prevented the growth of any cohesive unifying national aspiration. Mudoola focussed on religious groups, ethnic groups, student/youth groups, trades unions and, up to a point, the military (Mudoola 1993: 2,3). Awareness of such groups does contribute to our understanding of colonial and post-colonial Uganda – for example, the absence, after 1962, of institutions capable of *managing* such groups was clearly significant – but we need to look more closely at their provenance. Mudoola asserts that 'the colonial conquest process, the carving up of Uganda into administrative units and subsequent socio-economic changes, conditioned the emergence of interest groups which were eventually to play critical roles in the post-colonial political processes' (Mudoola 1993: 6). It is not clear whether 'conditioned the emergence' means 'caused'. In fact, religious division – into Protestant and Catholic (and Muslim) – pre-dated the establishment of colonial rule in Buganda by at least 15 years. It was certainly not intended, either by the missionaries them-selves or by officials in contemporary Britain, to be part of a 'colo-nial conquest process', either in Buganda or more extensively. It is only in retrospect that it might look that way. Meanwhile, ethnic diversity, the raw material for ethnic group formation, was of im-measurably longer (also *pre*-colonial) ancestry. Moreover Mudoola conceded that his other interest groups – student/youth groups and even trades unions – barely figure in the colonial period itself. [If anything he is perhaps too dismissive of the early trades unions, of motor drivers and farmers.] And we might add that a colonial army numbering a few hundred was not yet the 'interest group' which African politicians of the first years of independence were deliber-ately to make it. To conclude, colonial administrators came to ac-quire – that is, inherited – different religious and ethnic 'interest groups' within the newly and arbitrarily demarcated Uganda: they did not have to be, to use Berman's term, 'promoted'.

These competing interest groups had to be accommodated. And Mudoola found that the British were rather successful at the busi-ness of 'accommodation'. Until 1962, he conceded, the colonial power was able to act as an arbiter among conflicting interest groups. Given that arbitration is not a synonym for, or consistent with, aggravation – in fact it is the opposite – his analysis hardly sustains Kabwegyere's contention that the British deliberately intensified division. Overall, while we may question the extent to which Mudoola convincingly blamed colonialism for causing the emergence of religious and eth-nic interest groups, we may conclude that his overview of the colo-nial period remains the more convincing for not charging the British rulers with the political intent to promote dissension.

Religious differences, germinated before the establishment of co-lonial rule, proved durable and divisive in Uganda. African political parties formed in the decade before 1962 took on something of a religious character in terms of their constituencies, and this remained the case afterwards. But the available evidence suggests that British administrators may have been more even-handed in their handling of religious difference than they have sometimes been given credit for. In Buganda, for example, 10 per cent of *saza* chiefs in 1943 were Muslim: 2 out of 20. Moreover, in both these *sazas* (counties) Muslims were actually in the minority.[6] Meanwhile, among the majority Christian chiefs, Catholics were not invariably treated worse than Protestants. When two Ganda chiefs were selected to visit England in 1948, one was a Protestant (qualified by a knowledge of agriculture) while the other was a Catholic, a former Makerere graduate and at the time an assistant to the Chief Justice, who was described by the Resident, the most senior local British official, as 'the most able of the younger Catholic chiefs'.[7]

And from outside Buganda we find some evidence of strong *pro-Catholic* sympathy within the British colonial administration. The acting Assistant DC in Kitgum was not inhibited in writing to his senior, in 1958: 'I must emphasize that it is desperately difficult to be fair in this county. One's sympathies are so much with the Roman Catholics.... The Catholic intelligentsia are friendly and civil. The Protestants on the other hand are irredeemably unpleasant. Their majorities in the district council and committees ride rough-shod over every Catholic aspirant'.[8] It would be possible to assert that the situation being described here was a regrettable consequence of previous British manoeuvring – though anything other than a Protestant bias at the end of the nineteenth century would have been a self-inflicted wound in view of competition with the Catholic French. But as a statement of official sympathies it is forthright enough (along with the Buganda examples referred to above) at least to question and to counterbalance the conventional twin generalisations: that the British always 'divided and ruled' by favouring Christian over Muslim, and Protestant over Catholic.

Uneven development

The major contention of the 'divide and rule' school, however, relates not to religious but to ethnic differences; and it criticises the way in which British colonial rule allegedly exploited and aggravated these, particularly in the creation of army and police forces. So it is to this claim, and to the charge of deliberately engineered uneven development – as distinct from the observation that uneven development was an unintended outcome – that we must now turn. It is neatly articulated by Martin Doornbos. In the course of blaming British rule for the excesses of Amin and Obote, he claims to identify 'a legacy of the colonial regime that had sought to create a power balance, divide and rule model, through concentrating military and police recruitment on Acholi, Lango and West Nile in the north, away from the economic, educational and administrative central region of the country' (Doornbos 1988: 265). For an even pithier version of this opinion, we may cite once again Phares Mutibwa, who alleges that army and police recruitment 'was reserved for northerners and people from the east ... lest the Baganda became too strong and colonial rule was endangered' (Mutibwa 1992: 6).

Such a version of British colonial rule has to be modified. It treats the colonial period as a monolithic whole and makes no allowance for changes over time. It presents British administration in terms only of cynical conspiracy rather than in terms of an anxious search for viability, especially financial viability by the easiest means. In the Doornbos case, it subtly distorts the reality of the colonial legacy, by implying that the colonial army was far bigger and more narrowly tribal – and hence far more menacingly significant in 1962 – than it in fact was. In the Mutibwa case, it implies that there was a threat to colonial rule from the Baganda. But, notwithstanding the disturbances of the late 1940s, arising from specific economic grievances, it should be stressed that for the most part it was the Baganda who were the prime collaborating, consenting, acquiescing, *beneficiaries* of British rule in the protectorate.

Furthermore, this portrayal ignores the preferences, even options, of Africans concerned – particularly in the case of the Baganda. Above all, it ignores three important facts: the colonial army was, for the most part, small and insignificant; (yet) the Baganda played a significant part in this army when they chose to; and, far from being neglected throughout the period, the north experienced a measurable degree of economic development over time. Such development in Uganda was no more equally or evenly distributed than it was anywhere else, including Britain itself. [It is not customary in British history to regard the siting of ship-building in the north-east, the cotton industry in the north-west – or cider production in Somerset – in terms of 'divide and rule' conspiracy rather than in terms of simple and reasonable convenience: where was the coal, where was the damp climate, where were the ports – and where were the apples?] To focus on unevenness of development in Uganda as evidence of sustained 'divide and rule' intention, rather than as an inherently probable outcome (because easy and appropriate, from the point of view of British officials), misrepresents the record of British colonialism.

We must remember the size and significance of the colonial army, which were both slight. It comprised a single battalion. As to its importance, we are reminded that in the inter-war years 'the Uganda army was not very active within the country ... little used' (Omara-Otunnu 1987: 35). After the Second World War it was reduced to its prewar strength. Though deployed twice during the late 1940s disturbances, it was idle during the whole of the 1950s and not needed again inside the country until the 1960 Bukedi riots. At independence in 1962, as we have noted earlier, it numbered just 700 men.

It is often implied that the Baganda were deliberately kept out of the army – a simplification that needs to be challenged on two grounds. First, we should recognise that the Baganda largely absented themselves from service in the peace-time army. The Baganda here illustrate Bayart's point that Africans, albeit within a strange and uninvited colonial context, could to an extent make their own decisions about their own futures. Because they were indeed in a region where opportunities for education and employment were most numerous and varied, there was no need for them to enlist in the army if they did not choose to. And for the most part they did not choose to. Peace-time service in the colonial army had little to offer them; and even during the Second World War many remained reluctant. As the Resident noted at the time, their ambition lay elsewhere: 'In Buganda, the demand for higher education is becoming more and more evidenced'.[9] The fact that Swahili, for which the Baganda had a certain disdain, was the language of the British armed forces in East Africa, probably made service still less popular, as perhaps did the wearing of shorts. The minimum height requirement may have ruled out many. The delayed Africanisation of the colonial army proved a more serious disincentive in the 1950s: service in the ranks continued to appear unattractive and unnecessary. Thanks to Governor Cohen's neglect, the army still offered no inducement to potential officers; as 'the military establishment was isolated from the tide of progress and liberalization', so the Baganda chose in general to isolate themselves from it.[10]

How different it had been during the Second World War! It is as hard to find particular evidence of Ganda reluctance to enlist at this time as it is of official British reluctance to recruit them. In large numbers, too: by 1943 there were nearly 12,000 Baganda on military service – three times the number of Acholi. The Baganda were, of course, a relatively large tribal group, but even in proportional terms the statistics are quite revealing. Although at this time the proportion of enlisted men to total adult males in Acholi was double that in Buganda – 1:8 compared with 1:18 – the Ganda figures are very similar for those of the other so-called 'warrior' northern tribe, the Langi at 1:16.[11] In 1939, the British colonial authorities had sought to recruit men for a Uganda territorial battalion: advertisements and posters quickly produced 800 applicants for 100 places, and 60 out of the 100 selected were Baganda.[12] The 'official mind' certainly had recourse to stereotyping: but there is no evidence of anti-Ganda discrimination here.

As we have already noted, after the Second World War the colonial army shrank again to its prewar size. Much later on, we can again see evidence of a considerable southern element in the military. A career in the officer corps was only belatedly and briefly opened up, just before and after independence. The figures are interesting: there were 16 Ganda officers in the Ugandan army in 1966 (compared with 26 Acholi and 23 Langi); but as many as half of all the officers who found themselves discharged from this newly independent Ugandan army between 1963 and 1969 were Bantu speakers (Omara-Otunnu 1987: 80,84). We may conclude that the overall picture of the composition of the army in Uganda is more complicated than it is often depicted. If Baganda were relatively under-represented in the colonial (and post-colonial) army this has more to do with Ganda choice (and ultimately the politics of independent Uganda) than with any enduring determination of British officials to keep them out as part of a policy of 'divide and rule'.

Even more in need of reconsideration is the general charge that the British deliberately underdeveloped the northern districts of Uganda, in further pursuit of 'divide and rule'. A recent re-statement of this view is to be found in Yoweri Museveni's memoirs. He writes, 'The colonialists marginalized some parts of the country, including northern Uganda. Instead of introducing commercial agriculture there, as they did in Buganda, they just kept the area as a reservoir for cheap labour ... and also as a source of recruits for the army'. He adds, 'the people in the area did not get into the habit of generating wealth through cash-crop production' (Museveni 1997: 211). Once again, the (albeit brief) period of colonial rule in Uganda is here taken as a unit, rather than as a process involving much change. The early days of British rule offer some grounds for such a view, when an understaffed administration had little ambition beyond retaining overall possession and following the most convenient path towards making the protectorate pay for itself. But the picture thus painted bears little relation to reality by the middle of the colonial period, and is a distortion by the 1950s.

Official annual reports from the Department of Agriculture show us something rather more complex in the 1930s. Cotton acreage in Buganda exceeded by far the cotton acreage in the northern districts, but a detailed examination – of the 1938 report, for example – reveals some interesting variations. Cotton was concentrated in just one of Buganda's three districts, Mengo, which could claim 650,000 acres – 3 to 4 times the northern total. But Lango had over 100,000 acres under cotton cultivation – double the figure for Masaka district in Buganda – while Acholi had 45,000 acres, which was double that of Mubende district, also in Buganda. This does not look like 'marginalisation' by denial of cash-crop production opportunities. We must also again bear in mind the geographical variations within the protectorate which determined the productive potential of various cash-crops (as they did in the comparably sized metropolitan country).

This applied to food crops too: while the Buganda plantain acreage far exceeded the north's, so the reverse was true in the case of, say, millet. As for maize, still in its infancy in Uganda in 1938, Buganda's acreage was only double that of the north. Meanwhile, the northern economy was much more heavily dependent on livestock. The north could thus boast three times the head of cattle of Buganda. This was not so much 'marginalisation' as regional variation based on compatibility and experience. If the north did act as a 'reservoir for cheap labour', it was at least matched in this respect by a territory beyond Uganda's borders. The British did not cause thousands of immigrant labourers to cross into Uganda every year from Ruanda-Urundi: that is, there was clearly no deliberate British policy of neglect in relation to this area outside Uganda, under Belgian rule.[13] Nor is there any need to ascribe such a policy to the British colonial authorities in relation to the northern areas of their own protectorate.

During the Second World War the northern economy remained varied. West Nile's tobacco production received a stimulus; the Acholi continued to grow cotton; and there were an estimated 4000 ploughs in use in Lango during these years (Annual Reports, 1939-46: 84). Subsequently, what is striking about reports from both Acholi and Lango in the 1950s is the absence of reference to soldiers ... and the plethora of details on the very varied wider economy. When the ADC Kitgum wrote to his senior official in 1957 that 'by and large, crops are good and the cotton excellent, portending another bumper crop' he may have been inclined to make a favourable impression. But he could not exaggerate the extent of cotton production if there was none, nor could he refer to a previous year's bumper crop if there had not been one.[14] And there was more here than agriculture to report on: 'trading centres flourish ... out of reach of Asian competition'.

By 1955, there was sufficient cotton production in Lango district to sustain 10 ginneries.[15] In 1958, the number of trade licences for rural shops, issued to Africans outside townships, rose to 639. By this time there were in Lango 80,000 taxpayers. At a time when the colonial army numbered well under one thousand, it is quite clear that it was military service that was in fact on the margin as far as the economy and employment opportunities of Lango were concerned. Moreover, it appeared (to local officials, at least) that it was not absence of opportunity that served to hold back the Langi but inefficient practices (such as not picking all their cotton, or not grazing their cattle long enough). Even so, at this time 'considerable quantities of money' were available in the district 'even after taxes and school fees have been paid'.[16]

Conclusion

So none of the three main strands of this particular, insistent, latterday representation of British colonialism looks wholly convincing, in the light of the evidence; nor does the charge of 'uneven development' as a conscious design of British policy. The picture painted is at worst misleading, at best incomplete. This was not a regime which enjoyed 'absolute' power; it did as much to hold back as to promote capitalism; description of its policies simply as 'exploitative' is too crude; and there is far more to the real thinking of successive British administrators than a mere repetition of the 'divide and rule' mantra can ever convey.

It is, indeed, this 'reality' which one must strive to recover. Perhaps the main criticism of mythological critiques of British colonialism is that they do not tell us *what colonial rule was actually like*. It has not always been fashionable to try to describe the past, in the way that, say, in different centuries Thomas Carlyle and Simon Schama attempted to revive the experience of the French Revolution. Yet we do need, if only as a starting-point, to try to recapture that past – something of the texture of everyday life, the experience of normality, the rhythms of continuity (as well as the moments of dramatic and seemingly historic change). Otherwise we are more likely to fabricate a contrived history that bears little relation to its original subject. It is only through study of the untidy and confusing detail that we can see the past more nearly as it really was, and thence proceed, free of any desire to impose simple patterns on it, to analyse and interpret it securely enough to gain insights of value.

But can we, in a world of postmodernism, still set out to uncover past 'reality'? 'At its most strident', writes Edward Acton, in his editorial introduction to a major collection of recent works on the Russian Revolution, postmodernism 'repudiates the rules of evidence and the distinction between objective and subjective, denies our ability to study and understand the past, and is ultimately incompatible with the writing of history' (Acton 1997: 14). But all is not lost. As Acton goes on to argue, postmodernism has done more to discredit prefabricated models applied retrospectively to the past than to undermine historical enquiry itself. Moreover, as Richard Evans has recently written, it 'has restored individual human beings to history, where social science approaches had more or less written them out' (Evans 1997: 248). Thanks to postmodernism, there is in fact 'a heightened concern', adds Acton, 'to explore ... hard reality, the flesh-and-blood experience of men and women' ... duly armed now, we might add, with an awareness of the codes of language variously used by them and adopted by us who study them.

This study of Uganda under British rule rests where possible on the record of what people in the past did, and what they gave as their reasons for acting as they did. All players, of course, tended to act out of self-interest (or in the interest of groups with which they identified) –though not without restraints of one kind or another. Rulers and ruled all participated in this composite relationship: not as equals, yet equal in their ignorance of what the future would bring (and what labels historians would bestow on them and their deeds). All this is the subject of this book. And we are assured by Evans that 'we really can, if we are very scrupulous and careful and self-critical, find out how it happened and reach some tenable though always less than final conclusions about what it all meant' (Evans 1997: 253).

As the opening paragraph of this chapter attests, this study is not designed to exculpate British colonial rule in Uganda; it is intended, rather, to provide a 'moment of illumination', by detaching myth from reality.[17] Long ago, apologists of empire trumpeted the achievements of British rule in Africa and insisted that any sacrifices borne were those of the rulers, not the ruled. This view of Uganda's past is now duly buried; but so, too, should be buried the equally monochrome counter view which it gave birth to and which, as we have seen in this chapter, to some extent persists. It must be possible by now to work towards a fresh and balanced appraisal, a history generated more by light than by heat. Oliver Cromwell asked for his portrait to show 'warts and all'. Too many recent portraits of British colonial rule in Uganda have depicted warts a-plenty: it is time to complement these now with 'all' or at least some of the broader, fascinatingly complex, picture. We may even find that some of the warts do not look quite so ugly on closer inspection.

The proposition that colonialism was just one relatively short phase in Africa's long history – and one which presented a range of challenges, opportunities even, for two or three generations of Africans in Uganda to negotiate – does not deny for an instant the trauma of conquest, the humiliation of Africans' treatment as inferior subjects by their new colonial masters, or the countless frustrations presented by the multiple invisible ceilings to their advancement as the colonial situation matured. But this is a multifaceted subject. The history of all hitherto existing society is, perhaps, ultimately unfathomable. We delude ourselves if we think we can unravel such complex human interactions in a few simple and morally uncomplicated strands. But if we do look at both – all – sides of colonial relationships in Uganda perhaps we can get behind easy generalisation, reductionist phraseology, and lazy moralising. After all, the term 'colonialism' can be applied widely: to the rule of Belgians in the Congo, French in Algeria, Portuguese in Angola, and British in Nyasaland. But few would maintain that this single label denoted anything more consistent in those four locations than, say, 'democracy' denotes now in India, the USA, Switzerland or Peru.

What perverted representation of our own contemporary experience might some historians and commentators of a not-so-distant distant future peddle? Would the 1990s in Uganda, for example, be adequately and fairly characterised as a time of corruption, poverty and unresolved regional conflict – a picture not unlike the standard representation of independent Africa in the Western media over the last forty years – without reference to economic vitality, a stable currency, democratic experiment and a vigorous press ... or to the decades of trauma which preceded it? Accounts of the past that are devoid of balance in their assessment, taken out of context, and subjected to alien theoretical assumptions or simple prejudice, are not history: they are parody.

Certainly, colonial rule was unilaterally imposed on Uganda; and it made many demands of its inhabitants, over several decades. But the key to understanding the British colonial period, and learning from it, is an acceptance that 'governing Uganda' was not nearly as straightforward, uncomplicated and effectively authoritarian either as one might assume or as has sometimes been portrayed; and that in this context of limited capability (even in the heyday of empire), African calculation, initiative and enterprise 'from below' did much to minimise disadvantage, to shape the colonial relationship, and – often to the frustration of British officials – to determine the pace and direction of change.

---

1. Examples follow. Absolved from any such accusation are the many scholars, mostly of a somewhat earlier generation, whose works on Uganda are used in subsequent chapters and listed in the references.

2. See Introduction (Chapter 1, pp.5,6)

3. B.L.Jacobs, Lango District Annual Report 1955, Rhodes House MSS Afr.s.2227/1

4. See Chapter 3.

5. Walter Rodney's classic study proclaims its thesis in its very title: *How Europe Underdeveloped Africa*, London, 1972.

6. Resident to Chief Secretary, 28 October 1943, Uganda Protectorate Secretariat Minute Paper (UPSMP) R 51/2/19, Uganda National Archive (UNA), Entebbe.

7. Resident to Chief Secretary, 26 April 1948, UPSMP R 3/23, UNA, Entebbe.

8. H.J.B. Allen, ADC Kitgum to DC Acholi District, 2 April 1958, Rhodes House MSS Afr.s.1549.

9. Resident's note, 25 June 1943, on memorandum from the Uganda Civil Defence Board to the Chief Secretary, UPSMP, UNA, Entebbe.

10. O.G. Griffith, a personal note on Sir Andrew Cohen as governor, p.8, Rhodes House MSS Afr.s.2027.

11. Survey of Manpower, Military, 20 March 1943, UPSMP R 301/3, UNA, Entebbe

12. Progress Report, 21 June 1939, UPSMP F 78/14/2, UNA, Entebbe.

13. For the importance of immigrants from Ruanda-Urundi see Chapter 9.

14. H.J.B. Allen, Safari Reports, 29 September 1957, Rhodes House MSS Afr.s.1549.

15. B.L. Jacobs, Annual Report, Lango District, 1955, Rhodes House MSS Afr.s.2227/1

16. Ibid.

17. The phrase is used by Vladimir Bukovsky in *To Build a Castle,* London, 1978. In this record of his experience as a Russian dissident, Bukovsky describes how the Soviet media presented life in the West during the Cold War: 'There, the black forces of reaction and imperialism are grinding the faces of the workers and threatening us with war; here, the bright forces of progress and socialism are building a radiant future and battling for a stable peace'. But, he continues, 'sooner or later the moment of illumination comes . . . it percolates through to us that not everything (in fact nothing) in the West is as it is painted . . . and bang goes the belief in the radiant future.'

3
1894-1939: Uganda before the Second World War

Origins, purpose and form

Early in 1943, as the Second World War was fought around the world, a parade was held at the Old Fort, Kampala. It was April Fools' Day; but this was no joke. Just 50 years before, Sir Gerald Portal had raised the Union Flag at this spot to proclaim a British protectorate. Now, as if to emphasise the relative recentness of the protectorate's birth, a congratulatory telegram was received in Kampala from Lord Lugard who, as Captain Lugard, had first established a British official presence there in 1890.

The circumstances in which the British colonial state was established in Uganda throw light on its subsequent purpose and form. The first European missionaries arrived in 1877. Thirteen years later, by an act of 'paper partitioning' in European capitals, the area was provisionally reserved for Britain, and the Germans were excluded. By the end of 1891, however, the Imperial British East Africa Company, to which fell the responsibility of effective occupation in the British interest, 'was plainly on the rocks' (Robinson and Gallagher 1961: 309). A year later Harcourt, Chancellor of the Exchequer in Gladstone's British government, could think of no good reason for holding on to this inaccessible territory any longer: '*Cui bono?* Is it trade? There is no traffic. Is it religion? The Catholics and Protestants ... are occupied in nothing but cutting each others' throats..... Is it slavery? There is no evidence that there is any slave trade question in this region.... I see nothing but endless expense, trouble and disaster in prospect if we allow ourselves to drift into any sort of responsibility for this business' (quoted in Robinson and Gallagher 1961: 315).

When Sir Gerald Portal investigated the situation in Buganda at first hand on behalf of the British government in 1893, he found religious grounds on which to argue for retention: 'Everything, I fear, seems to point to a desperate and perhaps long continued struggle in the centre of Africa between the advances of European civilisation from the coasts on the East and West, and the old class of Arab traders.... In determining both the nature and the result of this contest, the position of the Christian country of Uganda [*sic*] is of vital importance' (quoted in Oliver 1952: 159). But Rosebery, the British Foreign Secretary, already favoured retention of Uganda within the British Empire because of a secular strategic argument. Since Lord Salisbury's decision that the British remain in Egypt in 1887, the security of the River Nile, and especially its source in Uganda, had preoccupied 'the official mind' in Britain. Robinson and Gallagher are at their most persuasive on Uganda. Specifically, a railway from the coast to Uganda might act as a springboard for the reconquest of the Sudan, which lay between Uganda and Egypt. The strength of Rosebery's strategic argument and of his position in the British government of the day – his continuing membership of it was essential for its very survival – were enough to determine the identity of Uganda's European overlord. Portal's proclamation in Kampala in 1893 was duly confirmed by the British government in London in 1894.

Uganda's strategic significance astride the headwaters of the Nile, at the mouth of which lay Egypt, remained the key to its remaining within the British Empire. Even as late as the 1930s, Uganda was excluded from consideration as part of any hand-over of territory in appeasement of Hitler's colonial aspirations. It should be stressed that in its early years, any specifically *economic* arguments for retaining the Uganda Protectorate were primarily related to 'India via Egypt' considerations, rather than to any perceived economic value in the territory itself. Britain's initial purpose was merely possession, rather than urgent economic exploitation. Indeed, in the aftermath of Uganda having been acquired 'nothing in the nature of a policy for its future was even considered' (Low 1965: 62).

This (lack of) purpose in a sense dictated the form of Britain's colonial presence in Uganda and also the scale of British colonial rule. The Protectorate government undertook no great economic development initiatives in the short term. The official British presence in Uganda was to be minimal, sufficient to maintain control and sustain order. Eventually, 'order' facilitated the establishment of cotton as a commercial crop during the first two decades of the twentieth century. This in turn enabled the colonial state to meet one further imperial requirement: financial viability. Within twenty years of its foundation, it was collecting sufficient annual revenue to cover its local costs. Sales of cotton enabled the peasants who produced it to pay a poll tax; and their consumption of goods, on the proceeds of sale, yielded customs and excise duties. Cotton represented 70 per cent of the total value of Uganda's exports by 1914-15 and it was thus largely cotton which freed the protectorate from financial dependence on imperial grants-in-aid after that year. From then on, Britain's officials on the spot were able to administer the protectorate on revenue raised from Ugandan peasant farmers.

Uganda as a colonial territory was, of course, an artificial creation and as such was to present problems for its administrators. The paper partition of Africa by European powers at the end of the nineteenth century had been largely decided in Europe, in ignorance of African geography. The resultant colonial frontiers therefore paid little attention to the existing distribution of indigenous peoples. Uganda is a sorry example of this general rule. Though relatively small, roughly the area of the British Isles in geographical extent, and with a population in the early twentieth century of perhaps three million persons, it nevertheless comprised a number of peoples – largely Nilotic-speaking to the north and Bantu to the south – of exceptional linguistic, cultural and occupational diversity.

The establishment of British rule on the ground furthermore tended to be *ad hoc* and piecemeal. Civil administration was not introduced into Karamoja in the north-east for the first time until the early 1920s. In 1926, Rudolf Province was transferred to Kenya: a belated admission that its administration within Uganda was impossible. It thus took over 30 years for even the colonial boundaries of the Uganda Protectorate to be defined. During the Second World War, as we shall see, they were to be called into question once more. Less than another twenty years thereafter, the Uganda Protectorate ceased to exist.

Colonial acquisition entailed force: to borrow from Mao Tse-Tung, conquest is no more 'a dinner-party' than is revolution. In the case of the British take-over of Uganda however, force was not widely or intensively used – because it did not need to be. Some peoples accepted British rule and collaborated from the beginning. In the case of peoples who resisted, as D.A.Low points out, the British 'had at their disposal weapons and forces that were overwhelmingly more powerful than anything which was locally available against them' (Low 1965: 109). Consequently, African casualty figures were relatively low from these albeit bloody encounters: in 18 months of confrontations in Lango, Teso and Bukedi, 174 were reported killed or wounded (Low 1965: 106). [By way of comparison: a dozen years earlier, over 11,000 Sudanese fell to British firepower at the Battle of Omdurman.] As the Lango figures for example suggest, in a number of cases – and in a manner familiar to them from their earlier experiences in India, and more recently in southern Africa – the British found themselves involved in clashes at the frontiers of their primary region of interest which served, in time, to *extend* that region. They came to be involved, too, in the perpetuation of existing local disputes before in turn determining their outcome. Thus they aided the Baganda against the Banyoro, eventually subjecting the latter to a period of military occupation.

For the most part it was a case of brief, small-scale but decisive military actions, typically described at the time by the British as 'punitive' operations. A small number of Sudanese and Swahili troops sufficed to impose British rule in Busoga; in turn, when Sudanese troops mutinied in 1897 over pay and conditions, the British were helped by local Africans – Baganda – to restore their authority and control. Much of the north-west and the north-east of the protectorate was brought under British rule in the first instance by the use of armed force – though northern peoples succumbed only to such an emphatically superior fire-power that they could still retain a reputation as 'martial' tribes. To keep African casualty figures in this period of 'pacification' and 'punishment' in perspective, we should perhaps remember that the really large-scale losses of life during the first two decades of British rule in Uganda were unintended: they came not from any fighting but from famine induced by drought and from endemic disease. As for the eventual outcome, Low writes sardonically of the acquisition of Teso: 'swift inclusion in a new economy of unimagined prosperity muted the harsher sensations of alien conquest' (Low 1965: 105). After all, '*Pax Britannica* was no figment. Its benefactions were in high demand' (Low 1965: 59). And nowhere was this more true than in Buganda.

Governing Buganda: political collaboration and 'indirect rule'
The kingdom of Buganda had been the initial core area of British interest in the interior of East Africa in the 1890s, and it formed thereafter the heart of the Uganda Protectorate into the 1950s. Its size, location and political character, not to mention its economic potential, gave it enduring special significance for British administrators. By the 1890s, it already had a highly developed and centralised political system and a chiefly hierarchy. This made possible a readily workable association with the British. Relations were formalised in the 1900 Uganda Agreement (Low, in Low and Pratt 1960: 3-159). This recognised the *Kabaka* as king of Buganda. It also recognised the *Lukiiko,* an assembly of chiefs, as his council; and it established the chiefs for the first time as a landowning class in the kingdom. It was practical, convenient and cheap for the British to exercise their overall control through such chiefs. Indeed, Buganda was to serve as a model for other areas of Uganda in this respect, where no satisfactory indigenous administrative apparatus was initially found. 'Baganda agents' were used therefore for some years in Bukedi, Teso and Lango, until local chiefs could be trained to take over from them and work with local British officials.

The Baganda were the main beneficiaries of Britain's search for political collaborators at the turn of the century (as they were to remain, up to the Second World War). With the Kabaka a minor in 1900, it was the three regent ministers and the administrative chiefs who gained most at that time. They not only had their authority confirmed and their assembly recognised, but also received generous grants of *mailo*, or quasi-freehold, land (measured in square 'miles'). Previously they had held land only in return for service to their king, and at his pleasure. The fragmentation of *mailo* land in subsequent years through its piecemeal purchase by growing numbers of peasant cultivators and, from 1927, the security of tenure enjoyed by tenants on all *mailo* estates, gave many more Baganda a stake in this unusual colonial system of land tenure. So arose, Fallers argues, a more general 'basic ideological acceptance' of the political framework defined by the Agreement, and of 'the legitimacy of the chiefs which entered into the association with Britain'. 'Most Baganda, most of the time,' he adds, 'have concluded that, everything considered, they drove a remarkably good bargain' (Fallers 1964: 180,181).

The British, too, considered it a good deal. But what had proved convenient to British authorities in 1900 was to pose huge problems for their successors. Governor Philip Mitchell lamented in April 1939 that 'the Agreement of 1900 is regarded by the Kabaka, the Ministers and Chiefs, and Baganda generally, as having an almost scriptural authority and inviolability' (quoted in Low 1971: 112). All three British governors of Uganda in the 1940s – Mitchell, Charles Dundas and John Hall – were to find the Baganda wedded to the Agreement to an extent that made changes in colonial policy towards the kingdom controversial and difficult to implement. In the cases of the other surviving pre-colonial kingdoms of western and southern Uganda, problems on this scale did not arise. Each had its 'agreement', but their privileges and autonomy were not on a par with those of the Baganda. It was Buganda's agreement with the British in 1900 which was to prove the perennial obstacle to the free operation and evolution of British colonial rule in Uganda.

How had the situation in Buganda evolved by the 1930s, the heyday of British colonial rule? Politically, chiefly collaboration appeared to be intact. Mamdani has written that the landlord-chiefs created by the 1900 Agreement by now formed 'an intermediary state bureaucracy', while the *Lukiiko,* in the hands of chiefs recently appointed from above, 'faithfully administered colonial policy' (Mamdani 1976: 127,147). Samwiri Mukasa was a good example of such a collaborating chief of the first colonial generation. Brought up in the Kabaka's household, he became a Christian and, as a chief under the British protectorate, took pride in collecting taxes, spreading cotton cultivation, getting roads built and, during the First World War, recruiting for the East African forces (Low 1971: 57-61).

Nevertheless, Mamdani's portrait of pliant collaboration in Buganda is not wholly satisfactory. If, as he argues, the Ganda chiefs were dependent on the British, so too were the British dependent on these chiefs. Also, within the kingdom there arose serious divisions which threatened to undermine the collaboration. Internal tension persisted between administrative chiefs in Buganda and rival figures who were symbolic of clanship, the *bataka* or lineage heads. This, as has been remarked, 'expressed itself politically in terms of land' but 'was at the same time a tension between the Christian pretensions of the new political system ... and the paganism to which the clan system essentially belonged' (Welbourn 1961: 19). The *bataka*, who had a special responsibility for clan burial grounds, were not, as such, beneficiaries of the land share-out of the 1900 Agreement. And by the 1930s, two Ganda ministers in particular – Martin Luther Nsibirwa, *Katikkiro* (prime minister), and Serwano Kulubya, *Omuwanika* (treasurer) – through their diligent commitment to goals defined by the British, made themselves unpopular and thereby provoked intrigue and faction within a chiefly class increasingly under strain (Apter 1961:203). Samwiri Mukasa himself became one of the Buganda government's most active critics: a leading figure in The Sons of Kintu, formed in 1938, he campaigned on behalf of farmers and traders, and sought the overthrow of the Nsibirwa administration. By the late 1930s, if not earlier, politics in the kingdom had already become a minefield for British administrators.

Governing Buganda was posing a universal political dilemma: how does the centre devolve responsibility while yet retaining influence, if not control, in the localities? And who thereafter takes the blame for the imposition of unpopular measures? By 1939, the legacy of earlier chiefly collaboration, and the subsequent theory and practice of 'indirect rule', needed urgent reappraisal. Mitchell grappled with the problem. He reiterated his belief in 'indirect rule', yet he argued that the British administration had to do its utmost 'to *change* the way of life ... in fact almost everything about our wards, as radically and completely as we are able' (Mitchell 1939: 29). There was indeed a contradiction in theory and aspiration here, between the desirability of continuity and the desirability of change. Meanwhile, even Buganda itself, Mitchell pointed out, did not actually enjoy pure 'indirect rule'. This was because British officers intervened in chiefs' concerns at the district level.

What was to be done? First, this 'direct' intervention must be removed, Mitchell insisted, in order to prevent the Ganda hierarchy's authority from being fatally undermined. Secondly, freed from such interference, the native government of Buganda must, along with native administrations in other provinces of the protectorate, take on further responsibilities: for finance, for appointments of officials, and for services. Mitchell hoped that there could then be an essentially organic development of African institutions towards 'the inevitable responsibilities of tomorrow' – a development nonetheless which would somehow remain open, he hoped, to guidance from above by British officials.

There was a further complicating factor: Governor Mitchell realised that there might not be enough time for this planned evolution. Buganda, once the Protectorate government's most prized partner, now posed the constitutional problem in practice in its most urgent form. In a secret memorandum devoted exclusively to relations with Buganda, Mitchell even urged a reconsideration of the 1900 Agreement. British officers, he wrote, must not acquiesce in the view that it should be interpreted 'in a narrow textual manner as if it were a statute enforceable in a court of law'. Rather, emphasis should now be given to the broad statement in Article 6 of the Agreement that 'the *Kabaka* of Uganda shall exercise direct rule over the natives of Uganda ... in the manner approved by Her Majesty's Government'. So the Agreement itself was open to differing interpretations.

What should Her Majesty's Government 'approve'? Mitchell's answer reveals considerable awareness of the problems, political calculation, and some apprehension:

There is indeed a fundamental incompatibility between an organisation under a Provincial and District Commissioners on the one hand, and the

constitutional status of the *Kabaka* and his Government on the other....
This incompatibility must become more prominent as a result of the
inevitable development which comes with education and a growing
racial consciousness. The fact has to be faced that as the Native Government progresses in experience and confidence, and the people in
education and interest in political questions, detailed intervention and
control is certain to become an increasingly difficult and in time politically dangerous method of discharging the responsibilities of the British Government (quoted in Low 1971: 112-115).

Mitchell was confronting what he considered to be an imminent
political challenge in Buganda, which made pre-emptive change essential. There were two particular political objectives behind his proposals to remove British officers from the detailed governing of
Buganda and to make the native government there more responsible.
First, in place of supervision through district commissioners, Britain
would substitute 'a less detailed but eventually more powerful and
effective influence'. This, he argued, would be done by means of
advisers at the centre of the protectorate under a provincial commissioner, now to be renamed Resident. Would the giving of advice represent power to promote change? Mitchell appears to have had in
mind a rather unsubtle means of resolving this residual problem. He
was insistent 'that the right to give advice should be coupled with the
right to ensure that such advice was put into effect' (Morris 1972:
309). Secondly, however, having taken on a wider range of responsibilities, it would be the native government and not the Protectorate
government that attracted the inevitable subsequent unpopularity and
criticism. The native government would not be able thereafter to 'shelter itself' behind the Protectorate government when, Mitchell shrewdly
predicted, 'particularly in the field of public health and agriculture,
progress may only be attainable at the cost of opposition and odium
and even organised agitation' (quoted in Low 1971: 117). His words
were prophetic. As we shall see later in this study, both Mitchell's
thinking and his anticipation of problems in the wake of any policy
development closely anticipated initiatives shortly to be taken by his
successor, Dundas, and their consequences. As the concurrent demands of the Second World War then sharpened the contradictions,

working political collaboration itself in Buganda was to be seriously threatened.

Governing Buganda was proving intractable in theory and in practice. Even Mitchell could not square the circle. While he hoped that he had formulated long-term answers to the problem of the evolution of 'indirect rule' which Buganda in particular posed, he already faced apparently insoluble questions relating to Buganda's constitutional and political relationships with British authority. For example, there was the current indigenous demand that the *Lukiiko* 'should be a representative body ... and not a group of government servants'.[1] This highlighted the limitations in Mitchell's thinking, and the contradictions entailed in any transition from 'indirect rule', or 'protected rule', towards more representative and, as he intended, more progressive rule. In this case, how could a British authority – distancing itself from Ganda affairs in order to inject 'responsibility' into its institutions – impress upon the Ganda *Lukiiko* the need to reform itself?

There was moreover already an 'emerging class composed of traders, cultivators and the like, which is seeking to acquire more definite avenues for voicing its own interests'; there was thus already 'an opposition' in Buganda (Hailey 1944: 188). This was opposed to those ministers and chiefs who most energetically collaborated with British rule and most closely identified with its culture. By the end of the 1930s, such opposition expressed itself in organisations such as The Sons of Kintu and the Uganda African Motor Drivers Association. Lord Hailey doubted whether the ruling class in Buganda would respond to the advocates of 'democratisation' and share political power with such groups. He predicted instead a cleavage between 'aristocratic' and 'popular' elements. Chiefs, 'aristocratic' or not, would indeed become increasingly detached from the mass of the Baganda by the later 1940s.

Hailey found some reassurance in the fact that 'popular' criticism was not currently being directed at the Protectorate government itself; and that opposition elements in Buganda were indeed still hoping for sympathy from British officials in the Protectorate government. Yet cautious steps towards realising the representative principle in the *Lukiiko* were not to be taken until after the Second World War. Meanwhile, the aspirations of Ganda 'opposition' served, as did the analyses of Mitchell and Hailey, more sharply to define divisions within Buganda than to reduce them. They also served more urgently to raise the question of Buganda's relationship with the rest of the protectorate. Formerly a lynchpin and model of Britain's colonial rule in Uganda, political collaboration there was now, in the 1930s, entering upon a deepening crisis.

Elsewhere, too, beyond Buganda, political collaboration between British officials and African chiefs was established between the wars, on the basis of the 1919 'Ordinance to Make Provision for the Powers and Duties of African Chiefs and for the Enforcement of African Authority'. However, the model had to be adapted to meet a wide range of local social and political circumstances – or *vice versa* – and even then it did not always fit. For example, while in some areas such as Bunyoro it was a case of recognising existing traditional authorities, in other areas such as Teso, where there were recognisable tribal units but no traditional centralised political system, strata of chiefs had to be superimposed.[2] Overall, the British were well served, as 'chiefs throughout Uganda ... were granted almost unlimited powers' – powers 'limited' in effect primarily by their accountability to British district officers (Burke 1964: 35). Yet governing the districts was not always easy. When a first generation of 'chiefs', often in fact prominent Baganda who had been sent abroad to spread the hierarchical chief system, came to be replaced by local men who had none of the traditional authority enjoyed by their equivalents in, say, Buganda itself, the new men might bear their responsibility only with difficulty. As Burke puts it, 'they frequently found their roles as government chief and clan leader incompatible'; and so, he adds, 'it is not surprising that the removal of Buganda agents was often followed by administrative chaos' (1964: 36).

The expatriate factor

For the time being, however, British officials in Uganda paid far more attention to the interests and opinions of their fellow Europeans (and of Indians, too) than they did to aspirations of Africans.

Indeed, the challenge to British colonial authority in Uganda at protectorate government level in the years immediately before the Second World War – when the situation was to be turned upside down – came not so much from African political demands as from British expatriates long established in the 'unofficial' community. At this time it was they, rather than Africans however eminent or numerous, who could to an extent determine the 'official' agenda.

British expatriates formed several very influential pressure groups. The Uganda Cotton Association, for example, existed 'to defend and further the interest of cotton ginners and traders in Uganda [and] to represent to the Government the general consensus of members' opinions on legislation and matters of policy'; and the Uganda Chamber of Commerce (UCC) sought 'to obtain the removal ... of all acknowledged grievances affecting merchants' (Thomas and Scott 1935: 517). Influence could be considerable. G.F.Engholm has argued that in this period immigrant pressures were successful in challenging, modifying and even blocking policies put forward by the Protectorate government. The rationalisation of the cotton industry in the 1930s, for example, was principally settled in discussions between the Protectorate government and the UCA that were 'screened from the public' (Engholm 1968: 206). Subsequently, a co-operative bill had to be withdrawn by the Protectorate government in 1937, following attacks by the UCC and others who played on official nervousness by arguing that African co-operative societies could grow and thus become politically powerful (Engholm 1968: 240-243).

Europeans had an institutionalised political voice through representation on the Legislative Council, founded in 1921. So too did other immigrants in Uganda at this time, in the form of the large Indian community which performed crucial functions in the protectorate's economy, especially in commerce. Both Europeans and Indians were largely representative of the cotton interest, ginning and exporting; yet overall there were as many bank-managers among the Europeans in the Legislative Council as cotton representatives during the 1930s. No 'unofficials' sat on the governor's Executive Council at Entebbe. As Beverley Gartrell has pointed out however, this Executive Council tended to be only a ratifying body (Gartrell 1979:

10). Actual decisions were hammered out beforehand, privately and informally, by a few men on an *ad hoc* basis. On economic issues, these would typically include Legislative Council unofficials (who included no African member before 1945).

The Protectorate government was shortly to become even more dependent on unofficials: their fellow Europeans were to enjoy what turned out to be their final phase of overriding local influence during the first years of the Second World War. Gartrell suggests that 'considerable power and wide discretion as to its use' were delegated by the Colonial Office to such British administrators in Uganda as the governor and the chief secretary and the financial secretary at Entebbe, on the northern shores of Lake Victoria, as well as to the officers of the provincial administration in the districts (1979: 44-45); and Gartrell considers that this made Entebbe a centre of decision-making and control. But unofficials clearly had influence. Later in this study we will have cause to observe that protectorate officials were very sensitive to – and even nervous of – the power of unofficial expatriate opinion at the start of the Second World War, especially on questions of finance and revenue. To this extent, Entebbe officialdom cannot be considered a wholly independent policy-determining agent in Uganda at this time.

The total European population of Uganda in 1938 was little more than two thousand (Annual Report 1938: 7). Shared identity and a high degree of common interest bound expatriate unofficials closely to the administration, and *vice versa* – if never as much as in neighbouring Kenya where the European settlers had a much stronger independent voice. The British *official* presence itself was numerically very slight. To rule a territory of approaching 4 million Africans and 17,000 Indians in the late 1930s, the Protectorate government of Uganda had a civil establishment of just 77 European officers in its administrative branch, and 53 in the police (Blue Book 1938). Such figures are consistent with Uganda's minor significance in the Empire and with Britain's being involved in what was essentially an inexpensive holding operation. They also suggest a considerable degree of acquiescence in, or collaboration with, British colonial rule on the part of Ugandan Africans. Yet, at the same time, these figures help to explain why, beneath the rhetoric, there was an under-current of apprehension among some Europeans within the British administration in Uganda.

Colonial rule in Uganda before the Second World War rested in fact on a certain congruence of political and economic interests between Europeans and Africans. At the same time, British authorities determinedly sought legitimacy and public acceptance on a variety of rhetorical fronts. Lugard wrote in 1922 that the British Empire could serve both Britain and its peoples: the benefit, he insisted, 'can be made reciprocal' and 'it is the aim and desire of civilised administration to fulfil this dual mandate' (Lugard 1923: 617). Thereafter 'trusteeship' was to be the watchword for the interwar period. The provincial commissioner of Buganda had even gone so far, as early as 1917, as to define the objective of British policy as 'self-government' – albeit 'under adequate and sympathetic guidance and supervision' (quoted in Low 1971: 51). 'Development' too started to become a familiar item in official British vocabulary in Uganda, during the 1930s. This perennial appeal to hearts and minds ran in parallel with the objective realities of the evolving colonial relationship, and sought to justify them.

Consent and collaboration did sustain a measure of confidence among British officials. Even so, when interpreting the public utterances of these functionaries, one must note that confidence was conditional and British complacency qualified. It took the Second World War to undermine this confidence. What we find among local British Uganda Protectorate officials in the late 1930s is a consciousness of present problems and of the undesirability, even danger, associated with alternative policy options or future scenarios. For example, the prospect of a wage-earning class emerging from the peasantry, based in towns and without land of its own, was an unwelcome one for British officials at this time. Were this to become a reality, 'unemployment, and maintenance in old age, conditions which are at present absorbed by the resilience of the tribal system, will claim State cognisance', observed a report in 1938 (Report on the Labour Situation 1938: para.157). This development was not to be encouraged.

Gartrell writes persuasively about officials who contemplated

African society and 'feared rootlessness, the destruction of restraining tradition, weakening of intermediate groups, the release of social control; they feared the mob'. In short, she concludes, 'administrators favoured tranquillity' (Gartrell 1979: 132). There were too few fellow expatriate Europeans on whom to rely, but at least in the end they too favoured order – notwithstanding the role which some from among the professional as well as commercial ranks of unofficials were to play as a critical opposition during the ensuing period of crisis. In the meantime, even before the outbreak of the Second World War there was clearly already a consciousness of the limits of state provision and state power in Uganda.

Economic collaboration: King Cotton

Although political collaboration in Buganda was under growing strain by the late 1930s, a more pervasive economic form of interaction between colonial state and African society was well established, in Eastern Province as much as in Buganda, and appeared durable. Indeed, as already remarked, the principal key to tranquillity in Uganda in the inter-war period was no longer the exercise of any coercive political power as such but the operation of economic relationships of apparently mutual benefit to state and society. This was because the most fundamental and enduring impact of colonialism in Uganda by the 1930s lay in the encapsulation of its life within that of the wider world. This profoundly affected its economic development. J.J.Jorgensen neatly remarks: 'Having been politically incorporated into the Empire to protect British access to the markets of India, Uganda was now to be economically integrated into the Empire to protect and expand Lancashire's supply of raw materials' (Jorgensen 1981: 53). The chronology is important here. It was only after Uganda had been acquired for particular strategic goals, and after the building of a railway from the East African coast to realise these goals, that the territory's economic potential could be properly tapped.

Thereafter, a familiar pattern soon became established. Africans in Uganda produced and exported raw materials, especially cotton, and with their disposable income they purchased imported manufactured consumer goods. By the 1930s, these links had achieved a normality, durability and consent which made tranquillity seem unsurprising. For African peasants, consumption was the spur – and thus the colonial state itself came to depend increasingly on the uninterrupted availability from overseas of soap and cigarettes, lamps and kerosene, matches and bicycles and, above all, of cotton piecegoods and other textiles.

The colonial administration's priority at the end of the nineteenth century was the *protectorate's* financial viability, rather than any direct pursuit of *metropolitan* economic advantage. This remained the case into the 1940s. Neither during the 'scramble' of the 1890s nor in the 1930s depression was Uganda regarded *primarily* by Britain as a captive source of raw materials for the metropolitan economy or as a captive market for British goods. Although Lancashire's appetite for cotton had indeed stimulated Uganda's raw material production in the early 1900s, by 1938 just 18 per cent of Uganda's exports went to Britain (Annual Report 1938: 19-20). Sixty-one per cent of them were by now destined for British India, which was economically independent of Britain for most practical purposes. At the same time only 47 per cent of Ugandan imports were of British origin, while 44 per cent came from outside the British Empire (most notably Japanese cotton textiles) (Annual Report 1938: 19-20).

As we have already noted, the Protectorate government's primary financial ambition had been achieved comparatively quickly and easily: by 1914-1915 Uganda was 'paying its way'. The key to this fairly early solvency, and the health of government finances up to the end of the 1930s, was the introduction of commercial fibres of cotton to Uganda in 1903, and cotton production in increasing quantities thereafter. While several other products were also sold abroad – sugar from the two Indian-owned plantations, for example, and increasingly African-grown coffee, too – it was above all cotton which by the 1930s yielded revenue for the colonial state in Uganda.[3] The poll tax and customs raised on imports were the two main sources of government revenue. In addition, there was the cotton tax, a valuable additional contribution to government finance.[4]

Initially, pressure had been required to promote African cotton production in Uganda. During the early 1900s, compulsion took the form of new taxes and promotion through intermediary chiefs. Subsequently, this pressure could be relaxed. Later British official expectations, and the options presented to local Africans, were expressed in the following telegram of 1924 from the chief secretary: 'Natives to be informed that three courses are open: cotton, labour for government, labour for planters – but no attempt is to be made to induce them to choose any one in preference to the others. Only one thing to be made clear: that they cannot be permitted to do nothing and be of no use to themselves or the country' (quoted in Mamdani 1976: 46). In time pressure from above merged with choice from below. By the 1930s, Ugandan peasants appear to have been growing cotton not only because they had to but also because they chose to. Tax obligations remained high, but still farmers chose to produce a surplus in order to purchase manufactured imports.

Uganda's peasant-based economy was able to withstand the inter-war depression more effectively than neighbouring Kenya's white-settler-based one. The African peasants' response in Uganda at this time has been commented on amongst others by Christopher Wrigley. 'It seems incontestable', he writes, 'that in the first and worst years of the slump African cultivators, taken as a whole, countered falling prices by increased effort, thereby maintaining their real incomes at approximately their former level' (Wrigley 1959: 61). Enjoying the security of subsistence from their own food crops, peasants increased cotton acreages to maintain their income and purchasing power. This benefited the colonial state too, and officials were thus able to find sufficient funds to spend on modest development projects in the latter half of the decade. As Brett remarks, 'the whole political and economic superstructure depended on their willingness to produce a cash crop' (Brett 1973: 245). In 1938 cotton exports amounted to 80 per cent in value of all Uganda's domestic exports, a figure not untypical for the decade (Annual Report 1938: 22). We may note in passing that post-colonial governments in Africa were not the first on the continent to experience the vulnerability of dependence on the cultivation of one or more primary export products.

In Uganda in the later 1930s the 'wants of the people were gradually widening in range and deepening in intensity' (Wrigley 1959:

62). In some respects, the necessary prior production of cotton was relatively undemanding. Overall, farming has been a reasonably secure occupation in much of Uganda, on account of fertile soil and rainfall which is generally well distributed. Cotton-growing could be notoriously vulnerable to any variations in that rainfall, but it entailed a manageable cycle of plot preparation, planting, harvesting, and marketing (stretching from, say, April to February). Certainly it was hard work, but increasingly in the 1920s and 1930s migrant labourers, especially from Ruanda-Urundi, were available in large numbers for help – in Buganda, at any rate – with the heavy chores.[5] While some cotton plots could be as large as 20 acres, a mere 'tablecloth' might suffice (Thomas and Scott 1935: 137). By 1938 cotton was grown on over one and a half million acres, in every province, and in 14 out of the 17 districts of Uganda (Agriculture Department Annual Report 1938). By 1939, the promotion of cotton required little official effort and no exercise of coercive power on the state's part.

However, the cotton industry occasionally also called for a degree of management and arbitration among the various locally based interests. The colonial state thus became decisively involved in the tensions between producers and processors, the sellers and buyers (and exporters) of cotton. Most notably, the Cotton Ordinance of 1933 defined zones within which cotton had to be sold and processed. This led to the rebirth of ginning associations, approved by the Protectorate government, which were able to engage in monopoly buying from African producers within their zones. The colonial state in Uganda thus proved to be 'much more than a neutral referee' (Brett 1973: 245). On the other hand, as Lonsdale and Berman have argued, 'the character of the colonial state cannot be reduced simply to that of a loyal minister to capital's needs' (1979: 487). Ehrlich criticised the British colonial administration for making the concessions to the European and Indian ginners and exporters which reduced prices paid to African cultivators (Ehrlich 1965: 456-7). But Mamdani persuasively endorses the contemporary official argument that the quality of product, and thus its value, was being put at risk in the absence of such regulation (1976: 73-4). And, anxious to ensure continued production, the administration did insist on minimum prices for growers. Perhaps these qualify as 'brakes fitted by the state' (Lonsdale and Berman 1979: 489). The overall outcome however was certainly a reduction of opportunity for individual African enterprise. Other crops became organised on similar lines and, as Mamdani rightly remarks, 'with the Native Produce Marketing Ordinance, the monopolisation of both marketing and processing structures was complete' (1976: 107). Regulation characterised the colonial temper ... but officials took care that cotton production, especially, was not stifled by administrative controls.

Cotton had thus become the Uganda Protectorate's life-support system. Cotton cultivation was, in contemporary British parlance, 'native enterprise'. Apart from the two large sugar estates and a handful of tea, coffee and tobacco plantations, productive activity in Uganda remained African. It also remained individual, and small-scale. This gave the Uganda Protectorate a wholly different character from the colony of Kenya, lying to the east. The central place – and officially protected status – of the African farmer in Buganda was emphasised in 1927 when the *Busulu* and *Envujo* laws gave tenants security of tenure and restricted their obligations to their landlords. By then the ideal of an independent and prosperous peasantry – governed by a collaborating salaried bureaucracy of indigenous chiefs – had crystallised in official British circles (and experience of protecting peasant interests in Buganda came to be applied elsewhere in the protectorate). Even so, the British had not found – and were never to find – an infinitely durable colonial formula. And the Second World War was to highlight the serious *dis*advantages of the colonial state's dependency on the 'production-for-consumption' of its numerous, anonymous peasant farmers.

A limited colonial impact

For the decade or more up to the Second World War, Uganda gives the appearance of a state and society which had established for the time being a relationship that was broadly satisfactory – if not quite 'essentially static' as Ehrlich has described it (1965: 468). Britain itself was preoccupied with other matters in the 1920s and the 1930s.

It had, in short, 'too few resources, too many commitments' (Gallagher 1982: 128) to pay new attention to far-flung African dependencies. It has been said of the early 1920s that the protectorate government still 'had no grand design, no master plan of the Uganda it wished to create' (Pratt 1965: 483). Indeed, the inter-war years are marked by a kind of *ad hoc* evolution in a context of, as it were, sustained absent-mindedness on the part of British imperialism.

Uganda's peasant producers came to enjoy the central place not only in economic practice but also in official valuation. Officials came retrospectively to accept as ideologically desirable practices which had emerged piecemeal from the preceding years. These included the peasant-based economy of Uganda, and the 'indirect rule' of its administration. The world market after the First World War had ensured the ruin of settler plantations in Uganda and confirmed the position of the peasant farmer there. Characteristically, however, British colonial authorities wished to appear to be responsible for what happened and, as Wrigley remarks, 'the policies which were originally adapted as a matter of practical expediency hardened gradually into a political doctrine' (1959: 43).

The colonial state had not made – for it had not needed to make – a profound impact on Uganda. Beyond the establishment of its ultimate responsibility for law and order, and financial viability through the interlocking of Uganda's economic life with more developed capitalist economies, British rule had few ambitions and made few demands other than fiscal. The reference of the handbook of Uganda in 1935 to 'a revolution which has in twenty years transformed Uganda' represents a judgement which needs to be tested against a longer perspective (Thomas and Scott 1935: 273). If we take peasant cotton producers as typical, we must note that neither their productive effort nor their subsequent purchase of goods entailed major change. In Buganda in particular, women could continue as before to provide subsistence by work on food crops, while men might employ migrant labourers for the more onerous tasks of cotton cultivation. In return consumer goods – whether cotton clothes, cigarettes and tobacco, domestic building materials, hardware, tools, or bicycles – could be enjoyed and absorbed without essential disruption to the existing social context. The lives of Uganda's peasants in the 1930s have been described as 'settled', 'quiet', 'unexciting', and 'unexacting'. The 'normal stuff of rural life' was seemingly undisturbed by pressures associated with British colonial rule (Wrigley 1959: 56-58).

By 1939 there were therefore few obvious signs of major economic dislocation in Uganda. 'Industrialisation' largely consisted of cotton ginning, in which seasonal workers would be casually employed without written contracts, and local mining in Western Province. Among the plantations, the sugar estates were by far the largest employers. However, the estimated total monthly average figure for employment of unskilled labour in 1937 was only 83,000. This represented just 9 per cent of the total of adult males in the protectorate, and half of this 9 per cent worked for the British colonial government or for native administrations (Report on the Labour Situation 1938: 34). The towns were few and small and had comparatively few African residents. Only about 500 Africans had their own dwellings in Kampala, the commercial capital of the British protectorate, while a further 4000 'commuted' there on a daily basis (Thomas and Scott 1935: 276). While by 1938 a class of labourers entirely dependent on wages was coming into existence in the protectorate, the number was still relatively small. Any 'proletariat' that existed was still essentially rural and consisted typically of migrant labourers, mostly from outside the Uganda Protectorate.

The structure of Ugandan society at this time was one in which Africans were engaged in a rather narrow range of perennial pursuits which reflected a degree of regional differentiation – a degree of *de facto* 'uneven development'. As noted earlier, the north and west of Uganda have been described as comprising – albeit not necessarily by design – something of 'a labour reservoir for the cash economy of the south' (Mamdani 1976: 52). Many from here migrated (or sought employment locally in government or private employment) to earn their cash 'target' for tax payment, bride-price or consumer purchase. The north also provided men for the very small peacetime British colonial army. Meanwhile, peasant farmers throughout most of the rest of the protectorate – especially in Buganda and Eastern Province, which were best served by communications with the East African coast – could participate in a modestly profitable 'subsistence-plus-cash-crops' economy (Tosh 1978: 415-416), without enormous capital outlay or technical innovation. They thus had little need to seek work elsewhere in mines, on plantations, or in the army or police.

Alternative opportunities for Africans in 1939 were limited. They were excluded from the processing of cotton, and they received no encouragement for the forming of co-operatives, of which there were a mere 15 in 1938. Small-scale trading was possible. 'The Muganda' was once officially described in 1938 as actually 'less a farmer than a trader' (Report on Labour Situation 1938: para.185). But it was Indians who dominated trade as well as cotton processing; and it was typically from Indian stores that Africans purchased their imported goods.[6] A contemporary observer wrote that 'the great ambition of almost every Muganda boy is to be a motor driver' (Lillingston 1934: 18), and this indeed became the occupation of some. However, the Uganda African Motor Drivers Association remained the only registered trade union in Uganda before the Second World War.

The British colonial state in Uganda above all valued order, continuity and predictability, in the economy as in all aspects of life. While the state at this time still made relatively few demands on its subjects, so too an established economic order, which enjoyed a considerable degree of acceptance, made few demands on the British administration. The British were still engaged at the end of the 1930s in little more than a holding operation. The colonial state was more willing – and more able – to prevent change than to generate development. Attempts to introduce the plough and permanent rotations into peasant agriculture in the 1920s had failed. In spite of its 'long-sustained badgering', Wrigley remarks pertinently that the administration's initiatives succeeded only when they were going 'with the grain' of peasant volition (Wrigley 1959: 66).

For the most part the British eschewed upheaval. As officials put it in 1935, 'It has been the object of the Administration to superimpose an appropriately coloured version of our own civilisation on the structure of native society *without causing any serious dislocation of its foundations*' (Thomas and Scott 1935: 272. My italics). Capitalism had been allowed only a limited penetration of Uganda's economy and society. Ehrlich remarks that 'the government which had begun as an active initiator of economic development had been transformed into an administration that valued stability above economic progress' (1965: 469). The description 'paternalism rather than exploitation' also implies an essentially passive rather than active role for the colonial state (Brett 1973: 42). Yet as Brett points out, there remained a contradiction. The political need was for order, exercised through largely 'traditional' forms. Yet the longer-term economic need was for a more expansive cash economy, potentially corrosive of African society. In parallel with the inevitable political manipulation of 'indirect rule', here in the economy too there was a dilemma for the colonial state: change was both essential and dangerous.

Seen from 'below', the impact of British colonial rule had been as limited as the administration's ambitions. It lay first in the payment of taxes. Beyond requiring a monetary income, this meant regular contact with officials: not European but the various layers of African authority in native administrations. In the particular case of Buganda's native government, an African kingdom also retained a judicial responsibility and passed its own legislation. There was continuity here with the pre-colonial past. In addition, the Buganda government now carried out a range of new executive functions. At heart it neatly reflected the two colonial priorities: it had its own staff of armed police to maintain order, and a hierarchy of chiefs to collect taxes. The upkeep of roads was a devolved responsibility; so too was the publication of Protectorate government ordinances, relating to matters such as sleeping sickness control and treatment of dead cotton bushes. All this could impinge on daily life but it was as yet only a hint of the demands that subsequent years would soon bring. Meanwhile, in the 1930s the presence of 'government', in its ultimate form of the British colonial authority, remained not only remote but also largely unquestioned and publicly unchallenged.

While colonial rule in the Uganda Protectorate entailed taxation (which required some kind of income-bearing occupation) and officialdom, it did not call for forced labour. There had been a phase, lasting from 1909 to 1922, when the colonial government had imposed *kasanvu,* a form of forced labour, to ensure that roads were built and cotton carried to railhead. It involved working for a month for the Public Works Department for a set wage. In 1938, 16 years after *kasanvu's* abolition, officials acknowledged that Uganda had 'already passed the stage when direct action to induce the labourer to seek employment might yield any useful results' (Report on the Labour Situation 1938: para.18). While there was on paper enough manpower for the labour needs of the protectorate, the British authorities resigned themselves to the fact that it was not actually forthcoming in sufficient numbers. Most Africans in Uganda, it was observed, had enough land on which to produce their own food and to enable them to satisfy their tax obligations and consumer wants by growing cash crops. In this sense and as far as the labour needs of the protectorate were concerned, the spread of the cash crop economy had been a little too successful. By 1938, even the 'traditional and less objectionable' obligatory labour for local purposes had been commuted everywhere into a money payment (Ingham 1962: 348).

Another impact of colonialism by this time was predominantly cultural. Cultural change is impossible to measure accurately and cannot be fully investigated here, but some trends were visible by 1939. The impact of Christianity in Uganda preceded the arrival of colonial rule (and was independent of it). The work of the churches then expanded further. It was associated with that other great medium of cultural change and access to a wider world, book-based education, which was in the hands of mission schools. 'The African of today', it was noted in 1934, 'is coming to realise that education is the key which will unlock the gates leading into that world of wonder and mystery.... In Buganda at any rate ... they are determined to have the best education possible, and that this shall be of a definitely Christian character' (Lillingston 1934: 42). And it has been suggested that 'the Christian Ganda to a large extent adopted the European view of the virtue of work and progress and economic development' (Wrigley 1959: 18). Christianity and the new education opened doors of opportunity. It is very hard to agree with Mamdani's charge that missionary education amounted to 'not liberation, but enslavement' (1976: 161). By contrast, a notable and prophetic contemporary official observation was that education was potentially dangerous, because 'manual labour will come to be regarded as beneath the dignity of one who has learned to read and write' (Report on the Labour Situation 1938: para.184).

The materialism behind the African aspiration for a higher standard of living, which hinged on the purchase and consumption of foreign imports, could be welcomed by the British colonial state as an incentive to work or produce. But already there were alarms being sounded about some aspects of cultural life in Uganda in the 1930s. The British were blamed. Daudi Chwa, Kabaka of Buganda, wrote a pamphlet in 1935 which condemned 'foreignisation'. He considered that a new generation was discarding 'its native and traditional customs, habits and good breedings'[*sic*], and abandoning 'a very strict moral code', in favour of 'the worst foreign habits and customs of the Western people'. He singled out prostitution and promiscuous relationships for particular disapproval (quoted in Low 1971: 105-7). Other contemporaries emphasised excessive drinking as 'a real threat to the moral and material future of the people' (Report on the Labour Situation 1938: para.259). Though similar comments also came from expatriates (whose own intake of spirits was not inconsiderable) some damaging phenomena, associated by contemporaries with the advance of 'civilisation', were unmistakable.

Yet at the level of what has been termed 'the ground floor' of history (Braudel 1974: ix) there was, despite all, a considerable degree of continuity to African life under British colonial rule in Uganda. In some respects this *dismayed* successive British governors, being itself a comment on the slightness of the colonial impact. Mitchell wrote in 1939, 'If ... we look at modern East Africa as it really is, the picture is disturbing' (1939: 29). He deplored the continued prevalence of poverty, ignorance and disease. Colonial rule thus far had had little impact on housing, the quality of water supplies or the methods of cultivation. Educational advances had been limited, and Mitchell's successor, Dundas, lamented a shortage of trained African staff which in turn reduced the effectiveness of colonial rule.[7] The most limiting factor of all however was perhaps the British insistence that the financing of 'development' projects should be met fully by Uganda itself, out of local taxation. Gartrell reminds us that 'the essence of the paternalism characteristic of Uganda officials was their firm belief that they were taxing the Africans for their own good' (1979: 204). But such revenue could achieve little if not supplemented. In fact, 1939 brought the welcome news that British funds would be made available for a new hospital and medical school at Mulago, Kampala.[8] But such a health project could no more disguise the general low level of health provision in the territory than the existence of Makerere College could disguise widespread and continuing deficiencies in education.

Having created an arbitrarily defined 'Uganda', British colonial rulers did not create an integrated society within its borders. They did not set out to; nor in the circumstances could they have done. As a government minister in independent Uganda later reflected: 'Indirect rule did not help the multifarious tribes of Uganda to understand one another better, or at all' (Ibingira 1973: 28) – yet 'indirect rule' was the cheapest and thus perhaps the only credible option for the British. As protectorate officials Thomas and Scott observed in 1935, economic development had not altered the basic pre-colonial pattern of African population distribution; and dietary factors among others had helped to inhibit a lasting drift of people from less productive to more productive areas (1935: 274). As it happened, Africans nearer the heart of the British protectorate, in Buganda and Eastern Province, had greater opportunity to 'advance' than some others, so variable was the access to communications, viability of certain cash crops and availability of education and other services. Ways of life remained separate and distinct. So did languages. Swahili had a degree of utility as a *lingua franca*, especially in aiding communication between Indian employer and African employee. But in general not only African peoples but even to an extent whole races, too, lived, as they conversed, *separately* – just as in a sense they worked separately, within 'the three-tier system' (European/Indian/African) obtaining in the protectorate (Mangat 1969: 172).

While the persistence of local identities perpetuated possibilities of local foci for political aspirations, there was very little interest among Africans for representation in the Protectorate's Legislative Council. In the case of Buganda there was positive hostility to such representation, in case it eroded the kingdom's special status derived from the 1900 Agreement. The Legislative Council remained therefore the preserve of Europeans and Indians, typically Europeans like H.R.Fraser and R.G.Dakin, representative of coffee and cotton interests respectively.

On a different level, there was no overt African sense of identification with the rest of British East Africa. Debate about 'closer union' with Kenya had been shelved in 1931. Since then economic links continued to function, if to Uganda's comparative disadvantage. Specific grievances such as discriminatory railway rates, affecting all races in Uganda, fuelled a general suspicion, particularly strong among Africans and Indians, of the white settlers of Kenya Colony. There would be widespread opposition to proposals for closer union – which Europeans in Kenya would seek, and be expected, to dominate – when these re-emerged during the Second World War. 'Closer union' would have entailed a colonial impact on Uganda far more extensive and intensive than anything the protectorate had so far experienced.

In reality, the weight of colonial rule on society in Uganda in the 1930s was evidently bearable. There was of course no equality between British and African, but collaborative relationships were established and sustained by a degree of mutual self-interest at political, economic, and even cultural levels. Taken as a whole and seen within the context of its time, the evidence does little if anything to suggest 'absolutism' and 'exploitation' as the defining hallmarks of the inter-war British administration in Uganda.

---

1. J.Mukasa, 'Why British Administration Fails', *Uganda Herald*, 15 April 1936.
2. See Fred Burke's introductory survey in *Local Government and Politics in Uganda*, 1964, especially p.3.
3. Blue Book, 1939.

4. *Report of the Uganda Cotton Commission*, 1938, paras. 344, 345.
5. For detail on Ruanda-Urundi immigrants, see Chapter 9.
6. For a book-length discussion of the Uganda situation, see H.S.Morris, *The Indians in Uganda*, London 1968. For a study of one Indian community of particular significance and influence, see Gardner Thompson, 'The Ismailis in Uganda', in Michael Twaddle, ed., *Expulsion of a Minority: Essays on Ugandan Asians*, London 1975.
7. Dundas to Dawe, 6 September 1943, PRO CO 536/209/40100/3/43.
8. Report, *Uganda Herald*, 16 August 1939.-

4
1939-1945: Phoney War or Total War?

The question

Just three weeks before Britain declared war on Hitler's Germany, in August 1939, Namirembe Cathedral witnessed a unique religious service. It was designed to articulate sentiments that were shared by both rulers and ruled in Uganda. There in Kampala, at the historic heart of a Protestantism introduced less than a lifetime before, a multiracial congregation gathered to unveil a window dedicated to the late King George V – 'Father of all his Peoples', as Governor Mitchell described him. 'Very large numbers of Europeans, Africans, Indians and Goans watched' as Mitchell drew back the Union Flag to reveal the memorial.[1] It depicted the royal arms, the arms of the protectorate, and the arms of Buganda, Bunyoro, Toro, Ankole and Busoga, all linked by a twine of blue ribbon. African rulers and county chiefs sat in the cathedral alongside officers of the Protectorate government. The national anthem was played by a band of the 4th (Uganda) battalion of the King's African Rifles, and Handel's Hallelujah chorus was sung in Luganda.

What can be made of such a scene? Was the whole occasion an instance of what one historian of seventeenth century France has called 'government by spectacle' (Treasure 1966: 296) – an illusion, fragile and as fruitless as its prayers for the peace of the world? Or was the service proof of a more substantial colonial achievement?

Any adequate answer must recall the very limited aims and objectives adopted by British colonial rule in Uganda before 1939, and the comparatively slight demands and dislocation occasioned by them.

68

It must be stressed that up to this point the British had tried only to *administer*, rather than to *govern* in the sense of fully exploiting the human, financial and material resources of a territory acquired – for no reason other than its location – around half a century earlier. The British had sought, since the 1890s, a marriage of convenience with the peoples of Uganda. Spasmodic displays of force had been converted into the steady exercise of civil administration. Coercion had been replaced by consent. So far, the establishment of a colonial order and the collection of taxes had entailed reorientation rather than revolution. Political and economic collaboration had been instituted and sustained, with relative ease, to the benefit of the colonial state and that of many of its indigenous citizens. Yet reflective British officials already recognised that the future – even a future of continuing international peace – would bring challenges which they would find difficult to meet.

For in Uganda, at the start of the Second World War, it was easier to identify the themes and preoccupations of British colonialism than to predict its future there. A contemporary Colonial Office view of British East Africa was guarded, if honest: 'We have introduced to the country, with enormous rapidity, the wonders and horrors of European civilisation; and no-one can tell how the experiment will turn out'.[2] As observed earlier, it can be in the interests of even well established states to govern *little*, and to make *few* demands upon their subjects. But the Second World War now ruled out such an option in Uganda, and instead obliged the British to make demands there on an unprecedented scale.

In Europe, the earlier global conflict of 1914-1918 had for the first time made sense of the concept of 'total war'. Could there be a comparable undertaking in colonised equatorial Africa, twenty years on; or would the war be so unreal there as to remain 'phoney'? To this question there was to be no simple answer. But the British attempt to mobilise all Uganda's resources, in order to make a contribution to the war effort which would be anything but phoney, exposed the limits of the power of their colonial state as no enterprise of theirs had done previously. On the one hand, the war was to unmask perplexing continuities in the anatomy of the under-powered colonial state; yet on the other hand, it was to contribute to irreversible changes, notably in the relationship between government and governed in the protectorate. What we will notice is not that demands were refused, but that Africans defined the nature and extent of their compliance with the government's exhortations. To a marked extent, Africans continued to fulfil their established role in the colonial relationship. But while doing so they became frustrated by the failure of the colonial state, for its part, to fulfil what was for them its own key self-justifying function – the provision of sufficient imported goods at affordable prices. The resulting disturbances of January 1945 marked the historic emergence of African (rather than expatriate European) interest groups and voices, and their crystallisation as the dominant political force in the protectorate thereafter.

The service in Namirembe may therefore be said to have symbolically marked the end of the beginning of Uganda's colonial history. So soon afterwards, the effects of the Second World War were to mark the beginning of its end.

Phoney war

For Britain itself, much of the first year of the Second World War was 'Phoney War'. This is partly because nothing could be done in September 1939 to prevent the Poles from being overrun and partly because except for engagements and losses at sea there were no significant encounters between Allied forces and the Germans. The Norway campaign in the spring of 1940 brought the war nearer, but what made the conflict suddenly and alarmingly 'real' was Hitler's push west and the quick fall of France. There then followed the Battle of Britain and the Blitz, and four full years of total British commitment – first to survival and then, as part of a great alliance, to the defeat of Germany.

It could be said that there was a comparable period of phoney war in Uganda, too; one which ended, also, at about the same time as Britain's, if for a slightly different reason. On seeing the fall of France, and greedy to participate in the spoils, Mussolini finally declared war on the Allies in June 1940. Italian-held Ethiopia thus became at once a hostile neighbour for British East Africa. Subsequently, with the fall of Singapore in February 1942 there was to be an even greater need for all Britain's overseas possessions, even those formerly most neglected, to come to its aid.

Yet there is a sense in which Uganda's war remained 'phoney'. This was not the case for its British personnel, of course, who clearly felt closely associated with it, but it was for its African (and Indian) population. The protectorate experienced no fighting and no civilian casualties. Some Africans left Uganda to fight abroad, and there was nothing phoney about the losses they suffered in battle or on campaign overseas. But the real struggle in the territory lay in the British colonial state's belated attempts to govern: to mobilise and to exploit Uganda's potential for the imperial war effort ... and to do so without undermining the layers of collaboration, political and economic, on which the administration had come to rest.

There was perhaps something unreal, at the outset, about Mitchell's efforts to explain and to justify the war against Germany to his African subjects. As one of Britain's African dependencies, Uganda was technically at war from 3 September 1939. A message from Governor Mitchell on that day was intended to inform Uganda's Africans, and to justify Britain's decision to fight the Axis powers. The Danzig question was explained by a rather contrived regional analogy: 'Although not in Poland [it] is the seaport for Poland, as Mombasa is for Uganda, though not in Uganda'. Hitler's aim, the message continued, was to destroy Poland – 'as Uganda would be destroyed if Kenya were a hostile foreign country'. Mitchell ended on a reassuring, if somewhat ironic, even desperate, note for a colonial dependency: 'There can be only one end ... liberty and independence will survive'.[3]

Readers of the *Uganda Herald* had already been told how to respond to the twin horrors of gas and aerial bombing. In the event of a gas attack, the advice was to 'urinate on a handkerchief and hold it over your nostrils and mouth'; and if 'Wop planes' raided Jinja, Entebbe and Kampala, Britain's subjects were to 'lie down quietly out of doors and wait till the trouble is over'.[4] So was there nothing to worry about? Privately, Mitchell fully recognised that the repercussions of Britain's war with Hitler could be destructive for Uganda, and he sought to protect the protectorate from them. He wrote in his diary: 'To bring war here would be so wicked'.[5]

The outbreak of war in 1939 prompted the Colonial Office and Mitchell to advocate differing priorities for the Uganda Protectorate. In the new context, the Colonial Office was more than ever concerned with accountancy rather than with economic advance – with continuing to balance Uganda's books rather than with stimulating development. It expected Uganda initially to help Britain's war effort merely by 'paying for itself'. The instruction was largely negative: to avoid using up foreign exchange (specifically, by seeking self-sufficiency in food) and to avoid making any demand on Britain which 'deflects men, material and shipping from war purposes'.[6] Meanwhile, normal services and any existing development policies were to be sustained in Uganda, but only if they could be financed from local sources. All colonies were urged to budget cautiously, to expect no aid in any form from the British taxpayer, and to consider raising taxation, especially in the wake of the 'drastic' war budget now introduced in Britain. Mitchell, in the last year of his governorship of Uganda, did what he could to resist such belt-tightening and to protect the interests of Uganda's producers and consumers by more expansive policies. But the war, and London, inhibited him; and frustration in this key area of policy made him all the readier to move on to Nairobi in June 1940.

In the meantime, having recognised the need to justify Uganda's participation in the war, Mitchell also adopted a longer-term strategy to win over public opinion. While the postmaster general was appointed chief censor, makeshift information services set out 'to circulate news and to counteract idle rumours and mischievous propaganda' ('War Effort' [1] November 1939). Broadsheets were distributed and broadcasts made. Mitchell noted in his diary on 8 September that 7000 people daily listened to news through loudspeakers in Kampala. By mid-1940 the information officer employed eleven full-time workers, and a mobile cinema service was said to attract audiences of 5000 in and around Kampala ('War Effort' [2] July 1940).

But this was not a government which could control information or opinion. Illiteracy was one obstacle; and British efforts at wartime propaganda were doomed from the beginning in a country where rumour, not radio, ruled. There were just 30 wireless sets in African possession in Uganda in 1939 (Twining 1939). News of the collapse of France did eventually become known, and it proved damaging. As a high-ranking British official in Uganda later recalled, 'the natives got to the state of believing that it was useless planting food or economic crops, as the Germans would soon come and confiscate the lot'. He continued, 'The Africans were becoming truculent; any who had lost their cases in court or had been admonished by government were immediately anti-British. "We are tired of this harsh British rule; we would like to have the Germans over us .... Germany will take over Uganda in three weeks." And so it went on' (Temple-Perkins 1946: 61-62). Against this type of enemy – alienation – the British colonial state's propaganda potential in Uganda was meagre.

Relations with the Baganda were especially uneasy. Temple-Perkins, subsequently the Resident, noted 'reports of subversive talk from all quarters.... One month in a small area my detectives reported 43 cases. My enquiries at the native government (Buganda) headquarters, however, elicited the fact that they also had detectives out, and their total for the same month was 166' (Temple-Perkins 1946: 61). In the light of this situation, Governor Mitchell decided not to attempt to raise direct taxation in Buganda, despite having recognised clear financial grounds for doing so. Meanwhile, the current Resident – the senior protectorate official for the kingdom – expressed a jaundiced view of the Baganda at this early stage of the war. He said he was 'disappointed' with them, adding that 'there was an irresponsible section which indulged in anti-British talk.'[7]

As noted earlier, there was already some 'opposition' in Buganda, before the implications of the Second World War gave further grounds and impetus for disaffection. For many Baganda meanwhile, there were two events more immediate and perhaps more significant than anything connected with the outbreak of war. These were domestic, seemingly parochial, issues, but they were of considerable moment. First came the death of the Kabaka, Daudi Chwa, in November 1939. Then came the prosecution of one Ignatius Musazi by the Lukiiko in June 1940. Both events were to contribute significantly to a new and turbulent – wartime but not war-related – episode in Buganda's dealings with the Protectorate government, to be considered below.

There was still a lingering unreality about the war itself, as late as June 1940. Mitchell's diary entry for Sunday 2 June illustrates this. First, he portrayed the humiliating evacuation of British troops from France at Dunkirk, under the threat of annihilation at the hands of the Germans, as 'surely an almost unparalleled military and naval achievement'. Immediately following, he made another favourable comment, this time on the Entebbe Club's annual flower show – 'a very large turnout of people and altogether it went very well'. The *Uganda Herald* actually reversed the order, giving the flower show a front-page coverage dwarfing that of Dunkirk.

Within a few days, much was to change. The June 1940 'Blitzkrieg' telegram arrived from London, calling for a 'maximum positive contribution' from the colonies.[8] And by the end of the month, Mitchell himself was in Nairobi. At the same time, Mussolini's declaration of war had brought hostilities directly to East Africa. Mitchell was prompted, in a memorable comment on a rival European country's power in Africa, to make a last advisory address to Ugandans: 'Do not be afraid. It is possible, but not likely, that you may see an Italian aeroplane or two over some part of Uganda. If you do, do not be frightened. Sit quietly in your banana groves, or under any trees, until it has gone away. It will do you no harm'.[9] We do not know how frightened the African population of Uganda was by the Italian declaration of war; perhaps they were reassured by Mitchell's message. In fact, this danger to Ugandans never materialised. Instead came an intensified pressure on them to wage a form of economic warfare on Britain's behalf.

Total war

By the end of 1941, there was no doubting the reorientation of British colonial policy in Uganda to meet wartime demands. Uganda's new governor, Charles Dundas, even observed in December 1941: 'I judge that we are now approaching, if we have not come to, the limit of state-organised effort'.[10] And in the same month, an anonymous letter in the press exclaimed, quite simply: 'now we have total war with a vengeance'.[11] Both statements deserve close examination. What were the 'limits of state-organised effort' in Uganda? When, if at all, were they reached? Did the war effort in Uganda during the Second World War amount to 'total war'? What could 'total war' mean in the context of this British colonial state?

For a definition of total war we must look outside Uganda. It has been said of the British war effort in the Second World War that 'the theory and practice of total war was developed to a much further extent than in 1914-18' (Marwick 1971: 97). What theory? The war was an emergency, and total war in Britain was no more than a series of practical responses to the critical circumstances of the time. We must thus consider total war in Uganda by examining practice, not by reference to theory. How did Uganda's war effort compare with contemporary practice elsewhere?

British experience provides a suitable point of comparison. Britain's total war reveals two main characteristics. First, there was an unprecedented mobilisation of the nation's human, financial and material resources for war purposes. Secondly, a central part in mobilisation and direction was played by the state.

At first it was not realised that Britain's colonies would need to undergo changes of a similar kind. But by June 1941 it was clear that colonial states would indeed have to play an unprecedented role in the process of mobilisation for war. Perhaps, as it has been suggested, 'the British Empire in Africa was marginal to total war for Britain' (Cowen and Westcott 1986: 25). Nonetheless, June 1941 marks the moment when the policy of 'total war' was exported, as a practical strategy, to Britain's colonies.[12] Henceforth, Uganda's war effort in many respects mirrored Britain's.

Thus in the Uganda Protectorate, too, there was both mobilisation of resources and an enhanced role for the state. By 1944 the Civil Defence Board could claim that 'practically every man and woman in the country, who could be usefully employed for the furtherance of the war effort', was making a proper contribution.[13] Financial policy served, and fiscal measures closely resembled, Britain's. New 'ministries', such as the Department of Labour and the Department of Supply, were created. Additional controls over the economy as a whole were introduced, so that it could be claimed in 1943 that 'commerce is gradually being shaped into what might almost be called a vast public utility organisation ... control is taking the place of competition'.[14] And Uganda, like Britain, had its own officials planning for post-war development.

Yet it is the contrast between British and Ugandan experience which should be stressed. Some policy objectives had different priorities, or posed different challenges. For example, import control had particular significance in a colonial state, whereas rationing proved to be impracticable on a wide front. And savings schemes had little chance of success in a territory where there was no sustained habit of saving to exploit.

There were other differences, of great importance, too. The British government in Uganda, unlike its metropolitan counterpart, did not come to embrace interests and institutions in society which had previously been 'outsiders'. For example, there could be no party-political coalition: the British colonial state remained a 'one-party' state. Although there was a still closer association with the unofficial expatriate community in Uganda during the Second World War, there could be no equivalent of the British incorporation of the trade union movement into partnership. Society as a whole, especially African, was not drawn into the corridors of state power in Uganda. Even when the British administration there drew up its local plans for welfare and development, it did so without reference to representatives of this wider African society. Britain's programme for Uganda for the later 1940s was conceived without discussion with its intended beneficiaries. It was imposed on them from above.

The state in Britain exercised authority over a society which largely accepted wartime regulations as reasonable and necessary. This is partly because the British people were fully at war, in a sense never replicated in East Africa. It was 'their' war, not least because it was local and immediate. In Uganda, in the military sense at least, the war was always 'phoney' because its principal theatres were so far away. Among the various peoples in Uganda, only British expatriates could fully identify with the British war experience in Europe. Nor, most significantly, did Africans in Uganda enjoy the improvement of real income, and standard of living, which for many people in Britain made restrictions in the later war years tolerable. Indeed, quite the opposite was the case.

The relationship between ruler and ruled in Uganda could not sustain such a degree of 'total war' as obtained in Britain. In Uganda there was neither the necessary degree of consensus within society, nor the sense of a common purpose shared by society and state. Moreover, civil society in Uganda had no 'tradition of compliance' with state interventionism (Prest 1948: 17). It has been said of the *First* World War that 'real conscription was possible only where a partnership existed between people and administration' (Stone 1975: 214). Such a partnership did not exist in Uganda during the Second World War. Again it has been written of the earlier conflict that 'the history of the state and of the people merged for the first time' (Taylor 1965: 2). Something of this can be seen in Uganda in the Second World War, but it was an uneasy merger between ill-suited partners.

The Protectorate government in Uganda was inexperienced in assuming new responsibilities, and proved to have limited competence. Subsequent chapters of this study will seek to explore the means it adopted to mobilise men, money and materials, and to measure the extent of that mobilisation. We will see that in none of these areas had 'the limit' been reached by December 1941 – which makes the observation by Dundas quoted above appear both overcautious and premature.

In Uganda, as in Britain, total war had a further dimension, beyond the mobilisation of resources. The British colonial state sought to protect society in Uganda from the worst economic consequences of the war. In Uganda it concentrated on two aspects of economic warfare in particular: import control and price control. Within the protectorate, British success in waging total war was to be measured against its ability to maintain imports of goods, at prices which African consumers could afford. In the event, attempts at control failed this test.

We must note, again, that the British in Uganda had very little freedom of movement – and in this respect, one might add, they were in a similar situation to that of successor African governments of the territory. They operated in a context which was always unfavourable. They had, of course, no more influence over world economic conditions during the Second World War than they had had during the 1930s depression – or than independent Uganda was to have subsequently over, say, the global oil crisis of the 1970s. Conditions progressively worsened, at least to 1942. Thereafter, supplies improved but world prices continued to rise. At the end of 1943, for example, the financial secretary was drawing attention to 'the considerable increase in the landed cost of imported goods'.[15] Moreover, as we shall see, in the later years of the war Nairobi-based institutions emphasised the merely peripheral significance, within British East Africa, of the Ugandan administration.

And this colonial state did not have an effectiveness comparable with that of the mother country. For the state in Britain, 'total war' was realistic as a strategy. In respect of price controls, it could pay subsidies to producers in order to help control prices in the shops; and it could operate a rationing scheme for a wide range of foods and other articles. And it did not have to confront such a critical primary supply problem as its colonies faced. The British in Uganda however could subsidise neither the foreign manufacturers of imported goods, nor the countless small producers of local foodstuffs. The Protectorate government did succeed in rationing petrol, the distribution and purchase of which was relatively easy to monitor. But its only other experiments in this field were marginal in range and importance. Bread, flour, rice and butter were rationed to 'non-natives' from June 1943. When stocks of butter were then left unsold, the *Herald* characteristically chided the Protectorate government, urging it to 'realise its limitations and leave rationing alone'.[16]

The British declaration of war against Germany on 3 September 1939 had automatically included the colonies. Mitchell's response then was unequivocal: 'The whole resources of the country have been placed unreservedly at the disposal of the common cause'.[17] What resources? During the five years from June 1940 during which the Protectorate government sought to mobilise Uganda for war, the territory's contribution had three main constituents: men, money and materials. Africans served in the armed forces either as soldiers or in a variety of auxiliary roles. Money contributions took the form of gifts and loans to Britain. Materials comprised not only staple products such as cotton but also a range of food products and, with the loss of British possessions in the Far East by early 1942, strategic war materials such as rubber. Once we have seen how the war affected the administration itself, this contribution deserves to be measured – if only to indicate the extent to which one remote British African dependency, following years of minimal government, could yet be of value to an empire engaged in a world-wide struggle for survival.

But we will learn more about the British colonial state in Uganda if we ask not only what was the contribution, but also how was it effected. How were Africans incorporated into the forces, to serve 'the common cause' as far away from their homes as Burma? Where did the money come from, which multiplied former aggregates of annual revenue? And how were peasant farmers induced to grow crops, to produce not only greater quantities but also new varieties of materials for export? Further, what factors determined the extent of this overall contribution? In short, what was the extent – and what were the limits – of the power of the colonial state in Uganda to exploit the territory and mobilise its people, now that it was summoned to do so for the first time?

Subsequent chapters will clearly illustrate that the British authorities were by no means masters of their own agenda. In no theatre of war – or mobilisation for war – were they to be autonomous agents. Between urgent metropolitan demands and judicious African responses there was to be little room to manoeuvre. In terms of the expectations placed upon it (and indeed its subsequent accomplishments), the colonial government's war, after 1940/41, cannot be described as 'phoney'. Even so, its ability to fulfil those expectations by the exercise of state power over its African subjects was to prove very far from 'total'.

1. *Uganda Herald*, 16 August 1939.
2. Sir Arthur Dawe, Assistant Under-Secretary of State, Minute, 19 January 1940, PRO CO 822/103/15.
3. Published in *Uganda Herald*, 6 September 1939.
4. Diarist 'Nemo', *Uganda Herald*, 30 August 1939.
5. Mitchell, Diary, 6 September 1939, Rhodes House MSS Afr.r.101.
6. Secretary of State to Colonies, 15 September 1939, PRO CO 854/178.
7. A.H.Cox, reported in the Executive Council Minutes for 17 May 1940, PRO CO 536/206/40099/1.
8. Secretary of State to Colonies, 5 June 1940, PRO CO 854/117.
9. 'Message to the People of Uganda on the Outbreak of Hostilities with Italy', reproduced as Appendix B to 'War Effort' [2], July 1940.
10. Address to the Legislative Council, 9 December 1941.
11. *Uganda Herald*, 17 December 1941.
12. Secretary of State to Colonies, 5 June 1941, PRO CO 854/120.
13. Uganda Civil Defence Board Minutes, 23 May 1944.
14. Financial Secretary to the Legislative Council, 9 December 1942.
15. Financial Secretary to the Legislative Council, 15 December 1943.
16. Editorial, *Uganda Herald*, 23 June 1943.
17. 'Message of Loyalty from the Uganda Protectorate to the King', 3 September 1939, published in *Uganda Herald*, 6 September 1939.

5

Crisis in the Administration

Undermanned

The British were not well placed to exercise effective – let alone 'absolute' – authority over Uganda in 1939, and the war itself further weakened their capacity to do so. Until now, demands on the Protectorate government in Uganda had been slight. A few British expatriate officers had governed with comparative ease, committed to little more than the fostering of low levels of peasant production and consumption, and good bookkeeping. There was no sudden hiatus in 1939. The initial impact of the Second World War was cushioned by Uganda's peripheral involvement in the conflict. Later, strains multiplied and the administration suffered something of a crisis.

The distorting effects of war made the full exploitation of the protectorate's resources doubly impracticable. More and more tasks had to be carried out by fewer and fewer men. The Protectorate government could not realistically hope to fulfil its redefined dual mandate. 'Total war' in the service of Britain was doomed, while the search for a new legitimacy in Uganda by way of development programmes could not succeed, in the absence of sufficient official expatriate manpower. The Second World War put British colonial rule in Uganda to the test. Weakened by loss of manpower and wearied by the accumulation of commitments, the British administration proved ill equipped to pass.

The total expatriate manpower of the British colonial state in Uganda in 1939 was 574.[1] British personnel were distributed thinly through several departments, only nine of which had as many as 20 European staff. In 1938, the provincial administration – responsible for governing over three and a half million Africans – was in the hands of a mere 74 expatriate officials (Blue Book 1938). More

81

numerous were the Europeans in two of the specialist departments, Medical (80, plus nursing staff) and Public Works (106). The Agriculture Department had 54 Europeans – which exceeded by one the number of European police spread throughout the protectorate. Next in numerical order came Education (32) and Survey (30), followed by the Legal (25) and Veterinary (21) departments. As tasks multiplied, these numbers were reduced. And by the end of the Second World War, assistant district officers and the Public Works Department were each reduced to two-thirds of their pre-war figures (Blue Book 1945).

After war broke out in 1939, official policy was to release men from departments 'while retaining the nucleus necessary for the continued efficient performance of essential departmental duties' ('War Effort' [1] November 1939). Such hopeful assumptions were challenged as soon as Britain's phoney war ended. Thus by the end of May 1940, 90 officials had been released for military service. The Agriculture Department had lost 9 of its staff to war service, while several of its officers were doubling up as assistant district commissioners and its Director was preoccupied with the Supply Board. There were additional duties for the officials who remained at their posts; and there was less leave. Increased workloads as well as the news from Europe lowered morale. It was a depleted, overworked and demoralised British staff who were now to confront the daunting tasks of wartime government in Uganda.

The 90 officials re-deployed were publicly described as 'the maximum contribution' which the protectorate could make immediately ('War Effort' [2] July 1940). In the company of just his senior advisers, Governor Mitchell was trying to calculate the higher, total number of men he could part with *'in extremis'*.[2] In due course far more than this 90 were in fact released. By October 1942, there were 122 officials enlisted, plus another 35 European officers on special war duties other than military service. This figure of 157 represented over a quarter of total pre-war manpower.

Perhaps the most significant 'release' had occurred in June 1940, when Uganda's own governor, Philip Mitchell, transferred to Nairobi. He was ready enough to move, on at least two grounds. First, he was irritated by the Colonial Office's injunctions on how he should, and should not, spend modest amounts of Uganda's revenue. He resisted the suggestion that he appoint a labour secretary, on the grounds that a Labour Department could only tell him what he already knew: for example, that wages in Uganda were too low, or that housing and levels of nutrition were poor.[3] That particular suggestion was dropped, for the time being. But his own proposal, to spend £1000 on experimentation with flax and jute in order to reduce Uganda's dependence on cotton, was turned down in London on grounds of expense.[4] Secondly, Mitchell realised at once that, with Italy's entry into the war, a central authority in British East Africa, in Nairobi, would be 'very desirable', even 'essential'.[5] He had become not only frustrated but also bored by his governorship in Uganda. He told the Colonial Office 'there is very little work for the Governor of Uganda to do here'.[6] His diary confirms his sense of being only a marginal figure in the conflict, with entries such as: 'I had very little to do' (19 June) and 'I had literally nothing to do' (22 June). As Kenya's Governor Moore wrote to London, 'Mitchell, I think, feels himself out of the hunt in Uganda'.[7] Mitchell was not to return to Entebbe. He spent only six months in Nairobi before moving on to Cairo, but his dynamism left its mark on the British East African war effort. His place in Uganda was taken by Charles Dundas, a newcomer whom the Colonial Office was to treat with less respect, and whose record suggests that he lacked something of Mitchell's drive and capability.

By the time of Dundas's arrival in late 1940 'all energies had to be directed to the war effort', and the new governor's aim was to 'keep the machinery of government going as best one could' (Dundas 1955: 215). By the end of 1942, departments generally had been 'handicapped by depletions in their European staff and the natural difficulties of replacements from overseas' and the reduced staff were said to be 'so busily occupied on current affairs' that they could spare no thought for the future.[8] Emergency organisations connected with the war effort had to be manned. Among these, at the height of the war, were the Civil Defence, Transport and Supply Boards; the Uganda Industrial Committee; the administration for internee camps and the directorate of refugees (which struggled to find enough staff to supervise and provide services for several thousand displaced Poles); the Information Office; the Central Recruits Depot at Tororo; Security Intelligence; the Police Service Company; the Secretariat of the Governors' Conference; and the East African War Supplies Board. So European manpower was 'extremely scarce' by 1943.[9] A year later, by which time the Protectorate government was planning to expand its longer-term peacetime activities, it could not find the men to do so. And the ending of the war changed nothing. It was not only development programmes that suffered in 1945. 'Shortage of staff and shortage of materials', said Hall, 'have gravely impeded and circumscribed all departmental activities throughout the current year'.[10]

The experience of the provincial administration illustrates clearly that such pronouncements were no mere excuses for underachievement. The officials of this department were the local agents, the personification, of the British Empire. The provincial commissioner was 'personally and directly responsible to the Governor for the peace and good order of his province and for the efficient conduct of all public business therein'.[11] Among the duties of the provincial administration – 'being the organisation most closely in touch with the native population' – were the promotion of increased cotton yields and the conservation of the soil. Specialists, such as those of the Agriculture Department, were meant to supplement, not replace, the district officers' efforts. There was more than just agriculture to care for. The DO could be described as 'certainly the backbone of the service.... He is the guide, philosopher and friend of, say, a quarter of a million Africans and a few hundred Asians; he is Administrator, Commander-in-Chief, Judge, Advocate, Registrar, Mayor of all Townships and Jack-of-all-Trades. He is, to a large extent, Monarch of all he surveys' (Temple-Perkins 1946: 11). Elspeth Huxley conveyed a similar image in her wartime survey of East Africa. 'Over every district of all these territories presides the white official, the District Officer, the possessor of great powers and great opportunities to guide and shape the destiny of black men and women' (Huxley 1941: 43).

'Great powers and great opportunities'? The role of the provincial administration, already central and many-sided in peacetime, became yet more crucial and varied, but above all more onerous, during the Second World War. It was to be here, in this department, that severe shortage of expatriate manpower in Uganda was to be most keenly felt. Even in peacetime, Governor Mitchell had considered the provincial administration to be understaffed, and he had sought to relieve his senior staff of excessive paperwork. There followed in February 1940 Lord Hailey's exhortation to East Africa's governors that administrative personnel should be out of the office, 'promoting development in their areas' and attending to 'the special problems with which they are called upon to deal as a result of war conditions'.[12] But officers could do neither if they were away, fighting. By the end of 1940, the secondment and departure of 16 officers meant that already the effective number of administrative officers had been reduced by almost a quarter.[13] Far worse was to follow. Within two years, 32 officers were seconded to the armed forces or to other special duties. This was exactly half the approved 'establishment' figure for this department. As a result, a year later the provincial administration could be described as 'down to bedrock and without reserves of any kind'.[14]

Overburdened

Meanwhile, the war brought numerous additional tasks. In Buganda, for example, September 1939 'saw a sudden and almost complete change of focus in the duties carried out by administrative staff' so that, even in the first month of the war, 'one administrative officer was struggling to organise control of petrol and the issue of coupons, while another was endeavouring to organise the sale and distribution of trade goods in the face of a steadily and rapidly deteriorating supply position' – while the third had been commissioned to the 7th KAR battalion. Regular touring 'suffered greatly' as military affairs came to dominate in all parts of the kingdom, and in the later stages of the war, the number of officers was so seriously reduced that 'it was possible only to undertake the more essential duties calculated to maintain the war effort' (Annual Reports 1939-46: 1). A Resident of Buganda was later to argue that the shortage of European officers contributed to the failure of Dundas's constitutional reform in October 1944, analysed in a later chapter. This reform was designed in fact to withdraw such personnel from the administration of the kingdom; but without sufficient staff available to explain and prepare the Baganda for the new arrangement, its chances of success were much-reduced (Boyd 1949: para.13).

The manpower shortage was not confined to Buganda. In the Western Province staff were reduced to the extent that it was difficult to do more than 'maintain the *status quo* and to attend to the greatly increased duties caused by the War'. In the later stages, with depleted and overworked staffs 'the administrative machine suffered severe breakdowns at times' and without the appointment of military affairs officers in late 1945 to help with demobilisation 'it would have been almost impossible for the machine to function properly' (Annual Reports 1939-46: 66).

District officers were made responsible for soldiers on leave and for remittances of pay to the families of soldiers on active service.[15] More problematical still was the tracking down and return of deserters. It was also intended that the provincial administration would staff the Central Recruits Depot at Tororo. It could not. Eventually instructions had to be issued from Britain at cabinet level that the army should provide the manpower which the Ugandan administration simply did not possess.[16] Nor was there staff to carry out London's instruction in 1943 that the cases of all the aliens in the protectorate be reviewed. Later, the task of 'civil reabsorption' meant that the ending of hostilities in 1945 brought no respite.

The experiences of J.R.N.Elliott, recorded in his personal diary, are instructive. As district officer in Teso, Eastern Province, he had to carry out a multitude of tasks, some directly involved with the military and with security, and others concerning the production drive. Here as elsewhere the provincial administration 'had to concentrate on essentials only'.[17] Extra war work included attending to the RAF and the aerodrome, and helping with the choice of sites for military staging-camps for troops proceeding to Ethiopia. One particular internees' camp entailed 'constant trouble with complaints and problems'.[18] These could lead to bizarre events: one day in this camp,

Elliott was occupied in the marrying of 14 couples, who had apparently calculated that they would thereby enjoy better conditions. Meanwhile he became district commander of the Uganda Defence Force of 30 to 40 men, 'most of whom did not know one end of a rifle from the other'.[19] New wartime controls had to be given priority. A typical early diary entry reads, 'Much of the day on price-fixing'.[20] Charged with maximising Teso's contribution to the war effort, Elliott had to spend time exhorting local inhabitants, through their chiefs, to produce groundnuts for export. In 1942 and 1943 he was busy recruiting. By 1944, he had to direct his district's attention to famine measures.

Officials senior to Elliott similarly found themselves with a huge increase in responsibilities which diverted their attention and sapped their energy. Temple-Perkins had to adapt to a sequence of different posts, including director of civil intelligence and labour commissioner, before being appointed Resident of Buganda. As Resident he had to sit on 4 councils, 8 boards and 8 committees – all of which he found less agreeable than taking the young Kabaka on hunting trips. Disagreeable, too, was constant correspondence with the increasing number of critics of British rule. In this colonial state, criticisms had to be answered, as they could not be silenced. It was said of Temple-Perkins 'that nowhere in the whole of Uganda ... has he heard so many complaints as here in Buganda'.[21]

No government department was unaffected by shortage. A quarter of the European medical officers were away fighting or involved with war work by the end of 1941.[22] Others were later seconded to the refugee administration. An investigation into malnutrition had to be suspended, because during the war neither medical nor agriculture officers could be spared. The Veterinary Department lost 'close on 50% of the staff to part or whole-time war work outside the department' (Simmons 1942). It was not possible, subsequently, to place quarantine restrictions on areas affected by an epidemic of rinderpest. Nor could the still understaffed department cope with the spread of trypanosomiasis in 1945. The departure of teachers left the two government technical schools understaffed. Makerere College 'made do with a tithe of the necessary staff' (Huxley 1948:266).

The Survey Department could not carry out its normal functions. The Second World War has been described as 'an unmitigated tragedy' for *mailo* land registration in Buganda. 'Severe staff shortages, and departmental preoccupation with other commitments' meant that survey and registration of land came nearly to a standstill, while around 150,000 unregistrable transactions in land occurred. Thus, wrote Henry West, 'little was achieved except in the training of African surveyors' (West 1964: 38). But the department even had to suspend its one-year training courses – just a year after they began in 1940 – because of a shortage of supervisory staff.[23] The Survey Training School remained closed until 1944.[24]

The Public Works Department provides a further example of a department severely handicapped by staff shortages at a time when ever greater service was being demanded of it. In 1940, seven of its full-time officials were working for the army, on accommodation and road projects. Other wartime tasks stretched the department to its limits. In July 1943, the Labour Advisory Committee urged the building of camps for the immigrant labourers from Ruanda-Urundi. The committee was warned 'there will be difficulties in finding the necessary staff'.[25] And three years later, Hall had to explain that this work had indeed been seriously delayed, largely because of staff depletion. Part of the problem was post-war demands on the PWD for other constructional work. The ending of the war did not ease the problem of staffing but exacerbated it. Hall said of the PWD in 1945 that 'the daily duty strength ... has seldom exceeded 50% of the approved establishment'.[26] Yet this was the time of demobilisation, the construction of training centres, and the attempted implementation of post-war development plans.

Orde-Browne pointed out that in 1945 another department, the recently re-instituted Labour Department, was 'so understaffed and inadequate' that it could not undertake necessary touring inspection (Orde-Browne 1946: para.343). Early in the war, the inspector of labour had had to act as a reception officer in Kampala for the East Africa Military Labour Service recruits. Five years later, the post-war European establishment in the Labour Department was to be fixed at just five men. Before this, three Europeans (and one African inspector) had to confront the twin challenges of demobilisation of Ugandan troops and the relief of labour shortages.

An early blow to the Agricultural Department was the loss of its director, G.F. Clay. He went first onto the Uganda Supply Board and then to Nairobi where, in December 1942, he was appointed director of native production on the East African Production and Supply Council. Anxiety was expressed in April 1940 over the 'continued frequent absence' of the director from his normal duties.[27] By 1941, there were several unfilled vacancies in the department, nine European officers were away on war service, and several of those who remained had been appointed to act as assistant district officers in addition to their ordinary duties. Then 1942 and 1943 saw staff heavily occupied with the new production programmes. In 1944 an extra task for the 'greatly depleted staff' was famine relief, through 'the utmost encouragement of food planting'.[28] By the end of the war years there was 'an acute shortage of European staff', notably in Western Province; and at the same time, long delayed leave movements and staff changes were said to be having a damaging effect on production in Buganda.[29] The European manpower level in the department that year was 45 compared with 54 before the war. Normal services could not be carried out.

Consequences: 'a lack of government'

To a limited extent the problem of wartime colonial manpower shortage could be relieved. Members of the unofficial European community were brought into closer partnership with government and, in particular, served on the various wartime boards and committees. The potential for such co-operation was limited however, since unofficials, too, were greatly reduced in number through war service. By the end of September 1942 there were 149 'unofficial' enlistments ('War Effort' [5] October 1942). The Uganda Company alone saw 10 of its pre-war total of 23 European employees enter the forces.[30] Moreover, members of the commercial community could not replace district officers or specialist departmental personnel. In 1944, the manpower position was described officially as 'becoming increasingly difficult', despite the fact that 'Honourable Unofficia

Members' of the Legislative Council had been 'called into consultation with greater frequency than ever'.[31] There was a limit, too, to the amount of 'Africanisation' that could take place to compensate for the unavailability of European manpower. Although departments such as Public Works, Agriculture, Veterinary and Medical all made greater use of African personnel when Europeans became scarce, there were – for the same reasons – too few Europeans to teach or train any greater number of such African recruits.

So officials felt the strain. Overseas leave was suspended at once in September 1939. Reduced periods of leave had to be spent locally. Retirements were postponed. The 'strain placed upon officers in the field' took different forms in different periods of the war.[32] There was nothing imaginary about the 'general depression' in Entebbe around the time of the fall of France (Temple-Perkins 1946: 60). At a meeting of the Executive Council at this time 'the Governor impressed upon members that strong measures must be taken with civil officers who allowed themselves to indulge publicly in defeatist views, or gloomy prognostications, regarding the outcome of the present conflict'.[33] Temple-Perkins confided to his diary his own apprehension in May 1940, but colourfully went on to imagine his own final act of defiance: 'If it comes to the worst I shall be ready to fight to the last. With my wide knowledge of the game trails of this country I might raise a guerrilla band. It would take a deuce of a lot of Huns to outdo us in our favourite old elephant haunts' (Temple-Perkins 1946: 60). Mitchell indulged in no such bravado, and his own prognostication was gloomy. 'I had no doubt of the results for Uganda', he later wrote, 'should a few aeroplane loads of German officers arrive to take command in the Congo' (Mitchell 1954: 188).

The toils of war were a new experience, for which pre-war service in the protectorate had provided no preparation. Christopher Harwich described the Entebbe of earlier times. 'In those delightful far-off days before the war,' he wrote, 'work was never very arduous, and the first pairs could be seen driving off from the tee outside the club within minutes of the office clocks striking four' (Harwich 1961: 4). Also looking out-of-date by the end of the war was Elspeth Huxley's picture of a typical officer of the administration: 'Walking down the street with the assurance of a ruler ... he would radiate confidence in the mission of his race to civilise and remould the African' (Huxley 1941: 8).

Confidence was no longer the prevailing mood among British expatriate officials in Uganda by the later years of the Second World War. Although the military crisis passed, vitality was undermined by the additional pressure caused by absence of leave. It was noted that 'ever larger demands are being made on officers whose energy and health are bound to be sapped as a result of long tours and overwork'.[34] Temple-Perkins wrote that by 1944 he was 'tired out, nervy, and as near to collapse as I have ever been' (1946: 91). Dundas confessed in his final New Year message that 'many of us are weary; for not a few of us the trying influence of climate and the effects of long separation from home, family and friends is hard to bear'.[35] And the scramble to apply for leave when the chance arose in September and October suggests war-weariness and exhaustion, among expatriates, rather than Huxley's 'assurance' and 'confidence'.

Neither the extent nor the significance of this manpower crisis, of depletion and demoralisation, can be measured accurately. Yet the impact on the British administration in Uganda was clearly damaging. Uganda's own attempt at 'total war' was undermined. So, too, was the search for a new legitimacy in 'development' in the later stages of the war and in its aftermath. Some contemporaries argued that the dilution of the European presence generally – and in particular the reduction in the expatriate ranks of officialdom – put the colonial presence itself at risk. G.C.Turner, principal of Makerere, wrote in February 1945: 'A country like this needs relatively few competent men for its administration, but during the last few years their number has been reduced *below safety level,* while those who have been left have been distracted, by special needs of wartime, from those personal contacts with the people which are, I believe, a most important part of work in Africa'.[36] In the same month, Turner wrote in a similar vein to the Colonial Office. 'Close contact . . . has been interrupted', he wrote, and 'the salient cause of this is our dangerous shortage of European staff in all departments'. Tired men were the least able to 'listen sympathetically', he added, and 'I should guess that the availability of officials to any but a few Africans has never been less than it is today'.[37] Here Turner touches on a significant theme to which we will later return. We should merely take note, at this point, of his assumption as to how officers of this particular colonial state were expected to interact with their African subjects at this time: they were to 'listen' to them, and to do so 'sympathetically'.

Turner's analysis was echoed by others. As the Muganda critic, Regimental Sergeant-Major R.H.Kakembo put it, 'We need *more* contact with you (Europeans). Come down to us and do your job of Trustee to your ward' (Kakembo 1946: 34. My italics). It was recognised that, because the number of administrative officers in Buganda was so seriously reduced, 'the administration began to lose touch with the chiefs and people. Only after the disturbances in 1945 did the staff position improve sufficiently to enable routine touring to be recommenced' (Annual Reports 1939-46: 1). Major Orde-Browne was in Uganda doing research for the British government between October 1944 and March 1945. He considered that a labour problem lay at the root of the disturbances, and suggested that a properly staffed Labour Department might have anticipated them. But, he wrote in his wide-ranging report on labour conditions, the department was 'at present constituted on a very modest scale, and this undoubtedly formed a contributory cause in events leading up to the recent disturbance' (1946: para.348). The Police Department, reduced by 25 per cent early in the war, was unable to manage the unrest. In these two respects at least, the manpower crisis in the administration may have contributed to the disorder of 1945.

But we must be careful not to adopt the 'public relations' delusion which the British colonial administration suffered at the end of the Second World War: that if only they had enough men, doing enough informing and explaining, all would be well. For what ultimately mattered was not so much personnel as policy. It is significant that the Agriculture Department was able to report a record acreage under crops in the protectorate in 1943 – thanks to price-manipulation – 'despite the absence of a not inconsiderable proportion of [European] manpower in the army'.[38] Again, it is doubtful whether any number of British expatriate officers would have succeeded, in the aftermath of the Second World War, in persuading aspirant African entrepreneurs to accept their continued exclusion from processing; or farmers to accept the perennially depressed prices for their produce. Yet the expatriate manpower crisis in the wartime administration did matter. It made policy goals harder to attain. Inadequacy and failure undermined not only confidence within the administration, but also respect for it among Africans. A regime rendered less capable of satisfying public expectations – above all, the import and distribution of consumer goods at accessible prices – was severely undermined.

In short, at the end of the Second World War, the colonial state in Uganda scarcely looked capable of exercising 'absolute' power. In fact, for some contemporaries at least, it was scarcely visible at all. Turner remarked in 1945 that 'we have suffered from a lack of government for some years past'.[39] Other expatriates drew a similarly bleak picture. An unofficial European critic wrote of 'the lack of administration. At the moment there is almost none'.[40] Turner himself identified two very serious consequences of manpower shortages and exhaustion. First, policy was 'made in the dark' by officials ignorant of African realities.[41] Secondly, and for similar reasons, British administrators found themselves being taken by surprise, as in the case of the January 1945 disturbances.

There seems to be an irony, even a paradox, here. Officials had been forced to adopt many extra administrative roles during the war. Yet at the level of imaginative understanding of prevailing African conditions and of African aspirations, British rulers remained remote. They had not been able to wage total war. Nor were they to prove capable of making informed policy responses to a range of major wartime developments, prompted by Uganda's war effort, within African society.

---

1. 'Vital Statistics of European Officials', Returns for 1939, (Crown Agents, 1941), PRO CO 822/103/18.
2. Executive Council Minutes, 18 May 1940, PRO CO 536/206/40099/1.

3. Mitchell to Dawe, 13 January 1940, PRO CO 536/202/40100.

4. Secretary of State to Governor, 22 February 1940, PRO CO 536/202/40100.

5. Mitchell to Secretary of State, 11 June 1940, PRO CO 822/103/15.

6. Mitchell to Secretary of State, 7 July 1940, PRO CO 822/103/15.

7. Moore to Dawe, 21 June 1940, PRO CO 822/103/15.

8. Chief Secretary to the Legislative Council, 9 December 1942.

9. Uganda Civil Defence Board, 'Developments in 1942'.

10. Hall to the Legislative Council, 4 December 1945.

11. 'Administrative Instructions' (Entebbe,1940).

12. Memorandum for the East African Governors' Conference, June 1940, PRO CO 962/15.

13. Acting Financial Secretary, Memorandum on the 1943 Draft Estimates, PRO CO 536/206/40100.

14. Chief Secretary to the Legislative Council, 15 December 1943.

15. Uganda Civil Defence Board, minutes, 7 December 1943.

16. Uganda Civil Defence Board, 'Report for the Year, 1943'.

17. J.R.M.Elliott, Diaries, Notes and Memoirs, RH MSS Afr.s.1384, p.78.

18. *ibid.*

19. Elliott, Teso District Diary, 20 October 1940.

20. Elliott, Diaries, 23 October 1939.

21. Letter from 'The Buganda Farmers' and Dairymen's Union' to the Governor, undated, containing notes of interviews with the Resident, Temple-Perkins, in October 1944: Rhodes House, FCB List 13 Box 125.

22. Acting Chief Secretary to Under Secretary of State, 23 December 1941, PRO CO 536/208/40100/1941.

23. Financial Secretary, Memorandum on the 1941 Draft Estimates, PRO CO 536/208/40100/1941.

24. Report, *Uganda Herald*, 23 February 1944.

25. 'Organisation of the South-Western Labour Migration Routes' (Entebbe 1943) para.13.

26. Hall to the Legislative Council, 4 December 1945.

27. H.A.Cannon, Unofficial Member, Minutes of the Proceedings of the Legislative Council, 1 April 1940.

28. Annual Report of the Department of Agriculture, 1943-44, pp.2,9.

29. Annual Report of the Department of Agriculture, 1944-45, p.24.

30. Chairman's Address to the AGM of the Uganda Company, 26 February 1942.

31. Acting Governor to the Legislative Council, 5 December 1944.

32. Chief Secretary to the Legislative Council, 15 December 1943.

33. Executive Council Minutes, 18 May 1940.

34. Chief Secretary to the Legislative Council, 15 December 1943.

35. Published in *Uganda Herald*, 5 January 1944.

36. G.C.Turner to Lord Finlay, 8 February 1945: Rhodes House, Turner Correspondence, MSS Afr.s.643. My italics.

37. G.C.Turner to Sir George Gater, 14 February 1945 *ibid.*

38. Annual Report of the Department of Agriculture, 1942-43, p.3.

39. G.C.Turner to Marjory Perham, 6 July 1945: Rhodes House, Turner Correspondence.

40. A.W.Turner-Russell to Rita Hinden, 1 April 1946: Rhodes House, FCB File 2, Correspondence II Box 125.

41. G.C. Turner to Bishop of Lichfield, 3 November 1944: Rhodes House, Turner Correspondence.

6

Uganda's War Effort: Men

Recruitment

What does the process of recruiting men for the war effort tell us about the problems of governing Uganda in the early 1940s? At the end of June 1940 there were 3491 Ugandan Africans enlisted in the armed forces ('War Effort' [2] July 1940). By the end of July 1945 – by which time the war in Europe was over, but the war in the Far East continued – as many as 55,000 were serving.[1] Total Ugandan African enlistments throughout the war amounted to around 77,000. Of these, 279 died in battle, while another 1615 died of 'other causes' (Annual Reports, 1939-46: 6). 'Other causes' of death on campaign were as varied and unpredictable as in peacetime: the most common cause was disease, but accidents (driving and other) took their toll. Many of the men who died are buried or commemorated in cemeteries in Uganda maintained by the Commonwealth War Graves Commission: in Jinja, in Tororo, and on the outskirts of Kampala. There is also the simple memorial in Kampala's City Park.

What does the figure 77,000 signify? Population statistics of the period are unreliable and can only be regarded as approximate. There had been no full census since 1931. One official wartime estimate was that the total male African population aged between 18 and 55 (and thus embraced by Compulsory Service regulations) was 760,000 ('War Effort' [5] October 1942). On this basis we may calculate that around 10 per cent of Uganda's available manpower served in some capacity in the British armed forces during the Second World War.

These tens of thousands who 'in the ordinary course would never have left Uganda, nor even in many instances their villages',[2] experienced service not only in Ethiopia and Somaliland but also in Madagascar, in the Middle East, and in Ceylon, India and Burma. An early experience for askaris was facing Italians in East Africa – but, as the historian of the King's African Rifles laconically observes, 'a high proportion of Italian bombs and shells failed to explode, and this factor greatly helped the process of battle innoculation' (Moyse-Bartlett 1956: 572). Until the fall of Pearl Harbour no unit of the King's African Rifles saw action outside East Africa. Then the call came for African troops to enter the widening sphere of operations. Four of the fourteen battalions of the KAR in S.E.Asia were Ugandan. In Burma they faced with others 'the most strenuous test', and passed it: 'in many aspects of jungle warfare African troops proved outstanding' (Moyse-Bartlett 1956: 679).

There were several stages in the administrative procedure for procuring recruits. These began in Nairobi where, in a series of manpower conferences, officials from Uganda, Kenya and Tanganyika agreed quotas for each territory in order to meet the requirements of East Africa Command, the local military authority. Within the Uganda Protectorate, the chief manpower authority which had to realise these quotas was the Uganda Civil Defence Board (UCDB). It had sub-committees responsible for each of the three main racial groups, and these functioned in different ways. While the European and Asian sub-committees embraced unofficials of the respective race, the African sub-committee comprised the Resident of Buganda and the other provincial commissioners ... and no African member.

A further procedural distinction exposed a lack of administrative competence. While Europeans and Asians had to register individually with the national/compulsory service authorities, Africans did not. The registration of Africans could not have been put into operation or subjected to official checking, because sufficient British official personnel and an adequate infrastructure did not exist. In the Africans' case, goals had to be redefined. In the absence of detailed statistical information, it was stated that 'for all war purposes to which Africans may be assigned, it is possible to meet requirements by direct recruitment of specified *numbers*'.[3] Governing Uganda was sufficiently problematical for the UCDB later to have felt a sense of achievement in merely having counted the number of men actually recruited, and found that there was 'a close concurrence with the figures submitted by the army'.[4]

By the end of 1942, the Board felt that they had a basis on which military requisitions could be accepted from Command HQ and allocated to provinces. Quotas sought to take account of each tribe and district. So in Buganda for example, recruiting was arranged in rotation at the *saza* (county), and sometimes *gombolola* (sub-county), headquarters (Annual Reports, 1939-1946:1). In this context, Uganda's district officers, operating with chiefs of the native government (Buganda) and Native Administrations, were left to translate mathematical expressions into flesh and blood recruits. These recruits were then sent to Tororo, in Eastern Province. Conveniently close to the Kenya border, this town became from January 1941 the Central Recruits Assembly Depot.

This procedure evolved piecemeal through trial and error. In early 1942, some recruitment was still being undertaken by individual military recruiters 'who toured the protectorate taking what men they wanted for their own units'.[5] One European KAR officer later recalled being posted in late 1940 to Bombo, north of Kampala. On arrival, he found a commanding officer, HQ staff, company and platoon commanders, and NCOs – but 'of troops there were none'.[6] They had yet to be enlisted, and so 'the officers set forth to scour the country for volunteers. This proved to be easier than might be imagined', continues this account, 'for liaison with DOs and chiefs and village headmen in those areas of the West Nile where fighting tribes were to be found soon produced numbers of eager volunteers'.[7] These *ad hoc* methods were clearly flawed, however. Hence responsibility to recruit for military service generally passed to the already overstretched provincial administration and local chiefs, leaving Tororo to allocate to military units.[8]

Compulsion or consent?

We noted, above, 'numbers of eager volunteers' in West Nile. In this mobilisation of Ugandan manpower for the British military forces, what was the ratio of compulsion to consent? Did the administration conscript 77,000 able-bodied Africans into the army against their will? Did it have the power to do such a thing? Is there evidence here of 'absolute power', and of 'exploitation'? Or was this a 'volunteer' army?

An assessment of the extent and limits of power in this particular British colonial state requires that we should at least seek answers to such questions, however elusive certainty may turn out to be. We need to investigate generalisations such as David Killingray's, that although 'official and semi-official accounts of African wartime service in the army ... refer to enlistment as largely voluntary ... this was far from so' (Killingray 1986: 75). The sources are seldom specific on such matters, but it is possible to reach some provisional conclusions as to where the dividing line between consent and compulsion lay.

In Uganda, officials did indeed claim that they could rely on volunteers. Thus Governor Dundas was subsequently to write that 'although power existed for compulsory enlistment of Africans for the forces and many thousands were recruited, those powers were never invoked' (Dundas 1955: 224). And a British army officer was to claim that in Uganda 'recruiting parties toured the country, and no difficulty was found in obtaining the necessary numbers' (Whitehead 1950: 2). Indeed, Sir John Shuckburgh, in the official history of the war, claimed for British colonial Africa as a whole that 'the great majority of colonial recruits for the army were volunteers' (Shuckburgh 1948: vol. i 42). By contrast again, Michael Crowder maintained forty years later that 'few were true volunteers' (Crowder 1984: 32).

However, this contradiction between official assertions and the subsequent assessments of historians may be more apparent than real. As we will see, officials seem to have experienced more difficulty in raising men for non-combatant roles than for active service as soldiers – resorting to compulsion more commonly in the former than in the latter case. Secondly, as we shall also see, there was no simple distinction between volunteer and conscript, since 'volunteers' in some cases may have had little choice but to present themselves for employment by the army.

Claims and counter claims have to be tested by the available evidence, which varies from territory to territory. Only one of David Killingray's own illustrations, to support his generalisation for British colonial Africa, comes from Uganda. This is the (short-term) drying up of the flow of labourers from Ruanda-Urundi in 1939, apparently caused by their fear of being rounded up in Uganda as porters in support of the military (1986: 75). [There may have been *fear* of being rounded up, but there was no round up.] As for the official version of events, some sources are more revealing – and more convincing – than others. The diary of one district officer, J.R.M.Elliott, describes recruiting in Teso in 1942 as follows: 'Dunlop and self recruiting all day; we got 168 men out of over 400 youths who volunteered. To Bukedea where we were recruiting all morning again getting 137 men. I supervised the entraining of 303 recruits leaving for the Depot down country. Minns and Dunlop recruiting at Bugondo for remaining 35 men required for the draft which they got very quickly.' This is persuasive evidence. It is the record of an 'official', but it is not an official record. The officer was off-duty when writing these notes in his personal diary, and there is no hint here of problems such as resistance or non-co-operation which might have required the exercise of coercive powers by the British colonial state which he served. Meanwhile, a form of recruiting continued to take place at times which sidelined the District Officer. 'Very successful recruiting' of volunteers in Western Province in 1942 was attributed to the visible presence in the recruiting party of the actual army officers and NCOs under whom recruits would subsequently serve; and the judgement at the time was that this 'flow' might not have occurred if the task had been left to DOs.[9]

To estimate how extensive and typical volunteering was, it is helpful to distinguish between different kinds of service with the forces – not least because Africans themselves appear to have done so. The four principal formations in which Africans from Uganda were to be found were: the battalions of the King's African Rifles (KAR); the East African Army Service Corps (EAASC); the African Auxiliary Pioneer Corps (AAPC); and the East African Military Labour Service (EAMLS). In addition, there were specialist units such as Signals, Artillery, Medical Corps and Ordnance. The records of these various branches of the African armed forces are not open to easy generalisation. There was certainly conscription in Uganda – the significance of which we return to later in this chapter – but while chiefs were indeed leaned on to produce men, in some cases and at some times, such practice must not simply be taken as typical.

There is no doubt, for example, that volunteers abounded at the outset. The new 1939 companies of the KAR were oversubscribed. 'Military service was popular and there was great competition to join the new units', Moyse-Bartlett reports (1956: 475); and the evidence strongly suggests that this was – and remained – a volunteer army. In the early summer of 1939, a 7th (Uganda Territorial) battalion of the King's African Rifles was created. Posters and advertisements in the press raised 800 volunteers in a week.[10] When a second company of the 7th battalion had to be raised, in July, not only was this accomplished in a day but, it was later claimed, 'if it needed increasing a hundred-fold, the recruits would be available at once'.[11] Similarly, at the end of 1940, it was said of the Acholi that 'a call for recruits always produces numbers far in excess of those required'.[12]

This readiness to serve made mobilisation relatively simple, and the British administration was grateful for that. Six months on, the governor paid general public tribute to the Africans 'who with alacrity have responded to every call and have even come forward in numbers considerably in excess of requirements'.[13] In 1942 the Uganda Civil Defence Board reported that 'from a large number of recruits called for interview the recruiter would only take a small proportion'.[14] There was no conscription in force for the KAR at the time when the UCDB was reconstituted in mid-1942. Three-quarters of the KAR's twenty-eight battalions then in existence had been formed since the outbreak of the war (Moyse-Bartlett 1956: 574). And there is no reason to believe that compulsion became necessary thereafter for the KAR, especially in view of the reduced call for fighting men by the end of 1944.

Relatively popular also was the EAASC. This unit had its own recruiting centre, at Kololo in Kampala, and here artisans and drivers volunteered for service. By the end of 1939, over 1500 Africans were already serving as drivers, artisans, clerks and storekeepers, or as ambulance drivers in the Medical Corps. All appear to have originated as volunteers. In particular, hundreds of motor-drivers volun-

teered: by June 1940, 1361 had passed out of the Kololo Motor Training School ('War Effort' [2] July 1940). In late 1943, when a call for
greater numbers came through from East Africa Command, there
was concern that, with such service still remaining attractive to Africans throughout the protectorate – including the Baganda – 'this
volunteering might compete undesirably with the filling of conscript
quotas for other units'.[15]

Of these remaining units, the AAPC (Pioneers) was more attractive than the EAMLS (Labour Service). The former were volunteers, at least into early 1942, or volunteers from the ranks of the
latter. Personnel in both units served as batmen, cooks and other
personal servants, pick and shovel men in camp construction, load-
ing and unloading, and road-making. The differences lay in deploy-
ment, terms and status. The AAPC were in forward positions and
armed, while the EAMLS remained in the rear. The AAPC saw service abroad, while the EAMLS stayed in East Africa. The AAPC
enjoyed better terms of service, two-year volunteers receiving seven-
teen shillings a month, for example, as opposed to fourteen shillings
if they remained in the EAMLS. So well were the AAPC considered
to have performed, in such theatres as the Middle East, that in 1944
the term 'Auxiliary' was dropped from its title in recognition of the
contribution it had made.[16] There was some distinction in being a
Pioneer, whether originally volunteer or conscript.

So it seems that the main application of conscription was to the
EAMLS, a minority within the protectorate's overall military manpower contribution. Discriminating Africans who chose to serve,
tended to choose other units. Until January 1942, the application of
compulsory powers was limited to EAMLS recruits.[17] This service
was originally for a 12 to 15 month period, but later 27 month and
'duration' terms came into force.[18] EAMLS men were classed among
the 'C' category, the lowest category of manpower at Tororo, and
considered unsuitable as fighting men. In June 1940 it was reported
that all appeals for personnel were satisfied – except for 'an urgent
request at the beginning of the year for African stretcher-bearers.
The Africans of Uganda were not attracted by this form of service,
and the need was met by recruiting in Kenya' ('War Effort' [2] July

1940). Noteworthy here in this report are the term 'request' and the action – or rather lack of action taken locally – when offers were not forthcoming. Even EAMLS recruits received army uniforms and accommodation, rations and health care, pay of 14 shillings a month and a pension.[19]

From the start, enthusiasm for war service was less than universal; and from the start it was selective. Yet even after 1942, when the urgency of the war situation led to a sudden rise from 18,000 to 40,000 in the number of serving Ugandan Africans, there appears to have been little difficulty in recruiting for armed service. Why did so many Ugandans volunteer for service, or at least accept the call for service so readily, and thus relieve the local British colonial state of the need to explore the extent of its power to compel them to do so? It would be rash to attempt a simple generalisation for thousands of individuals whose motives are likely to have varied greatly according to personal inclination and circumstances. But we can identify some deciding factors.

It must be stressed that there was no clear-cut distinction between 'compulsory' and 'voluntary' service. In reality, there was a spectrum of response; and 'compulsion' could take a variety of forms. In his study of war in the early modern period of European history – when continental states struggled to fulfil their own 'absolutist' aspirations – Geoffrey Parker has provided a useful comparison. According to Parker, of Louis XIV's huge armies in the early 1700s 'by far the majority ... were volunteers'. Yet he shows that among the reasons for choosing to join up, 'hardship and want were the most prominent' (Parker 1988: 46). Thus alongside any attraction of novelty and adventure lay the promise of cash and clothes. Perhaps many of Uganda's army recruits, too, had little real choice. Volunteering may have been forced upon them by economic factors, just as economic factors led labourers to choose to leave Ruanda-Urundi in search of employment in Uganda.

The part played by 'hardship and want' can be illustrated to some extent by reference to the tribal origin of those that joined up. Men from northern and western areas came forward in greater numbers, as a proportion of their total tribal numbers, than men from more southerly, central, and eastern districts. The Acholi and the Baganda provide something of a contrast. Acholi enlistments during the war as a whole numbered 6071, compared with 18,820 Baganda. Yet the Acholi number 'amounted to nearly 20% of the tax paying male population, while nearly three times that number of men actually offered themselves for service' (Annual Reports 1939-46: 68). On the other hand, the Baganda enlistment was only around 7 per cent. Thus the overall Acholi number was proportionately two to three times higher than that of the Baganda; and it is reasonable to suggest that the former experienced more 'hardship and want' than the latter.

That said, we must not understate Ganda involvement. During the Second World War, around a quarter of all recruits were Baganda. Can this indicate, as is sometimes inferred, a conscious British policy *not* to recruit from this area because the Baganda were deemed unreliable?[20] There were good reasons why many Baganda chose not to serve in (even) larger numbers: access to post-secondary education, or employment in civilian government service, for example. The main point here is that in the end they, the Baganda themselves not the British authorities, were deciding on the degree of their participation.

Officials at the time, however, tended to explain variations in terms of tribal character. They noted a contrast of responses within Western/Northern Province. They observed that 'it was the able bodied men of the Nilotic area' who immediately came forward in large numbers 'as recruits for the essentially "fighting" units of the Army. The Bantu areas were much slower in starting in this respect'. The explanation was thought to lie in 'the difference between a fighting race and one which prefers to follow more peaceful pursuits' (Annual Reports 1939-46: 65). The Second World War could thus confirm existing stereotypes. It was claimed that the Nilotic tribes were again responding in such large numbers, because 'they like the military life'.[21] By contrast with other provinces, the official account of Buganda in wartime is the only one which does not stress the keenness of men to offer themselves for service. Acholi soldiers won proportionately more medals and mentions in despatches than their Ganda counterparts, but this clearly imperfect measure of ultimate courage – or recklessness? – is open to a range of interpretations other than 'tribal character'.[22]

'Hardship and want' provide a rather more convincing explanation of the enlistment pattern than contemporary tribal stereotyping. Broadly, less economic development had taken place in the north than in the south during the first forty years or so of British colonial rule in Uganda. There were far fewer alternative employment opportunities in Acholi than in Buganda. But everywhere taxes had to be paid; and everywhere, too, there was an appetite for basic consumer goods. Even before the First World War, the largest contingents of recruits for the army came from the districts of Acholi, and later Lango (Omara-Otunnu 1987: 31,32). Although Lango suffered a sustained outbreak of cerebro-spinal meningitis which virtually stopped all recruiting from 1942 to 1944, it was not surprising that, during the Second World War, it was again men from the north and west who presented themselves in relatively large numbers for army service.

We must recall that East Africans serving with the British forces were able to make regular payments from their wages to their families at home. When the time came for demobilisation, 'it was decided at the outset that at whatever cost these men must not be kept waiting for their pay' (Annual Reports 1939-46: 3). For that was why, in so many cases, they had joined up. Soldiers were to be rewarded further at the end of the war. In April 1945, it was estimated that up to 5000 of the currently serving 14,000 Baganda could be expected to take advantage of a government scheme to offer mortgages to returning askaris, to enable them to buy 10 acre plots of land, as these came onto the market.[23] In general, of course, farmers such as many in Buganda were in a good position to respond to a demand not for recruits but for a variety of cash crops – a demand which moreover increased at just about the same time as the call was made for more recruits for the armed forces.

There remains, even so, some evidence of enlistment more 'voluntary' than that prompted by simple financial or occupational need. One serving soldier attributed his fellow Africans' 'remarkable' readiness to get into the army and take up arms to 'devotion and loyalty' – not to King and Empire, nor even to the cause of freedom which they were being told they were fighting for, but to one or other of the two or three Europeans (missionary, district officer or doctor, for example) that they had ever met (Kakembo 1946: 8). This source has to be treated with care. The writer was seeking publication of a pamphlet, and may have been anxious to make his observations acceptable to the censors. On the other hand, an implicitly pro-colonial view does not have to be discounted. And the source is the more remarkable for referring to the Baganda, given their reputation for being less than enthusiastic about service in the armed forces.

An equally vivid insight into voluntary enlistment is to be found in the recollections of a serving European officer. Of the so-called 'fighting tribes' in West Nile, he wrote: 'Service with the KAR carried with it in normal times not only the prospect of permanent employment with an elite body of men but also the distinction, in time, of being able to return to the village with a pension and an assured place in the local community. To all this was now added the prospect of fighting, of travelling and adventure in far distant lands, and of returning to his [*sic*] village with exciting tales to tell'.[24] So the army offered not only a paid occupation and economic security but also status and adventure, along with the opportunity for proud recollection in the village in the years to come.

The authorities recognised the propaganda potential of the example and experience of those already enlisted. A 'Message to the Peoples of Uganda from the KAR' claimed: 'The men of your tribes in the newer battalions of the KAR are beginning to feel themselves soldiers. They are stronger, heavier and smarter than when you last saw them in the villages. They are well fed and well exercised'.[25] Kakembo confirms the positive effect on those at home of men returning from service. And the UCDB decided to have accounts of East African troops in Burma published in the vernacular press as they 'would rouse interested attention from African readers with possibly a favourable stimulus to recruiting'.[26]

It would be fanciful perhaps to imply that Africans volunteered in order to be properly fed, but the role of diet in visibly transforming the physical well-being and potential of men in the forces can only have worked in favour of further recruitment. The extent of ill health and malnutrition in the protectorate was clearly shown by the large numbers of volunteers turned down on medical grounds. In their survey of a few years earlier, Thomas and Scott had described leprosy as 'widespread' and malaria as 'universal' (1935: 303-310). The army operated its own definition of 'able-bodied'. So, for example, there was a shortfall to the EAMLS in 1944 when the army rejected an unusually high proportion of recruits from Western Province.[27] An army marches on its stomach, and a major function of Tororo was the 'building up' of recruits, to render then fit for military duty. Many food items supplied daily in the army were 'only rarely included in tribal diet, and ... normally considered as luxuries'.[28] In fact the UCDB, conscious of 'the already exhausted livestock population of Uganda', came to regret that there were seven 'meat-days' a week in the army.[29] The army, and the recruits, reaped the benefit. It was claimed that 'the effect of a balanced ration combined with army training on the recruit is often spectacular'.[30] Contemporaries understandably assumed that 'many serving soldiers must be feeling positively fit for the first time in their lives'.[31]

We may conclude that service with the armed forces was attractive enough to have led to widespread volunteering, or at least to ready co-operation with recruiting agents. The introduction of the 5ft 8in height qualification for soldiers in 1939 suggests that no shortage of volunteers was anticipated. Mobilisation of men in Uganda during the Second World War demanded little of the British colonial state by way of new institutions or legislation, sanctions or means of compulsion. It proved to be a task which even a greatly depleted staff could accomplish. The high overall level of recruitment is a measure not so much of the effectiveness of the colonial state in directing its subjects, as of the Africans' readiness to enlist.

Limits

What defined the limits of the colonial state's ability to recruit? There seem to be two main answers and they refer us back to two of the fundamental themes of this study. We shall see that there were administrative shortcomings and political constraints: it was unwise to over-use chiefs as recruiting agents of the reluctant. But first, we must note that there were perceived economic limitations, too. The British Empire required commodities for export in a production drive to help the war effort, especially from 1942. But Uganda could not fully satisfy simultaneous imperial demands for both soldiers and exports (as well as subsistence) – especially against a background of acute local food shortage in East Africa in 1943/44. Again, the Uganda Protectorate government had its own financial position to worry about. Less concerned about the articles produced than with the act of production, it needed its peasant farmers to earn an income by production, and then to spend it on consumption, in order to sustain government revenue. During the early years of the war especially, this question of financial viability was of the first importance. In the later war years, when finances were buoyed by other factors, the Protectorate government was to be embarrassed by its own success at promoting production. By this time, African farmers had money enough to spend but, because of the inability of the government to secure goods from outside, too little to spend it on. So this put at risk the economic collaboration on which the protectorate rested.

Official sources point to economic considerations as the factors which mainly determined when and where compulsion in recruitment was applied. When Dundas spoke against lengthening service in the EAMLS to 'duration' terms, he argued on grounds of social and economic stability, rather than grounds of political urgency. Discussing the matter in private with senior colleagues, he expressed the wish that men might be able 'to go home at the end of their year's service and resume their family life and cultivation' – notably omitting any political argument that the shorter period might make recruitment easier.[32] Subsequently, we are told that in the Eastern Province conscription was introduced 'not on account of any reluctance on the part of the African to serve, but rather to spread as evenly as possible between all the tribes the call-up of manpower' (Annual Reports 1939-46: 35). This statement, unlike that of Dundas, was for public consumption; but it is still reasonable to attribute such an official call-up strategy to cautious assumptions about the viability of local economies.

Similarly, on the occasion of the review in 1942 of overall man-power availability, the implementation of compulsory powers was seen not (only) as a means of forcing a sufficient number into service but as a mechanism for spreading the implementation and impact of call-up. From its inception, the UCDB sought 'to select and provide ... personnel for military and emergency services ... having due regard to the economic conditions prevailing, the necessities of civil life'.[33] It was thought necessary 'that there should be power to assign quotas fairly throughout counties, parishes and villages, so that there may be an even distribution of the burden entailed by withdrawal of man-power from what is an almost entirely rural economy' ('War Effort' [6] November 1943).

We have already noted that approximately 10 per cent of Uganda's able-bodied Africans came to be enlisted. The UCDB, using its own figures, specifically proposed that military manpower recruitment should not exceed 57,000, a figure 'representing ten per cent of our original estimate of 570,000 able-bodied Africans'.[34] It was claimed that 'a figure representing one-tenth of effectives is generally regarded as the highest percentage of military mobilisation compatible with the maintenance of reasonable or required levels of social and economic activity in the protectorate, particularly when account is had of intensified production for war purposes' ('War Effort' [6] November 1943).

There are difficulties here. There is nothing in the records to suggest that the figure of 10 per cent was anything but arbitrary. Further, it seems questionable in the light of the variety of economic activity in Uganda and the variable rates of enlistment, in the event, from different districts. Nor does the figure appear to take account of prevailing patterns of labour and production. The dependence of many enterprises in Buganda on immigrant labour, and on women for food production, meant that there was no simple correlation between numbers of recruits and size of productive output. Nor was there a direct link between numbers of men who were able to labour or produce, and the numbers of those actually willing to do so.

Convenient half-truths abound in much of the surviving official documentation. Yet the repetition and consistency of such economic assumptions in the records as are referred to above strongly suggest that they were an important determinant of the official mind in Uganda and hence of government policy. The commissioning of Temple-Perkins's manpower survey in October 1942, to identify availability for military service and essential war effort production, followed logically from the assumption that manpower not recruited into the armed forces would contribute to production. The Labour Department assumed a direct interchangeability of military and civilian manpower when it noted that demands for recruits in late 1940 had been counter-balanced by a larger supply of immigrant labour. The UCDB expressed a similar belief when it made the unconventional suggestion in November 1943 – turned down by the War Office – that former Italian POWs should be enlisted into Pioneer units in the Middle East on the grounds that 'African soldiers might thus be replaced and restored to the production effort'.[35] The existence of 'reserved' occupations, in transport for example, testifies to the same preoccupation in British official thinking.

Warned in 1943 of 'the approaching exhaustion of Uganda's available manpower', the British authorities in Nairobi proved sympathetic to Uganda's economic 'safety margin' and reduced military manpower demands accordingly. There was concern 'at continuance of military recruitment at the current rate, for fear of repercussions on the production programme'.[36] Men who stayed at home might serve the 'production drive', if only as employer. A possible food producer was preferable to a certain food consumer. It would appear that the British authorities in East Africa felt that there must be a limit to the calling up of African manpower for active service. This limit should not be breached for fear of failing to export vital resources – and for fear of undermining the local economy and local revenue.

The second limit to recruitment lay in the fact that the colonial state in Uganda simply lacked the political means to sustain compulsion beyond a modest level. As Killingray has observed, in 1939 colonial governments 'assumed extensive powers, especially over the mobilisation and direction of labour for military and war production purposes' (1986: 68). But in the case of Uganda it was one thing to assume a power, and another to exercise it.

There was, as we have seen, some conscription in Uganda, particularly into the less attractive branches of military service. The local agents of this compulsion were the chiefs. It has been argued that 'although military enlistments ... were supposedly the fruit of spontaneous loyalism, in practice pressure from chiefs ... counted for more than civic spirit' (Hargreaves 1988: 52). Whether it counted in fact for 'more' is arguable, but chiefs were certainly called upon to play an important role in recruitment, not least because of the acute shortage of British expatriate personnel in the provincial administration during the war. In Western Province, for example, it was admitted that 'without the assistance of the African rulers and chiefs ... it would have been impossible for the administrative machine to have worked as smoothly as it did and without serious breakdown.... Most important of all, the Province contributed large numbers of men for the services' (Annual Reports 1939-46: 66). And we are offered other glimpses of this chiefly role. When Governor Dundas toured Toro in August 1944, he took the opportunity to thank local authorities. 'You, Mukama, and your chiefs', he said, 'have done a good deal to help the war, especially in recruiting'.[37]

Few details of the local operations of chiefs are recorded, though 'fit tax defaulters' were conscripted.[38] More important, we cannot accurately measure the effect that this particular wartime role had on the chiefs' local standing – or would have had if the Protectorate government had continued to instruct chiefs to compel men to serve far beyond the level at which they were ready to come forward 'voluntarily'. British officials would have risked exposing and undermining the effective local authority of these men, whose political collaboration was essential to the normal working of the British colonial state. This is no mere speculation. One of the first jobs of the regents responsible for Buganda after the death of Kabaka Daudi Chwa in November 1939 was to persuade Baganda to join the ranks of the British army. According to one highly educated Muganda, this proved 'a very difficult task and it made them unpopular at once' (Mulira 1950: 23). Such unpopularity as was engendered by this process, among others, endured and proved damaging in the longer term.

David Killingray has shown that in the Gold Coast – in many

respects comparable with Uganda in size and character – there was a heavy dependence on chiefs in the process of recruitment during the Second World War, which 'contributed to the lowering of the esteem of the chiefs in the eyes of their people and to a weakening of their authority' (1982: 91). Nor was recruitment through chiefs desirable in other respects: it was arbitrary and inefficient, and Killingray quotes a British district commissioner who considered it 'a beastly job, this recruiting by pressure. . . . A rotten system for we don't get the best men'. Meanwhile, it was 'a fairly widespread practice' for chiefs not to co-operate, and even to shelter deserters. The full extent of the parallels between the Gold Coast and Uganda in these respects perhaps needs further research, but the picture Killingray has sketched is clearly recognisable. The chiefs' role as intermediaries in the colonial situation led to competing demands being made of them. Yet recognisable, too, is the research finding that a majority of Second World War veterans, interviewed during an oral history project in the Gold Coast, claimed to have volunteered for their wartime service, and not to have been subject to such chiefly pressure (Holbrook 1985: 358).

There remains another measure of the British colonial state's limited competence in the field of recruitment in Uganda. Like anywhere else, service with the forces did not prove universally popular, whether for disillusioned volunteer or reluctant conscript, and a significant proportion of Uganda's serving men chose to abandon the army, thus flouting the authority of local officials both civilian and military, British and African. Killingray notes 'high figures for desertion' among Gold Coast recruits (1986: 78). Uganda was no different in this respect.

Unrest among Ugandans was not unknown even in the volunteer ranks of the KAR. At the end of the Abyssinia campaign in 1941, Ugandan askaris assumed they were going on leave. 'Many of them asserted that they had only taken military service for the defence of their homes in Africa, and should be given the chance of volunteering afresh if they were required to serve abroad'; and they now demanded higher rates of pay (Moyse-Bartlett 1956: 568). 'Adventure in far distant lands' was no enticement for these particular men. Earlier, a propagandist 'message' from the KAR had confessed that 'a few weaklings have run away to their homes' – though it had added hopefully, 'they will get their reward in the villages where the women will laugh at them'.[39] In 1944, General Platt spoke about 'absentees or deserters' and announced that 'there were daily some 5,000 African soldiers away from their units on these grounds'.[40] It was estimated in May 1945 that as many as 15,000 African troops were absent without leave from E.A.Command – a figure equivalent to nine months' supply of new recruits. 3532 of the absentees were Ugandans.[41] This figure represents the accomplishment by this time of a sizeable exercise in voluntary, premature, unofficial, demobilisation.

Baganda deserted in some numbers. Among Ugandan Africans, the Baganda represented around 25 per cent of all enlistments – and an estimated 85 per cent of all deserters. When Governor Hall complained to the *Lukiiko* in April 1945 that there were 1100 deserters in Buganda alone,[42] he seems to have been underestimating the true figure. A later official report put the figure for Baganda deserters at 'some 3000', with 2100 of them from the single district of Mengo (Annual Reports 1939-46: 2). D. K. Sekkuma is one example of a reluctant conscript, and of one who succeeded in returning himself to civilian life. This aspiring trader claimed to have been forcefully recruited while in Ankole on business. However, the frustrated entrepreneur turned political activist was evidently a free man again by the time he began to correspond with the Fabian Colonial Bureau. Significantly, Sekkuma (a Muganda) had an alternative occupation.[43]

By contrast, E.M.K.Mulira, one of the most accomplished Baganda of his generation, readily volunteered – but he observed later that his was not a wholly typical response. 'Some of us, who knew what was involved, volunteered at once to save the situation, and we were severely criticised for that action' (1950: 21). We have already noted some of the tensions and divisions in Ganda society in the 1930s. Former Governor Mitchell, keen to raise recruiting levels in 1941, implied there was a readiness to serve but that problems had been caused by recruiting 'many of the wrong type' – the type who, for example, resented being addressed in Swahili rather than in English.[44] The record of some Baganda is likely to have reinforced official British colonial perception of them as an unreliable group, and added to concern for the future of the protectorate's relations with the kingdom. But clearly, as we have seen, there was no single response to the war among Baganda. It should be pointed out that in mid-1940 none of the nine vernacular Luganda newspapers was advocating opposition to service.[45] And five-sixths of Baganda recruits did *not* desert.

How did the Protectorate government in Uganda respond to the challenge to its authority which desertions posed? The contest between deserter and the authorities was an unequal one, given the British administration's shortages of information and of manpower. Even as General Platt urged East African governors to encourage their District Commissioners to help, it was acknowledged that the latter were 'very much overworked, and many of them are already doing all in their power to help in getting back these men to their units'.[46] Fewer than a third of the Mengo deserters were apprehended and returned to the forces. The only sanction ultimately available to the British authorities was deprivation of benefits; the only deterrent, wider knowledge that this punishment would apply. Not surprisingly, in May 1945 the East African governors agreed merely to 'write off' all men who had overstayed their leave by more than three months, who thereby lost their benefits.[47]

We may conclude that, just as the British would probably have found it very hard to raise any more Africans for the war effort in Uganda (had they actually attempted to do so), there was also little they could do to counter a desertion rate which amounted to far more losses to the forces than were suffered on military service. Taken as a whole, the story of the mobilisation of men in Uganda for the war effort tells us much about governing Uganda in the early 1940s. The shortage of British personnel, and the dependence locally on chiefs, would have rendered large-scale mobilisation quite impossible had it not been for the readiness of so many Africans to enlist as 'volunteers' of one kind or another. The evidence suggests a great variety of response – and such a complex picture overall that simple talk of an 'absolutist' colonial state becomes meaningless.

1. Hall to the Legislative Council, reported in *Uganda Herald*, 4 December 1946.
2. Uganda Colonial Annual Report, 1946, p.3.
3. *Uganda Gazette*, 15 June 1942. My italics.
4. Uganda Civil Defence Board 'Report for the year 1943', p.4.
5. Uganda Civil Defence Board, 'Developments in 1942', p.3.
6. C.L.Holcom, 'The Crested Crane – Uganda Recalled', unpublished typescript, p.140: Rhodes House, MSS Afr.s.1823.
7. *ibid.*
8. Uganda Civil Defence Board, 'Developments in 1942', p.3.
9. African Manpower Committee Minutes, 2 September 1942, F 78/5/6, Uganda National Archive, Entebbe.
10. Progress Report for the Chief Secretary, Entebbe, 21 June 1939, F 78/14/2, Uganda National Archive.
11. Columnist Nemo in *Uganda Herald*, 18 October 1939.
12. Commentary on the War Fund, *Uganda Herald*, 11 December 1940.
13. Dundas to the Legislative Council, 17 June 1941.
14. Uganda Civil Defence Board, 'Developments in 1942', p.2.
15. Uganda Civil Defence Board, Minutes, 5 October 1943.
16. Central Office of Information, 'News from the Colonies' no. 92, RH FCB Box 77 file 1.
17. East African Governors' Conference, Secret Proceedings, January 1942, PRO CO 822/107/8.
18. *ibid.*
19. *East African Standard*, 13 September 1940.
20. See also p.32.
21. Official Communique in *Uganda Herald*, 12 February 1941.
22. Civil Reabsorption Progress Report, Entebbe 1948, p.3 and p.32.
23. Reabsorption and Rehabilitation Committee Minutes, April 1945, F 23/35/1, Uganda National Archive.
24. Holcom, *op.cit.* p.140.
25. Published in *Uganda Herald*, 12 February 1941.
26. Uganda Civil Defence Board Minutes, 28 November 1944.
27. Uganda Civil Defence Board Minutes, 27 September 1944.
28. Nutrition Committee, 'Review of Nutrition in Uganda', 1945, Rhodes House, FCB Box 126, File III.
29. Uganda Civil Defence Board Minutes, 31 March 1944.
30. East African Medical Journal, July 1943, Rhodes House, FCB Box 77 File I.

31. Chief Secretary to G.C.Turner, 22 November 1944, in Turner Correspondence, *loc.cit.*

32. East African Governors' Conference, Secret proceedings, PRO CO 822/107/8.

33. Uganda Civil Defence Board Minutes, 22 May 1942.

34. Uganda Civil Defence Board Minutes, 10 September 1943.

35. Uganda Civil Defence Board Minutes, 2 November 1943.

36. Uganda Civil Defence Board Minutes, 7 December and 10 August, 1943.

37. Reported in *Uganda Herald*, 16 August 1944.

38. Uganda Civil Defence Board Minutes, 20 April 1943.

39. Published in *Uganda Herald*, 12 February 1941.

40. East African Governors' Conference Proceedings, November 1944, PRO CO 822/13/2.

41. African Manpower Conference, Secret Proceedings, Nairobi, March 1945, PRO CO 822/117/6.

42. Reported in *Uganda Herald*, 18 April 1945.

43. Correspondence in Rhodes House, FCB Box 125 File I and Box 127 File I.

44. East African Governors' Conference Secret Proceedings, January 1941, PRO CO 822/107/7.

45. Letter from F. Ziwa, *Uganda Herald*, 3 July 1940.

46. East African Governors' Conference Proceedings, November 1944, PRO CO 822/113/2.

47. East African Governors' Conference Proceedings, May 1945, PRO CO 822/113/2

7

Uganda's War Effort: Money

Policy

The colonial state in Uganda was no more a free agent when raising revenue than it was when mobilising manpower. In making funds available to metropolitan Britain, it remained throughout the war subject locally to both economic and political restrictions. These prompted caution and ultimately set limits on its operations. In fact it was primarily political constraints – real or imagined – which determined the character of its behaviour in the field of wartime finance. Initially, European expatriate opinion caused more concern than African, though by 1945 the latter could no longer be ignored.

Meanwhile, British officials did achieve much, in an area – financial management – which was familiar and in which they had some previous experience. Between 1940 and 1945, Uganda – that is, Ugandans – contributed considerable sums of money to the British war effort. At first these took the form of 'free gifts', but this practice was soon replaced by loans in the form of Uganda's sterling balances. Before 1943, this money was raised in Uganda by means of conventional forms of taxation, selectively applied. From 1943, however, money became more readily available from the rise in world prices for Uganda's exports – and from the Protectorate government's response, which was to amass funds by denying African peasant farmers the full financial return for the sale of their produce. This particular practice came to be seen by African farmers as a form of exploitation; and when the funds continued to be augmented even after the war was over it proved a major grievance in the later 1940s. It took the widespread disturbances of 1949, as well as a new economic climate at the start of the new decade, to persuade the British

117

to drop the policy. This had served them financially for a while, but the political price proved in the end unbearable. When this colonial state seriously sought to 'exploit', it was forced to think again.

Governor Mitchell understood the relationship between finances, on the one hand, and the economy as a whole, on the other. At the start of the war, he foresaw dangers in retrenchment and belt-tightening, and he challenged the thinking behind his London masters'instruction to balance the books. He was preoccupied with the overall economic viability of the protectorate – which underpinned the poll tax and customs that represented almost two-thirds of total tax revenue in Uganda. He recognised Uganda's vulnerability. His concern from the start was 'the maintenance and, where possible, increase of African purchasing power, which is as important to British interests as it is to their own welfare'.[1] He repeatedly argued his case. 'The most valuable contribution which this small country can make,' he wrote to London in December 1939, 'is to increase its consuming and purchasing power.'[2] This would stimulate production locally, and in the case of imports it would augment customs revenue. He noted in his diary, on 30 September 1939, 'We must be careful lest in trying to raise more money we bring consumption to a stop.' These are not the words of a governor relishing a 'good deal of power'.[3]

And though the Colonial Office remained respectful, it was not persuaded. Disagreement came to focus on a single shibboleth. Six months before war in Europe, Uganda was told not to allow its liquid surplus balances – that is, the sums left in reserve at the end of any single year's working of revenue and expenditure – to fall below £1 million. For Mitchell, this freezing of financial resources was damagingly deflationary, and he wanted his development projects to be accepted as legitimate charges against them. Arthur Dawe at the Colonial Office insisted on the freeze, and admitted to being 'unduly sticky on the matter'.[4] Dawe's argument rested on Ugandan cotton's vulnerability: he wrote of all Uganda's eggs being in one basket. His nightmare was the disaster that would befall Uganda should there be difficulty over the disposal of her principal export. But Mitchell was not convinced. 'We cannot lock up a million pounds.' he said. In the spirit of Joseph Chamberlain, he went on to speak of the need to develop 'our great and fertile estate', as well as merely 'stand securely on our own financial feet'.[5]

Mitchell ultimately had no choice but to do what he could within London's parameters. He introduced three new revenue measures in Uganda, but their chief characteristic was their lightness of incidence, especially on the African population. Income tax, new to Uganda, was to apply only to non-natives, who were also hardest hit by increased customs and excise rates on beer and spirits. The third imposition fell exclusively on African producers: the export tax on cotton was raised from one cent per pound to two. This was, of course, a form of income tax to those who sold cotton for export, but it amounted merely to the restoration of the rate in force in the later 1930s. Significantly it was re-introduced only in the confident expectation that prices to be paid for cotton in 1940 would be as much as 50 per cent higher than the previous year. And it was soon reported that the price offered in Busoga had risen by just that degree. This tax was considered by Mitchell's British colleagues in Uganda to be justified by 'the ability of the cotton producers, whose direct taxation is not being increased, to bear the burden without hardship'.[6]

Mitchell seemed to have succeeded in leaving in circulation the means of African consumption. But his pet policies were to prove impracticable. At the Colonial Office's insistence, his development policies were among early casualties of the war. He had had three particular plans in mind in September 1939: the new hospital at Mulago; the provision of rural water supplies (on New Deal grounds of providing new employment and purchasing power); and the improvement of Uganda's roads. But these were only a small part of Mitchell's grander vision. 'In such an undeveloped place as this', he wrote to Dawe, 'there is no limit to the schemes that could be devised'.[7] But Mitchell had to accept cuts, and the proposal to spend on Uganda's roads was soon dropped.

For a while there was new hope, in the shape of the £5 million Colonial Development and Welfare vote of February 1940. This held out the promise of a £230,000 allocation to Uganda. Mitchell was ecstatic and justifiably incredulous. 'Your new development policy', he wrote to the Colonial Office, 'is so great an event and a break with tradition that it takes us a little time in these distant places to become convinced that you really mean it'.[8] In the event, by May 1940 London was emphasising the hypothetical nature of the figures. The water scheme was soon judged insufficiently urgent to justify British funding. The Mulago Hospital plan survived on paper, and the government was authorised to begin spending on this – but shortages of men and materials were to lead to prolonged and unavoidable delay.[9] Major expenditure and work on Mulago could not be taken up until after the war.

Then in the summers of 1940 and 1941 came the big squeeze. Uganda, like the other British African dependencies, was given its strategic wartime instructions on financial and economic policy in two major despatches from London. One was sent in June 1940, when Mitchell was leaving Uganda; the other in June 1941. The former advocated direct taxation 'upon those best able to bear it', especially to maintain 'existing social and other services'within the territory.[10] The 1941 despatch was much more explicit and emphatic in its financial clauses. It declared that 'an increase of taxation, especially direct taxation, should be a definite object of policy'.[11] Metropolitan thinking was simply that higher taxation would serve a financial, and book-balancing, function: to replace lost revenue, or to meet new wartime charges. But this call from London in 1941 to *reduce* local purchasing power had serious implications. If taken too far, it could threaten the stimulus to production on which, as Mitchell had insisted, a British colonial dependency such as Uganda rested.

While neither British despatch laid emphasis on direct financial support for the mother country, the 1941 instruction continued along lines full of significance for the subsequent wartime role of Uganda and other colonies. 'It may well be that in some dependencies at least the effect of such increases of taxation would be to increase the surpluses available to the governments concerned. The question will then inevitably arise of what is to be done with such surpluses, and whether they should be transferred in whole or in part to His Majesty's Government in aid of general war expenditure'.[12] Any such transfer of funds, it was suggested, might take the form of free *gifts*; but this was not to be encouraged since 'it is most undesirable that there should be any suggestion that taxation is being imposed ... if its proceeds are in effect to be handed over to His Majesty's Government'. Interest-free *loans* from the colonies to London were to be preferred.

And so the June 1941 despatch inaugurated a policy of central significance in the wartime experience of both Britain and its Empire. Dependencies such as Uganda made their surplus funds available for British use. This, it has been argued, 'was the major contribution which the Empire made to the British war effort' (Cowen and Westcott 1986: 40). Britain fought the war indebted to the USA; and 'the corollary of minimising British external dollar debt was to maximise sterling debt' (Cowen and Westcott 1986: 28). A.J.P.Taylor was to describe the sterling balances subsequently accumulated in London as 'virtually forced loans' (Taylor 1965: 514). However, the colonies were assured in 1941 that, having lent their surplus funds to Britain during the war, they would nonetheless be able to resume the use of their financial resources 'when they are required for post-war purposes'.[13]

British officials in Uganda energetically set about their task of helping to fund Britain's war effort, their diligence reinforced perhaps by their knowledge that revenue accumulation was one administrative function that they could carry out with relative ease and success. More familiar with raising revenue and book-keeping than with mobilising men and materials, the Protectorate government accepted British policy proposals and adopted the reasoning behind them as its own. Governor Dundas claimed that the June 1941 despatch held 'the foremost place in the minds of his government'.[14] For the next two years Uganda budgeted for big surpluses to loan to Britain and eventually reclaim for post-war development. It was only in the framing of the estimates for 1944 that Dundas proposed to budget not for a surplus but for a deficit on a year's account.[15] Yet the 'development uses' to which 1944 revenue was to be put were themselves in tune with the paternalist final clauses of the 1941 despatch. This had referred to 'the obligation to raise the standard of living of all those classes in the Colonial Empire whose standard is at present below the minimum that can be regarded as adequate'.[16]

Taxation of expatriates

What do we learn of the official mind in the protectorate from the particular measures adopted for raising its revenue? In the case of direct taxation – increases of which were to account for as much as a third of all the additional revenue being raised by 1944 – there are two telling indications of government apprehension. First, direct taxation increases fell almost exclusively on the non-native population – it being a political and economic assumption, elevated almost to an article of faith, that Africans could not, or would not, contribute more by this means. Second, even in the case of Europeans there was trepidation. Would British expatriates consent to additional taxation measures, even to finance and sustain 'their' war?

Mitchell was not confident. In October 1939 he wrote: 'I fear the tax may be very unpopular here'.[17] Already the introduction of income tax had been successfully resisted, in 1932, though now, added Mitchell, 'it is possible that because of the war it may be swallowed'. How loyal or generous would the European community be? It seemed to depend on the bank-managers. Governor Mitchell singled them out as 'naturally very influential people'[18] – the manager of the National Bank of India in Kampala sat on the Legislative Council – but he hoped that they could be persuaded to come into line. Mitchell was haunted by his awareness, or fear, of 'a deeply rooted political objection to income tax in non-official circles in Uganda'.[19] But the governor worried too much. In the event, the *Uganda Herald* – a paper which was frequently highly critical of the Protectorate government during the war – expressed approval of the measure. And two years later, it approved a further increase in the levels of income tax. This whole episode demonstrates a degree of unwarranted government nervousness in dealings with its own expatriates. For, despite looking for it, Mitchell 'found no opposition' (Engholm 1968: 231).

That official apprehension was misplaced may be illustrated by the sizeable voluntary money contribution which expatriates were ready to make. In November 1939, a War Charities Appeal was launched. In seven months it collected £6,470.[20] In July 1940 it was succeeded by the Uganda War Fund. Reluctant to inflict a more demanding rate of income tax on non-natives, the government settled on the War Fund as a way to avoid the risk of raising the formal tax demand. This Fund forwarded money direct to the British Government. In six months it raised £80,000. It succeeded in raising £100,000 by the middle of 1941 – so that in one year and by voluntary effort, Uganda enabled Britain to build a squadron of Hurricane Fighters – named 'Uganda'– at £5000 per plane.[21] Governor Mitchell seems to have been seeking to raise by invitation and exhortation what he was reluctant to demand, for fear of dissent.

Expatriates were not the only contributors to the War Fund. Indians secured a prominent place in the lists of contributors, notably cotton ginners and the sugar manufacturers; and there was particularly extravagant official praise for African gifts, especially 'the few shillings or few cents which continue to be received from individuals throughout the country'.[22] Curiously, Tarsis Kabwegyere has focussed on this fund, suggesting that it was a significant, even sinister, means of taxing Africans during the Second World War. But even if there were evidence of pressure to pay – which Kabwegyere does not provide – the fund amounted to only a fraction of the sum of the subsequently appropriated proceeds of cotton sales from 1943, which Kabwegyere ignores. His preoccupation with the War Fund is rendered more bizarre by his accusation that its district-based organisation was a deliberate device to encourage separatism and to prevent the emergence of a Ugandan 'collective identity' (1974: 207-8). What alternative means could an over-stretched administration have adopted?

Meanwhile, of the various communities in Uganda, Europeans were evidently under the most pressure to make donations to the War Fund. The pressure was indirect and informal and was applied through the expatriates' newspaper the *Uganda Herald.* Here, week by week, names of contributors to the War Fund, and exactly what they gave, were publicised. Although the precise overall European contribution is lost in the overall figures for areas such as Kampala, Entebbe and

Eastern Province, we may conclude that it was substantial. For example, the Jinja Club raised £425 in a single evening for the War Fund shortly after its launch.[23] In such ways voluntary giving supplemented the involuntary. The 1940-1941 War Fund total of £100,000 almost matched the aggregate of the first and second year's non-native income tax totals – £29,000 and £83,000 respectively.[24] Nor was this the end of donations. A further voluntary 2 per cent levy on European officials' salaries equalled the cost of a further Hurricane by March 1941.[25]

The Protectorate government had raised taxation very cautiously, at 'the shallow end of the bath'.[26] And rather than risk any further increase in direct taxation in mid-1940, Mitchell chose the less painful option (for tax-payers) of making a free gift of £100,000 to Britain simply by taking the sum out of surplus protectorate funds. However, in January 1941 and again in January 1942, when voluntary contributions began to wane and income tax rates were doubled, neither occasion prompted the uproar which Mitchell had earlier appeared to fear. The 1944 Blue Book shows that a year's revenue from this source, first introduced in 1940, exceeded £320,000. We may conclude therefore that, in spite of early British official doubts, Europeans and Indians in Uganda made a substantial difference, at first through voluntary sums and later via direct taxation, to the Uganda Protectorate's wartime financial support of Britain. And we may deduce from the amendments made to income tax legislation in October 1943, in order to counter companies' evasion of tax, that by this time tax demands had begun to bite ('War Effort'[6] November 1943).

Expatriates were subsequently asked to pay further charges – some of which were more acceptable to them than others. After June 1941, companies were subject to an excess-profits tax, which applied to firms, mines, plantations and ginneries throughout East Africa. Its purpose was to give financial aid to Britain. The new tax was presented as a complement to the 'very inadequate' income tax'.[27] If officials hoped it would be more palatable than higher levels of income tax, the responses of unofficial opinion must have reassured them. The *Uganda Herald* accepted it uncritically, and the Uganda

Chamber of Commerce did not complain. By 1945, the special fund established for the excess-profits tax stood at £364,218 – which approximately matches the annual income tax receipts of the time. Proceeds from wartime commerce were considerable enough for such taxation to represent a tolerable sacrifice. For the Uganda Company, for example, wartime trading profits climbed steeply towards a level four or five times that of the late 1930s depression years.[28] By contrast, a measure which provoked much hostility in the business world was the compulsory war-risk insurance scheme. This 'curious and somewhat anomalous'[29] measure operated from 1 January 1941. The Uganda Chamber of Commerce immediately launched a challenge to what it regarded as an 'excessive' compulsory insurance rate of 7 shillings and 50 cents (7/50) per £100 value of goods. The challenge was successful. The rate was reduced to a mere 1/- per £100.[30] Clearly, expatriate protest could on occasions still produce a climb-down by the local British authorities.

Local politics came first. Aware of the high profile of expatriates in neighbouring Kenya at this time, the government in Uganda had neither the wish nor the means to try to extract from the unofficial community more than it readily consented to donate from the proceeds of its wartime operations.

Taxation of Africans
If the Protectorate government was apprehensive and hesitant in levying income tax on non-natives, it was still more reluctant – alarmed, even – to contemplate an increase in the direct taxes paid by indigenous Africans. There are no hints of 'absolutism' here. Neither the onset of war in 1939 nor the imperial crisis of 1940-42 could induce the British administration in Uganda to shed its opposition to any suggestion that direct taxes on Africans should be raised, or African income tax be introduced. Economic and political issues here both related to fundamentals. As always, African spending-power needed to be sustained, because spending-power promoted production. This was at the heart of African acquiescence in colonial rule in Uganda; and at the same time, the purchase of imported goods in turn yielded customs revenue. Political factors similarly dictated caution. The

Africans best able to pay more in taxation were those – especially landlord chiefs in Buganda – whose collaboration the colonial state could least afford to put at risk, especially during a war, and whom it could thus least afford to alienate.

In order to understand wartime fiscal issues, we need to recall the state of African taxation before 1939. Direct taxation of Africans took two almost universal forms in Uganda. First, there was the poll tax. This ranged from 5/- (five shillings) to 21/- per annum, the level being related to the overall prosperity of a district. The poll tax, collected by chiefs in the native administrations, was essentially a Protectorate government tax, though a fifth was rebated to the local African authorities from where it had come, to pay chiefs' salaries and for local projects. Secondly, there was the native administration tax, ranging from 5/- to 10/-, again depending on the district. Both these taxes were at flat rates per individual, the rates fixed by the governor. The thirteen native administrations, financed by the latter tax and by the poll tax rebate, were not deemed competent to set and levy their own rates. When the financial secretary in the protectorate conceded in 1943 that they would one day do so, as 'preliminary training in the working of free institutions', he was assuming – as other local officials typically did at the time – that there would be at least 50 years of British rule in which to make such experimental governmental changes.[31]

In Buganda, as elsewhere, these two taxes or their equivalents were in force. But Ganda peasants had a further burden in the form of tribute or rent paid to landlords. This was the residual *busulu* and *envujo* obligation, the nature and extent of which had been summarily altered by Protectorate government intervention in 1927, but which still amounted to a basic 10/- per annum per plot, plus a surcharge per acre under economic crops. The landlords who were recipients and beneficiaries of these payments in turn paid only a small proportion to the native government, namely 15 per cent per tenant. The total tax obligation was a considerable burden for Ganda peasants. E.M.K.Mulira attributed African poverty to this perennial burden of direct taxes. Through the *Uganda Herald* he publicised the fact that in Buganda a cotton-producer might have an annual income of 50/-

to 60/-, yet well over half, 35/-, was handed over to some authority or other: 15/- poll tax, 10/- native government tax, and another 10/- to the landlord.[32]

The tax burden did not end with direct taxation, of course. On top of licence requirements, such as for trading or owning a bicycle, there were two major forms of less visible, indirect taxation in operation. Cotton producers paid the cotton export tax – reduced, as we have seen, just before the war but restored to 2 cents per pound as soon as war broke out. And all purchasers of foreign manufactured goods paid customs duties on imports.

Who benefited from this long-established tax revenue accumulation? The beneficiaries were local. In part the taxes sustained the British colonial bureaucracy and the services of central government in Uganda. Yet more significantly, and notably in Buganda's local government, they sustained that class of chiefs and landlords with which British authority had collaborated since the turn of the century and who, as a result of their central political importance – and by contrast with the peasantry – were themselves relatively undertaxed. During the Second World War, apprehensive local British authorities ensured that they remained so.

In this particular context, the British appeared to have little room for revenue-raising initiatives when the Second World War commenced, judging as they did that African taxation generally was too high and that it should not, or could not, be raised further. This was an assumption so widely shared that it appeared to require little public amplification or justification. In 1939 the financial secretary simply claimed that 'the policy of government in recent years has been to *reduce* taxation, on the African in particular, and this policy is unchanged'.[33] The following year, increase in direct taxation of Africans was contemplated but advised against. In July 1941 Dundas wrote that there should be no rise in taxes on Africans since they were highly, 'if not excessively', taxed already.[34] He told his fellow East African governors that there was no question of 'native' taxation being increased in Uganda. And there was sympathy for this view in London, where Lord Hailey observed that the Baganda were the most heavily taxed Africans in East Africa (1944: 177-8).

In Uganda, powerful economic arguments lay behind this consistent official line. Governor Mitchell argued that the introduction of income tax for Africans was inappropriate in a country where there was generally an even spread of wealth, and that flat-rate taxes at the existing level could suffice. More significantly, as we have seen, on the outbreak of war he expressed his overall conception of what the Uganda economy required: not less money in circulation but more. A year later attention was drawn to the 'economic equilibrium' that would be upset if higher taxes on peasant producers were not matched by higher prices for their products.[35] If higher taxation was not balanced by buoyant commodity prices, not only peasants' purchasing power but also the incentive to produce might be adversely affected.

And there were conclusive political reasons, too, for not introducing income tax on Africans in Uganda. Some Africans were more equal than others and, as we have noted, could certainly have paid more in taxes. Successive governors wanted to tap the wealth of the richest Baganda, but neither Mitchell nor Dundas felt that they could risk the attempt. In private, Mitchell revealed the nervousness of his administration at the prospect of changing or increasing African taxation. He confided to Dawe, when income tax for non-natives was about to be introduced, an observation which unconsciously but persuasively shows us how far away this colonial state was from even the pretensions of 'absolutism'. He wrote, 'We shall have to exclude Africans, for I certainly could not have a full dress political row with the Baganda in the middle of a war'.[36] The association of 'Africans' and 'Baganda' is no accident. Mitchell knew that wealthy Baganda landlords could pay more – but feared that any move in this direction would raise the whole question of the permanency of the post-1900 settlement in Buganda. The 1900 Agreement, it has been observed, had given rise to 'a generation not of farmers but of rentiers' (West 1972: 29). Although after 1927 the burden of rents and tribute payable by peasants to rentier landlords was limited by law, in 1943 Dundas could still denounce 'a class of landowners fattening on the land ... indifferent to anything but their rentals'.[37] This situation was 'neither healthy nor just', he went on, insisting that these Africans at least would be able to pay more to the colonial state.

But what could be confided to Dawe in London in a confidential letter could not be proclaimed in Entebbe or Kampala, let alone be translated into public policy. After all, the larger Baganda landowners were 'the real centre of importance locally' (Mair 1936: 171). So public official utterances reveal a quite different emphasis from that which both Mitchell and later Dundas privately confided. Mitchell went so far as to declare that the land tax contribution of Baganda landlords was already high.[38] It was conceded that currently 'rich and poor are liable to pay the same tax'. But, it was officially argued, there were only a few wealthier Africans who could be taxed further – and even they could be excused further taxation in view of the fact that they had heavy social obligations, and school fees to pay ('War Effort'[4] September 1941).

The acting governor in 1940 confessed that 'the essential need is to maintain confidence and a sense of security, which would hardly be fostered by a definite addition to direct taxation'.[39] For the most part however, British officials in Uganda disguised their political apprehensions and preferred to blame insuperable administrative obstacles. Mitchell preferred stressing the difficulties of estimating and collecting a universal income tax, to acknowledging in public any lack of political will and confidence on his part.[40] The relationship with Buganda was highly sensitive and, at a time of factionalism within the landlord and chiefly classes in the kingdom, the Protectorate government could not afford to alienate upholders of British rule there by taxing them more heavily. They could not afford to alienate 'loyal' chiefs further from their local rivals, opponents of British rule, by having them introduce a general income tax which augmented the existing tax burden. Thus in addition to arguments related to the 'economic equilibrium', this fusion of administrative and political weaknesses limited the power of a colonial state which at all levels relied on acquiescence, consent and co-operation.

Nor was it only the wealthier Baganda landlords who might resist new or further direct taxation. New tax demands might threaten peace on the plantations and, particularly, in the towns. Thus in August 1940 the editor of the *Uganda Herald* criticised the idea of a general 10 per cent per month income levy, arguing that it would be too much for 'an average African income of 25/- per month' to bear.[41] He repeated the view that the African wage-earner was taxed highly already, and he warned that an increase in his burden of taxation would bring hardship and 'a protest that would be quite legitimate'. Government in the Uganda Protectorate during the Second World War was an exercise in avoiding protest. Thus no new income tax was introduced which might have either shaken relations with senior Baganda or brought crowds onto the streets of Kampala.

For similar reasons, a 1941 proposal to introduce a native liquor tax was not implemented. It was suggested that a liquor tax would tap the wealth of prosperous Baganda landlords and chiefs who were the main beneficiaries from local African brewing and distilling.[42] But the Standing Committee on Finance reported that a liquor tax would be too difficult to administer 'in a country where every staple food is capable of being fermented into an alcoholic liquor'('War Effort'[4] September 1941). It added that the native administrations might explore the idea. But this evasive alternative was soon made to look particularly unpromising. Native administrations did not in general possess powers of taxation, and therefore the proposal – to impose a tax locally on all liquor brewed in excess of family requirements – raised a constitutional problem.[43] The matter was dropped. As we shall see below, the British did go on to introduce a measure of prohibition in March 1943, but to little or no effect.

In the event, the Protectorate government stayed on familiar ground. Neither of the two major fiscal changes that were introduced before 1943 was itself an innovative measure. Rather, both entailed higher rates of existing tax forms. While both fell heavily on the cotton producer, the first did so only indirectly. Customs and excise rates were raised, as for example in the 10 per cent surcharge on all imports in August 1940.[44] Some taxes were easier to administer than others. Customs revenue was relatively easy to collect; but the increased excise rates proved not to be. So, purchases of excisable tobacco dropped immediately after the excise was raised in December 1942.[45] Africans simply turned instead to unprocessed leaf – in defiance of the colonial state and in defence of their purchasing power.

The second measure was the increase in the cotton tax. Restored to 2 cents per pound in January 1940, it was raised again to 3 cents a year later and it stayed at that level until 1945. This proved to be the Protectorate government's principal alternative to African income tax. The financial secretary claimed that the tax 'in its effect was similar to an income tax on the African community';[46] but in two respects this was not quite true. Just one (albeit sizeable) group of Africans, the cotton producers, was subjected to this demand – selected on the grounds, it was officially argued, that they could afford to pay more and their 'direct taxation is not being increased'.[47] Secondly, the cotton tax did not tap the wealth of that class of Baganda landlords whom both Mitchell and Dundas and their officials identified as the Africans best placed by income to contribute more to it.

Needing to raise revenue but reluctant to impose any new taxation demands on African producers, British officials in Uganda showed a degree of particular sensitivity towards the operation of this cotton tax. Mitchell had regretted the rise to 2 cents and told his Legislative Council that he hoped it would last for only one year.[48] When the acting financial secretary announced the further increase, he chose the moment to state that this was the tax that must eventually be reduced at the earliest possible opportunity, prior to any other war tax reductions.[49] In fact, officials had to witness the proceeds of the cotton tax subsequently diminish by two-thirds between 1941 and 1943. The shift away from cotton cultivation at this time, as peasant producers voted with their hoes, may have been accelerated by this higher level of cotton tax. Only in the later war years did cotton again prove relatively rewarding as a product to African farmers in Uganda – and only then could the government venture to raise the tax yet again, from 3 cents to 5, as we shall see shortly. By this time however, cotton growers had a far greater financial grievance, which took the form of the Cotton Fund.

The Cotton Fund
The origins of the Cotton Fund lay in the fortuitous transformation of the taxable capacity of the African peasant farmers of Uganda in the later war years. After 1942, when the military threat to Britain and the empire was easing, the income of African primary producers

was increasing. The prices paid for Ugandan raw cotton exports more than doubled between 1942 and 1945, as the value per cental of raw cotton rose from £3.03 to £6.64.[50] As the world economic context changed, so in time did the perspective of the British authorities in Uganda. African peasants who had formerly been regarded as worryingly overtaxed appeared after 1942 just as seriously to be under-taxed. The size of the cotton crop in 1945 was a mere 10 per cent greater than in 1942. What had changed was the price being offered: instead of earning Uganda £3.2 million, as it would have done at 1942 prices, the 1945 crop earned £7 million.[51] On the back of this dramatic change, major new revenue measures of taxation were introduced in Uganda. They resulted in massive accumulations. But success was bought at a high price. The new taxation strategy of the later war period and beyond came to represent a widespread political grievance among African producers in Uganda which threatened at times in the later 1940s to undermine the stability of the protectorate.

How did the Cotton Fund come into being? The Protectorate government feared inflation. A warning was sounded as early as November 1942. Then the financial secretary saw that the combination of two wartime phenomena – increased prices to exporters of raw materials, and diminished supplies of purchasable imports – might require new measures of taxation.[52] As a generator of inflation, high commodity prices did pose a problem. But for a government that was concurrently seeking to increase its own revenue there appeared to be only benefit. It was a simple administrative act to have the Cotton Exporters Group pay into a Protectorate government fund a substantial proportion of the proceeds of cotton sales, which might otherwise have rewarded the producers. Subsequently and consequently, the albeit improved prices that were paid to the producers from this time were only a fraction of what they might otherwise have been, given the higher prices prevailing in India to which most of the crop was actually sold.

There thus appeared in the official Blue Book colonial accounts a vast sum: over £3.5 million by as early as 1945. This sum was equivalent to over half the total proceeds of the cotton crop in that year. The

Protectorate government expressed the hope that the Cotton Fund would please all interests: it fulfilled Uganda's imperial obligations by providing an interest-free loan to the British government; and also, by holding down inflation, it might provide some financial stability for the protectorate. The Fund was presented to the producers themselves as a short-term protection against possible international price fluctuations, a 'stabilisation' fund for their benefit. And as for the longer term, the Fund was 'under pledge given by this government, reserved for expenditure on projects beneficial to the cotton industry and cotton-producing areas'.[53] Moreover, it was argued, all other Africans would indirectly benefit if, by restricting profits from the production of cotton, the Fund indirectly helped to sustain the production of food. There seems even to have been a moral dimension, for the administration had argued in 1940 that it was right 'to take to revenue a proper share in any abnormal advances of prices of export commodities beyond reasonably high levels ... when enhanced values of colonial exports may fairly be ascribed to the emergence of conditions peculiar to war *and not to any effort on the part of producer* or to improvement in the quality of the product'.[54]

Things were not so agreeably simple, however, and not all interest groups were readily convinced. The effectiveness of the Protectorate government was limited by its inability to recognise that its own rationalisations and moralising might not be widely shared. It was now insured against poverty of financial resources, but it could not be rescued from its own poverty of imagination. One problem had been solved only to create another. Thousands of peasant producer-consumers faced an acute rise in their cost of living, notably in the price of imported goods during the latter years of the Second World War. They had a more particular and short-term perspective than was convenient to their colonial rulers. They wanted to exercise purchasing power, and yet they were being denied much of their means of doing so. In Buganda, their grievance was not yet significant enough politically to play more than a minor part in the 1945 disturbances. But continuing adherence to the Fund policy after the war certainly helped to produce the subsequent and more widespread crisis of 1949.

The Fund also proved inadequate to the huge task of containing inflation. Yet the Fund continued to grow – and to be regarded by those whose labour made it possible, not as a welcome insurance against a sudden collapse in world prices (which never occurred in the colonial period), but principally as a tax and a grievance. British officials and African peasants had different and conflicting priorities. And against a background of incipient complaints from farmers, the Protectorate government now introduced a further increase in cotton export tax, from 3 cents to 5 in July 1945. As before, such an act could be presented as 'just and reasonable' in view of the higher prices anticipated.[55] Governor Dundas had even claimed that the growers would pay no part of the tax.[56] Like the Fund payments, the money was to be collected from the Cotton Exporters Group, and thereby withheld from the growers. However, since this money was being taken out of cotton profits before the payments were made into the Fund, in effect cotton producers were indeed being taxed. Unlike the Cotton Fund, the raised cotton export tax was intended as a simple fiscal device, to reduce the budgeted deficit for 1945. Unintentionally, it became one additional means of undermining political consent.

Uganda's coffee producers were also threatened with a similar export tax in 1945. The growers faced having nearly three-quarters – £210,000 – of the estimated surplus proceeds from their crop sales in 1946 denied to them and diverted, not into their own war-time fund, but into the general protectorate account.[57] The Protectorate government judged that the coffee growers would be well able to pay such a sum. Coffee prices were even higher than cotton prices, relative to their respective pre-war levels, and income from an acre of coffee was calculated as 50 per cent more than that from an acre of cotton. Governor Hall could thus claim that the price currently paid to coffee producers was 'regarded generally very satisfactorily'.[58] Here was an alternative to an increase in direct taxation which, he added somewhat naively, the coffee growers would not even notice.

It was the Colonial Office which did not agree and which expressed its concern. By this time, the January 1945 disturbances had taken place. The uncharacteristic bullishness of the Protectorate government in the wake of its apparently successful responses to that crisis was not shared in London. The Colonial Office, embarrassed by the disturbances and anxious to maintain calm in the protectorate, urged caution on the local British administration. £210,000 looked too high a sum and too high a proportion of coffee proceeds to deny the producers. The secretary of state asked Hall to assure him that 'this is not likely to lead to grave dissatisfaction on the part of the producers concerned'.[59] Hall did his best. He pointed out that the June rise in cotton tax had been successfully instituted; that coffee growers were fewer in numbers than cotton growers; and that the new African members of the Legislative Council had approved.[60]

Colonial Office anxiety was not so easily dismissed. London requested a reduction, by up to a half, of the proposed sum. It seems that Colonial Office concern was infectious. In the event, the Protectorate government imposed even more than the required cuts on its original proposal. Hall reduced the target figure to a mere £96,350.[61] This was a partial and belated recognition, following the events of January 1945, that the accumulation of revenue in Uganda should not result in the accumulation of grievance.

Conclusion

We may conclude that during the Second World War as a whole, money did flow out of the Uganda Protectorate to the mother country. This was made possible by the fact that annual protectorate income by 1945 was very nearly double what it had been in 1939. Design and accident both played their parts in bringing this about. That is, new administrative measures were undertaken – while at the same time extraneous wartime conditions beyond local British government control, such as higher prices for colonial commodities, had a huge impact.

The British colonial state in Uganda took no conscious risks. It was aware of the limits of its power over its local inhabitants. Taxation increases for Africans were kept to realistic proportions in an attempt to avoid serious curtailment of purchasing power or erosion of the incentive to produce. Wartime tax initiatives were broadly targeted at Africans better able to bear them – the cotton and coffee producers – except that this targeting excluded those Baganda of the chiefly-landlord class who were most clearly *under*-taxed but whom the British could not afford to alienate.

Though resultant taxation could be a grievance, it seems to have been not so much taxation levels as prices which generally determined productive effort and output in Uganda during the 1940s – as we shall see in the following chapter of this study. If the price promised was sufficient to allow both payment of tax and purchase of goods, then productive effort continued to make economic sense to producers. The Protectorate government kept tax demands in line with what it judged to be capacity to pay, and in the later years of war did ensure that cotton producers received higher prices – though they were not as high as they would have been without the Fund, nor high enough to match the raised cost of imports.

What did limit the Protectorate government in its raising of revenue was the need to keep money in circulation, and to maintain African spending-power as well as tax yields. Above all, however, British officials were influenced by political factors. There would be opposition and protest – whether from expatriates or from Africans – if levels of tax rose too high in Uganda. There were no effective coercive means available for the routine collection of tax. Inevitably, the local administration's greatest success at revenue raising, the Cotton Fund, was achieved at a considerable political cost in the longer term. It proved to be a grievance of disturbing potential in Uganda – and a symbolic illustration of what happened when the British colonial state overplayed its hand.

---

1. Mitchell to Secretary of State, 19 September 1939, PRO CO 536/202/40100/1.
2. Mitchell to Secretary of State, covering letter attached to 1940 Draft Estimates, PRO CO 536/202/40100.
3. See Governor John Hall's claim, in Chapter 1.
4. Dawe to Mitchell, 13 March 1940, PRO CO 536/202/40100.
5. Mitchell to the Legislative Council, 29 November 1939.
6. Financial Secretary, Memorandum on 1940 Draft Estimates, PRO CO 536/202/40100.

7. Mitchell to Dawe, 28 March 1940, PRO CO 536/202/40100.

8. *ibid.*

9. Chief Secretary to the Legislative Council, 9 December 1942.

10. Secretary of State to the Colonies, 5 June 1940, paras. 8,9, PRO CO 854/117.

11. Secretary of State to the Colonies, 5 June 1941, para. 7, PRO CO 854/120.

12. *ibid.* para. 10.

13. *ibid.* para. 11.

14. Dundas to Secretary of State, 23 December 1941, PRO CO 536/208/40100/1941.

15. Dundas to Secretary of State, 3 November 1943, PRO CO 536/208/40100/1943.

16. Secretary of State to the Colonies, 5 June 1941, para.12, PRO CO 854/120.

17. Mitchell to Dawe, 19 October 1939, PRO CO 822/99/11.

18. Mitchell to Secretary of State, 16 December 1939, PRO CO 822/99/11.

19. Mitchell to Secretary of State, 9 November 1939, PRO CO 822/99/11.

20. Reported in *Uganda Herald*, 24 July 1940.

21. Reported in *Uganda Herald*, 21 May 1941.

22. Reported in *Uganda Herald*, 19 March, 1941.

23. Reported in *Uganda Herald*, 3 July 1940.

24. Blue Books, 1940, 1941.

25. Report, *Uganda Herald*, 19 March 1941.

26. Acting Governor to the Legislative Council, 6 August 1940.

27. Dundas to the Legislative Council, 17 June 1941.

28. Uganda Company Ltd, Minutes of General Meetings, Rhodes House, MSS Afr.s.1523.

29. Editorial in *Uganda Herald*, 2 July 1941.

30. Uganda Chamber of Commerce, Annual Report, in *Uganda Herald*, 18 February 1942.

31. Financial Secretary to the Legislative Council, 15 December 1943.

32. Letter, *Uganda Herald*, 28 January 1942.

33. Financial Secretary to the Legislative Council, 6 December 1939.

34. Dundas to Secretary of State, 29 July 1941 PRO CO 536/208/40100/1941.

35. Acting Governor to Legislative Council, 21 November 1940.

36. Mitchell to Dawe, 19 October 1939, PRO CO 822/99/11.

37. Dundas to Dawe, 7 September 1943, PRO CO 536/209/40100/3/43.

38. Mitchell to the Legislative Council, 29 November 1939.

39. Acting Governor to the Legislative Council, 21 November 1940.
40. Mitchell to the Legislative Council, 29 November 1939.
41. Editorial, *Uganda Herald*, 14 August 1940.
42. Anonymous letter, *Uganda Herald*, 3 December 1941.
43. Financial Secretary to the Legislative Council, 12 December 1941.
44. Acting Financial Secretary, Memorandum on 1941 Draft Estimates, PRO CO 536/206/40100.
45. Financial Secretary to the Legislative Council, 15 December 1943.
46. Financial Secretary to the Legislative Council, 12 December 1941.
47. Uganda Government to Colonial Office, 4 November 1940, PRO CO 536/206/40100.
48. Mitchell to the Legislative Council, 29 November 1939.
49. Memorandum on 1941 Draft Estimates, PRO CO 536/206/40100.
50. Appendix IIIa, Annual Report of the Department of Agriculture, 1945-46.
51. *ibid.*
52. Financial Secretary Memorandum on the 1943 Draft estimates, PRO CO 536/208/40100/1942.
53. Dundas to Secretary of State, 22 November 1944, PRO CO 536/212/40100/1944.
54. Memorandum from the Government of Uganda for the East African Governors'Conference, June 1940, PRO CO 962/15. My italics.
55. Acting Chief Secretary to the Legislative Council, 18 December 1944.
56. Dundas to Secretary of State, 22 November 1944, PRO CO 536/212/40100/1944.
57. Hall to Secretary of State, 23 November 1945, PRO CO 536/212/40100/1945.
58. Hall to Secretary of State, 23, 30 November 1945, PRO CO 536/212/40100/1945.
59. Secretary of State to Hall, 28 November 1945, PRO CO 536/212/40100/1945.
60. Hall to Secretary of State, 30 November 1945, PRO CO 536/212/40100/1945.
61. Financial Secretary to the Legislative Council, 4 December 1945.

8

Uganda's War Effort: Materials

Produce of the estate

The coming of the Second World War led Britain to treat Uganda for the first time as a 'tropical estate'. Joseph Chamberlain had long ago advocated, as colonial secretary, investment in Britain's tropical dependencies as strategic sources of raw materials in an increasingly competitive world. Only minimal steps had been taken along this road before 1939. Now, in a global conflict, Uganda could not produce weapons; but by 1942 'the foodstuffs and minerals' of African dependencies could themselves be described as 'a vast armoury for the war effort'.[1] So while the foundation of Uganda's economic and financial viability remained the export of such pre-war staples as cotton and coffee, the protectorate was forced in addition to adopt novel wartime production programmes. From these initiatives and their outcomes we may learn more about the true nature of colonial rule in Uganda – whether it had 'absolute' power, say, or how far it could 'exploit' the country.

But first, what was required of Uganda; and what in fact came to be produced there? We note at once the Protectorate government's limited capacity to determine its own future. Policy and production programmes were formulated by external authorities, in London and Nairobi. Moreover, some of these policies were adopted with considerable reluctance by local British authorities who considered them to be in conflict with the protectorate's own interests.

Indeed, in some important respects Uganda under British rule was now to suffer economic pressures, and one dilemma in particular, comparable with the predicament of the territory long after the British departed. Some demands changed over time, but for the duration of the war imperial requirements posed continuing and intractable problems. Above all, local British officials were instructed to promote *both* self-sufficiency *and* a high level of exports. First, in September 1939, all colonies were instructed to replace imported goods of all kinds, especially foodstuffs, with local produce wherever possible. And while pursuing self-sufficiency in food, the British administration in Uganda was also urged to export cotton and coffee to the limit of its capacity (thereby conserving foreign currency when selling within the empire, and earning foreign currency when selling outside the empire). At the outset, planting of the 1939-1940 cotton crop had to be delayed to ensure sufficient food acreage. In such ways could production for domestic food self-sufficiency, and production for export, compete with each other during the colonial period – as they have done in Uganda and elsewhere since the end of that era.

The so-called 'Blitzkrieg' telegram of June 1940 was less a policy document than an emergency British cry for help from the colonies. Because of the 'deepening gravity' of the war situation in Europe, the colonies had to make 'a supreme effort in the next few months'. A 'maximum positive contribution' of supplies was called for, especially of 'raw materials of importance to the war effort'.[2] How was such a demand to be interpreted in Uganda? The British Empire clearly could not defend itself with cotton or coffee. But Uganda could provide raw materials for use by local military forces now that Mussolini's declaration of war was bringing hostilities to both North and East Africa, and in response troops were being mobilised. Thus 2000 tons of timber were exported from Uganda for military railway construction during June and July 1940. But this was just a start: in the first nine months of 1942, for example, another 18,000 tons of timber followed.[3] The personal needs of the soldiers in East Africa had also to be served, and Uganda supplied its territorial quota of tea and sugar, and tobacco and cigarettes, for these requirements, too.

Two events in 1942 further underlined Uganda's wartime role and importance: the failure of Britain's defences in the Far East; and the failure of the short, late, rains in East Africa. The former led to renewed and intensified demands for Ugandan products, including specific raw materials of war; the latter led East Africa towards famine. As a result, at the end of 1942 the East African Production and

Supply Council was instituted in Nairobi to harness East Africa's resources, not only to meet the requirements of the British global war effort but to stave off acute food shortages in its own territories. Thereafter programmes essentially designed in Nairobi shaped Uganda's wartime production drive. From 1943, the Director of Native Production on the EAPSC drew up plans and targets for British East Africa. Prices, marketing, and distribution procedures were all laid down.[4] And in Uganda itself production plans were worked out for each district and province.[5]

In time, burdens on the British administration multiplied. In March 1942 there came a renewed instruction from Britain to 'intensify all forms of local production which assist the war effort'.[6] So in Uganda again policy was amended: to include the export of all available foodstuffs, while maintaining a normal cotton crop. Uganda should indeed feed itself. But it had now also to supply foodstuffs to its neighbours, to imperial forces in the Middle East, and to Britain. Oliver Lyttelton had said, 'All you can produce will be taken'.[7] The British Ministry of Food now requested maximum production of oilseeds, especially groundnuts (an extra 10,000 tons) and sesame seed (an extra 5,000 tons).[8] In the spring of 1942, the acreage of groundnuts planted by African farmers in Eastern Province nearly doubled the previous year's.[9] The export of 25,000 tons of cotton seed went further towards meeting the ministry's raised requirement for vegetable oils ('War Effort' [5] October 1942). The Agriculture Department in Uganda sought also to promote more cultivation of rice and soya beans, and even of wheat and 'European' vegetables.[10] There was also a demand for further tonnage of sugar to be produced by Uganda's Indian-run plantations.[11] Tea from European-owned estates, such as the Uganda Company's at Mityana, and African-grown coffee were described at this time as 'commodities essential to the war effort'; so too were the 15,000 head of cattle exported to Kenya during July and August 1942, mainly for Messrs Liebigs canned meat factory. Liebigs were not the only beneficiaries: the Karimojong of north-eastern Uganda benefited so much from the wartime cattle trade that, in recognition of their new prosperity, they had their poll-tax rate raised ('War Effort' [5] October 1942).

Japan's entry into the war at Pearl Harbour was of particular significance. Once Malaya was lost, British Africa had to find substitutes for commodities formerly drawn from the Far East. So the great broadening of Uganda's food production effort in 1942 was supplemented by a focus on raw materials of a different order. Uganda's mineral deposits, such as they were – tin, wolfram, mica and tantalite – were to be fully exploited; and above all there was to be new activity on Uganda's rubber plantations.[12] Many rubber estates were found to be in a neglected condition following years of low prices during the 1930s depression.[13] As a step towards an intended doubling of Uganda's production, an official survey was also carried out into wild rubber resources.[14] The British Ministry of Supply now offered credit for the rehabilitation of former estates ('War Effort' [5] October 1942).

Thus in 1942 the Second World War introduced a new set of priorities and a new pattern for Uganda's productive efforts. So too did local shortages following the failure of the 1942 short rains. But this particular famine was caused only partly by the vagaries of the weather. It was also man-made: a consequence of the war, and of wartime conditions. Military recruitment represented some loss of producers to the army; and the army itself in turn consumed 350,000 bags of East African maize annually.[15] In addition, officials noted a serious shortage of consumer goods – which reduced the incentive for African peasant farmers to aim at maximum production, or maximum sale, of food crops.[16] As a result a famine commissioner was appointed in the Uganda Protectorate in 1943. Other steps were taken too. The presence of Polish refugees at camps in Uganda (there were 4719 of them by February 1943) meant more mouths to feed, and the rate of their arrival had to be slowed down on account of local food shortages.[17] Meanwhile, 'to provide an additional supply of food', prisoners of war held in Jinja were allowed to go fishing on Lake Victoria.[18]

As demands on the productive capacity of the Uganda Protectorate became more intense, the local British administration's essential dilemma grew steadily more acute. Maximum production of war materials for export could not easily coexist with maximum production of food urgently needed throughout East Africa. Yet as well as this tension there was a degree of interdependence between the two undertakings. Labourers engaged on rubber and sugar plantations had to be fed; and if there was insufficient maize to feed them, production of such commodities would have to close down. Various expedients were now tried. EAPSC's chairman proposed a reduction of the number of such labourers in order to avoid expensive imports of maize into East Africa.[19] This proposal implicitly 'solved' the problem created by the demand for war materials, by sacrificing a proportion of the production of war materials itself. A possible alternative was to eke out supplies of food by giving labourers less to eat; and in June 1943 the EAPSC did indeed recommend to all East African colonial governments that the maize ration to employed labour should be limited to 1.5 lbs. per head per day, a 25 per cent reduction.[20]

The Uganda government itself took unilateral action in January 1944. Calculating that there was not enough food available both for the indigenous population of the protectorate and for the immigrant labourers from the south-west on whom so much production in Buganda depended, the local British authorities closed the border with Ruanda-Urundi. But this could hardly be a long-term solution. While such government intervention could ease the food problem, it aggravated the labour problem, and thus starved in turn the farms, mines and plantations of the labour they relied upon to produce the required war materials. By the latter half of 1944, a more normal flow of labour was restored.

The story of maize in Uganda is a paradigm: it exemplifies the contradictions in British aspirations and the recurrence of undesired outcomes. The only satisfactory long-term policy was to increase the amount of food available; thus more of East Africa's territory was allocated to maize. But such a solution to one problem entailed the creation of another. The local government in Uganda now found itself unavoidably committed to a productive effort which it had long resisted. Uganda was capable of growing maize, but maize caused soil erosion. In 1940, Uganda's G.F.Clay had bluntly told his fellow British East African Directors of Agriculture, 'I consider that maize is an undesirable crop'.[21] His preference was for Uganda to remain an importer of maize grown in Kenya, as was the case until April 1942. But then it was decided that Uganda should produce enough maize for its own consumption – partly at least to avoid congestion on the railway link with Kenya. Worse was to follow. In 1943 Uganda's officials reluctantly undertook, as a war measure, the cultivation of maize on a large enough scale to meet the greatly increased demand throughout East Africa.[22]

There was clear tension here between short-term needs and long-term interests. It was recognised by the protectorate's agriculture department that Uganda had no choice but to 'sacrifice some of its precious fertility in order to provide foodstuffs for the common East African Pool'.[23] Having failed to parry the demand for maize, British officials in Uganda were similarly unable to dampen the subsequent enthusiasm for the crop shown by growers in the protectorate. A forecast that there would be considerable difficulty in preventing the continued production of maize on a large scale was borne out in Eastern Province. There in 1946, the Busoga maize crop 'exceeded all expectations and intentions'.[24] In Buganda maize production flourished too, so that ginners became concerned at the waning interest in growing cotton. Buganda contributed most to Uganda's increase in maize production at this time.[25] By 1947 maize had become the third cash crop of Buganda. The protectorate's record 1944 crop was 'unexpectedly large'. It brought to light storage difficulties, and – another unintended consequence – it jammed the railways.[26] Uganda was by now producing a third of East Africa's total crop.[27]

Each successive reference to maize in the annual reports of the Uganda Protectorate's agricultural department recorded damage to soil fertility. It may have benefited the British administration in the short term, that a proportion of the maize crop was eaten within Uganda and thus helped to keep famine at bay and minimise the need for further costly imports of food during the Second World War. But by the later 1940s, maize-meal was a permanent feature, a staple article of diet, in much of Uganda; and cultivators found it 'an easily grown, remunerative, cash crop'.[28] Thus the war brought about a major productive and dietary change in Uganda, neither willed nor welcomed by the local British government department ostensibly responsible for agriculture and for soil conservation.

The later years of war saw further new commitments, reluctantly undertaken. Sugar was exported to Britain as before, but now Uganda had to provide sugar for the rest of East Africa, too, to the extent that it was permitted to retain only one-seventh of its total crop. As a result, Ugandans went short of sugar. The Uganda Protectorate government asked the EAPSC early in 1945 for an increased allocation of sugar for local consumption 'as the Ugandan natives were finding it difficult to understand why they could not obtain sugar easily in Uganda, which was a producing area'.[29] This request was turned down by Nairobi.

Rice provides another illustration. In May 1940, Clay had argued that 'it would be completely wrong as a wartime policy to stimulate rice production' in Uganda.[30] He advocated the creation of an East African economy in which each territory produced the crops most suited to it, and in his view, Tanganyika should produce the rice. Despite Clay's view, there was an abrupt rise in rice production in Uganda as the war progressed. In 1942-43, fewer than 100 tons of rice were produced in Uganda; by 1943-44, however, the rice target set for the protectorate was 4350 tons, and for the next year it was 8800 tons. As it turned out, weather and disease greatly reduced crop totals and hence exports, though rice locally milled in Eastern Province did contribute locally to the protectorate's overall food supply. By 1944, Uganda had 28 times the rice acreage it had in 1938.[31]

Problems thus arose from Uganda's attempts to fulfil its new productive obligations as a colonial state on the periphery of an empire at war. Uganda struggled to produce cotton, too, the main pre-war export commodity. Here there were sharp falls in exports in 1942 and 1943, and recovery was incomplete by 1945. Between 1938 and 1944, the cotton acreage in Uganda fell by a third.[32] But, as we have already seen, one needs to set against this the higher monetary value of the cotton that was exported, and also the maintenance of both coffee and sugar exports during the same period. And from 1942 onwards there were considerable increases in the quantities exported of a wide range of other products, notably groundnuts and beans;

tea, tobacco and rubber; and cattle and timber, too. New exports from Uganda during the Second World War included wolfram and pyrethrum. Overall acreages of not only rice and maize but also cassava increased markedly.[33] 'Even remote Kigezi' was involved, producing flax as well as tobacco now (Huxley 1948: 214).

All this was unprecedented in its range and extent. Some of the potential of the estate was being tapped. But the colonial state in Uganda was never entirely free to choose how to respond to the British war effort. Its fate here lay largely in the hands – and interests – of others: whether the authorities in London and in Nairobi, or the thousands of immigrant labourers, or its own African population. The British in Uganda could at best make only a series of piecemeal responses to the war, in the grip of changing situations – themselves seriously affected both by wartime conditions and by the forces of nature.

Price and wage manipulation

How was this 'tropical estate' being made so productive? What actually happened in Uganda between the request for, and the export of, such material products as we have identified? How effective was the British colonial state? One thing was certain: goals defined in London or Nairobi could be reached only if Uganda's African farmers and labourers were mobilised to achieve them. How was this done?

We gain a glimpse of the real situation 'on the ground' in a remark made by Uganda's Director of Agriculture shortly *before* the war began. With the value of Uganda's cotton in the world market lower than ever before, he wrote: 'With unrest in so many parts of the world due to low prices that have perforce been paid ... it is of no little importance to find out if possible where the cotton danger line may be in Uganda'.[34] Apprehensive mention of 'danger' emphasises the centrality and the delicacy of this price-centred relationship, between Uganda's Africans and the world economy, on which the British in Uganda necessarily depended.

In the absence of sufficient effective means of compulsion, British authorities had recourse to stimulation by incentives. One means of increasing peasant production of raw materials was the manipulation of prices. Prices paid to peasants represented both power to meet tax obligations, and power to purchase desired consumer goods. East African governments appreciated the potential of 'price-stimulated production' and exploited it with a degree of success. Its partial effectiveness as a policy device is well illustrated by the story of cotton, long-established as Uganda's major export.

In 1941-42, the Protectorate government faced a crisis. Successive years of low and uncertain prices – apparently arising from falling demand in India – led to a slump in cotton production. A sharp fall in cotton prices (and their subsequent unpredictability) was accompanied at this time by the further disincentive of a rise in the price of imported consumer goods – though also, in some areas, by the availability of alternative cash crops, such as groundnuts in Eastern Province, offering higher rewards for farmers. In both 1941 and 1942 the price of cotton in Uganda fell to such an extent that the Protectorate government stepped in to suspend marketing. Rescue operations took the form of bulk purchase agreements negotiated in both years by the Protectorate government with the Ministry of Supply in Britain. These bulk purchases enabled prices to recover. But immense damage had been done, as farmers responded to price reductions by neglecting their cotton crops and reducing their cotton acreages. By the end of June 1942, only 104,000 acres had been planted, compared with 372,000 acres a year earlier. This was a 72 per cent reduction, the result of two successive years of uncertain prices and interrupted marketing.[35]

British authorities in London and in Uganda were primarily concerned neither with cotton nor with cotton-producers as such but, as always, with the financial viability of the protectorate. The Ministry of Supply's *ad hoc* bulk purchases of 1941 and 1942 had this in mind. Such purchases were usually undertaken by Britain for Britain's own direct benefit. But 1941 was one of the exceptions. That year's agreement was 'to relieve the Ugandan Government of the territory's cotton crop' when sale in the usual manner had become impossible (Leubuscher 1956: 61). The war thus produced, in the colonial context, a prophetic illustration of the potential perils, for independent African states, of monoculture.

A dramatic policy change was announced in December 1942 which was intended to achieve both price maintenance for cotton producers and a sufficient financial reserve for the protectorate.[36] It was indeed to have long term repercussions. Each immediate year thereafter, the Protectorate government was to buy all Uganda's cotton from the local ginners, employing as agents a Cotton Exporters' Group of existing established exporters such as the Uganda Company. The Ministry of Supply in Britain could take as much of this crop as it wished; and would take any of the crop which Uganda proved unable to sell on the world market. The key ingredient in this scheme was a price guarantee. Before each cotton season, local British officials would announce a price which would apply to producers throughout the marketing period.

Since the whole purpose of the scheme was to promote recovery of cotton production and export – and thereby of protectorate finances – the new prices had to compare favourably with the poor levels of recent experience. The guaranteed price, however, was to reflect a reserve price fixed by the Ministry of Supply – and this was considerably below world prices which were, at just this time, beginning to rise. In the event, Uganda was to sell less than a third of its cotton crop to Britain (Ehrlich 1958: 286). But the Ministry of Supply's reserve continued to influence the price paid to peasant producers. The government's proceeds, which arose from the difference between what the government was paying to the producers and what the crop was making on world-wide sales, were paid into the Cotton Fund (which we encountered in the previous chapter). The scheme represented a form of further taxation of Ugandans during the 1940s; and 'centralised marketing was to be used to tax the low-income peasant, while the foreign-owned ginners and exporters worked on generous margins of profits' (Zwanenburg and King 1975: 215).

Nonetheless, the newly guaranteed prices worked, to a certain extent. The first purchases under the new arrangements were of the 1943 crop. This had been planted before the announcement of the new measures, but the price of 13/- (per 100 lbs) had an effect in encouraging diligent picking, and the crop 'was marketed expeditiously'.[37] The June 1941 price had been a mere 7/-. Planting for the next (1943-44) season showed a marked improvement. By the end of June 1943, the acreage of planted cotton was over three times that of a year earlier.[38] Farmers were responding as intended. Prices continued to rise in 1944 and 1945, if slowly; also to exceed, albeit modestly, the Ministry of Supply's reserve price, though Uganda's Cotton Fund grew and grew. Dundas's view in 1943 was that 'the introduction of fixed prices ... undoubtedly provided a stimulus to cotton planting'.[39]

European self-satisfaction proved myopic. Success came at a heavy price. Schemes which were working in financial terms were to prove expensive politically. 'Strong protests are being voiced by all sections of the community,' reported the *Uganda Herald* on 10 February 1943. What the government wanted – and claimed to be in Africans' interests – was not universally welcomed by African producers themselves. The *Herald* published letters from aggrieved Africans. One of these admitted in 1943 that a rumoured official price of around 15/- would be the best for many years; but he added that growers had been expecting as much as 20/-, given the current strong demand for cotton in Europe and India. If growers received the full value of their produce, the correspondent went on, it would not only be fair but it would compensate them to some extent for recent increases in the cost of living in Uganda.[40] By contrast, an official British claim in 1945 was that 'the prices paid (to growers) are proper and reasonable. They are far higher than what the growers used to receive before the war' (Whitley 1945: para.31). Cotton prices were indeed higher. But they might have been higher still; and they did not catch up with the prices for imported goods. Africans' purchasing power was being undermined. We must thus agree that 'the growers were considerably worse off than they might otherwise have been' (Ehrlich 1958: 287).

The administration's defence of its policy was many-sided, but it failed to convince those most affected by it. Whitley argued that the chosen official price levels helped to keep inflation in check (1945: para.41). The Uganda Company considered that 'without this scheme, the price of cotton might have been higher but the grower would have been tempted to use his larger income in trying to acquire a strictly limited amount of consumable goods. The result would in all probability have been ... the sowing of seeds of future discontent and unrest'.[41] African growers in Uganda did indeed work at this time not to save but to spend. But the origins of wartime inflation lay rather with the shortage of goods – about which the British colonial state could do little. The Protectorate government in Uganda still faced a policy dilemma. If it permitted the cotton growers to enjoy the full profits of their crop, then inflation might indeed worsen for other sections of the community, such as labourers on plantations or in the towns. But as long as it continued to depress cotton prices artificially, it fuelled grievance among the growers. 'Discontent and unrest' already existed, among cotton producers more concerned with the present than the future. One African complaint in Uganda in 1944 was that 'the present prices barely cover tax obligation'.[42]

Local British officials lacked the confidence to allow open debate on this issue, and so resorted to censorship. The *Uganda Herald* thus did not print a letter from a highly critical expatriate, George Foster, writing on behalf of African producers. He had to turn to *The East African Standard* instead. On 29 January 1943, Foster alleged that on the Bombay market African growers could be earning 30/, while in Teso 'the native is being forced by the Ugandan Administration to accept 10/50'. The outraged Foster concluded: 'This is what I call an Administration three-card trick, damn it, Sir.... The little racket just stinks and must stop'. It did not. There is little overt evidence, as already noted, that 'vehement' opposition from African cotton growers in Uganda made an 'important' contribution to the 1945 disturbances, as alleged by Ehrlich (1958: 304). Yet the 1949 troubles certainly demonstrated that growers remained unconvinced by the official case for the continuing price stabilisation fund. By 1949 it could be argued strongly that the Fund had been retained, and the money withheld, for too long – at a time indeed when postwar world cotton prices were soaring. The Protectorate government clearly failed to persuade cotton producers of the Cotton Fund's perennial necessity.

While the institution of the Cotton Fund was one official British response to the cotton crises of 1941 and 1942, another was the officially sanctioned *diversification* of Uganda's productive effort. War promoted diversification, not only by emphasising the seriousness of excessive dependence on cotton, but also by providing a ready wartime market for a variety of other raw materials.

The central mechanism in the promotion by government of alternative crops was once again price stimulation. Here in fact was an opportunity for some African cotton growers to put a brake on the decline in their real incomes: one reason for the very low 1942-43 cotton crop was a switch in 1942 to groundnuts and simsim (sesame seed). These were crops which the administration was adopting under pressure of wartime need; and they were promoted by prior price guarantees to growers. In December 1943 it was observed that 'the Provincial Administration appears to have had less trouble with the collection of native poll tax than ever before, a fact which clearly indicates that, in spite of the poor cotton crop, there must have been a great deal of money in African hands from the sale of other produce'.[43]

Price stimulation of course posed difficulties of its own. It was recognised that prices for one product required for the war effort had to be closely related to prices for others, in order to balance production. Thus in the case of groundnut cultivation in Buganda, it was suggested that 'little expansion in cultivation is likely without a considerable increase in the price to the producer, particularly as it has to face competition from maize'.[44] And price stimulation could prove *too* successful. Launched on the basis of approved imports of seed and, especially, guaranteed official minimum prices, maize production (as we have seen) came to defy government control.

During the Second World War, British officialdom was not alone in recognising the need for and the value of diversification. Expatriates in commerce, especially exporters of cotton, also had to reconsider their position. In 1939 the Uganda Company had regarded cotton as 'by far the most important department' in its business. But 1941 was found to be an 'exceptionally difficult year for trading'; and the small crop of 1942 led the company to sell 9 of its 16 ginneries – and to conclude that 'in the immediate future, cotton will contribute less to our profits'. By contrast, the Company's interest in motor cars flourished and was responsible in 1944 for 54 per cent of its trading profit; while there was also a record crop on its Mityana tea estate in 1945, following wartime investment and expansion.[45] Although its cotton fortunes did recover after 1943, by the end of the Second World War cotton had become a product of reduced, if still considerable, importance in the dealings of the Uganda Company – as in those of the Uganda Protectorate.

Price manipulation did work. In the light of this, the British East African authorities considered that their food production campaigns would succeed only if attractive prices were guaranteed before planting. African opinion agreed. Africans foresaw little problem if sufficient cash incentives were offered. One Muganda advised the government to promote production through the newspapers – 'and offer favourable prices' (Kakembo 1946: 47). Events provided confirmation. The Nutrition Committee observed that first efforts to encourage soya beans and rice met with little success, but 'when it became possible to offer an attractive price, they were readily grown as a cash crop'.[46] From November 1942, relatively high guaranteed prices for African-produced coffee led to more plantings, better cultivation and higher yields, especially in Buganda where 'stabilised prices ... encouraged continued expansion of cultivation'.[47]

Yet, as we have already noted, the policy had its limitations. Weather conditions were another factor in determining yield per acre of cotton in Uganda. As the chief secretary lamented in December 1943, 'the vagaries of weather and war are relentless in their demands'.[48] As we have seen, the failure of the short rains could threaten famine. Also, carefully conceived official price-stimulated production programmes could founder on producers' preference for the black-market: 'price-stimulation' of an unofficial kind. Refugee Poles provided enterprising local farmers with one such opportunity. The farmers locally chose to produce, and the Poles to buy, chickens, eggs, fish, pigs and milk, which amounted to 'an element of unregulated sales and black-marketing *vis-a-vis* the refugees'.[49]

Moreover, it remained a somewhat perverse fact that higher prices could on occasion deter rather than stimulate production. It has been pointed out that if both commitments and tastes are static, higher prices may induce less production, since the sums required for payment of tax and purchase of goods are acquired more easily (Prest 1948: 12). Furthermore, there was no point during the Second World War in working for additional consumer goods if they were so scarce, and their prices so high, that greater efforts and higher output would still be of little avail. A specific instance of success breeding failure may be seen in the Bwamba county of Toro district in Western province. In 1942-43, coffee prices were raised from 23 cents to 28 cents a pound, and they so stimulated coffee cultivation that Bwamba produced a record crop. The following season however, despite raised prices, Bwamba sales fell. According to the Agricultural Department, this was 'as a result of the record' of the previous year.[50] Tax obligations had thereby been covered, and there were insufficient goods available at accessible prices to warrant further efforts at coffee production by these particular Ugandans. So no single means of promoting production always worked.

Just as prices were used by government to encourage farmers to produce export crops, so both government and private employers needed to offer more cash reward to attract labourers to the Public Works Department, the ginneries, the plantations and the mines. Employers were indeed officially urged to attract labour by improving pay and conditions. It was recognised that 'in a country in which the vast majority of its male population has for many years been taught to derive an adequate and pleasantly earned income from the soil, it is not surprising that the African does not take readily to employment as a wage earner'.[51] Peasant farming with hand tools may not have been as 'pleasant' for the farmer as it was described by British officials. However, a good example of 'wage-stimulated' employment appears to be the ginneries. In 1940 they were short of labour, partly because cotton growing was more rewarding. Five years later in Buganda, where there was most competition from price-stimulated peasant agriculture programmes, wages in ginneries were 49 per cent higher than they had been in 1939.[52]

Similarly, labour for the rubber plantations could only be attracted 'by the offer of varying rates to suit the varying conditions of different plantations, and by the grant of special bonuses for continued

regular attendance'.[53] Absenteeism on the sugar estates on the other
hand was on occasion met not by wage rises but by 'forceful recruitment of unsophisticated immigrants' by private recruiting agents.[54] But
this was no long-term solution to labour shortage. The use of force was
likely to deter immigration. Plantation labourers proved especially vola-
tile during the January 1945 disturbances – without having been conscripted. But it was the mines which had the greatest difficulty in acquiring labour, though the largest tin mining company 'was eventually
persuaded to appoint a welfare officer and institute a canteen'.[55] Indeed, when the 'famine' came, the greatest inducement that employers
could offer was not higher wages but food.

We may conclude that during the Second World War prices and
wages in Uganda had to be raised to levels which were attractive
enough to encourage both peasant farming and other forms of labour. We have noted that this stimulation was not free of complications or limitations. By far the most important condition for the success of price stimulation was, of course, the availability of goods.
This is what ultimately motivated farmers and labourers to work
beyond the requirements of subsistence and payments of tax. There
was no purchasing power if there was nothing to purchase.

The limits of pressure and propaganda

During the Second World War, the British colonial state in Uganda
was threatened not by the presence of enemy soldiers in the streets
but by the absence of purchasable goods in the stores. This view is
sustained by a persuasive contemporary analysis, to be found in the
1938 Cotton Commission report, of what motivated Ugandan cotton
producers, just before the war.

> Formerly cotton cultivation was regarded by the African cultivator as
> a convenient means of providing for the payment of his taxes. This
> outlook has become very much modified of recent years. Cotton culti-
> vation is looked upon as a means of providing for many things for-
> merly regarded as more or less unobtainable luxuries. A moderately
> high standard of dress is the rule, and there has been a notable im-
> provement in housing conditions and much greater diversification in
> diet. The large number of bicycles is another symptom of increased

prosperity, and school fees are recognised as a regular item of the family budget.[56]

That is, production of a cash crop had formerly been an imposition, once indeed a matter of coercion; now, although financial obligations still had to be met, it seemed that it had become more a matter of choice. Peasant farmers now produced their cash crops, or rather decided to increase their level of production beyond an estimate of their minimum needs, in the expectation of purchasing goods and services.

As we have noted, it was primarily customs and excise revenue, as well as the poll tax, which peasant producers furnished, that paid for the colonial state in the years before the Second World War. The British therefore relied on the continued availability of the imported goods which peasants wanted to purchase, and for which they would produce crops, or for which labourers worked. There existed a delicate link between work, goods and prices. Goods had to be available at affordable prices. The protectorate's fortunes thus depended on a further link *between* price levels: that is, on the extent to which peasants' income represented effective purchasing power. If the prices peasants were paid for their produce did not match prices of imported goods, the whole mechanism – and hence even the foundations of the colonial state itself – would be undermined. Local British officials could manipulate prices paid to peasants as producers. But they could not control the prices (or the availability) of the imports that peasants sought as consumers. Without the prospect of goods to buy at affordable prices, the attractiveness even of higher producer prices (and the potential of 'price-stimulated' production) waned.

All this was well understood among British East African officials at the time – but at the height of the production effort during the Second World War, we are able to observe the widening gap between their objectives and their capabilities. On 17 April 1943, J.V.Lewis, the senior statistician working for the East African Governors' Conference, wrote a letter to the chairman of the War Supplies Board. With a mixture of wishful thinking and pragmatism, he neatly summarised the prevailing position:

You stressed at the last Production Council meeting the importance of propaganda to encourage native production. The success of propaganda, however, must depend largely on the degree to which there exists a concrete incentive to produce, for however much we may pride ourselves on the loyalty of the African in his desire to assist the war effort, there is still a human side to him and the practical results will fall far short of the maximum possible so long as the present shortage of trade goods continues.[57]

Lewis thus recognised the essential relationship between voluntary production and the availability of goods. Similarly, in 1939, the financial secretary of Uganda had urged his colleagues to try to sustain imports 'at prices within the means of native consumers', because 'an abrupt change might affect the stimulus to production'.[58] And after Uganda became committed to the maximum wartime productive effort, the chief secretary noted that, in tackling what he termed African peasants' 'natural reluctance to sustained effort', there was 'no substitute for material incentives'.[59]

But where were the goods? Uganda's difficulty in securing imports is explored at a later stage in this study; one illustration of the problem must suffice here. 'The present shortage' referred to by Lewis in April 1943 caused grave anxiety to the EAPSC. The level of imports into East Africa of cotton piece-goods had dropped from 125 million in 1941 to a mere 60 million in 1942; and the expected 1943 quotas, mainly from India, again amounted to only about 60 million. Yet the estimated annual 'minimum essential requirement' for such items was 90 million.[60] The gloomy forecast was that 'stocks will be rapidly depleted and a position of acute scarcity will develop.... The general result will lead to a further excess of purchasing power, which must have a grave effect on production and upon the disposition of wage-earners to seek employment'.[61] It is a mark of the gravity – and the irony – of the situation that the council added an expression of relief at the *low* level of the most recent cotton crop, since a higher level of output would have further emphasised to producers the dearth of items to buy.

The crucial importance of the availability of goods was well expressed by Uganda's Eastern Province commissioner at the end of

1946. The problems of the war period still persisted, so that:

> the only effective stimulus to production of cash crops and the more thorough picking of cotton is likely to be given by increased imports, of bicycles and their spares, hoes, fair quality clothing, and household utensils such as cooking-pots and crockery. *It is not that people have more money than they know what to do with, but that the majority are not anxious to have more money than they can spend.*[62]

The fate of the British colonial state in Uganda hinged on the aggregate of considerations such as these. And a specific case at the end of the war seems to illustrate the point well. Simsim sales in Western Province fell in 1946. It was said that 'the dearth of consumer goods was again largely responsible, since the producers chose to eat the crop themselves rather than acquire more unwanted money' (Annual Report 1946:33). There seemed to be purchasing power, but nothing to purchase. At the end of the war, the official British verdict on levels of production was that 'unfortunately the monetary incentive was, in Uganda as elsewhere, to some extent nullified by the continued shortage of consumer goods' (Annual Report 1946: 32).

Levels of employment were affected, as well as levels of peasant production. In 1944 and 1945 employers in sugar, sisal and tin concerns all struggled to meet the maximum production requirements laid down in Britain and Nairobi. In 1944, the Labour Department described man-power shortages as 'acute at times' and attributed them in part to 'a shortage of imported attractive goods of all kinds'.[63] Some observers argued that Africans must be encouraged to desire *more* goods at which to target greater efforts. This deduction was ironic in the context of prevailing shortages. At the time, it was the considered view of E.B.Worthington that 'the average African ... does not show much desire for improvement – in fact he has too few wants of any kind for a country which hopes for increasing prosperity' (1946: para. 143). After the Second World War, Uganda's Governor Hall suggested that African 'indolence' arose from 'the psychological effect of an almost complete absence of consumer goods in the shops and stores'.[64] He too felt that it was an immediate task of government to 'create in the

African wants, healthy and progressive wants ... stronger than his present love of leisure'.[65] Here the distance between ruler and ruled was perhaps essentially cultural: and another example of a gap between hopes and achievements, which the absence of purchasable goods in Uganda so clearly demonstrated.

What about 'absolute' power? We might expect the British colonial state to have resorted to some form of compulsion: a stick in place of the elusive carrot. Yet according to official sources of the war period currently available, there was no compulsory labour, and little compulsion to produce crops. When Governor Moore said in 1942 that conscription of labour for agriculture was about to be instituted in Kenya, Dundas insisted that 'there was no question of introducing a similar measure in Uganda'.[66] The issue was not as clear-cut as this, however. The Uganda Civil Defence Board in fact discussed at some length the questions: 'should Africans be conscripted for agricultural and other industrial purposes'; and 'should there be power to compel an African to grow on his land the kind and quality of crops which government might require?' Though the minutes are rather bare, the recorded conclusion was clear. 'The Board reaffirmed its view ... that compulsion generally was unworkable'.[67] This implies that if it had been 'workable' it would have been permitted. Why was compulsion regarded as not so, in Uganda? The two questions formulated above require separate answers.

Plantations, industry and the mines depended to an extent on immigrant Banyarwanda labour, which would not have been forthcoming if the pay and conditions of work proved inferior to what they would have accepted voluntarily. The colonial state could hardly conscript labour which resided outside the protectorate, and which entered Uganda only out of choice. There had been a brief drop in immigration in 1939, apparently for fear of military conscription. Moreover, there would not have been sufficient European supervisory personnel to handle such a labour force effectively. Disturbances during the war years, especially on the estates in January 1945, gave some indication of how difficult conscription would have been. Labour shortages persisted.

Secondly, was the compulsion of peasants on their own land workable – or in fact practised? There is little evidence available and the language in such sources as we have is frustratingly ambiguous. So, for example, the Baganda were 'exhorted' to grow more food.[68] Native authorities launched an 'energetic campaign' to that end, and soy beans were promoted by 'intensive propaganda'.[69] Meanwhile, the Agriculture Department reported – for example – that cultivation of oilseeds was 'encouraged'; and 'active dissemination' of policy on soil conservation was carried out. What do these phrases mean?

We must remember in whose hands these promotional campaigns lay. The acutely understaffed Agricultural Department could do little more than launch a scheme and then observe from afar. It tried to tackle manpower shortages by increasing the number of African agricultural assistants, and by creating a new category of rural assistant. But the former joined the service at the rate of only three or four a year.[70] And the quality of rural assistant students was so poor that a quarter of the twenty who began a two-year course at Bukalasa in July 1944 had soon to be dismissed, while most of the remainder could not adequately understand or speak English.[71] So despite such efforts as these, the department still did not have in the districts the personnel which it required. This could in practice be provided only by the native government in Buganda, and by the native authorities elsewhere – that is, by chiefs.

British officials confirm this central importance of chiefs. J.R.M.Elliott, district officer in Teso, mentions 'a long meeting with chiefs, with especial emphasis on groundnut production' and, again, 'long meeting with chiefs on famine measures'.[72] Similarly, Governor Mitchell recorded in his diary, on 3 June 1940, a conversation with the highest ranking Buganda minister: 'I took the opportunity of stressing the importance of cotton cultivation' which the Katikiro said 'he would not neglect'. In fact, of course, it was the minor chief who came into contact locally with the peasantry and on whom responsibility for the production campaign tended to fall. Cotton quality control was thought to be improved by the posting of sub-chiefs at each buying centre. Soil conservation was served by co-operation between the Agricultural Department and chiefs in the native administrations. In Buganda 'many badly gullied areas were dealt with, as the result of efforts by the chiefs'.[73] The Agricultural Department sought to enhance the chiefs' role further by providing short training courses at their research stations, Bukalasa in Buganda and Serere in the Eastern Province. By the middle of 1943, 300 muruka chiefs from Buganda had attended such courses. This confirms the chiefs' perceived significance not only in 'encouraging' the cultivation of certain crops, but also in 'instructing' how this should be carried out.

And the methods adopted by chiefs could amount to a form of 'compulsion'. What otherwise did the Katikkiro of Buganda mean when he spoke of the 'zeal' of his chiefs in stimulating cotton production?[74] Or what did the Kabaka mean, when he told his chiefs to 'spare no efforts' in promoting cultivation?[75] European officials occasionally provide a glimpse of reality. When in May 1940 the East African Directors of Agriculture discussed the 'relative merits of coercion and persuasion as a means of seeing effective action by natives', they agreed that normally compulsion was not only undesirable but also likely to be ineffective – 'unless introduced with the backing of the Native Authorities'.[76]

This qualification tends to subvert subsequent official statements denying compulsion; and it is reinforced by unofficial comment from the post-war phase of 'production drive'. Thus, for example, R.H.Blackie, president of the Caledonian Society in Uganda, said in 1947 that he could not see how the country could develop 'unless some of the 4 million can be encouraged to pull their weight' – and added that this could only be accomplished by chiefs using their tribal authority.[77] The editor of the *Uganda Herald* was even more explicit when he urged other native authorities to follow Buganda's example in laying down rules to enable chiefs to ensure maximum production. He concluded, 'if a maximum crop is to be obtained, some measure of compulsion is necessary'.[78] As the Agricultural Department's former chief research officer later put it, 'Uganda has always employed a relatively small number of expatriate administrative officers, and this was only possible because of the highly organised system of local government' – and a corollary of this was the important role which fell to local chiefs in generating the export of crops (Jameson 1970: 4).

We must ask, moreover, what the authorities meant when they used the term 'propaganda'? Nowhere is the haze of official ambiguity and euphemism more closely encountered, for there seem to have been at least four different meanings. First, propaganda was *informing*. When the Resident of Buganda undertook 'to spread propaganda' for rubber tappers, this consisted of advertising the various rates of pay and special bonuses available to workers on the plantations. [79] Secondly, propaganda was *educating*, through demonstration farms and work in the schools, by posters and articles in the vernacular press. Thirdly, propaganda was *persuading*, which would incorporate 'exhorting' and 'encouraging' in their more innocent forms, and arguing the advantages to be gained from the adoption of a new crop or new methods. And finally, propaganda was *commanding* – in other words, compulsion.

Resort to an element of compulsion by chiefs was probably most common in the production of food; and peasant farmers were being urged, throughout the war period, to grow more. But the kind and the degree of compulsion are both immeasurable. Furthermore, there must be doubt about the effectiveness of any of the methods used to promote food crops in Buganda: officials concluded in 1945 that 'the recurrent near famines of recent years in Buganda are an indication that food production as a whole is inadequate'. [80]

Such compulsion as took place bore a heavy political cost. Peasant farmers became increasingly aware that they were no longer masters of the pace and direction of their own efforts. Already before the Second World War they were subject to interfering chiefs. Lord Hailey wrote that 'government' for a typical Muganda peasant meant just this form of contact, when the local chief visited him with instructions to burn his dead cotton bushes or to stop cutting trees on a hillside (1944: 179). Mitchell too regretted that government was represented by offensive and 'hectoring' local officials (1939: 6). In the early years of the war, chiefs were engaged in promoting early planting of cotton and soil conservation schemes, and as the exigencies of wartime production increased such contacts multiplied and intensified. Dundas could be a shrewd observer. In a letter to London in 1943, he maintained that 'the native is forever being preached at, admonished, instructed, and probably bored'.[81] Later C.H.Bird, representative of European unofficial opinion, said that the peasantry had been pushed to the limit. They had become 'bewildered' as well as exhausted – 'due to prolonged stimulation to increase production over the past three years'.[82]

Here we encounter the true extent – the limits – of British colonial authority 'on the ground' – in Buganda, at any rate, where colonial rule was in so many respects centred. A consequence of compulsion was a degree of alienation from chiefs as the interfering agents of colonial government in this remorseless production campaign and in others. The effect in Buganda was to reinforce a widespread attitude of resentment. David Apter writes:

> of annoyance at the active intervention in veterinary, health and agricultural services of protectorate officials who issued orders and forced people, through the chiefs, to carry out unpopular but important measures in public health and agriculture.... Thus both expatriate protectorate officials and senior Baganda chiefs found it difficult to work with the Baganda (1961: 191-192).

Perhaps we need to bring forward the start of what has come to be termed 'the second colonial occupation' (Low and Lonsdale 1976: 12-14). The 'great intensification of government activity' and the beginning of 'the decisive strains in the colonial relationship' were Second World War phenomena in Uganda, not post-war. And recourse to compulsion was not infinitely repeatable.

When Uganda's British officials claimed that there was no compulsion, they were not necessarily engaged in a conscious act of deception. Their repeated assertions that compulsion was unworkable, rather than unacceptable, are significant and tend to confirm this. They appear to have judged the forcing of peasants to adopt new crops, or to extend their acreages, to be on a lower level of significance than, say, settlers' use of conscripted labour elsewhere in East Africa. In Uganda, diligent chiefs could be thought to be acting within the limits of local custom and precedent. In any case, excessive 'zeal' would probably not come to the attention of an overworked and undermanned – and unsympathetic – British colonial administration.

Indeed, it remained the firm conviction of British officials that peasants would be the beneficiaries of their own more energetic production, and their acquisition of new productive techniques. Thus Worthington was prepared to countenance some form of compulsion during the 10-year 'production drive' which he advocated in 1946, on the ground that only if production outpaced population growth could the standard of living of the people of Uganda rise and their public services expand (1946: para. 12).

After the Second World War, Governor Hall preferred educative propaganda to compulsion, because his view was that in none of its forms would compulsion work in Uganda. He was quoted in his introduction to Worthington's Plan as favouring 'precept and example, exhortation and demonstration, supervision and propaganda'. But there were few grounds for any faith in these approaches. After all, such methods had been tried during the wartime production drive, and clearly they had tended not to work. In Busoga there was 'very little to show' for six years' instruction in progressive agricultural practice.[83] The 1946 Annual Report had to acknowledge that although two major centres had been chosen for wartime demonstrations in rural reconstruction, 'the examples shown have not yet been copied to any great extent even by neighbouring farmers'. The Baganda proved least responsive. Though they were urged to introduce strip-cropping, and to plant elephant grass as a guard against erosion, progress in both respects was disappointingly slow. It seemed to one contemporary at least that Banyarwanda were drawn to seasonal work on Baganda farms because of the 'attractive conditions' and 'easy-going employment' (Orde-Browne 1946: para.28). These immigrant labourers, like their employers, do not appear to have welcomed 'instruction' in newer methods of production.

In the light of such disappointing wartime experience, it is remarkable that those in a position to influence future policy seemed to retain confidence in methods which had previously failed. Governor Dundas had been under no illusions in this respect. But his successor Hall put his faith in a much enlarged Agricultural Department, more officials in the provincial administration, and the new Public Relations and Social Welfare Department and its mobile propaganda units.

Worthington similarly trusted that Uganda's productive capacity was 'likely to increase in direct ratio to the number of trained technical officers who are employed to supervise the agricultural process', and that the embryonic PRSWD would 'help greatly in the production drive' (1946: paras. 97, 178, 385).

Yet only when spurred by the prospect of the availability of goods at affordable prices did peasants respond to propaganda and adopt both new crops and even new methods, if they were simple and seen to have immediate effect. Strip-cropping thus succeeded in some areas by virtue of costing nothing in money and little in labour; it was seen to work and it required minimal supervision. Propaganda and pressure from chiefs, not underpinned by the prospect of such material benefit, were tried during the Second World War and did not wholly fail. It was nevertheless unwise of Uganda's policy-makers after the war to draw conclusions which ignored wartime experience. Above all, it was short-sighted to give primacy of place to interventionism, through Protectorate government departments and chiefs – which was no substitute for autonomous peasant motivation based on availability of goods to buy at accessible prices, and which in practice tended to discredit both indigenous authorities and the British colonial state which they served.

Finally, who was determining the pace and direction of change – rulers or ruled? Was the wartime mobilisation of materials a paradigm for 'exploitation'? Nicholas Westcott has written of the Second World War in Tanganyika that 'to increase African production, the government generally preferred to use a stick rather than a carrot' (1986: 148). This seems inherently unlikely; and there is no present evidence of such a preference among British policy-makers in Uganda. The latter were keenly aware of the need to promote production and to attract labour, by price stimulation and, above all, by making goods available. When all else failed, and in the face of famine, compulsion through chiefs does seem to have been used as a last resort, however politically hazardous to the colonial state this could prove. Nonetheless, Michael Crowder's generalisation, too, must be queried. He wrote that the 'demand for Africa's raw materials was secured not by higher prices, but in many cases by various forms of coercion'

(1984: 33). It would be misleading to include Uganda among such cases. The evidence there is that the colonial state possessed only very limited power to compel either production or labour. And it was Africans as producers, and as consumers, who ultimately determined the dimensions of Uganda's material achievement during the Second World War.

---

1. Secretary of State to Governors of African Dependencies, 21 March 1942, PRO CO 822/111/29.
2. Secretary of State to Colonies, 5 June 1940, PRO CO 854/117.
3. Chief Secretary to the Legislative Council, 9 December 1942.
4. East African Governors' Conference 'Report for the Year 1943', PRO CO 962/15.
5. Agriculture Department Annual Report, 1942-43, p.2.
6. Secretary of State to Governors of African Dependencies, 21 March 1942, PRO CO 822/111/29.
7. Report, *Uganda Herald*, 17 December 1941.
8. Agriculture Department Annual Report, 1941-42, p.1.
9. *ibid*. p.3.
10. Agriculture Department Annual Report, 1941-42, p.1.
11. East Africa Supplies Board Minutes, 19 December 1941, in East African Governors' Conference Proceedings, January 1942, PRO CO 962/15.
12. Dundas to the Legislative Council, 25 May 1942.
13. Agriculture Department Annual Report, 1941-42, p.4.
14. *ibid*.
15. East Africa Production and Supply Council Minutes, 8 June 1943, PRO CO 822/111/30.
16. East African Governors' Conference 'Report for the Year 1943', PRO CO 962/15.
17. Uganda Civil Defence Board Minutes, 16 February 1943.
18. Uganda Civil Defence Board Minutes, 18 May 1943.
19. East African Governors' Conference Proceedings, November 1943, PRO CO 822/107/13.
20. EAPSC Minutes, 8 June 1943, PRO CO 822/111/30.
21. Conference of Directors of Agriculture, May 1940, PRO CO 822/106/5.

22. Agriculture Department Annual Report, 1942-43, p.6.

23. *ibid.*

24. B.F.C.Childs-Clarke, Report on the Eastern Province, 1946, Rhodes House MSS Afr.s.424. My italics.

25. Nutrition Committee, 'Review of Nutrition in Uganda', Entebbe, 1945, RH Box 126, file III.

26. Agriculture Department Annual Report, 1944-45, p.27.

27. EAPSC Minutes, 8 June 1943, PRO CO 822/111/30.

28. Agriculture Department Annual report, 1949, p.30.

29. EAPSC Minutes, 4 April 1945, PRO CO 537/1525.

30. Conference of Directors of Agriculture, May 1940, PRO CO 822/106/5.

31. Agriculture Department Annual Reports, 1938, Appendix VII p.64; and 1944-45, Appendix II p.41.

32. *ibid.*

33. *ibid.*

34. J.D.Tothill, Some Notes on the Uganda Cotton Crop, 10 October 1938, in J.D.Jameson Papers, Rhodes House MSS Afr.s.1032.

35. Agriculture Department Annual Report, 1941-42, p.2.

36. Report, *Uganda Herald*, 23 December 1942; official communication, *Uganda Herald*, 3 February 1943.

37. Agriculture Department Annual Report, 1942-43, p.4.

38. *ibid.*

39. Dundas to Secretary of State, 28 December 1943, PRO CO 536/208/40100/1943.

40. 'Muganda Enquirer', letter, *Uganda Herald* 10 February 1943.

41. Chairman's Address, 4 May 1944.

42. P.Tamukede, *Uganda Herald*, 2 February 1944.

43. Financial Secretary to the Legislative Council, 15 December 1943.

44. Agriculture Department Annual Report, 1944-45, p.28.

45. Chairman's Addresses, 27 April, 1939; 27 August 1942; 1 April 1946.

46. 'Review of Nutrition in Uganda', 1945, Rhodes House FCB Box 126, File III.

47. Agriculture Department Annual Report, 1944-45, p.26.

48. Chief Secretary to the Legislative Council, 15 December 1943.

49. Uganda Civil Defence Board Minutes, 25 July 1944.

50. Agriculture Department Annual Report, 1943-44, p.3.

51. Labour Report, 1943, para. 15.

52. Labour Report, 1945, para. 7.

53. Uganda Civil Defence Board Minutes, 18 December 1942.

54. Labour Report, 1944, para. 12.

55. Labour Report, 1943, para. 11.
56. Report of the Uganda Cotton Commission, 1938, pp.29-30.
57. Lewis to Norton, 17 April 1943: J.V.Lewis Papers, Rhodes House MSS Afr.s.1147.
58. Proceedings of Secret Conference of Financial Advisers, Nairobi, 23-25 October 1939, PRO CO 822/95/5.
59. Chief Secretary to the Legislative Council, 9 December 1942.
60. Lockhart, memorandum for the EA Governors' Conference 31 May 1943, Proceedings, June 1943, PRO CO 822/107/12.
61. _ibid._
62. B.F.C.Childs-Clarke, Report on the Eastern Province, 1946, para. 9. My italics.
63. Labour Report, 1944, para.3.
64. Hall to Secretary of State, 27 July 1946, PRO CO 822/130/2.
65. Address to the Uganda Chamber of Commerce, reported in _Uganda Herald_, 26 February 1947.
66. East Africa Governors' Conference Proceedings, January 1942, PRO CO 962/15.
67. Uganda Civil Defence Board Minutes, 18 December 1942.
68. Kabaka to the Buganda Lukiiko, reported in _Uganda Herald_, 25 October 1944.
69. Acting Director of Agriculture to the Legislative Council, 20 December 1943.
70. Agriculture Department Annual Report, 1941-42, p. 9.
71. Agriculture Department Annual Report, 1944-45, p. 31.
72. J.R.M.Elliott, Teso District Diary, 29 January 1942; 25 February 1943.
73. Agriculture Department Annual Report, 1941-42, p. 8.
74. Report, _Uganda Herald_, 9 July 1941.
75. Speech at his coronation, reported in _Uganda Herald_, 25 November 1942.
76. Conference of Directors of Agriculture, May 1940, PRO CO 822/106/5.
77. _Uganda Herald_, 2 December 1947.
78. _Uganda Herald_, 4 May 1948.
79. Uganda Civil Defence Board Minutes, 18 December 1942.
80. Agriculture Department Annual Report, 1944-45, p. 30 .
81. Dundas to Dawe, 7 September 1943, PRO CO 536/209/40100/3/43.
82. Report, _Uganda Herald_, 16 February 1944.
83. B.F.C.Childs-Clarke, Report on the Eastern Province, 1946, para.24.

9

Uganda and its Neighbours: Kenya and Ruanda-Urundi

There was no reason to suppose in 1939/40 that Uganda had anything to fear from any of its neighbours, apart from perhaps Italian-held Abyssinia. Other British possessions lay to the north, east and south, while clearly Belgian-ruled territories to the west and southwest would be friendly. Nevertheless, British power in Uganda was to be subject to a dual local wartime dependency. In their very different ways, both British officials – and settlers– in Nairobi, and African migrant labourers from Ruanda-Urundi (now the two independent states of Rwanda and Burundi), proved unpredictable and uncontrollable neighbours. A study of these twin vulnerabilities will reveal a colonial state in Uganda where power was anything but 'absolute'. It will also reveal, in the case of Kenya, that close regional co-operation in East Africa was tried, under British auspices, long before independent African governments discussed such matters in the later decades of the twentieth century. Serious consideration was even given at this time to the radical redrawing of territorial boundaries in the region. Perhaps the difficulties and obstacles identified during these stressful years, when the two main territories concerned were still under the same overall political authority, throw light on subsequent tensions and inform current debate.

Kenya

The Second World War's exposure of the limits of the British colonial state's regional competence was nowhere more dramatically illustrated than in Uganda's dealings with Kenya, especially in 1942. Wartime conditions gave birth to a succession of institutions in Nairobi which assumed a wide responsibility for regional production and for guaranteeing supplies for East African consumption. In the event, the latter function proved beyond their competence. Meanwhile, the territorial administration in Uganda proved unable, through these councils located beyond its own borders, either fully to determine its own production programme or to acquire its due share of such scarce (and highly priced) imported goods as were available for its farmers and labourers to 'consume'. Previously, Uganda's subservience to Kenya had been at least partially disguised. Now, in the global crisis of the Second World War, subservience proved both visible and damaging.

Before 1939, the British East African territories were only loosely linked to one another, by the East African Governors' Conference. Once a year the governors of Kenya, Uganda and Tanganyika took turns to host and to chair joint meetings. Additionally, there were annual meetings of such departmental heads as financial secretaries and directors of agriculture. Uganda, Kenya and Tanganyika were also linked by a customs union, by a common currency, and by a common posts and telegraph service.

Would the Governors' Conference prove an adequate inter-territorial institution in the event of global war? There had already been signs that it would not. Relations had not always been harmonious. Rivalry born of competitive interest could lead to friction. In 1938, there was a sign of things to come when there was a marked divergence of opinion on the question of the territorial allocation, within East Africa, of a tea quota which the region had recently won.[1] There had also been continuous unease on the Ugandan side concerning the running of the railway which was administered jointly with Kenya.

The outbreak of war in Europe led to a spurt of *ad hoc* interterritorial activity, prompted by the British imperial government. Meeting in Nairobi in November 1939, the East African governors agreed to a number of immediate revenue-raising measures: the increase in non-native income tax (indeed, in the case of Uganda, its introduction); and an immediate rise in customs and excise rates. Some price control measures were also initiated through the combined agency of the Kenya and Uganda Supply Boards.[2]

There was no hint at this stage of any moves towards any overall

East African authority, but the ending of the 'phoney war' in Europe in 1940 was to have far-reaching consequences for the British territories in East Africa. So, too, did Italy's involvement. Apart from responding to Britain's plight, especially its enhanced need for colonial produce, British East Africa now had to face a hostile belligerent on its northern borders in Abyssinia and Somaliland. At a secret meeting in Nairobi in late June 1940, the three East African governors consequently recognised the need for new administrative arrangements.[3] Governor Henry Moore of Kenya now became permanent chairman of the Governors' Conference and Philip Mitchell, until now governor of Uganda, became permanent deputy chairman. This entailed his moving from Entebbe to Nairobi, to co-ordinate the war effort.

While it was the pressure of circumstance which clearly prompted these developments and appointments, the personal initiative and energy of Mitchell played a major part in them. In an earlier analysis of Uganda's economic situation, he had noted that 'nearly every aspect involves Kenya'.[4] This was particularly true in the case of the availability and price of goods imported for African peasant producers, among others, to consume. Mitchell had also forecast that the entry of Italy into the war would make a 'central authority in East Africa very desirable, and for Uganda essential'.[5] Mitchell stayed in Nairobi for six months. In this time he introduced a new intensity into inter-territorial co-ordination. His East African Economic Council was an assembly of official and unofficial representatives from the three territories, which he visualised as a planning and directing staff. They would allocate duties, functions and business to the various agencies which had so far come into existence, such as the Kenya and Uganda Supply Boards.

Nothing could better symbolise the peripheral position of Uganda, and the onset of its subjection to Kenyan influence during the Second World War, than the governor of Uganda personally organising his own departure from the protectorate in order to position himself at the heart of affairs in the capital of the neighbouring colony. Although he augmented institutions there for the British East African war effort, Mitchell was still not satisfied when he moved on to Cairo in

January 1941. East Africa still lacked a central authority. Mitchell regretted the 'objections and opposition' to fuller integration which he had encountered, adding later that 'one good air-raid would have been a great help' (Mitchell 1954: 191). But, until Japan's attack on the USA in December 1941 and its simultaneous threat to the British Empire – across the Indian Ocean perhaps – provided a fresh impetus for more institutional change, there would be insufficient pressure to take interterritorial co-ordination any further.

*   *   *

1942 was the critical year in the evolution of Uganda's wartime relationship with Kenya. For several months in that year Uganda found itself part of an East African institution which claimed considerable authority over its affairs, yet over which the protectorate's officials had little influence and still less control. Dominated by Kenya's European settler-expatriates, this new body so alarmed the Colonial Office in London that the secretary of state had to intervene quickly in order to retain metropolitan authority– and thus incidentally restore to Uganda its own separate identity and voice.

This was a drama in which local British officials responsible for Uganda had no more than a walk-on part. It was Governor Moore of Kenya, chairman of the Governors' Conference, who observed in January 1942 that the war experience had 'shown up the administrative weaknesses inherent in a system whose constitution provides for no overriding executive authority empowered to take prompt and final decisions'.[6] Moore's views represented a political movement so powerful that within a few weeks an institution was born which threatened to render any further discussion about closer union irrelevant.

The controversial body came into being in the last week of March 1942, as the Civil Defence and Supply Council (CDSC). It partly represented a response to the fall of Singapore and the approach of the war nearer to East Africa. It also partly arose as a response to the secretary of state's declared readiness to approve emergency measures in the interests of production. These twin military and economic pressures both clearly acted on Moore. East African Command's chief military officer was advocating the appointment of a central authority in East Africa. Also it had already been recognised, since the successful conclusion of the Abyssinian campaign in the autumn of 1941, that British East Africa's main wider wartime role was to lie in production for the war effort. That requirement was underlined from December 1941 by the new Japanese' threat to imperial supplies and to Indian Ocean shipping, after the attack on Pearl Harbour. Fear of a Japanese assault on East Africa itself even led to discussion of the possible evacuation of Mombasa.[7]

Six of the original eight men appointed to serve on the CDSC, under the presidency of Moore, were Kenyan European unofficials. Nonetheless, Charles Dundas, governor of Uganda in succession to Mitchell, immediately sought to associate Uganda with the new council. Dundas reasoned that its decisions and measures were bound to have their repercussions in Uganda, and that participation would give Uganda 'a voice in determination of matters which would otherwise be consequentially prescribed by decisions taken in Kenya'.[8] In the event, the Ugandan element amounted to the inclusion in the council of just two officials of the Uganda Protectorate government. Even with their inclusion, the CDSC remained dominated by Kenyan unofficials. Moreover, CDSC decisions were to be implemented through direct correspondence with appropriate officers in Uganda–a procedure which threatened to undermine, because it bypassed it, the entire governmental structure in the Protectorate: Governor, Executive Council and Legislative Council. The *Uganda Herald* asked apprehensively whether Uganda had not surrendered too much of its autonomy.[9]

The Colonial Office, while welcoming the CDSC's potential for harnessing East Africa's economic potential for the imperial war effort, was quick to perceive the seriousness of the constitutional dimension and its implications for Kenya's neighbours. Sir Arthur Dawe, assistant under-secretary of state for the colonies, thought that the body that Moore had instituted– without London's prior approval– presented a dual threat. First, it was 'another important step towards the subordination of the Executive Government in Kenya to white settler control'; and, secondly, the settlers sensed 'the possibility of the executive power of the Kenya government being extended over the other governments in East Africa'.[10]

Uganda's separate constitutional position was indeed now precarious. Regarding the CDSC, Dundas admitted in a confidential letter to the Colonial Office: 'I recognise that in agreeing to participation thereon I am to some extent committing the territory to direction from Kenya'.[11] But the question of the CDSC's relationship with Uganda was dwarfed by that of its relations with the British government itself. This crisis of authority had to be resolved, before the government in Uganda could recover its own position. In the summer of 1942 it was. Dawe soon came to the conclusion that 'we have reached a position in which the new council is, in effect, an executive cabinet'; and this did represent for British East Africa a 'constitutional change'.[12] It was thought that the CDSC's control of affairs, which it was rapidly acquiring through *ad hoc* wartime organisation, would lead to the creation of an East African Dominion at the end of the war. Dawe's Colonial Office perception seems to have been more politically acute than that of Dundas, when the latter so speedily volunteered Uganda for inclusion in the council's sway.

By the end of the year, however, the political and constitutional threat posed by the CDSC had been dealt with. The council was abolished. The secretary of state could not tolerate its members taking binding decisions, and to an extent thereby eliminating the governors of East Africa from effective participation in these decisions. Another body, the East African Production and Supply Council, was therefore formally instituted to succeed it on 27 December 1942; and this was placed under the authority of the Governors' Conference. Moore and his fellow governors were to share responsibility for the new body. Uganda thereby was saved, constitutionally. Whatever the threat to Ugandans' economic interests the new council might pose – by imposing its own production targets on the territory in due course, or by neglecting (as it did) Uganda's critical need for consumable imports – by the end of 1942, the protectorate's governing authorities had been in large measure restored to their previous political and constitutional position. However, the colonial state in Uganda had failed to determine its own fate in 1942; and thereafter, with its relative subordination to Kenyan interests latent no longer, it faced the prospect of further subservience to an East African institution sited in Nairobi.

The rise and fall of the Civil Defence and Supply Council in 1942 marked a turning point in East Africa's wartime government. Previously there had been a period of loose co-ordination of policy and limited economic direction; afterwards, for the remaining three years of the war, came close co-ordination and a measure of centralised control. For after the drama of 1942 the need for economic co-ordination remained. The CDSC's successor council lacked independent institutional ambition, and constitutionally it was subject to the East African Governors' Conference. Nevertheless, during the second half of the Second World War, Uganda's protectorate administration continued to find itself less a free agent than ever before. Uganda was now merely one unit in an inter-territorial East African political economy which was increasingly subject to the East African Production and Supply Council (EAPSC) in Nairobi.

*   *   *

There were no activities more central to the colonial purpose, and to the fundamental economic relationship with colonial peoples through which that purpose was fulfilled, than those which the EAPSC was commissioned to carry out at the end of 1942. As its name indicated, it had to 'produce'– that is, to promote the extraction and multiplication of the material resources of East Africa; and to 'supply'– that is, to ensure the availability of imported goods which were the incentives without which ultimately such extraction and multiplication would not be undertaken. War made production all the more urgent; and in the process it made supply all the more problematical.

Neither Ugandan peasant farmers nor British officials in Uganda had much leverage on the workings of a body on whose decisions and effectiveness their own future prospects now hinged. Uganda enjoyed little representation on the EAPSC. G.F.Clay, as Director of Native Production, was the lone Ugandan British official within the inner circle of the EAPSC. As a concession to territorial sensibilities, there were to be one or two extra nominated members per territory, who might be either officials or unofficials. In practice however, the Ugandan presence at the dozen full meetings of the council from 1943 to 1945 was slight. Although there certainly were times when Ugandan voices were heard, there was little continuity of representation. No single member from Uganda even attended as many as half of the meetings; and on at least two occasions Uganda had only one person in attendance.[13]

The European community in Uganda drew the conclusion that the presence on this board of only one Ugandan representative, the protectorate's former Director of Agriculture, was inadequate. In the full January 1944 meeting, a prominent Ugandan expatriate, H.R.Fraser, an unofficial member of the Legislative Council in Uganda who was attending for the first time, asked whether an additional Ugandan representative might be appointed. The reply of Charles Lockhart, former financial secretary in Tanganyika, now chairman of the EAPSC, was unsympathetic. He 'could not see the necessity for territorial representation on this Board', but if, at the appropriate time, a Ugandan 'happened to be in Nairobi, there would be no objection to his attendance'.[14]

Did 'the East African connection' work overall to the advantage or the disadvantage of the Uganda Protectorate and its inhabitants during this period? The EAPSC, theoretically subservient to the Governors' Conference though in practice operating independently of it, attracted much criticism in Uganda at the time. Yet there were some occasions when the EAPSC proved responsive to concerns expressed by Ugandan representatives, especially those related to the interests of African consumers – though the council never of course came within earshot of an African voice. For example, in February 1943 the Uganda Supply Board persuaded the EAPSC to keep more local tea in East Africa because otherwise 'the African would be affected in particular' since tea was one of the few locally produced articles on which the African could and did spend his money.[15] It was difficult enough for the authorities to acquire goods imported from abroad. To have exported more than was obligatory of whatever consumer goods were produced locally, would indeed have been short-sighted.

On a later comparable occasion, when arguing the case of European commerce in Uganda before the same council, H.R.Fraser shrewdly played 'the African card'. Aware that Africans needed the goods which merchants wished to import, Fraser urged that their spending power should no longer be restricted, Africans 'having been most affected by the restrictions of supplies and the high prices ruling for such as have been available'.[16] Changes were shortly made. In July 1945, 24 items which were specially in demand by African consumers were taken off the lists of 'controlled' imports (that is, imports for which the issue of import licences was restricted), including bicycles, cheap clocks and watches, cooking pots, cheap knives and crockery, lamps and torches, mirrors, primus stoves and umbrellas.[17]

But this measure was clearly too late. Six months earlier, in January 1945, Uganda had suffered a series of strikes and civil disturbances. These, as we shall see in a subsequent chapter, were essentially protests against wartime shortages, inflation and a fall in real wages. While the July measure was taken, officially to 'remedy a real hardship' and to 'absorb excess of currency', there were other considerations behind it too.[18] In seeking to make imported goods more readily available, the EAPSC seems to have been responding more immediately to the need to sustain civil order, by improving the prospects for African consumption (and thereby re-establishing the incentive to produce). It thus appears to have been consideration by the EAPSC of African motivation and interests, and the dependency of local British colonial power on them, which were belatedly making first major breaches in the structure of wartime import controls.

However, it was one thing to change policy occasionally, and quite another to change the context in which policy decisions were made. No local British government authorities, neither the Uganda Protectorate government nor the EAPSC in Nairobi, proved capable during the Second World War of exercising adequate control over the underlying conditions determining imports and prices. It was easier to appoint a 'director' of imports than to guarantee their supply in practice.

*   *   *

The Uganda Protectorate had been in danger of losing its autonomy and identity during the Civil Defence and Supply Council episode in

1942. When the 'closer union' debate– the question of amalgamation of the British East African territories which had been dormant since the early 1930s– sprang into sustained life once more in the wake of that year's experience, the protectorate faced a threat to its very existence as a separate state. This too proved to be a drama in which Uganda was not in a position to be much more than a bystander. The real struggle once more was between Kenyan Europeans and the Colonial Office. The former set the pace. But it was the latter which formulated a solution to the problem which preserved Uganda's identity. In the event, the East African High Commission– that is, the form which closer union eventually took in 1948– was to be one of the more tangible institutional results of the Second World War in East Africa.

A brief glance at the closer union controversy, from the Ugandan point of view, is illuminating in a number of respects. First, it provides further evidence of the fragility of the colonial state in Uganda itself: that its very existence could so easily be questioned, and its fate decided by political forces external to it. Secondly, it provides the context which helps to explain the heightened political sensitivity of public opinion among all races in Uganda in the later war years: whether traders complaining about Kenya's handling of imports, or Baganda leaders concerned for the future of their kingdom's protected status. And thirdly, it shows how fragile and provisional were Uganda's borders– even the existence of 'Uganda' itself– forty years after the territory came under British rule (and barely twenty before that rule ceased).

Officially, the debate over closer union had been closed since 1931. In the following decade, the Colonial Office had been keen that it should remain closed, in view of African perceptions. It was recognised that 'not one of the natives of Tanganyika, Kenya or Uganda desires closer union and Asiatic opinion has all along steadfastly opposed it'.[19] Even a limited union would extend Kenya politics into Uganda. But now global conflict inevitably raised the question again. Kenyan settler pressure for administrative change in East Africa did not die with the demise of the Civil Defence and Supply Council in 1942. In fact, it was at that very moment that the Colonial Office itself decided to reconsider closer union, seeking both to regain the political initiative in East Africa and to lay foundations for the post-war era.

In his contribution to the resurrected debate in July 1942, Sir Arthur Dawe identified three options. The first was to 'leave things as they are'. But this might allow East Africa to drift towards a *de facto* dominion under white settlers, at the expense of African inter-ests which the British government was pledged to uphold. The sec-ond was to institute a unitary state. But this was open to 'obvious and insuperable' political objections of a similar nature. The third was to adopt a federal scheme. That was Dawe's preference at this time because he thought it could secure a balance between African and white settler aspirations in the region. But he recognised that 'formidable obstacles' lay in the way of this course too.[20] However, Dawe was certain of one thing: closer union was far too important to be defined only by the local Europeans who most wanted it.

These included at governor level both Moore and, strangely per-haps, Dundas. Moore wanted major constitutional changes to be made promptly. For his part, Dundas explained that 'in the end, Moore and I could see no workable half-way measure between a complete union and the existing system'.[21] Dundas thus tacitly ignored sensi-tivity about Uganda's current subjection to Kenya – though com-plaints about import control were to continue throughout the war, and were voiced by all races in Uganda. There were other complaints, too. For example, given that Uganda was East Africa's major pro-ducer of sugar, why were its Africans denied supplies so that Ken-yan sweet-makers had sufficient?[22] And why were prices paid to African maize growers in Uganda only a third of those paid to Euro-pean producers in Kenya?[23]

In the meantime, existing territorial boundaries within British East Africa became the subject of radical review and considerable specu-lation. Moore had observed that the 'boundaries as at present drawn are out of line with both economic and ethnological frontiers and ... it is desirable that they should be redrawn'.[24] On this topic, the Colonial Office sympathised with Moore and produced some imaginative proposals for change. Thus Dawe's proposal retained 'Uganda' as one of five provinces, while dismantling Kenya and Tanganyika.[25] But Uganda as such did not survive at all in another metropolitan British official's plan: one of his six units would have been a 'Lake Victoria Basin' comprising pieces of Kenya, Uganda and Tanganyika.[26]

There are two points of importance here. First, the British Protectorate of Uganda clearly appeared so shallow rooted to Colonial Office officials that it might easily be dug up, transplanted or indeed discarded completely. Secondly, in the retrospective light of the concern with this issue shown by African states since independence, we may note that in the 1940s British authorities in London, Entebbe and Nairobi were not only fully aware of the unsatisfactory nature of the colonial boundaries but also ready to contemplate sweeping changes to them. And yet, even on this occasion of radical reappraisal by a single European colonial power, no change was effected. In such a way did state frontiers in East Africa assume a permanence– once divergent courses of development were established, as had already become clear within the Kenya colony and the Uganda Protectorate. Thus was finally sealed the territorial definition of the 'Uganda' which gained its independence in 1962.

The paper partitioning of 1942-43 therefore proved to be all paper and no partition. By March 1944, the Colonial Office concluded that 'none of the difficulties appears to be nearer a solution'.[27] It was Mitchell's proposal in November of that year which brought thinking back to earth. Focussing on what was possible, as ever, Mitchell left the boundaries where they were, and proposed a structure that was 'a natural outgrowth from the existing state of affairs'.[28] Taking shape eventually as the East African High Commission, it had the virtue of concentrating on services which wartime experience had confirmed to be best operated in common. What Mitchell termed 'the bogey of loss of territorial identity' would be removed. It is ironic that closer union finally took a form which created some distress in Kenya but was welcomed in Uganda. The *Uganda Herald* was able to reassure its readers then that 'Uganda has nothing to fear from these proposals'.[29] Having survived both the actual inter-territorial intrusions of the war and the proposals which at one time threatened it with virtual euthanasia, Uganda was thus to pass intact into the post-war world as a colonial state with a separate and continuing territorial identity.

Unofficials of all races in Uganda feared domination by Kenya. Europeans felt they would suffer further, having already 'suffered sufficiently from the stranglehold of Kenyan interests'. Indians in Uganda felt that their fellows in Kenya were 'kept in subjection'. Finally, Africans knew that over the border European interests were 'paramount and ruthlessly maintained'.[30] Oddly, however, Dundas had not concluded as the *Uganda Herald* did, that 'progress in this country can best be achieved by retaining our identity, and not by losing it in a union'.[31] Instead he had sided on this matter with Moore.

Uganda had not been in existence as a territory for long by 1942. Dawe judged that East Africa was still at something of an 'experimental stage'.[32] Would it have been of any significance if 'Uganda' had indeed disappeared from the map at this time? Having in mind Uganda's general commitment to the preservation of African agriculture, not to mention the 1900 Agreement, Dawe recognised the essential East African question. 'Is it possible', he asked, 'to resolve the conflict of forces between the settlers, and the advocates in Great Britain of a pro-native policy?'[33] If Uganda were to be absorbed into a settler dominated 'unitary' state, how secure would the Africans be in possession of their land? How free would they be from pressure to labour on European farms? And would they be able to defend their interests as producers – and consumers – if the settlers had total control over the railway to the sea? It was precisely the conflict between the Ugandan and the Kenyan colonial traditions and possible outcomes which pressured the Colonial Office during the late 1940s to establish a milder form of closer union – which retained existing East African divisions and distinctions; and which amounted to a mere common services administration which did little more than formalise and augment practical arrangements developed during the course of the Second World War.

What did Uganda's wartime relationship with Kenya reveal? First, it made clear for all to see that the British authorities in Uganda had little power to determine their territory's destiny in its dealings with its neighbour. It thereby emphasised the differences, in character and relative potential, between an administrative protectorate and a settler colony. Limitations on the Uganda Protectorate's power internally were thus paralleled in its external relations. Although it was far from any substantial military danger, the Uganda Protectorate very nearly became an institutional casualty of the Second World War.

Secondly, and more specifically, the task of nurturing the economic relationships on which the colonial state in Uganda depended came to be based in Nairobi. Perhaps unsurprisingly in the context of global war, institutions there failed Uganda in the crucial area of supply, and, as we shall see later in this book, even appeared to aggravate Uganda's plight further in this regard. Meanwhile however, these institutions, by the very character of their functioning during the Second World War, probably served at the same time to render the eventual 'closer union' of 1948 less harmful to Uganda than it might have been; and to ensure the protectorate's survival as a separate entity.

Ruanda-Urundi

'Purposeful, silent, not readily to be deflected, they may be seen in groups on almost any day in the year on the south-western roads pressing relentlessly towards Buganda, reminiscent of nothing so much as a stream of ants' (Labour Situation 1938: para. 206). These 'ants' were the migrant labourers, known in Uganda as Banyarwanda, who provided the labour on which, by 1939, much of Buganda's perennial production of materials for export depended. They came from Ruanda-Urundi, the former German colony on Uganda's south-western border which had been mandated to the Belgians after the First World War.

The relationship with Ruanda-Urundi received far less public attention at the time than the links with Kenya – and it has received even less attention from historians since. But this small neighbour had a comparable significance in Uganda's wartime experience.

Moreover, this relationship, so clearly revealed in all its intractability during the war, also helps to explain subsequent issues and controversies – concerning land ownership in Buganda, for example – which have concerned Ugandan government and society long after the ending of British colonial rule.

The 'ants' exerted an influence over Uganda's destiny as profound as, and arguably longer lasting than, that exercised by expatriate European settlers to the east in Kenya. We are reminded of Tolstoy's rather disturbing depiction of History, in *War and Peace*, as 'the unconscious, universal, swarm-life of mankind [which] uses every moment of the life of kings for its own purposes' (Tolstoy 1866/1957: 718) – except that in this case, as we shall see, there was nothing 'unconscious' about these migrations. What disturbs the historian here is that Tolstoy appears to render the attempt to identify 'cause and effect' in history as futile: Providence and Predetermination is all. But we do not have to accept this gloomy conclusion to see the sense of directing our attention away from 'kings' and towards the masses of mankind. In the case of Uganda during the Second World War, these masses included not only the anonymous thousands of indigenous producers and consumers of the protectorate (whom we have already encountered), and indeed the anonymous thousands of askaris who went away on war service and subsequently returned (whom we meet in a subsequent chapter), but also these migrant labourers from Ruanda-Urundi.

The Second World War highlighted some discomforting characteristics of Uganda's economic life, several of which related to Banyarwanda migrants. First, by the 1940s Uganda's economy – notably in Buganda – was heavily dependent on this labour supply from outside, and it became increasingly so as war progressed. Secondly, the British administration in Uganda proved quite unable to control this mass movement of migrants: officials could not dictate either the numbers of migrant workers or their choice of direction and occupation. British officials could not guarantee public order in places where migrants congregated. Nor could they provide adequate food and health services for them. In short, during the war years the previously 'largely untouched labour problem of Uganda' [34] could remain untouched no longer. But it proved beyond the competence of the British colonial state to solve it.

Contemporaries saw that the most intractable feature of the labour problem was the annual migration of approximately 100,000 Banyarwanda. They sought work, primarily in order to meet Belgian tax obligations. Uganda offered more work opportunities: better paid and less arduous than in Ruanda-Urundi, and free of compulsion. Migrants from Ruanda-Urundi could also escape from 'congestion of population' to a neighbouring territory where there was even an opportunity to settle permanently, which many migrants took. This was the case specifically in Buganda. In 1948, Elspeth Huxley was to describe Banyarwanda migrants as 'poor, thin, ill-clad and uncouth, not at all like the prosperous citizens of Uganda' (1948: 197). Yet Buganda could represent to such migrants as these in the 1930s and 1940s 'what the United States did to the Irishmen of the 19th century' (Report on the Labour Situation 1938: para. 79).

Migration into Uganda, and especially Buganda, began to develop on a large scale in the mid-1920s. Baganda farmers, unable to hire enough fellow Baganda, were increasingly employing labourers from outside to grow cotton for them. Andrew Roberts has argued that the increase in cotton production in Buganda in the 1930s was made possible by this availability of Banyarwanda immigrants – who thus also played a key role in· sustaining protectorate revenues (Roberts 1986: 696-697). The seasonal peak of the movement of labour tended to be March/April, as migrants broke up new land for local Ugandan employers before cotton planting. Thereafter they were engaged in harvesting or, under Indian and European employers, ginning. Thus the cotton industry in Buganda also became increasingly reliant on them: 75 per cent of labourers in Buganda ginneries were of Ruanda-Urundi origin. Sugar became a second industry dependent on this source of labour from the 1920s. The two largest individual private employers of migrant labour were Indian-owned sugar plantations and factories: at Lugazi, in Buganda, and Kakira, just over the provincial border in Eastern Province. Forty-nine per cent of labourers on these sugar estates were, likewise, of Ruanda-Urundi origin (Report on the Labour Situation 1938: paras. 57, 54).

In addition to African agriculture and various non-native enterprises, government departments in Uganda were heavily dependent on such labour from outside the protectorate. This applied notably to the Public Works Department and to the native government of the kingdom of Buganda. Both of these employed migrants for tasks such as building and road construction. This pattern of migration and employment did not grow out of any colonial calculation but out of the wider regional socio-economic context, in which the initiative lay not with officials but with the migrants.

Perhaps more serious than this dependency of key sectors of the Ugandan economy on migrant labour was a lack of official control over where the migrants worked. Banyarwanda did not necessarily go where they were most needed, by the colonial state or by private employers. Migrants voted with their feet: and the great majority of them chose to work for Baganda farmers. Ironically, what seemed to others like low wages and poor conditions brought these migrants to Buganda and to the attention of a British administration which was both paternalist and anxious about the potential for disorder. In 1943 the acting labour commissioner described the situation 'of immigrant labour employed by Africans' as 'deplorable'. He condemned overcrowded and insanitary accommodation; and he went on to propose that the Buganda government should be persuaded to legislate (while recognising that many in the Lukiko were chiefs who benefited from the existing arrangements).[35] Even so, this type of employment proved the most popular– because, it appeared in 1946, 'the worker lives very much as one of the employer's family, and is well fed, while the task expected is modest' (Orde-Browne 1946: para. 340).

The same could not be said, for example, of employers at Uganda's mines, where a difficulty in attracting labour was to have serious implications during the Second World War. The British did not and could not control the distribution of migrant labour: the diaspora occurred independently of government. As Audrey Richards subsequently pointed out, it took place without labour exchanges (Richards 1954: 76). Instead, it was shaped more by kinship ties with former migrant-settlers; the location of the best farming areas; the availability of land for eventual settlement; and simple convenience. In the competition for labour in Buganda, between Baganda farmers on the one hand, and non-African employers (including government) on the other, the shorter hours, availability of food and shelter, and the greater prospects of long-term settlement ensured that the small Muganda cotton farmer had the edge over alternative employers (Richards 1954: 218). This remained the case after the Second World War, despite the intervention of local British officials. For after 1945, the Protectorate government attempted to prevent farmers from recruiting along the migration routes (which non-African enterprises were free to do). Yet migrant labourers still chose to work for Baganda farmers and, ignoring colonial borders which were nothing if not permeable, simply turned up at the place of work, as before (Orde-Browne 1946: para.340).

*　　　*　　　*

The uncontrolled and uncontrollable dependence of important segments of the Ugandan economy on migrant labourers, established between the wars, assumed a seemingly benign aspect at the start of Second World War. In 1940 a larger than usual supply of labour from Ruanda-Urundi, in the wake of a change in the franc-sterling exchange rate, was welcomed by British officials in Uganda and believed by them to have counterbalanced the manpower demands of military recruitment. Dependence on Banyarwanda was subsequently such that by 1941, the number of Ruanda-Urundi employees at the two sugar estates of Lugazi and Kakira was three times that of men from West Nile (which was the main source of migrant labour from within the protectorate). The ratio at Lugazi was 8250 to 2747; and at Kakira, 10,200 to 3738 (Labour Report 1941: appendix). However, from 1942 onwards labour problems multiplied as a result of a complex interplay of wartime conditions – over which the Ugandan Protectorate government was powerless to exercise control, and for which solutions were to prove elusive.

By 1942, for example, there were too many migrant labourers from Ruanda-Urundi in Uganda. They were fewer in number than the previous year, but since then their main source of employment in Uganda had diminished. For as we have seen in 1942, in response to falling prices, Baganda farmers reduced their acreages devoted to cotton. As the supply of Banyarwanda labour now exceeded demand for it, there was unemployment among migrants. There had been a warning in 1938 of the possible danger of 'many 1000s of strangers being stranded without means of subsistence in Buganda, with possibly untoward consequences' (Report on the Labour Situation: para. 266). Now indeed, just four years later, 'the problem of destitute Banyarwanda' reached beyond Buganda into Eastern Province, putting pressure on supplies of food and, with their 'appalling state of health', on hospitals and dispensaries, too, in that part of Uganda.[36]

Added to this was a problem considered just as serious: the threat to order. There were disturbances on the sugar estates. A strike at Lugazi in 1942 over working hours 'developed into a riot'. An enquiry revealed that conditions on the perimeter of the Lugazi estate, where most labourers lived, represented a 'potential area of danger both to public order and to public health' (Labour Report 1942: para. 5). There followed an incident at Kakira, when a European government officer was murdered by a group of migrants, this time of northern Ugandan origin.[37] In response to such disturbances, the British authorities in Uganda decided by the end of 1942 to re-institute a Labour Department– the former department having been downgraded to a single-man inspectorate as an economy measure during the 1930s depression (Report on the Labour Situation 1938: para.262).

It was also decided to instruct the Labour Advisory Committee to consider the problems associated with the south-western labour migration routes. This committee was deeply conscious of what government could not do. It judged that it would be unwise to try to control immigration by any form of registration, for this would probably deter potential workers from entering Uganda. Moreover, it added, 'the administrative difficulties to be overcome are so great that no attempt should be made at present' to introduce any scheme for the regulation of labour supply.[38] Registration had already been ruled out as impracticable and undesirable in 1938, when it was acknowledged that migrants could not even be counted accurately (Report on the Labour Situation 1938: paras.49, 213). Now the committee turned instead to the provision of rest camps along the migration routes. These, it was thought, would at least prevent the physical condition of the migrants from deteriorating before they arrived at their place of work.

A second purpose of such camps would be to demonstrate clearly to non-native employers how to attract workers by improving conditions of employment by better provision of food, shelter, and medical care. The British administration had earlier insisted that the employer alone could guarantee the supply and quality of his own labour. The fact that, in the 1942 conditions of overall labour surplus, some employers at mines, plantations and raw mills still experienced labour shortage, may be seen as an illustration of the limits of employers' as well as officials' competence to direct labour within the wartime economy. Local labour shortage was also a serious obstacle to the urgent production drive which was being launched at this time, after the fall of Singapore. At the end of 1942 it was reported that 'the supply of labour to essential war undertakings, such as rubber production and tin mining, is a problem of first concern' (Labour Report 1942: para. 5).

Already the twin themes of the Labour Advisory Committee's report in 1938 were 'the high degree of dependence' of the Ugandan economy on the migrant labourers and, typically, the problem of order (perhaps the perennial colonial preoccupation, above all others). The latter applied not only on the fringes of the sugar estates but also 'en route' when migrants were frequently 'waylaid, robbed or swindled'.[39] General concern was also expressed that 'these large bodies of men should be roaming about the country without coming under the cognisance of any public authority' (Report on the Labour Situation 1938: 213). In the 1943 context, the only possible remedy seemed to be the provision of a series of rest camps along the migration routes as soon as possible.

Would the provision of 14 rest camps be a sufficient solution to this pressing wartime problem? It was as much as the government considered practicable. But the question was never answered. Camps had first been suggested in the 1920s and 1930s, but when the wartime committee began its deliberations just one camp existed, at Mbarara where the two routes from the frontiers met. And by the end of the war and into mid-1946, only one more had been added: at Merama on the Ruanda-Urundi border. All that Governor Hall could tell the Colonial Office was that 'a start has been made'.[40] The British protectorate administration had not reached by 1946 the essential minimum (determined by officials eight years earlier) of three camps.

Why had only 'a start' been made? Finance was not the major problem, and officials accorded the scheme high priority. Dundas described the scheme as 'a work of development ... too urgent to be postponed until the post-war period'.[41] His concern was not only for the migrant labourers themselves– 'on which the industries of the territory so greatly depend'– but also for tranquillity.[42] He was influenced by the Kakira incident and saw the need for some 'preventive action', since such large numbers of migrants remained 'under little effective control'. Order could not be taken for granted. Hence, provision was made for a labour commissioner to head the reborn Labour Department; and £42,100 was set aside in 1943 for the Public Works Department to build camps.[43]

A huge problem, as we have seen, was the shortage of expatriate British staff. The Second World War made great demands on the manpower of the administration, and the Public Works Department was one of the hardest hit. The ending of the war did not reduce the need for work on the camps, since labour was required for 'development' and the sustaining of the territory's productive effort. But when European staff did start to become available, they had to be directed to other, even more pressing, tasks. No financial provision was made for the camp programme in the estimates for 1946, because it was clear by the end of 1945 that progress was ruled out by the lack of PWD staff (as well as a shortage of materials). The priority now, for those staff available, was the demobilisation and re-absorption of ex-soldiers.[44] Shortages of tyres and of petrol had already meant that it was impossible to reduce dependence on camps by accelerating the pace of transport from border to employment.[45] And the shortage of appropriate available expatriate manpower was to continue to hold back the growth of the Labour Department itself.

The Protectorate government had defined a problem and determined a solution. But the Second World War, which had underlined the need for an improvement in the regulation and quality of migrant labour, had thwarted official attempts to meet this need with the provision of camps. And on one occasion the war itself seemingly played a further trick on Uganda. Just when the wartime production drive rendered the territory's 'economic crops' increasingly dependent on migrant labour, the Protectorate government was forced to close the border with Ruanda-Urundi. This was because, as we have seen, by the end of 1943, the whole of East Africa was faced by a serious food shortage. Uganda, although perhaps the least affected territory, had had to appoint its own famine commissioner in February 1943. Migrant labourers leaving Ruanda-Urundi in search of wages during that year were also accompanied by women and children seeking food. There was no official welcome in Uganda for such 'ineffectives',[46] and it was decided instead to close the Ruanda-Urundi border, on 1 January 1944.

How serious would be the implications for Uganda's labour supply? The Director of Supplies had referred to 'difficulties being experienced in meeting the essential needs for labour of such vital industries as sugar, rubber, timber and sisal'.[47] There was no escaping the British administration's dilemma in Uganda. Closing the border to conserve food stocks would, and did, worsen an existing problem of labour shortage. In fact, the border was reopened as soon as March 1944; but official restrictions on the Ruanda-Urundi side meant that a normal flow of labour was interrupted for six months in all. Shortages caused inconvenience, as seen in complaints from the sugar estates. In some cases, firms resorted to 'forceful recruitment of unsophisticated immigrants' in order to acquire a share of the migrant labour which was available (Labour Report 1944: para. 12).

Clearly it proved impossible to turn off the tap of population movement in the south-west completely. Dundas referred to the 'not inconsiderable drift to and fro' after the border was closed.[48] Powseland subsequently described the closure, which was 'enforced' on both sides, as only 'fairly effective' (1954: 47,48). As Audrey Richards wrote too, 'it has always been impossible to control all the byways which may be used by the travellers, and particularly by those from Ruanda-Urundi' (1954: 201).

*   *   *

To sum up, the Second World War greatly increased Uganda's reliance on immigrant labour and heightened official and general awareness of this unpalatable fact. But the period saw no related administrative achievement. The colonial state remained, as it had been before the war, unable to regulate effectively the supply of labour on which it depended. In 1942 there were too many migrants; in 1944, too few. The flow and direction of migrant labourers into Uganda was not open to control by local British officials. The Protectorate government could not police its own borders. Indeed, it could scarcely even monitor the immigrants, let alone count them.

Its two most notable wartime decisions clearly illustrate, if in different ways, the limits of its competence. First came the policy decision to go ahead with a major, priority, camp-building programme. Even had it been fully implemented, this would have affected only symptoms of the problem and not causes. In the event, the programme foundered on wartime shortages which the Protectorate government could not remedy. Then came the closure of the border. This was a negative measure, prompted by a wartime crisis of a different order, which ironically served only to worsen the already existing problem of labour shortage.

In the later years of the war and beyond, the pattern was to change little. Large numbers of migrants crossed the border annually, but now still more intended to settle in Buganda. Those who chose to work for others continued also to choose for whom they worked. Post-war reports recognised some fundamental continuities. Orde-Browne's terms of reference required an investigation into labour immigration from Ruanda-Urundi. He reported that Uganda would be 'gravely inconvenienced' if the normal flow were interrupted (1946: para. 28). Another British official also reported at this time that 'not only is a high proportion of export production from the central parts of Uganda dependent on this itinerant labour, but a good deal of food in Buganda is likewise dependent on labour employed by Buganda landlords' (Worthington 1946: para. 187).

As we shall see later, at the end of the Second World War demobilised Africans returning to Uganda chose not to replace the migrants by seeking immediate employment themselves, but instead to enjoy for a while the financial rewards of their military service. Other Ugandan Africans were deterred from presenting themselves in the labour market by the absence of consumer goods in the stores. As the opportunities for consumption diminished, so the incentive for potential local labourers to look for work evaporated, and thus the protectorate became dependent to an even greater extent on Ruanda-Urundi for its wage labour supply. The Second World War had made the Protectorate Government more conscious of the labour problem. But – as in the case of political and economic subordination to Kenya, its neighbour to the east – the British colonial state's continuing vulnerability in these areas was more easily perceived than remedied.

---

1. East African Governors' Conference (EAGC) Proceedings, June 1938, PRO CO 822/84/21.
2. EAGC Proceedings, November 1939, PRO CO 822/93/11.
3. EAGC Proceedings, June 1940, PRO CO 962/15.
4. Mitchell to Secretary of State, 3 October 1939, PRO CO 536/202/40100.
5. Mitchell to Secretary of State, 1 June 1940, PRO CO 822/103/15.
6. Moore, Memorandum for EAGC, 5 January 1942, PRO CO 822/107/8.
7. EAGC Proceedings, April 1942, PRO CO 822/107/9.
8. Dundas to Secretary of State, 14 April 1942, PRO CO 822/111/29.
9. Editorial, *Uganda Herald*, 24 June 1942.
10. Dawe, minute, 30 April 1942, PRO CO 822/111/29.
11. Dundas to Secretary of State, 14 April 1942, PRO CO 822/111/29.
12. Dawe, minute, 3 June 1942, PRO CO 822/111/29.
13. EAPSC Minutes, PRO CO 822/111/30; CO 822/111/29.
14. EAPSC Minutes, 12 January 1944, PRO CO 537/1525.
15. (Anonymous) Memorandum for the EAPSC, 15 January 1943, PRO CO 822/111/30.
16. Memorandum for EAPSC, undated (?October 1944), PRO CO 537/1525.
17. Memorandum from the Assistant to the Director of Imports Kenya/Uganda for the EAPSC, 2 July 1945, PRO CO 537/1525.
18. *ibid.*
19. Seel, minute, 14 December 1939, PRO CO 822/103/15.

20. Dawe, Memorandum, July 1942, PRO CO 822/111/33.
21. Dundas to Secretary of State, 7 December 1943, PRO CO 822/108/20.
22. Editorial, *Uganda Herald*, 23 June 1943.
23. Letter, *Uganda Herald*, 14 July 1943.
24. Moore, Memorandum, 20 April 1943, PRO CO 822/108/20.
25. Dawe, Memorandum, July 1942, PRO CO 822/111/33.
26. Seel, Notes on East African policy, March 1943, PRO CO 822/108/20.
27. Seel, minute, 1 March 1944, PRO CO 822/114/7.
28. Mitchell, Memorandum, November 1944, PRO CO 822/114/7.
29. Editorial, *Uganda Herald*, 19 December 1945.
30. Dundas, Memorandum on Closer Union, 3 October 1943, PRO CO 822/108/20.
31. Editorial, *Uganda Herald*, 13 October 1943.
32. Dawe, minute, 19 January 1940, PRO CO 822/103/15.
33. Dawe, Memorandum, July 1942, PRO CO 822/111/33.
34. Labour Advisory Committee, *Organisation of South-Western Labour Migration Routes*, Entebbe 1943, para. 5.
35. Uganda Protectorate Secretarial Minute Paper, R 306/4, Uganda National Archive, Entebbe
36. *ibid.* para. 4.
37. Report, Uganda Herald, 11 November 1942
38. Labour Migration Routes, para. 1
39. *ibid.* para. 11
40. Hall to Secretary of State, 27 July 1945, PRO CO 822/130/2
41. Dundas to the Colonial Office, 7 August 1943, PRO CO 536/209/40100/2/1942
42. Dundas to the Legislative Council, 9 December 1942
43. Dundas to the Colonial Office, 7 August 1943, PRO CO 536/209/40100/2/1942
44. Financial Secretary to the Legislative Council, 4 December 1945.
45. Labour Advisory Committee, *Organisation of South-Western Labour Migration Routes*, Entebbe 1943, para.10.
46. Official communique, *Uganda Herald*, 22 December 1943
47. Official communique, *Uganda Herald*, 24 December 1943
48. Report, *Uganda Herald*, 14 June 1944

10
Import and Price Control

Imports

The Uganda Protectorate was from the outset dependent on a wide range of imported goods – and thus vulnerable to any dislocation of supply. From 1940, 'total war' implied import control. But during the Second World War, the British administration in Uganda could not control imports.

From the first months of conflict the complexity of wartime economic issues became evident. So did the limits of officials' competence. When the Protectorate government instituted petrol rationing, a 40 per cent reduction in consumption followed. Among a small number of rationing initiatives, this looks like a success story (albeit a solitary one). But even this achievement was deceptive, because it reflected the sudden loss of the means of transport. By mid-November 1939, as many as half the total number of lorries in Uganda were in the process of being requisitioned for the army and sent to Kenya. The resulting exodus – by December, 580 lorries had left the country – automatically reduced the demand for petrol ('War Effort' [1] November 1939). Unfortunately, it also damaged local trading activity: an adverse side-effect of fewer lorries around Kampala was a rise in the price of bananas there, banana plantains being the staple diet of Baganda and others among the local population.[1]

By contrast, the exclusion of some imported goods by selective licensing brought few complications, and helped to conserve currency. It was given a further function, a moral one, when in June 1941 Britain sought to prevent the 'wrong' use of colonial spending-power in 'unnecessary consumption'. Self-denial was being urged: to economise on shipping, to avoid misapplication of Britain's productive capacity and, as before, to save foreign exchange. The British metropolitan government felt that it was time that 'efforts much

193

more nearly commensurate with those now being made in this country should be made by all those inhabitants of the Colonial Empire who enjoy a comparatively high standard of life'.[2]

At this stage, expatriate opinion still had to be courted. How would they react if they were denied such goods as the refrigerators, gramophones and toiletries which were still being imported from sterling sources at the end of 1940? Dundas privately assured London that he would check 'that we have done all that is reasonable'.[3] But what was 'reasonable'? Expatriates were certainly affected by controls. The number of cars imported into Uganda in 1941 was 159 – only a fifth of the 1938 figure ('War Effort' [5] October 1942). And from July 1941 there was a prohibition on the import from Britain of a number of luxuries such as leather goods and furniture, glass and jewellery, cameras and watches.[4] Yet there is evidence that by late 1942 the expatriates' sacrifice was still minor. The secretary of the Uganda Industrial Committee bemoaned 'the really staggering apathy and indifference' of the public to the question of cutting consumption.[5] The fact that this official was reduced to exhortation – appealing to expatriates not to demand import of articles into Uganda – suggests that the weight of official restrictions had by no means become intolerable by this time. Even in 1942, imports of wine and spirits were sustained at 60 per cent of 1941 levels, suggesting consumption of arguable necessity.[6] While waging economic warfare on behalf of the empire, it would appear that the British colonial state could not wholly ignore the political pressure upon it of expatriate consumer demands. But then an unprecedented shortage of shipping capacity in July 1942 prompted a review of all existing import licences, and the Uganda Supply Board had to publish a list of 44 totally prohibited imports, 17 of which – ranging from soap to confectionery, musical instruments to firearms, zip fasteners to fishing-rods – were being banned for the first time.[7]

By this time, the war context had deteriorated and was forcing a reconsideration of what kind of control should, or could, be attempted in Uganda – a small protectorate on the periphery of the British empire, entirely dependent on a shipping life-support system which could no longer be taken for granted. War was exposing the vulnerability of Ugandans of all races to a major disruption within the world economy – into which it had become increasingly integrated, and on which it had become increasingly dependent, during the previous fifty years. Import control in a practicable form, concentrating on *exclusion,* had been imposed on Uganda by Britain between 1939 and 1942; import control of a quite different order, entailing *acquisition*, was imposed on Uganda by wartime conditions thereafter. From 1942, the Uganda Protectorate was no longer merely serving the British empire. It was now struggling to survive.

The capacity of the Protectorate government to control imports was put to the severest test – as was the case, of course, elsewhere in Britain's African empire at this time (and as it had been in the First World War, a generation earlier). Although the British administration had been able to exclude goods, it had no means now to acquire them. At the outset, officials had proved able, if reluctant, to conserve currency and reduce some consumption – though conscious that such a form of import control could provoke criticisms from local traders and consumers (especially European); reduce customs revenue; and even, as it affected Africans, threaten the chain of consumption and production. From now on, British officials in Uganda did not prove able to sustain a sufficiently high level of imported goods. Instead, from mid-1942 they could only seek to distribute such imports as did become available. But allocation was an inadequate substitute for acquisition. And British officials did not perform even this function without provoking considerable criticism and controversy.

As the Protectorate government transferred the balance of its attention from the keeping out of undesirable imports towards the allocation of desirable ones in short supply, it had to appear to be disinterested as well as efficient. The supply of imports had to be controlled, 'so as to ensure the distribution, fair alike in quantity and price, of commodities essential to the civil population'.[8] But who should be given licence to import, against the background of inadequate supply? Once involved in this delicate act of allocation, the Protectorate government soon found itself condemned by interested parties for its arbitrariness, discrimination and incompetence.

In official thinking, the roots of fairness lay in past performance: established pre-war importers were entitled to obtain a share of the restricted import trade. But this criterion discriminated against recently established traders, among them many Indians attracted into retail trade by prevailing higher prices. One particular problem, which was raised by a distinguished Kenyan Indian, was that traders who first took out licences in 1941 and 1942 were now being treated 'all as one class of speculators and price-enhancers'.[9] The Uganda Supply Board was dominated by government officials and European expatriates, and had been set up in 1939 without any Indian on the relevant executive committee – an interesting example of British discrimination against, rather than in favour of, Indians. In 1944, the Consumers' Co-operative Society of Kampala, an Indian body which sought collectively to import goods which were in short supply, still complained that the acquisition of 'provisions and other essentials of life was most difficult on account of the rigid system of past performances'.[10]

But the problem of allocating scarce import resources within Uganda was dwarfed by the still more highly sensitive issue of allocation between Uganda and its neighbour, Kenya. We have already noted Kenya's powerful local position and seen how in Nairobi a series of institutions in which settler views were powerful sprang up during the Second World War. From the outset, their responsibilities included equitable distribution of commodities between the territories. But, in practice, and in the eyes of interested parties in Uganda, distribution proved far from equitable. Thus for example Uganda had to accept that three-quarters of its cotton piece-goods would continue as before to pass through importing channels in Kenya; and in practice, importers of various commodities in Uganda remained convinced that they were not receiving their due share of specific agreed quotas.[11]

By 1943, commercial interests in Uganda were increasingly concerned with the question of the protectorate's overall share of imported commodities. On these goods depended not only the fortunes of trading interests but also levels of African production-for-purchase. 1943 was a year of heightened emotion and vigorous protest.

The year opened badly with the provocative news that a licence had been issued in Kenya for the import of 'essential' golf-balls – while it was claimed that firms in Uganda had had applications to import goods for legitimate trade purposes turned down by the Imports Controller in Kenya. The editor of the *Uganda Herald* launched a passionate and wide-ranging attack: 'There can be no denying the fact that Kenya today is controlling absolutely what can and cannot be imported into Uganda'. The article concluded: 'Kenya is not giving us a fair share of the goods imported'; and argued that 'a mutually agreed upon quota is the only justifiable way of allocating supplies to both countries'.[12] The editor added that this was a state of affairs 'for which our own government must share some of the blame'.[13]

Indeed, the Protectorate government shortly did admit official concern and even responsibility, accepting that there must be 'machinery for ensuring the fair inter-territorial allocation of goods received' ('War Effort' [6] 1943). Shortly afterwards, G.F.Clay challenged the East African Production and Supply Council on behalf of the Ugandan Protectorate government. He considered that Uganda should have 'a definite allocation of all bulk purchases'.[14] But nothing substantial came of Clay's pleadings. In February 1945, the new governor of Uganda, John Hall, confided to London that 'suspicion and bitterness have been given a new impulse recently because both the control of supplies and the control of prices have recently operated unfairly towards Uganda'.[15]

Hall was writing after the January 1945 disturbances in Uganda, which occurred in the wake of – and largely because of – successive years of distorted distribution and resultant shortages. At the time, C.H.Bird, president of the Uganda Chamber of Commerce, blamed the failure of import control for the riots. He pointed out that bilateral arrangements had been broken by importers in Kenya and that the Protectorate government had been too weak to prevent this jeopardising of Uganda's fundamental interests. His specific examples related to bicycles and to piece-goods, but he claimed that 'in nearly every line investigated the same results appeared'.[16] Thus when East Africa had to reduce its kerosene imports, Uganda had to suffer 70 per cent of the cut and Kenya only 30 per cent. The result, Bird continued, was that 'practically all our Africans are now without oil and are raising serious complaints'.

Bird and those he represented were interested parties, but official statistics on the distribution of imported goods between Uganda and its eastern neighbour provided support for those in Uganda who felt that they were suffering at the hands of rival interested parties within Kenya. Total volumes of imported cotton piece-goods held up well during the first three years of the war, but then came the huge reduction. In every category of imported cotton piece-goods, Uganda acquired a reduced share of the much reduced volume.[17] A severe shortfall of imports of agricultural implements into Uganda occurred in 1941 and 1943: again it was the wartime relative shift away from Uganda and towards Kenya which preoccupied contemporary critics.[18] Such figures all underlined the failure of the authorities in Uganda throughout the Second World War to secure a reasonable and adequate portion of available foreign goods for the peoples of the protectorate – especially for Africans.

Criticism of Kenya had some effect on the 'closer union' debate. Bird observed that 'it is extremely difficult to maintain any sort of goodwill towards closer union or inter-territorial combined action when this sort of thing is going on the whole time'.[19] Commenting on a paper sent in 1944 by the Uganda Chamber of Commerce to Lord Hailey to say 'No' to closer union, the *Uganda Herald* condemned 'wartime controls operated supposedly impartially from Nairobi, but in actual practice resulting in a distinct brake on Uganda's commerce'.[20]

Import substitution

One alternative response to the reduction in supplies of imported goods in Uganda was to try to manage without them. The story of import substitution in Uganda was no more than a sideshow of the hopeless struggle for import control. But it was to throw additional light on the narrow limits of Protectorate government competence during the Second World War – as well as perhaps on the prospects for local industrialisation in the longer term following colonial rule.

There was scope for using local rather than imported building materials in, for example, the construction of a bridge or a rest-camp for immigrant workers. But the general shortage of goods, especially consumer goods for Africans, required more widespread innovation – that is, import substitution. And there was soon some evidence that *private* initiatives had met with modest success. Drugs for medicinal purposes, formerly imported, were now manufactured from local resources; and cotton seed was being used as a fertiliser, as a cattle food and as fuel to replace coal ('War Effort' [5] October 1942). Meanwhile, a new variety of flour, 'adulterated' with 30 per cent maize flour to reduce imports of wheat flour, had become available locally. Termed 'national flour', it proved an unpalatable wartime sacrifice for the European community to endure, but it was said to have saved thousands of tons of shipping space.[21]

Perhaps the main achievement of import substitution during the early part of the war was the manufacture of hoes. But this was the result not of any European initiative in Uganda but of African enterprise in Kenya. At Kisumu, on the Kenyan shore of Lake Victoria, hoes were made by local blacksmiths from discarded car and lorry chassis. These hoes found their way into Uganda – until the supply of discarded chassis itself ran out.[22] Officials acknowledged in 1942 that 'while a Uganda Committee deals with the protectorate's potentialities and publishes reports as occasion demands ... native craftsmen make serviceable hoes out of scrap iron and ancient motor vehicles' ('War Effort' [5] October 1942).

The major official British initiative came in July 1942, with the setting up of a Uganda Industrial Committee. Its aims, on a budget of £800, were the co-ordination of efforts in Uganda 'to replace imported articles by local products' and 'the encouragement of village industries'.[23] By such means, there might still be goods to buy in local stores. Meanwhile, the overall strategic purpose of such enterprise was the saving of shipping space. As an official advertisement in the *Uganda Herald* put it, 'a ship of 10,000 tons could, in the time it takes to make the voyage to Uganda and back, land 60,000 fully equipped men in France'.[24]

In light of the crisis over imports of cotton goods, the Uganda Industrial Committee concentrated from the start on cotton spinning and weaving. It is on this project that the UIC may therefore fairly be judged. Within two years, the UIC had trained nearly 400 African spinners and weavers. But the enterprise suffered, fatally as it turned out, from the absence of both equipment and markets. There was inevitably a shortage of imported tools and machinery, so that in the Entebbe workshops trainees had to use machines improvised from scrap – by skilled internees specially drafted in for the purpose. In March 1944, the UIC was still insisting that the establishment of village industries was its first priority.[25] But who would buy the finished articles, if they were of poorer quality than available imports? Bird remarked that 'it would be wise to note that the African peasant is a very discerning buyer'.[26] The committee itself observed sadly that despite its own productive efforts 'the purchase of imported textile goods has been universal'.[27] And by December 1944, the decision had been made to abandon the promotion of village spinning and weaving. The committee's experiments had succeeded neither in substituting imports in wartime nor in establishing any viable prospect for a village industry for post-war Uganda.

Overall, the factors that worked against the development of manufacturing in Uganda earlier in the twentieth century – now reinforced in wartime by absence of equipment, inadequate financial investment by government, and acute manpower shortages in the British administration itself – ensured that import substitution could be no instant answer to the problem of import shortages. As a senior British official in Uganda plaintively observed, 'individual colonial governments are not in a position to shape their own individual policies. These must necessarily conform not only to the regions to which they belong, but to the higher pattern set in the councils of the nations at war'.[28] Import substitution was thus a wartime imperial requirement which Uganda could not fulfil. The shortages from 1942 onwards emphasised the need to *try* substitution, but served only to make any such effort less likely to succeed. Meanwhile the shortages became more acute.

The effects of shortages

Shortages of imported goods in Uganda were a feature of the whole period of the Second World War. Before the 1945 disturbances, there had been five years of relative scarcity. At the start of the war, there had been an immediate reduction in the volume of imported consumer goods for Africans, from matches to bicycles, from nails to corrugated iron roofing.[29] In time, cotton imports became the principal item of concern to officials anxious to meet African demand. One African claimed in 1943 that 'nearly 75% of the things we use are of foreign make'.[30] Few were unaffected by shortages in this year, when it was remarked that 'the question of supplies is by far the most thorny of all questions affecting Uganda today'.[31] In 1944, importers Gailey and Roberts (Uganda) Ltd had to announce to their customers: 'the shortage of supplies makes it difficult to meet all your needs'.[32] Orde-Browne too noted 'an almost complete cessation of imports of the type that appeal to the tribesmen', listing as examples cooking-pots, enamelled ware, knives, lamps, sewing machines and bicycles (1946: para. 40). By 1946, cycle tyres and tubes and fishing nets were all in short supply in Eastern Province. Indeed, the end of the war offered little immediate relief. Governor Hall acknowledged the 'acute shortage of imported goods' in Uganda in mid-1945.[33] There was only limited improvement even in 1946 'when the supply of the principal imported goods, especially textiles for African use, was still far less than the immediate requirements and consumptive capacity of the protectorate' (Annual Report 1946: 26).

This shortage of consumer goods for Africans directly threatened wartime production by removing the principal incentive to work or to grow export crops. There were other effects. From the outset shortages led to higher prices, a drop in 'real' wages, and to profiteering which, as we shall see later, proved immune to the local British administration's preventive measures. In due course shortages contributed to the cocktail of economic grievances which ultimately exploded in the strikes and disturbances of January 1945. And shortages also led to crime. For example, in 1944, thefts of bicycles dramatically increased. A general warning was published: 'Watch Your Property. The present shortage of certain goods has not only resulted in high prices, it has also caused a wave of thefts by house-breakers in Kampala and other towns'.[34]

It was not only Africans who suffered ... or were inconvenienced. The minutes of the Entebbe Club, a retreat for off-duty European officials, reveal that status and privilege were no protection against 'hardship' caused by wartime shortages. Members were restricted in May 1941 to one bottle of gin per week and, six months later, to a single bottle of whisky per month. Here was not only an example of wartime shortages but also evidence, rare elsewhere in the protectorate, of effective wartime rationing. [There had always been a race-specific dimension to official thinking about the connection between work and drink in the protectorate. It had been somewhat haughtily observed, before the war, that 'people who work for wages in offices, workshops, etc. and leave off at fixed and fairly early hours will inevitably drink if they have nothing else to occupy their minds; and if there is nowhere they can go except a sordid hut or shed they are tempted to get drunk as soon as they can'.[35]] But even the Entebbe Club could not ration what was not there: by March 1943, its supplies of whisky and brandy were exhausted. Meanwhile, the crisis of 1942 lay, for the Entebbe Club, in the shortage of spares for mowers for the golf course. This led to one imaginative but short-lived experiment in import substitution. The committee, although always reluctant to spend money, now decided to purchase 40 sheep from Teso district to 'mow' the greens. The experiment proved destructive of both club finances and sheep, while doing little for the improvement of members' golf. The death rate among the sheep was high, and as only one ewe was purchased, the birth rate low. Those sheep which survived their movement to Entebbe were eventually resold. Meanwhile nothing could be done about the shortage of cricket balls, other than to commission G.F.Clay – Uganda's Director of Agriculture, East Africa's Director of Native Production, and Entebbe's Captain of Golf – to seek supplies in Nairobi. In this Clay succeeded; but the scarcity of tennis balls at Entebbe was not solved until 1946 brought new imports. By this time however the protectorate-wide shortage of tennis balls had closed Nakasero Tennis Club in Kampala.[36]

Somewhat more significantly, government too was affected, and shortages over which they had no control threatened to have a more serious effect on officials when they were on duty. Bureaucracy itself was put at risk by the paper crisis of 1942. A stark general warning published in the *Uganda Herald* pulled no punches: 'When the present supplies run out in Uganda there is no possibility of getting any more from anywhere in the world'.[37] The writing and publication of some departmental reports were consequently suspended for the duration of the war ('War Effort' [4] September 1941). Newspapers were also reduced in size, and the issue of bank statements limited. Another problem was that movement around the protectorate was threatened in 1942. This was less the result of a shortage of petrol, which had been subject to strict and, it would appear, effective rationing since 1939, than of a shortage of tyres. The paper and tyre shortage became more critical after Japan entered the war. Purchase of tyres was at once made subject to permits, and these were only issued on grounds of necessity and the surrender of old tyres fit for reconditioning.[38] Even so, the Supply Board still had to confess that it could not meet the claims of those who had priority permits.

Uganda's economic performance was further endangered by the dearth of tools for agriculture. An acute shortage of hoes affected cultivation in Western Province. This widespread shortage 'gradually increased in intensity', while in Lango District there was still an 'acute' shortage of parts for its 4000 ploughs in 1946 (Annual Reports 1939-46: 84). African cultivators had already found by 1943 that the price of hoes had risen 'considerably'.[39] Reviewing the war period, the 1946 Annual Report admitted that shortages of agricultural implements had proved an important limiting factor in obtaining maximum production. Transportation of crops too was affected by shortage of twine and gunny bags from 1942 onwards. All that government could do in such cases was to urge economies.

Shortages also sabotaged the protectorate's development programme. Because of shortages of steel, work on Mulago hospital had to be postponed; and a road bridge over the Ora river in West Nile, which was to have been of steel, had to be made of wood. Road-making machinery was unavailable for intended improvements to the Kampala-Port Bell route.[40] Building, generally, was badly affected. Supplies of corrugated-iron roofing had virtually disappeared by March 1942.[41] In that year there was a total stoppage of all building work while a census was conducted on the availability of supplies. The PWD in Uganda could proceed only with projects that were not heavily dependent on imported materials – such as camp construction for migrant workers on the south-west route into Uganda. Lack of building material meant that there was an acute housing shortage in Kampala by 1944.[42]

The effects of wartime shortages in Uganda were varied and wide-ranging. Some were felt from the outset; many persisted into the post-war period. It was the widening of the war after December 1941 which produced a crisis in the availability and supply of goods. In this context, the Protectorate government in Uganda functioned with difficulty. It had to postpone its development plans; and its efforts to meet African consumer demands, upon which its production pro-grammes rested, led only to mounting failure. Uganda suffered short-ages, crime, and eventually widespread disturbance. The British in Uganda were seen to be failing: 'import control' remained in most respects a fiction, an aspiration never fulfilled.

Prices, profiteering and the Indian question
On 8 April 1942, an anonymous correspondent to the *Uganda Herald* observed that 'the shopkeepers are very clever and the law is not very strict'. This contemporary insight could act as a text for a ser-mon on 'absolutism' in colonial Uganda. As with import control, so with price control: attempts to wage 'total war' proved from the start to be largely ineffective. There was more than prices at stake here, though. The authorities' failure in this field inadvertently led to the emergence of a heightened racial consciousness, especially re-garding Indians as retailers. A generation later, Idi Amin expelled Indians from Uganda, charging them as a community with economic sabotage and exploiting their African customers. It is interesting in retrospect to see how critical assumptions about racial interest groups crystallised during the Second World War and how outspoken was their expression.

More generally, the Protectorate government seems to have quite misread the political situation. It did much to try to appease (and to involve) the unofficial expatriate community, while ignoring the hard-ship and grievances multiplying among Africans. Politically, it seemed to be preparing for past battles rather than the ones which might lie ahead. In spite of the sweeping responsibilities assumed on the outbreak of war by newly appointed British governmental institutions, and legislative changes thereafter, African consumers received minimal protection. The gap between legislation and enforcement remained unbridged – and unbridgeable. The British colonial state in Uganda was consequently seen to fail. The 1945 disturbances were, as we shall see, a direct consequence.

Yet at the start of the Second World War, the British in Uganda had appeared purposeful and decisive. Abandoning 'laissez-faire' for interventionism, they had sought to minimise the threat, and almost at once the reality, of price rises resulting from world shortage or local profiteering. At the end of August 1939, essential foodstuffs were among a number of items already subject to officially set maximum prices.[43] In September, a sub-committee of the Supply Board was commissioned to control the distribution and fix the prices of all trade products in Uganda, whether imported or locally produced goods. The first list of imports subjected to 'control prices' comprised a dozen items which included cotton goods, lanterns and matches, nails, hoes and corrugated iron sheets.[44] Such goods were among those most commonly purchased by Africans – commonly, from Indians. The British administration was publicly assuming responsibility for Africans as consumers. Even so, before the end of the year the first officially sanctioned rises in levels of 'control prices' were published. Such rises became a regular occurrence thereafter.

Governor Mitchell had to admit as early as November 1939 that 'attempts have been made by most improper means to profiteer at the expense of the public, especially the poorer members of it'.[45] Meanwhile, prosecutions had already begun. African retailers as well as Indian were exposed. An African butcher in Kampala was sentenced to 6 weeks hard labour for selling 2 pounds of beef for a shilling instead of 80 cents; and a Muganda shopkeeper was sentenced to 14 days hard labour for selling a bottle of paraffin oil at double the fixed pre-war price. In his defence, the latter 'stated that he thought that as war had been declared it was a good opportunity to put up his prices'.[46] The age of innocence soon passed.

Prices continued to rise, officially as well as unofficially. By the end of 1940, advertised (lawful) prices for clothes had risen by as a much as 33 per cent. By then, the ending of Britain's 'phoney war' brought a new price control measure. From August 1940 a new regulation entitled purchasers to complain if, for a 'wide range of necessities', they were charged an 'excessive' price. According to this ruling, goods might not now be sold 'above a price which gives the seller a normal pre-war profit', even though no maximum price for the particular article or foodstuff had been fixed.[47] This measure established what officials subsequently chose to term a 'comprehensive system of price control'.[48]

However, it was soon undermined by judicial interpretation in the courts. A case in December 1940 revealed how a retailer charged with profiteering could avoid conviction when goods not subject to fixed maximums were involved. Such were bicycle spokes, which a Mr Sultani was accused of selling above the 'permitted price': that is, at an 'excessive price'. The permitted price was further defined as a price which did not 'significantly' exceed the 'basic' price of the goods. It was left to the court to decide what was significant. The prosecution alleged that the 'basic' price was 3/- (three shillings) per gross. Though Sultani was selling at 6/50 per gross, he was acquitted.[49] The 'comprehensive system of price control' thus proved loose both in conception and in implementation.

Judgement could go the other way, however, and there were cases of profiteers being convicted. Service Stores of Kampala were fined 'for selling listed goods at prices above the basic price by an amount larger than is justified'.[50] But from the bench itself came admissions that fines were not succeeding as a deterrent. A magistrate in Lira explained that he was imposing a fine of 500 shillings on an Indian who had overcharged for bicycle rubber solution, because a fine of 250 shillings earlier imposed for a similar offence on another retailer had clearly not deterred.[51] Neither the number of convictions nor the weight of punishment undermined the black market. 'Judging by the frequency of the reports', ran a press commentary on profiteering in August 1942, 'cases are if anything on the increase, so the prosecutions do not seem to be having much deterrent effect'.[52] Fines, the commentary continued, were of no use because they represented only a fraction of the amount of money being made by profiteering. 'Surely', it concluded, 'the Government is not too weak to step in?'.

As if in response to the challenge – though insisting that the previous arrangements had operated with reasonable success – the Protectorate government introduced new measures within two weeks of this pressure from the expatriate press. The new policy was to be somewhat desperately described by Governor Dundas as yet 'more comprehensive and rigorous' than what had gone before.[53] First, harsher penalties were made available, including not only the removal of a trade licence in the event of a third offence (as had been specifically advocated in the press) but also prison sentences for 'those who secretly hoard trade goods for surreptitious disposal at black market prices'. Secondly, from now on all goods were to be covered: whether they were 'price regulated' (that is, subject to specified fixed maximum prices), or 'percentage fixed' (that is, subject to a formula of prescribed percentages over costs at each stage of distribution). Thirdly, prices were no longer automatically to sustain 'normal' (prewar) profit margins. And to prevent 'snowballing' (the practice of inventing extra links in the chain of distribution, to legitimise extra profit margins), there was a ban on the transit of goods through more than three handlers before they reached the consumer.[54]

What would be the impact of these new governmental initiatives? The Mbale Chamber of Commerce immediately condemned the new regulations and predicted that the new, depressed, profit margins would serve either to put traders out of business or drive them into the black market.[55] There is less evidence of the former consequence than of the latter. Much depended on whether the courts would adopt the new penalties. In some notable cases, they clearly did not. Within a month, an Indian director of Uganda Stores Ltd, Kampala, was found guilty on two counts of overcharging and failing to provide an invoice. This was his third conviction. Although the magistrate described Uganda Stores as 'the most persistent black market profiteer in Uganda' and one which was repeatedly 'sabotaging the war effort', the sentence was neither loss of licence nor a term in prison, but a fine of £300.[56] Nor was the campaign against hoarding being waged very vigorously. Known offenders were not being brought before the courts. A year after the 'comprehensive and rigorous' new measures, the *Uganda Herald* gave lengthy coverage to a case where two Africans, acting independently, had identified cases of shopkeepers refusing to sell goods, but the Supply Board had refused to prosecute.[57]

In any case, the new rules did not tackle the heart of the problem. As the Uganda Chamber of Commerce suggested in 1942, greater control at the coast was required to keep prices of imported necessities at a generally lower level.[58] When an Indian retailer near Mbale was convicted for selling nails at three times the legitimate price, his defence was that he had no option but to overcharge since he was forced to buy his goods from overcharging wholesalers.[59] A sympathetic Indian correspondent to the *Herald* took up this theme and accused the government of misdirecting its efforts. Hoarding began with the wealthy wholesaler, he maintained. This damaged the retailer as well as the consumer. The retailer had no real choice: he could not complain to the authorities about the prices demanded by wholesalers, for he would be boycotted; and so he had to pay the inflated prices and pass them on to the consumer. 'The black market thus starts from the top and not in all cases with the small fry'; and yet, the correspondent pointedly continued, 'cases of overcharging before the Uganda courts, so far, have been almost all of petty retail traders'.[60] He concluded that the government needed to prosecute the wholesalers, who withheld stocks or overcharged for them.

In 1943, little was done to intensify the struggle for price control. This was despite the financial secretary's tacit admission that the measures of September 1942 were insufficient, and his acknowledgement that something more effective was still required.[61] In March 1943 a report on the cost of living for government servants in Uganda implied that since the middle of 1942 – ironically, about the time of the introduction of the new measures – there had indeed been hardship.[62] As a result, war bonuses were added to government servants' salaries in 1943.[63] This payment of war bonuses, however, tackled symptom rather than cause. Furthermore, the government paid the bonuses only after repeated calls for such action in the press, and after private firms had led the way.

Once again, in December 1943, when further modifications to wartime price control regulations were eventually made, changes seem to have been prompted as much by press criticism as by direct official experience and response. Increasingly, criticism focussed in 1943 on the question of the enforcement of existing regulations and, specifically, on the shortage of inspectors. It was easier to introduce a succession of price regulations than to enforce any one of them. By mid-1943, the Price Control Inspectorate consisted of just four men. There were repeated calls for more inspectors, including Indians and Africans.

In the wake of such calls, in December 1943 one more new regulation and an expansion of manpower were announced. From January 1 1944, a number of specified goods could be offered for sale only if bearing a mark or label indicating the retail selling price 'marked in plain letters in English'.[64] The list of 18 items represented a catalogue of imported goods bought by Africans: far broader than the 1939 list, it included all household utensils and – a notable omission from its predecessor – bicycles, tyres and spare parts. As for enforcement, this refinement of the regulations was accompanied by an increase in the number of price controllers. There were now to be ten inspectors, concentrated in Buganda where the need was deemed greatest: Mengo District, especially, and Entebbe and Kampala. Meanwhile, all district, agricultural and senior police officers were also declared responsible for control of prices. Lacking trust no doubt in any but their own kind, officials took no action on the suggestion to appoint Indians or Africans.[65]

Meanwhile, the increase in manpower was more apparent than real. We have already seen how district officers, for example, were so heavily laden as to be in practice scarcely capable of assuming any additional responsibilities. Indeed, to a limited extent they had already been involved: it was they who set official maximum prices for their various districts. It was easier to announce a legitimate price (and declare that it be marked on the article concerned) than to police the act of retailing. The new measures and the new manpower failed to achieve the price control which had already proved so elusive.

Mutual recriminations proliferated with the continuation of widespread shortages and profiteering during 1944. The British colonial government appeared to blame, and continued to prosecute, retailers. For their part, retailers continued to blame wholesalers who forced them to raise their prices. Indian importers, in their turn, blamed retailers. Ralli Brothers, who imported cotton, rayon and haircord goods from Britain, paid for a newspaper advertisement which criticised retailers of their goods for selling them 'at prices that are far from justified'.[66] Meanwhile, the president of the Uganda Chamber of Commerce blamed 'rigid bureaucracy' generally, and especially the arrangement whereby Uganda accepted so much of its imports through Kenyan agencies which were allowed a far higher profit margin than any Ugandan firms enjoyed.[67]

On one further occasion, a press campaign appears to have had some effect on the operation of price control. A demand for tougher punishment of offenders seems finally to have led to prison terms being imposed for the first time – after they had been available to the courts for two years. A leader in the *Uganda Herald* on 28 June 1944 argued that the only way to deter 'the big Black Market men' was by removal of licences, confiscation of goods, and a prison sentence. Just one week later, the paper triumphantly reported that an Indian blackmarketeer had been sent to prison, and claimed this was the first time that imprisonment without option of a fine had been imposed for an offence of this nature. The victim of this tougher sentencing did not look like one of 'the Big Men' – he was sentenced to 14 days for hoarding saucepans, and overcharging for them – but this was a success of sorts, and shortly afterwards came another. Two Indian traders of Mengo were convicted for having overcharged for stocks of hoes, sugar and cycle spares. These were perhaps the three items most keenly sought and eagerly purchased by Africans at this time. The traders each received three-week prison terms.[68] Yet there was no evidence that even sterner punishments like these would protect the African consumer from a black market which, by 1944, was firmly established in Uganda.

Already a member of the public had spotted an emperor with no clothes. 'It seems rather strange', wrote this correspondent to the *Herald*, 'for the well organised state like ours not to be able to overcome this evil .... Such an inability on the part of the state is amazing'.[69] This 'evil' was hoarding and profiteering on the black market. Voices, including those of African consumers, were raised in protest throughout the war at the British failure to control distribution and prices. Letters to the press achieved little for African consumers however, and were eventually, in January 1945, superseded by action on the streets.

How serious was the profiteering? During the period of the so-called 'comprehensive system of price control', from mid-1940 to mid-1942, the black market and profiteering which had started in 1939 flourished. Press coverage reveals something of the extent of this *absence* of price control. The *Uganda Herald* regularly carried reports of cases of overcharging, and of related crimes such as withholding stocks, not issuing invoices, or attempting to bribe the police to avoid prosecution. The scale of overcharging varied: price increases of 25, 50 and 100 per cent were frequently reported, while on some occasions consumers were charged many times the maximum permitted price. An Indian in Mbale in September 1942 charged 80 cents for a tube of Dunlop puncture solution, when the official price was 17 cents, while another Indian had earlier been convicted in Masindi for charging 100 cents (one shilling) for a similar article.[70] Such reported court cases were complemented by plentiful letters on the same subject. A correspondent complained in January 1942 that it was becoming impossible to buy 'cycle solution' and alleged that both Indian and African shopkeepers had the tubes in stock but were refusing to sell them for less than 1/50, which was about 9 times the legal price.[71]

The detailed if incomplete information that we have from the press can indicate something of the extent of the problem. For example, an Indian convicted in Kampala in March 1942 asked for 53 other, similar, counts to be taken into consideration.[72] Are we to deduce from this example that fewer than 2 per cent of cases came to light? We cannot be sure, but when two other Indians were convicted later that month, for overcharging for cigarettes and bicycle rubber solution, the magistrate drew attention to 'the prevalence' of such cases.[73]

The Protectorate government was a victim of circumstances;

but one could argue that the British administration did not make prosecutions an urgent enough priority. On a daily basis the African consumer was suffering, even if the items and sums concerned seem small. In the 70 or so cases of profiteering in town centres recorded in the *Uganda Herald* between mid-1940 and the end of 1942, the goods concerned were primarily for African consumption. Most frequently involved (about a quarter of the total) were bicycle parts, especially the rubber solution required to mend punctures. And bicycles were no mere luxury. On the ground-floor of Uganda's economy, they carried goods to market and they carried men to work, at a time when bus services were being curtailed and motor vehicles lacked workable spare parts. Other items for which African purchasers appear from this evidence to have been overcharged at this time included, in order of frequency of press mention: matches, cigarettes, soap, kerosene, cloth and nails. The aggregate of shortages and price increases acted as a disincentive to labour and production, and also reinforced a sense of grievance.

It was not only Africans in the towns who suffered. Peasant farmers who produced export crops perhaps experienced a less serious rise in their cost of living than town-dwellers in the later years of the war, but they did have to endure acute shortages, and they seem to have suffered from a near total lack of effective price control. In 1943, an African cultivator drew public attention to the situation in the countryside. 'Control of prices is quite a good thing if it is done reasonably, and everything would be alright if the prices of hoes and other imported things had not gone up considerably, and if there was no such evil as black-marketing and profiteering in our village dukas where there is practically no check on these evils'.[74]

Again, a greater racial consciousness is perceptible in some contemporary comments. A regular African correspondent wrote in July 1943 that 'profiteering has now become a national pastime with shopkeepers, particularly with Indians'. A subsequent letter from the same source distributed blame rather more widely – 'The Indian dukawallah is second to none in underhand business. The African is a close runner-up'[75]. However, there was an increasing tendency in discussion of the issue to imply that overcharging retailers were Indians.

One correspondent wrote of 'the extreme difficulty we Africans experience in buying certain goods. It is not a question of lack of supplies.... The shopkeeper will not sell them'. He could buy matches, he complained, 'only after many long prayers to the Indian deity in charge of the shop'. He concluded: 'The Indian shop-keeper is very cunning'; and he proposed to 'set an Indian to catch an Indian'.[76] This letter, notwithstanding its explicit racial dimension, was singled out for editorial support in the *Uganda Herald*. The leader made no attempt to challenge the assumption that Indians were to blame, and insisted 'there is no doubt whatever that this injustice to Africans is being practised on a very wide scale by a large number of shopkeepers today'. Some government measures possibly served to heighten racial consciousness. For example, in January 1944 Africans in Kampala were told to buy their sugar from any one of fourteen authorised retailers – all of whom were Indian. An anonymous critic subsequently accused Indians of victimising 'helpless and uninformed natives', and called for government-run outlets or registered African sugar retailers.[77]

On the question of the racial identity of profiteers, the columns of the *Uganda Herald* are illuminating, if tantalisingly inconclusive. Of the price control cases reported in the 24 months up to the end of 1942, Indian defendants outnumbered African by about 3 to 1. This may reflect actual malpractice. It is also possible that British authorities were choosing to concentrate their attention on the Indians and present them as scapegoats, but without sufficient evidence this remains speculation. In fact, during the next year, 1943, the number of Africans convicted was very nearly on a par with the number of Indians. This suggests not only an increase in small-scale trading by Africans during the Second World War but also that profiteering was not exclusive to any single racial group. In 1944, the apparent Indian/African ratio in prosecutions returned to around the 3 to 1 of the earlier war period. Cases in which Europeans were prosecuted were rare, though there was an instance of a European retailer being prosecuted for not displaying his prices.[78] It may be that the overall balance of prosecutions corresponds with the racial balance of involvement in commerce.

Very much more important than the actual figures, at the time and since, was the perception among Africans that they were being exploited by Indian traders on an unprecedented scale. Shortly after the Second World War an emotional attack on the Indians was published in the Luganda press. The writer claimed that the Indians 'rob us and make us poor. They are a millstone weighing many pounds around the neck of the African, and which would destroy us the people of Uganda. They trick us and they rob us saying that they are selling goods to us reasonably at proper prices whereas in fact they are profiteering'.[79] Smuggling rackets were meanwhile known to the authorities. When Nairobi made an urgent appeal for groundnuts for the army in 1942, the Chief Secretary in Entebbe replied by telegram that there were 'no groundnuts available' in Uganda. But a junior official was subsequently to report that three Indian firms had been sending groundnuts to Nairobi by train, into private sidings, hidden among other items. 'These people', he concluded, 'are moving heaven and earth to smuggle them out'.[80] It would seem that the wartime experience of badly interrupted supply, rising world prices and local profiteering could catch the official eye, as well as nourish a more general racial antagonism in Uganda which was to remain long into the post-war period.

The failure of price control had particular significance in 1944, the year preceding the disturbances. The themes were by now familiar, the variations slight. As many prosecutions for profiteering and related crimes were reported in the *Uganda Herald* during the first 10 months of 1944, as had been reported throughout 1941 and 1942 combined. Cases involving bicycle spares remained especially common. At the same time, imported hoes were by now scarce and highly priced. This represented a particularly serious problem for peasant cash-crop exporters and subsistence farmers in the rural areas; and for Africans working in, and residing on the edge of, the towns. Here was a further brake on Uganda's economic activity. In this year of famine in East Africa, however, most reported profiteering cases concerned sugar, while overcharging for other local foods like sweet potatoes and matooke also increased.

A note of urgency, even despair, entered the columns of the *Her-*

ald. In March 1944, for example, it was being claimed that 'in some places, an African cannot obtain any food at all unless he pays well in excess of controlled prices'.[81] Another editorial in June 1944 insisted that 'the Black Market is still flourishing in Uganda'.[82] By now, with the supply situation beginning to ease, price control was becoming a more urgent consideration than import control in the waging of 'total war'. 'However strongly the authorities might seek to deny it, it is an indisputable fact', claimed the editorial, 'that there is practically no article of everyday use – foodstuffs, medicines, clothing, even luxury goods – that cannot be bought in the Black Market in Kampala and other towns in Uganda if you know where to go'.

At the start of 1945, there was dramatic irony in the by now regular New Year editorial on price control. It represented a sustained indictment of the Protectorate government's record: 'We have had some sort of price control ... since the early days of the war but ... the regulations existing here do not in practice give much protection. There are too many loopholes for unscrupulous traders to exploit. Much more vigour is needed in enforcing the regulations. Once they were safely on paper, a sort of official inertia set in. Too many traders are breaking the law with impunity'. It concluded, just a week before the strikes, that 'the great mass of people' were shouldering an unnecessary burden.[83]

In its attempts at price control, the British colonial state in Uganda had very little freedom of movement. It operated in a context which was always unfavourable. It had of course no more influence over world economic conditions during the Second World War than it had had during the 1930s depression. These conditions progressively worsened, at least to 1942. Thereafter, availability of some commodities improved but world prices continued to rise. At the end of 1944, the Financial Secretary was drawing attention to 'the considerable increase in the landed cost of imported goods'.[84] Moreover, in the later years of the war, Nairobi-based institutions underlined the merely peripheral competence of the British Ugandan administration within East Africa.

And as we have seen, this was a state crippled by manpower shortage at a time of ever increasing demands. Effective price control at the point of sale would have required numbers of suitable personnel which simply did not exist: whether official or unofficial, and whether European, Indian or African. This problem of numbers was critical and insuperable. The available price inspectors and other officers had the responsibility for controlling a multitude of transactions which in practice they could not observe or count. They could measure neither the scale of the problem nor the level of their success in tackling it. And as Shuckburgh was to point out, 'no machinery existed at the time for calculating fluctuations in the African cost of living' (1948: vol. ii p 227).

But the British colonial state in Uganda did not even fulfil the limited potential for action which it did have. The bureaucracy achieved little and the manpower available might have been more effectively used, not least in touring the shops and recording stocks. Alternatively, one might argue that, by focussing on the retailer, British officials restricted what they could achieve. The profiteering started elsewhere and, this being so, occasionally successful prosecutions of retailers merely led to the redirection of goods to new outlets. Though energetic at the outset, the British administration thereafter proved sluggish and complacent, apparently persuaded to act only by cries of complaint and criticism from outside its ranks. It was left to the English-speaking press, well informed through its correspondence columns by an African as well as an Indian and European public, to remind the British administration that profiteering was flourishing throughout the war, in town and country, and in local goods as well as imports.

There was also a particular local political reason why the Protectorate government did not enjoy freedom of action in its war against rising prices. A consistent dimension of official price control policy and its operation during the Second World War was the close association of British officials with the unofficial commercial community, whose members served from the outset on the Supply Board and its sub-committees. The interests of established traders were thereby safeguarded in the regulations. From early in 1940, the Mengo District Commissioner was being advised on price levels by a panel appointed by the Uganda Chamber of Commerce; and maximum prices were to respect not only the Supply Board's price but also pre-war profit margins. In June 1942 a Standing Committee was appointed, consisting wholly of unofficials, to carry out the 'day to day business' of the Supply Board. There was no ambiguity of official intention here. The Standing Committee was to concern itself with questions of interpretation and application of regulations and control – routine and recurring problems which demanded immediate and expert attention – 'in the interests of the commercial community' ('War Effort' [5] October 1942). In August 1942, 'normal' profit margins were dropped as an official criterion for price-fixing; but the partnership of officials and unofficials continued.

The significance of these arrangements goes beyond the obvious point that some members of the commercial community were better able thereby to protect their interests. When a senior British government official expressed his appreciation of 'the active co-operation of the commercial community', we may confidently assume there was reciprocation.[85] A contemporary comment from the public in Uganda was less charitable: 'The Control machinery is directed under the advice of big business and it is natural that this branch of commerce will seek more protection for itself than for the small trader and consumer'.[86] Even so, a degree of partnership did not protect the British administration from criticism from an expatriate community which was by no means monolithic at this time.

In this context of wartime shortages in Uganda, we may finally note evidence of some rather inconsistent perceptions in an administration exposed as ever to competing political priorities. On the one hand, when the Supply Board was considering in 1943 how to allocate some scarce building materials, they opted to appease expatriates. 'Strong opinions were likely to be held by the public', it conceded, on the question of whether an African church upcountry or a cinema for Europeans in Entebbe should have priority. Adopting sound Benthamite principles, and deftly answering its own question while asking it, the committee decided that it 'would be guided solely by the greatest good of the greatest number: would it be more in the public interest to provide light relaxation for many hundreds of non-natives strained under war-time conditions, or to improve the amenities for worship of several dozen Africans?'[87] It is evident, in this somewhat un-Livingstonian policy preference, which 'public' mattered most.

On the other hand, there was already real concern among some officials at the possible consequences of a sustained supply crisis. In January 1943, a letter was sent out by Entebbe to all district commissioners, urging them 'to keep HQ carefully informed of any important developments of the supply position in their districts and the effect of such developments on African opinion'. And provincial commissioners were 'to draw attention to any economic unrest or disturbance' arising from 'such factors and influences as shortage of customary trade goods and the higher prices of piece–goods'.[88] Such perceptions perhaps serve to illustrate further the gradual shift of official concern from expatriate opinion to native African opinion. They also prove that, however reluctant the administration was to admit later that there were profound economic causes of the disturbances in January 1945, one or two individual officials at least were not entirely unaware of them.

And yet the administration as a whole seems still to have been removed from reality and not to have responded to the failure of its price control policies. General European detachment from the perspective of the consumer, especially the town-dwelling African, persisted. The evidence is clear: in addition to officially sanctioned and acknowledged wartime price rises, the consumer faced escalating rises at the hands of the profiteer, resented all the more when this was an Indian. We cannot of course precisely measure the scale of the black market – for which sound overall statistics are unavailable. Yet we may conclude that the Protectorate government failed to recognise the extent and importance of the hardship suffered by African consumers at the time. This was a failure not only of competence but of imagination, and it was to prove costly.

---

1. Letter, *Uganda Herald*, 29 November 1939.
2. Secretary of State to the Colonies, 5 June 1941, paras. 1, 3, PRO CO 854/120

3. Dundas to Moyne, 29 July 1941, PRO CO 536/208/40100/1941
4. Official note, *Uganda Herald*, 9 July 1941.
5. Report, *Uganda Herald*, 25 November 1942.
6. Official note, *Uganda Herald*, 22 July 1942.
7. *ibid*.
8. Financial Secretary, Memorandum on the 1943 Draft Estimates, PRO CO 536/208/111/30
9. R.Kasim (Indian member of the Kenya Legislative Council), letter, *Uganda Herald*, 6 January 1943
10. Report, *Uganda Herald*, 10 May 1944
11. Report, *East Africa and Rhodesia*, 12 April 1945 – which may be located in the papers of C.H.Bird, RH MSS Afr.s.1674.
12. Editorial, *Uganda Herald*, 9 June 1943
13. Editorial, *Uganda Herald*, 6 October 1943
14. EAPSC Minutes, 12 January 1944, PRO CO 537/1525
15. Hall to Secretary of State, 8 February 1945, PRO CO 822/114/10
16. Bird to Joelson, 5 June 1945, C.H.Bird, Papers.
17. Annual Trade Reports of Kenya and Uganda, in the yearly Blue Books.
18. See, for example, Bird to Joelson, 22 December 1944.
19. Bird to Joelson, 5 June 1945.
20. Editorial, *Uganda Herald*, 15 March 1944.
21. Official communique, *Uganda Herald*, 26 August 1942.
22. R. Kasim, letter, *Uganda Herald*, 8 July 1942.
23. Chief Secretary to the Legislative Council, 9 December 1942.
24. *Uganda Herald*, 19 August 1942.
25. UIC note, *Uganda Herald*, 8 March 1944.
26. 'Trade Prospects and Opportunities in Uganda', 1954, Bird Papers.
27. UIC Review, *Uganda Herald*, 28 July 1943.
28. Financial Secretary to the Legislative Council, 9 December 1942.
29. Details of volumes of imports can be found in successive war-time official *Blue Books*.
30. P.K.Wajjayu, letter, *Uganda Herald*, 20 January 1943.
31. Editorial, *Uganda Herald*, 6 October 1943.
32. Advertisement, *Uganda Herald*, 9 February 1944.
33. 'Hall to the Legislative Council, reported in *Uganda Herald*, 20 June 1945.
34. Note, *Uganda Herald*, 2 February 1944.
35. Uganda Protectorate Secretarial Minute Paper, R 120, Uganda National Archive, Entebbe.
36. Report, *Uganda Herald*, 5 April 1944.

37. Official note, *Uganda Herald*, 14 January 1942.

38. *Uganda Gazette*, 31 March 1942.

39. P.K.Wajjayu, letter, *Uganda Herald*, 20 January 1943.

40. Acting Financial Secretary, Memorandum on the Draft 1941 Estimates, PRO CO 536/206/40100.

41. Official note, *Uganda Herald*, 25 March 1942.

42. *Uganda Gazette*, 29 April 1944.

43. Official note, *Uganda Herald*, 30 August 1939.

44. *Uganda Gazette*, 17 October 1939.

45. Mitchell to the Legislative Council, 29 November 1939.

46. Reports, *Uganda Herald*, 20 September 1939, 20 March 1940, 10 April 1940.

47. *Uganda Gazette*, 31 August 1940.

48. Official note, *Uganda Herald*, 2 September 1942.

49. Report, *Uganda Herald*, 25 December 1940.

50. Report, *Uganda Herald*, 20 August 1941.

51. Report, *Uganda Herald*, 4 March 1942.

52. Editorial note, *Uganda Herald*, 19 August 1942.

53. Dundas to the Legislative Council, 9 December 1942.

54. Official note, *Uganda Herald*, 2 September 1942.

55. Letter to the Price Controller, published in *Uganda Herald*, 7 October 1942.

56. Report, *Uganda Herald*, 23 September 1942.

57. Editorial, *Uganda Herald*, 22 September 1943.

58. Annual Report of the Uganda Chamber of Commerce, published in *Uganda Herald*, 18 February 1942.

59. Report, *Uganda Herald*, 1 July 1942.

60. M.Khairu, letter, *Uganda Herald*, 4 November 1942.

61. Financial Secretary to the Legislative Council, 9 December 1942.

62. Quoted in editorial, *Uganda Herald*, 31 March 1943.

63. Editorial, *Uganda Herald*, 31 March 1943.

64. *Uganda Gazette*, 15 December 1943.

65. Editorial, *Uganda Herald*, 28 June 1944.

66. *Uganda Herald*, 3 January 1945.

67. President's Report to the AGM of the UGC, reported in *Uganda Herald*, 16 February 1944.

68. Report, *Uganda Herald*, 20 September 1944.

69. Anonymous letter, *Uganda Herald*, 11 August 1943.

70. Reports, *Uganda Herald*, 3 June 1942, 16 September, 1942.

71. Anonymous letter, *Uganda Herald*, 28 January 1942.

72. Report, *Uganda Herald*, 4 March 1942.
73. Report, *Uganda Herald*, 18 March 1942.
74. P.K.Wajjayu letter, *Uganda Herald*, 20 January 1943.
75. G.Kay letters, *Uganda Herald*, 7 July 1943, 8 September, 1943.
76. 'Patriot' (anonymous African) letter, *Uganda Herald*, 11 August 1943.
77. Letter, *Uganda Herald*, 1 March 1944.
78. Report, *Uganda Herald*, 22 March 1944.
79. G.R.Gizza, *Gambuze*, 26 April 1946; reproduced in D.A.Low *The Mind of Buganda*, 1971, pp. 131-132.
80. Uganda Protectorate Secretarial Minute Paper F 23/26/40, Uganda National Archive, Entebbe.
81. Editorial, *Uganda Herald*, 22 March 1944.
82. Editorial, *Uganda Herald*, 28 June 1944.
83. Editorial, *Uganda Herald*, 10 January 1945.
84. Financial Secretary to the Legislative Council, 15 December 1944.
85. Financial Secretary to the Legislative Council, 9 December 1942.
86. M.Khairu letter, *Uganda Herald*, 4 November 1942.
87. Minutes of the Twelfth meeting of the Standing Committee of the Uganda Supply Board, 11 June 1943, F 78/2/7, Uganda National Archive, Entebbe.
88. Note from the Financial Secretary to the Assistant Chief Secretary, 6 November 1942, F 78/108, Uganda National Archive, Entebbe.

11
The Struggle for Mastery in Buganda

Introduction

During the course of the Second World War, the British colonial state in Uganda all but lost control of its most important province: the African kingdom of Buganda. We have already noted features of the peculiar relationship between this kingdom and the Protectorate government, established and built on during the earlier twentieth century. This convenient relationship endured until around 1939. At its core lay a mutual dependency – a 'collaboration' in the morally neutral sense defined earlier, in the introduction to this study, based on shared or complementary interests. There was, at the overtly political level, British interaction with Ganda chiefs and landlords; and, at the economic level, general British promotion of African consumption and production.

The context of world war made the exercise of British authority in Buganda immensely more difficult. The mobilisation of men, money and materials brought Ganda chiefs into ever closer contact with their people as interventionist agents of British colonial rulers. Such contacts provided greater scope for friction and grievance. Moreover, the failure of the British administration's attempts to wage 'total war' served over time further to undermine its local standing, as consumer goods became scarce and prices soared. We have noted that there were already elements of discord and uncertainty by 1939, both within Buganda itself and between Buganda and the Protectorate government. Global war after 1939 aggravated these tensions. Issues were now sharpened, as the priorities and values of rulers and ruled came into conflict. Consent broke down.

While all this was happening, British administrators also unwittingly contributed to their weakening position in the kingdom. On three occasions, and over issues which did not directly arise out of the war, the colonial state in Uganda was gravely weakened by the flawed political judgement and initiatives of its senior British personnel. The war was responsible for taking away Governor Philip Mitchell in 1940, and many other expatriate officers too. But it was not inevitable that a new British governor and his much reduced staff would have so seriously mishandled three issues: first, the Namasole Affair in 1941; secondly, the land question; and, thirdly, the introduction of a new constitution for Buganda in 1944.

The decline of British authority in Buganda in this period may thus be said to have resulted partly from the Second World War, and partly from the incompetence of the British administration. At the heart of the matter, however, was a problem which appeared to have no solution. In its political form, the problem lay in the existence of Buganda as a distinct kingdom, reconstituted on its incorporation within the British colonial state of Uganda under the 1900 Agreement. As we have seen, before 1939, British officials were already finding it difficult in practice to manage the kingdom's affairs; and there was a broader constitutional, even theoretical, dimension too. As the institutions of this kingdom proved increasingly inimical to sustaining British interests during the Second World War, and incapable of containing its own emergent political forces, the British colonial authorities in Uganda were confronted as never before by the ultimate question posed by 'indirect' rule. How would it evolve? Or, in Buganda: how could the native government be transformed by British initiative into a more adaptable and pliable organ of colonial rule?

The issues which divided Baganda and British during the Second World War can be understood only by reference to the institutions and personalities of Ganda politics at the time.[1] Buganda was a hereditary monarchy; but political power within it was diffuse and fragmented. The king or *Kabaka* exercised his power through a number of selected ministers, notably the Treasurer (*Omuwanika*), the Chief Justice (*Omulamuzi*) and a Prime Minister (*Katikkiro*). Below these stood a hierarchy of chiefs appointed and promoted on the Kabaka's authority, though with the approval of the British Protectorate government. The parliament of Buganda was the *Lukiiko*. Originally the Kabaka's council, its position was formalised in the 1900 Agreement. The label 'parliament' must be applied to it with considerable caution, however. The Lukiiko represented and protected the interests only of the chiefs and large landowners, themselves essentially a class of officials. They were perceived by the British locally to be 'an extremely privileged class'.[2] In this 'parliament' the elective element was entirely lacking. Following a minor change in 1939 the Kabaka was to nominate one non-official from each of the twenty counties of the kingdom, but even after the greater reform in 1945 the 89-man Lukiiko was still primarily a chiefs' body.

The British official presence within Buganda was slight indeed. It was the 20 county (*saza*) chiefs, and the 175 sub-county (*gombolola*) chiefs, and the numerous parish *(miruka)* chiefs below them, who administered the kingdom. From the early days of British colonial rule, these chiefs were required – as elsewhere in the protectorate – to be its active agents. 'Chiefs became responsible to a government over and beyond their own ruler and were expected by that government to interfere in all kinds of ways in the lives of ordinary people'(Mair 1962: 222). They were collectors of taxes, local guardians of order and law and, like latterday *intendants*, general functionaries charged with the overseeing of everything from road maintenance to dispensaries, from cotton production to liquor licences. Their responsibilities were to be further multiplied and their interventions in local life made still more generally unwelcome during the course of the Second World War.

Dundas considered that the Ganda chiefs were 'selected purely on personal merit'(1941: para. 6). However, E.M.K.Mulira, not himself a chief but a Muganda and a closer observer than the governor, was to challenge this assumption and to cite 'the whole system of chieftainship' as a major cause of unrest in Buganda in the 1940s. In his portrait, patronage – and not merit – was the prime mechanism of an essentially unfair process. Clerks on the humble fringes of government service could indeed hope to become chiefs, but according to Mulira not in any open competition but through 'favouritism'(1950: 31).

In the absence of elections and of party, factionalism and personal rivalries pervaded Ganda politics and made British influence in the kingdom increasingly difficult to sustain. Divisions arose which had origins in the pre-colonial past or in the modernising effects of colonial rule itself. There were tensions between Catholics and Protestants; and between older conservatives and younger products of secondary and higher education. Rural class struggle (of tenants against landlords) seems not to have persisted in Buganda to any considerable extent after British intervention on behalf of the peasantry in 1927. Instead, the major divisions tended to crystallise over specific issues, which had in common what we may term 'the colonial dimension'. In the 1920s such issues were the early proposals for 'closer union' with Kenya, or the fall of Katikkiro Apolo Kagwa after a dramatic clash with British officialdom. In such a context, factional struggles within Buganda's political nation focussed increasingly on the divisive question of the 'loyalty' of leading protagonists – 'loyalty' to historic Buganda, or 'loyalty' to efficiency and progress as defined and prompted by British administrators.

To heighten the significance of such struggles, the 'middle class' (noted by Lord Hailey at the time) of perhaps 50,000 larger farmers, traders and skilled workers, comprised (or at least included) aggrieved and politically conscious Baganda with little stake in the existing social-political establishment (Fallers 1964: 187). Many of these Ganda farmers and traders were frustrated by their restricted roles in the cotton industry and in commerce, and by their enjoying no voice of their own in the Lukiiko. They tended to resent British policy and practice – and sought the removal of senior Baganda whose collaboration with British overrule struck them as subservience and disloyalty. It was claimed in one popular pamphlet that 'Europeans have their own agents amongst our own selves who report to them matters: who are in receipt of large remunerations, and who are promoted to respectable chieftainships in our country, whereas they are actually the traitors'.[3]

The only officially recognised trade union in Uganda, the Uganda African Motor Drivers Association (UAMDA), was preoccupied from its foundation in 1938 with political affairs in Buganda. According to David Apter, 'For the first time the younger elements around Kampala, particularly motor drivers, were brought into close liaison with those whose economic grievances were strong and whose antipathy to the Buganda government leaders had reached a new high' (Apter 1961: 204). In the early 1940s, the leaders of the UAMDA, James Kivu and Ignatius Musazi, did not lack mutually reinforcing support within the hierarchy. Moreover, James Kivu's correspondence during the war years with Rita Hinden of the Fabian Colonial Bureau in London demonstrated clearly how the political energies of Baganda could no longer be contained solely within the established institutions of the kingdom.[4]

Musazi, too, was later to develop contacts with foreigners in pursuit of his causes. His activities are of considerable interest and significance. He achieved early wartime notoriety when in 1940 he was convicted for acts of deception linked to his campaigning. First he petitioned on behalf of Africans wishing to break an Indian monopoly of certain bus routes; secondly, he petitioned against the appointment of three Baganda ministers to the regency for the young Kabaka, Mutesa II. A former teacher at Budo and assistant school inspector, Musazi became a prominent critic of Indians and of the Baganda establishment – and of the British government, too. When a British judge upheld the sentence passed on him in Buganda, he spoke of Musazi in headmasterly tones typical of disappointed paternalism. 'He has had the benefit of a good education, and has seen fit to make use of this advantage for the purpose of imposing upon the less enlightened of his fellow natives in order to endeavour to deceive the government'. He went on to describe Musazi's alleged criminal methods of collecting signatures and petitioning the Kabaka and the governor as 'a wicked and dangerous offence'.[5]

But at heart, this was simply politics. In the 1940s, Musazi both represented and personified critical African opinion on a whole range of central issues. [He was shortly to be deported from Buganda in the wake of the January 1945 disturbances, in which he had participated.] Less obviously, he also demonstrates the relative lack of ruthlessness of the Protectorate government in dealing with the perennial problem of articulate political criticism. The regime tolerated irritants such as Musazi – to the extent, for example, that he was released in October 1946 following his 1945 conviction, and was thus free to further his career. He helped in 1947 to form the Uganda African Farmers' Union, and once again articulated wide-ranging criticisms of the Buganda and British governments during the major troubles of 1949. By 1952 he was campaigning across the territory on behalf of the newly formed Uganda National Congress; by 1957 he was an outspoken member of the Protectorate's Legislative Council. In the event, he was not silenced. If colonial regimes can be said – in parallel with the bourgeoisie in Karl Marx's analysis – to have brought into being their own 'grave-diggers', Musazi's relationship with the British in Uganda looks like a case in point.

To the increasing discomfiture of British officials, such Ganda outsiders and critics concentrated their political attacks in the late 1930s and early 1940s on two men in particular who still served Britain well: the Katikkiro, Martin Luther Nsibirwa, and the Omuwanika, Serwano Kulubya. Kulubya had insisted on rigorous tax collection and the rooting out of peculation throughout the 1930s depression. This helped to make him 'the chief butt of agitators' in Buganda (Welbourn 1961:22). His acceptability to the European community, on the other hand, was shown when in 1942 he became the first African President of the Uganda Society, and in the same year was awarded the MBE. Mitchell regarded Kulubya as 'shrewd and good'.[6] To James Kivu, however, Kulubya was a 'trickster' in league with the Resident.[7] At the same time, as Katikkiro of Buganda, Nsibirwa sustained Apolo Kagwa's tradition of leadership in both state and Anglican church in Buganda. He and Kulubya had both been friends of Kagwa; and Apter portrays them as all appearing in the same mould of 'firm, capable, progressive, autocrat' (1961: 183). Both Nsibirwa and Kulubya were widely regarded as 'men of character' by officers of the Protectorate government.

Unfortunately for the British colonial state, it was just this reputation which brought into question their acceptability within Buganda. Both were unable, or unwilling, to satisfy the demands of aspiring entrepreneurs. Thus the 'Sons of Kintu' had come into being in 1938, 'with the primary aim of securing the dismissal of Nsibirwa and

Kulubya' (Welbourn 1961: 26). Musazi had been the first secretary of this organisation, closely linked with the frustrated Bataka movement of the 1920s. The 'Sons of Kintu' joined and intensified attacks on the two ministers, stirring up support at parish level for chiefs in the anti-Nsibirwa and anti-Kulubya factions in the hierarchy. As Lucy Mair points out, local chiefs in such factions learned that they, unlike chiefs loyal to the British, should not 'disturb the tranquillity of life by harassing their people with orders from outside authorities' (1962: 224). It made sense for lower-level chiefs to lie low. Meanwhile, the 'Sons of Kintu' enjoyed widespread support in Buganda. Although they were labelled by Lord Hailey as 'far from representative', even Hailey admitted that three out of seven vernacular newspapers in Buganda supported them (1944: 189).

The Namasole affair

The first of the three great wartime issues was the Namasole Affair, which erupted in 1941. This was two years after the Second World War began; but its genesis owed nothing to the new global context, and everything to the peculiarities of the situation in Buganda. By the end of the 1930s, the British potential for directing political affairs in the kingdom was already open to question, and mutual confidence was giving way to suspicion among many Baganda. Indeed, the situation was highly unstable. Kabaka Daudi Chwa had ceased to interest himself in the affairs of his state and indeed had virtually retired, spending most of his time at his country palace. Long overshadowed by his ministers, he now 'became a rallying point for intrigue' against them.[8] Daudi Chwa resisted the Buganda Native Courts Ordinance which his ministers accepted in 1940. This matter was typical of the period. Substantially, it involved the posting of European magistrates to areas where hitherto saza and gombolola courts had enjoyed full jurisdiction; symbolically, to men such as Kivu it represented a further undermining of the Kabaka's position in the kingdom and of the 1900 Agreement itself.[9] Relations between Daudi Chwa and Governor Mitchell had deteriorated by 1939 to the point when Mitchell boycotted the Kabaka's birthday celebration and was even considering his exile.

It was as much by his death in November 1939 as by his reign that Daudi Chwa was to have an impact on the affairs of his kingdom. The succession – by his 15 year old son Mutesa – was controversial. Mutesa, as one colonial official confided to the Fabian Colonial Bureau, 'was an unpopular choice from the first: public opinion was almost wholly in favour of his half-brother, Mawanda'.[10] In the eyes of the Anglican church, however, Mawanda was illegitimate; and the Anglican church, the Protectorate government and, notable among others, Serwano Kulubya, ensured that the succession passed to Mutesa II. This did not prevent Mutesa's uncle, Prince Suna, from directing a campaign against Mutesa – and against Kulubya – which was supported by saza chiefs such as Samwiri Wamala and his faction.[11] Daudi Chwa's death and the succession of a minor required a regency. This appeared to suit the Protectorate government well enough, since it meant that responsibility remained with ministers with whom it had already been co-operating fruitfully, and in particular with Nsibirwa and Kulubya.

This regency, however, was to mark not the consolidation but the near evaporation of British influence in Buganda. Within two years Nsibirwa fell from power, essentially as a casualty of the Namasole Affair. This affair arose from another indirect consequence of Daudi Chwa's death, the remarriage of his widow, the Queen Mother (Namasole). This re-marriage was contrary to Ganda custom. It was acceptable, however, to the Anglican church, which approved the Namasole's remarriage and thus for the second time in two years appeared to be interfering with Ganda practice. It was supported, too, by Katikkiro Nsibirwa. Nsibirwa's enemies seized upon the issue to challenge his remaining in office, and the Lukiiko demanded his resignation. In July 1941 he was forced out and succeeded as 'prime minister' by Samwiri Wamala, the Lukiiko's choice. This episode proved to be a milestone in the history of relations between the kingdom of Buganda and the Protectorate government. For the Muganda author E.M.K. Mulira, it was 'the greatest storm this century' (1950: 23). For the British official Temple-Perkins, it was 'a crisis of the first magnitude' (1946: 118).

The episode was so important because, first, here was an issue

– the remarriage of the Namasole, to the commoner Simon Peter Kigozi – which symbolised the cultural gulf between Ganda traditionalism and 'progressive' British, or Anglican, values. In supporting the Anglican Church's position on the remarriage, Nsibirwa could be labelled disloyal and charged with failing to defend Buganda's cultural identity. According to one Muganda source, Nsibirwa was dismissed for 'breaking our nation's custom deliberately'.[12] Four years later, in Temple-Perkins' view he was 'still a marked man owing to his support of the remarriage' (1946: 141).

Secondly, the affair revealed the new assertiveness and effective power of the Lukiiko. It was unprecedented for chiefs in the Lukiiko to force the resignation of a minister and to choose his successor from among their own number. And the minister thus removed was one of two dominant figures in a regency closely identified with British colonial rule and which the British themselves had welcomed. In 1944 the Lukiiko was to pose another obstinate challenge to the Protectorate government on the question of land – by which time Governor Dundas had observed that this body had become 'the real and ultimate authority ... against whose wishes neither the Kabaka nor his Ministers and Chiefs can act' (1941: para. 6).

Thirdly, the Namasole Affair held great significance for the future of the British colonial state in Uganda. Relations between the kingdom of Buganda and the Protectorate government centred on effective co-operation of Baganda ministers and chiefs with British authority. Yet – as with chiefs all over British Africa – the more co-operative and interventionist such Baganda were, especially during the Second World War, the more they tended to alienate themselves from their own people. This was only one of the inherent contradictions in the Britain/Buganda relationship. Another lay in the fact that there was no mechanism for any guided evolution of Buganda's institutions. Governor Dundas inherited this problematical situation – and made it worse. Dundas had been in Uganda for only seven months, and had been wedded to the notion of 'indirect rule' on his arrival. This was because of his previous experience as a District Commissioner and Secretary for Native Affairs in Tanganyika in the 1920s. Since then he had been removed from the theory and practice of indirect rule by subsequent service in the Bahamas. Now, committed to the 1900 Agreement, Dundas appears to have hoped that a fully responsible Lukiiko would somehow usher in a form of parliamentary democracy in Buganda. Consequently, Dundas declined to step in to save Nsibirwa. The Katikkiro had indeed been a good servant of the British; but the Lukiiko appeared to be behaving like the parliament Dundas wanted, in removing a minister who no longer enjoyed its confidence. Dundas did nothing.

But Dundas's inaction served as a 'most important impetus to political agitation and to personal intrigue' in the kingdom (Pratt 1960: 277). In sacrificing Nsibirwa, Dundas had legitimised the growing authority of the Lukiiko, where opinion hostile to British interests was now dominant. This Lukiiko approved as his replacement Wamala, who was said to have 'a largely irrational dislike of European influence'.[13] Moreover, in accepting this, Dundas undermined the position not only of one Katikkiro, but of all loyal chiefs, who clearly now could no longer be confident of British support. He had thus sown 'a dangerous seed', encouraging challenges to other pro-British collaborators (Mulira 1950: 35). Ganda chiefs would now naturally deduce that courting support among their own people – if only by inactivity – was a better insurance policy for remaining in office than was active service under the Protectorate government. As a later British Resident noted when seeking the origins of the major crisis of 1949, the Namasole Affair 'showed that an unpopular official could be forced out of office if he lost the support of his fellow chiefs'.[14] The Protectorate government had acquiesced in this, and failed to stand by its man.

Not only the British colonial state but also the Anglican Church suffered. Bishop Stuart wrote of the Namasole Affair: 'The Government weakly gave way. I begged them to be firm'.[15] They were not. British authority was thus now being challenged not only at a political level but also at a religious level, and at a more broadly cultural one too. There was another illustration of this the following year, not far from Kampala, at King's College, Budo, the protectorate's pre-eminent (Protestant) boys' secondary school. Budo's intake of pupils was overwhelmingly Baganda. Here could be seen the cultural clash within Buganda in microcosm: on April 6 1942, a Mr Kaima lectured on the keeping of tribal customs while, on the same day, the headmaster gave a lecture an English table manners. Later in 1942, in the strained context of wartime shortages, relations between headmaster and staff finally broke down. A portrait of George VI was smashed, torn, and abandoned on the cricket field. Arson and riot followed this symbolic gesture, and then resignations and sackings, and finally the temporary closure of the school (McGregor 1967: 105-107).

Against this immediate background, Dundas's speech in November 1942 at the coronation of Mutesa, himself an Old Budonian, was the more remarkable. Was Dundas simply naive or was he disingenuous when he said to the young Kabaka: 'The allegiance you owe to our Sovereign Lord the King ... will never conflict with your duty to your people'? [16] The whole drama of 1941 had centred on just such conflicting allegiances. What Dundas said was simply not true: of the Kabaka, or of his ministers, or of his chiefs. As the Principal of Makerere subsequently remarked, 'The unpopular and suspect minister or chief is most often, I think, the man of some education, who speaks English fluently, and so seems to be a mouthpiece of the Protectorate: the man, in fact, who seems to us most convenient and enlightened'. [17]

By his inaction in 1941, Dundas made allegiance to the king of England all the more difficult, and politically dangerous, for Baganda chiefs and officials who had previously been prepared to work closely with their British colonial rulers. Kulubya was now exposed to unrestricted attacks by Wamala and his faction. In a sense, Governor Dundas was not governing. His inactivity in 1941 looked more like an abdication. Nsibirwa fell. Kulubya remained, exposed and vulnerable to future attack. Standing outside the native government, British officials had only a vicarious involvement in, and limited understanding of, the Ganda factionalism which was undermining their effectiveness. Governor Dundas had clearly not intended that fuller autonomy for Buganda, and especially the Lukiiko (by now in reality an agency of faction), would threaten his own British administration's hold on the Buganda kingdom. But it did. The governor was soon seriously to compound his wrong-headedness; but it can be argued that he had already surrendered the initiative in 1941, and that British overrule-by-collaboration in Buganda was irrecoverable thereafter.

The land issue

In 1943/44 a second issue arose around which Baganda factions crystallised, and which demonstrated further estrangement between the Baganda and the Protectorate government. The issue was land. It smouldered through 1944. It was unresolved at the time of the introduction of the new constitution for Buganda in October of that year, and still unresolved by the time of the January 1945 disturbances. No other issue could have been at once so substantial and so symbolic.

There is a sense in which most of the great issues in Buganda since 1900 had concerned land: the 1920s Bataka troubles, and the controversy over closer union, are the two best examples. Land questions were so sensitive partly because of the huge expansion in individual land ownership (and security of tenure) that took place in Buganda after 1900. Audrey Richards' estimate is that the 3700 landowners of 1905 had grown to around 50,000 by 1952 (1954: 173). And in the years of the Second World War, although survey and registration came virtually to a standstill, 'unregistrable dealings in land continued apace' (West 1964: 38). The Baganda were by now a nation of landowners.

But some of these suddenly found themselves under pressure to sell. By early 1944 it became known that Makerere College in Kampala, the premier higher education institution in the protectorate, required a further 200 acres of land for expansion; and that the Empire Cotton Growing Corporation was seeking to acquire land at Kawanda, to the north of Kampala, for an experimental cotton station (Temple-Perkins 1946: 98). In both cases, the land was currently in African freehold possession, and in neither case did the Ganda owners wish to sell. Under clause 15 of the 1900 Agreement, the Protectorate government could acquire land in Buganda for purposes of defence and communications 'and other useful public works'. Because this formulation was deemed not to cover the two proposed projects, the Buganda Resident was commissioned to change the wording of this foundation-stone of Baganda-British relations, as a step towards compulsory purchase of the two sites. Temple-Perkins wrote later of 'the immense difficulty I had in 1944 in trying to persuade the Baganda to revise one line of that Agreement. It was my unenviable task to try to persuade the Baganda to amend the words "public works" to the words "public purposes"' (1946: 139).

Resistance to this proposed change was immense. The Protec-torate government faced the determined opposition of all the Lukiiko – except for Kulubya and one of his assistants. The Lukiiko was summoned repeatedly in 1944 to amend the Agreement, but as fre-quently it refused – on the grounds that there was sufficient crown land available elsewhere. Meanwhile, the UAMDA leadership ap-pealed beyond Buganda and Uganda, to the Fabian Colonial Bureau in England. Kivu asserted that 'the Protectorate government's aim is to have free access to every inch of land in Buganda with impu-nity'. And he made two emotive allusions: to Kenya and to the war. The African in Buganda, he wrote, was now to be considered 'like a squatter in Kenya who is being pushed about to make room for white settlement.... We have joined arms in fighting for liberty and freedom against dictators and are at the same time being forced into submission by dictatorial enforcement'.[18] If the purchase went ahead, Kivu went on to claim, the 800 former tenants of the Kawanda site would find themselves 'wandering about the country like strangers', even though some of the 800 were soldiers 'away out on active serv-ice in His Majesty's Forces'.[19] One of Kivu's UAMDA colleagues complained that 'this particular Government has already unjustly taken 9000 square miles from us, and before these square miles are fully occupied now our own land is being taken by force'.[20]

The dispute raised racial questions. Most Ganda complaints in 1944 rested on the conviction that non-natives – European expatri-ates, or Indians – would be the main beneficiaries of such compul-sory land acquisition as was being considered at Makerere and Kawanda. Opponents were not convinced by the official Protector-ate government claim that both measures, for higher education and for improved cotton production, were to serve African development. One critic alleged that the cotton research station was for the benefit of immigrants: 'We are getting very little out of the cotton we grow. Only the Europeans and the Asians are enjoying our crops'.[21] There were additional contemporary fears about land: another Ganda critic of British policy claimed that the Polish Refugee Camp was currently being re-named the Polish Settlement.[22] There was also rising non-African pressure for land purchase in the Kibuga, an undeveloped area on the edge of Kampala assigned to Buganda in 1900 (Southall and Gutkind 1957: 9). With the renewal of debate over closer union, it seemed to D.S.K.Musoke that 'the time is not distant when we shall lose our land and become squatters on European estates.'[23] Kivu claimed that the very purpose of the imperial presence in Uganda at this time was 'to exploit the natives by making them work for very low pay and feed Goans, Indians, and what not of the other races.'[24] Perhaps it was not surprising that land issues, in these circumstances both real and imagined, should take on a racial dimension.

And divisions within Buganda were further aggravated. Kulubya, the Omuwanika who was almost alone in his support of the Protectorate government's attempt to change clause 15, was now singled out for a renewed campaign of defamation. The campaign was led by Wamala, Katikkiro since Nsibirwa's removal in 1941, who sympathised with the opposition on both land issues. 'Closely in touch' with Kivu and Musazi, Wamala was said by one British official to have 'acted as a focus for discontent'.[25] The January 1945 disturbances were eventually to bring Kulubya down. Mulira argues that the campaign against the Omuwanika at that time was especially concerned with the land issue, as when 14 saza chiefs complained about him to the Kabaka (1950: 25). And a War Office report of 1945 also recognised that land represented a main cause of the 'latent hostilities' within Buganda which 'boiled over' early in January 1945.[26]

The officers of the British colonial state displayed short-sightedness, lack of imagination and serious misjudgement over the Ganda land issue at this time. The late summer of 1944 saw the publication and circulation of a pamphlet, *Buganda Nyafe* ('Buganda Our Mother'), which concentrated especially on the land question. It was written after a political blunder by one of the Resident's assistants, who threatened landowners of Makerere Hill with compulsory purchase by the Protectorate government if they refused to sell. This threat of purchase, under 'The Indian Land Acquisition Act', in fact had no legal validity; and according to Mulira the landlords should have been approached through their chiefs (1950: 38). But the damage had been done. A British official visiting from Sudan wrote: 'The Uganda Government has made a complete mess of this land acquisition problem, by first getting a wrong legal opinion and then telling the Kabaka and Baganda about it'.[27] *Buganda Nyafe* exploited the mess. Chief Justice Whitley was later to focus his attention on the intemperate language of the pamphlet, labelling it 'most subversive', 'bitterly anti-British' and 'pernicious' (Whitley 1945: para. 18). But Whitley missed the point. As UAMDA's Maindi wrote, in a commentary on Whitley's Report, it was the land question which 'causes greatest anxiety among the Baganda'.[28]

The Resident, Temple-Perkins, was unsympathetic. He wrote that the Baganda met the request for their land 'with typical self-satisfaction and selfishness'; he blamed the 1945 troubles on 'the avarice of the Baganda as regards their freehold land' (1946: 104). This judgement recognised land as a cause of unrest, but it displayed a poverty of imagination. For nearly half a century, land had been a sensitive issue in Ganda affairs. To dismiss it now as mere selfishness and avarice was to reveal a fundamental political misconception. The issue not only coloured the January 1945 disturbances but remained alive long after Temple-Perkins's tenure of the residency ended. In 1948 it would be described as 'still the subject of much heated controversy by the politically minded' (Annual Reports 1939-46: 9). Temple-Perkins's attitude personified a failure at official level to take seriously the political issue which was, for Buganda, perhaps the most serious of all. Meanwhile, the magnitude of the obstacles which the colonial state faced in dealing with any land issues in this most favoured province illustrates the absurdity of any claim that such a remote, over-stretched and muddleheaded administration possessed 'absolute' power.

The 1944 constitution

The third major wartime issue in Buganda coincided with the land question. On 1 October 1944, a revised constitutional relationship between Buganda and the Protectorate government came into being. This represented a momentous folly by Dundas, far greater than that of 1941. On the occasion of the Namasole Affair there had been an error of omission: his not reacting firmly, or at all, to a crisis that had originated within Buganda. Now there was an error of commission, for the governor himself promoted a political crisis. This colonial initiative proved to be a self-inflicted wound, and it starkly revealed the limits of the British colonial state's capacity to dictate the pace and direction of change in Buganda at this time. It was, essentially, a short-sighted personal contribution by Dundas to the narrowing of the margins of what was politically possible in the Buganda kingdom. The disturbances three months later in January 1945 suggest that the breakdown of authority in Buganda was not stemmed by Dundas's October 1944 reform but hastened by it.

What was Dundas trying to do? Like Mitchell earlier, he thought that the positions of Kabaka and ministers were undermined if local British expatriate officers of the provincial administration in Buganda acted directly through chiefs in their districts. British officials had certainly been taking initiatives. As Fallers remarks, in the 1920s British administrators 'had come to be more interested in promoting the welfare of ordinary folk than in maintaining the power and dignity of their rulers' (1964: 186). It appeared to Lucy Mair too, in the 1930s, that 'Buganda does not manage its own affairs, but pays Europeans to manage them' (1936: 174). In the light of this, Dundas told the Baganda that 'the chiefs were under two masters; and the people ... looked to the District Commissioners as much as to your Government for adjustment of their affairs'. Formerly 'such was perhaps necessary', he went on; but now the time had come for the British presence to be reduced. 'I wish the Resident and his staff to confine themselves to advice and guidance, leaving inspection and control to your Government and its agents'.[29]

Mitchell had previously reduced the number of districts from four to three in Buganda; now the districts were abolished as centres of British oversight. There remained a British Resident, and two Assistant Residents, all based in Kampala. The latter were to tour; but only to observe and report to the Resident so that he could in turn advise the Kabaka, when called upon to do so. The business of the Protectorate government, as opposed to that of the native government, was to be carried out by two protectorate agents. So there would continue to be a British colonial administrative presence in

Buganda, but the two structures of authority – and this was the point – would be entirely separate.

So what purpose was this measure, especially the removal of British officials from the districts, intended to achieve? Dundas expressed his view that Buganda was lagging behind other parts of Uganda 'in progress and liberal government'; but that, given real responsibility and left to themselves, the Baganda would catch up. In time, the authorities there might voluntarily and autonomously introduce reform: the Lukiiko might reconstitute itself, chiefs might economise on their own salaries, large landowners might pay higher taxes and ease the burdens of the peasantry – and, one might have added, warthogs might fly. Dundas appears to have thought that a form of organic evolution would succeed – where heavy pressure from above, from an alien British governor and Resident, were failing and would continue to fail. By Dundas's gubernatorial act of will, as it were, a purified 'indirect rule' was to lead to efficient and democratic parliamentary institutions.[30]

Any chance the measure might have had of succeeding, however, was destroyed by the manner of its introduction. Ganda authorities did not receive adequate preparation or training for the work and the responsibility which was now to be theirs and theirs alone. They were evidently not even informed as to the actual nature of the changes, for it was only after their introduction that the Resident toured the 20 sazas where he 'explained at considerable length the meaning of what had been effected' (Temple-Perkins 1946: 36). Three weeks after the changes, the Kabaka regretted that some chiefs were still addressing letters to protectorate agents – 'just as they used to do before' – rather than to their own ministers. Meanwhile the people themselves still had to learn to 'lay all their problems to the chiefs responsible' and henceforth seek access to the Protectorate government only through 'the proper channels'.[31]

More important than the manner of its introduction were the nature of the reform itself and the contemporary perceptions of it. Baganda opinion at the time was divided. The Kabaka described it as a 'pleasant feature'.[32] Even Maindi of the UAMDA thought it 'promising'.[33] But Kivu claimed that 'Indirect Rule in British protectorates is only a veiled attempt or policy to keep us under'.[34] One Ganda rumour indeed maintained that the innovation was itself a plot to demonstrate that the Baganda were incapable of ruling themselves. In fact, not all Baganda had confidence in the diligence of their chiefs, in the absence of British overseers.

Meanwhile European opinion, official as well as unofficial, was overwhelmingly critical of Dundas's innovation. The President of the Uganda Chamber of Commerce described the scheme as 'unwise and hurried'.[35] Turner at Makerere regarded it as 'too *a priori*'.[36] Temple-Perkins wrote of the opposition not only of all his district commissioners, who regretted loss of contact with the people, but also of department heads, who wanted DCs on the spot. His own prediction was that the measure would promote either 'stagnation' or 'chaos' (1946: 94). Even the official Annual Report for the period admitted that 'inevitable confusion took place at first, since no clear dividing line between Buganda Government and Protectorate Government business can be made' (Annual Reports 1939-46: p 7). For Sir Keith Hancock subsequently, Dundas had proposed 'a fallacious form of dyarchy'.[37]

A considered judgement must take into account the question of timing. First, October 1944 was not a good time to bring in the measure. In a sense, Dundas was putting into practice plans outlined by Mitchell before him; but Mitchell had shelved his proposals on the outbreak of war (Mitchell 1939: 4-6, 10 and *passim*). The Second World War meant that Baganda authorities had to carry new responsibilities, such as recruitment, the potential unpopularity of which they would now have to bear more directly than before. By 1944, factionalisn within the Ganda elite was already proving divisive and destructive. The withdrawal of the colonial dimension from Baganda affairs could only nourish factionalism further and leave pro-British chiefs more exposed. Moreover, the land issue was achieving prominence at just the time that the new measure was announced. So Turner was perhaps over-generous when he described the timing of Dundas's initiative as 'unlucky'.[38]

At that particular time, too, the lack of experience of the leading actors – as well as the absence of a common sympathy among them

– did not bode well. On the Baganda side, there was a Kabaka only two years on from his minority. The relatively new Katikkiro, Wamala, was suspicious of the British and at odds with his Treasurer, Kulubya. Governor Dundas was still a relative newcomer, while his Resident, Temple-Perkins, was not well qualified to introduce and to lubricate the delicate machinery of this new relationship. 'At the end of December 1943', he later wrote, 'I received the truly astonishing news that 1 was to be the next Resident of Buganda' (1946: 91). European opinion at the time seems not to have held the new Resident in very high regard, and shared his astonishment. Turner felt that Temple-Perkins was 'ill-fitted to his job',[39] while Harwich noted that he was 'more famous for his hunting exploits than his administrative ability'.[40] In short, this was indeed a 'particularly precarious moment' (Ingham 1962: 372).

There is moreover a second, more theoretical, level at which we can consider the question of timing. Apter described Dundas's reforms as 'advanced for their time', and if anything 'premature' (1961: 226). This echoes a contemporary observation by the military that the measure was ahead of its time.[41] Is there anything in this interpretation?

We have noted that the British authorities in Uganda were facing one of the great dilemmas of indirect rule: how does it evolve? What happens next? Not even former governor Mitchell had been able to explain how an autonomously functioning organic community, such as he advocated, could be expected to reform itself ... and subsequently evolve in a direction considered appropriate and desirable by the British. If the British continued to define the overall political course, as Mitchell clearly intended, they could not avoid another damaging by-product of indirect rule – what Margery Perham later described as 'a tendency to warp and discredit chieftainship by making it too much the agency of alien power' (1961: 58). At the Colonial Office, Dawe had also predicted before the Second World War began that 'the doctrinaire adherents of the indirect rule principle may find themselves outmoded much quicker than anyone would have thought possible a few years ago'.[42]

Mitchell's successor as governor, Dundas, had a 'dogmatic faith' in indirect rule (Pratt 1960: 276). He seems not to have recognised that, as Margery Perham again later put it, 'the system tended to become static' (1961: 58). Dundas wanted it to be dynamic, but like Mitchell he had no answer to the question of how to induce desirable change within an order which, by definition, was now going to be allowed to function autonomously. He even conceded privately that within the existing arrangements the native government depended on having a DC at Mubende 'to uphold their authority'. Indeed, he went further and admitted that 'it is well nigh impossible to safeguard the interests of the mass of the people'.[43] Nonetheless, this did not stop him from going ahead with his experiment.

In the longer perspective of British colonialism in Uganda, Governor Dundas seems to have been moving in the wrong direction. His initiative was far from 'premature'. The time for indirect rule had passed, and its particular form in Buganda was already visibly breaking down and beyond rescue. Initiatives in a different direction were required if the kingdom was to be developed and integrated into the protectorate so that Uganda might be able to sustain itself as a self-governing entity at some time in the future. At best, the October reform could be described, as it was at the time by a visitor from the Sudan, as 'an interesting move, but dubious'.[44]

What resulted from Dundas's reform? The Resident, Temple-Perkins, though a critic of the new arrangement, declined to blame it for the disturbances of January 1945 which followed so soon after its introduction. 'The crisis had no connection whatever with that new constitution', he wrote, arguing that it had not been in operation long enough for any resultant loss of contact between British and Baganda to have occurred (1946: 97). This verdict, however, is not entirely convincing.

First, loss of contact was already an established fact in Buganda. To a degree, the 1900 Agreement decades earlier had institutionalised some distancing of the British administration from most Baganda. The remoteness of the British governor in Entebbe was highlighted by the fall of Nsibirwa in 1941, when Dundas did nothing. In addition, a more corrosive form of distancing was now noted. The collaborating Baganda elite themselves came to be 'completely out of touch, and in a large number of cases in direct conflict with the mass of the Baganda' and there was 'a gulf between governors and governed', during the war-time Residency of A.H.Cox, Temple-Perkins's predecessor.[45] The loss of contact with British administrators was reinforced in wartime by the general staff shortage among expatriate personnel. A later British Resident blamed this for the ignorance and inadequate preparation of those Baganda authorities who in October 1944 were supposed to be assuming new responsibilities.[46] Thus Temple-Perkins's point about loss of contact ought to be applied to the period before October 1944, not to the short period of three months which followed.

Secondly, even three months was time enough for a damaging impact on Ganda affairs to occur. At different levels of the Ganda hierarchy, those chiefs who had been inclined to work in co-operation with the British, even after the Namasole Affair, were now highly exposed and vulnerable. Because they could no longer be sure of British support, such chiefs now withdrew from 'positive administration', as David Apter saw (1961: 225). Baganda chiefs at the top of the hierarchy were now even more vulnerable to renewed agitation and intrigue. Kulubya was soon to be the principal victim of this. He tried to surround himself with dependable appointees. But his success in doing so, when his nominations were rubber-stamped by Governor Hall – Dundas's replacement in December 1944 – proved short-lived. They only served to make Kulubya even more of a marked man by January 1945. In the context of Ganda factionalism, it had become impossible for any minister to survive without the active support of British authority – 'upon which', as Ingham remarks, 'since they were required to carry out its directives, they had not unnaturally come to rely heavily for support' (1962: 372).

Thirdly, the reform did nothing to incorporate Hailey's 'emerging class'. Hailey had asked whether 'native administration' was not 'incompatible with the growth of a large educated urban population'.[47] Margery Perham subsequently noted that 'socially and politically displaced persons showed their discontent with indirect rule' during the 1930s, and that educated Africans already felt then that 'it led nowhere'(1961: 59). Bird commented, in the wake of the October reform, 'it is not surprising that a large number of intelligent Baganda, occupying positions of comparative responsibility outside the magic circle, in trade, in commerce, and as landowners, became completely exasperated'.[48]

Thus Dundas must be held partly to blame for the disturbances – at least in respect of their Buganda dimension. His governorship, as it applied to Buganda, was deeply flawed long before October 1944. As for the measure itself, it is hard to agree with Apter that it was 'extremely sensible' (1961: 226). No constitutional design can be judged in isolation, without reference to considerations of time and place. If the particular context is not appropriate for its introduction, then a policy initiative cannot be described as 'sensible'. It could be argued rather that what Buganda required of a British governor in the early 1940s was firmness and decisiveness, combined with a positive programme of both opening up Ganda institutions and breaking down some of the barriers to African commercial enterprise.

Dundas's record here may be set against two episodes later in the 1940s. First came the qualified democratising of the Lukiiko, in 1945, in the wake of the January disturbances; and then came the opening of opportunities for African commercial enterprise, in the wake of the 1949 crisis. Both reforms were politically overdue. Though they might have been initiated by Dundas in the early 1940s, they were only introduced eventually in the wake of successive dramatic signs of British weakness. Perhaps the major fault of Dundas's measure of October 1944 was that this, too, looked like the work of a British authority unwilling to rule.

Conclusion

Between 1939 and 1945, therefore, the British essentially lost control of Buganda. Having been considered so useful at the turn of the century, Buganda proved in time to be uniquely problematical. The British authorities proved incapable of operating within the strange constitutional framework that they themselves had created in 1900 and then modified in 1944. The Second World War was only partly to blame. It did not cause the political crises of the war period. Yet in a sense the war's impact was profound. The collapse of collaboration at the political level coincided with the war-induced failure of import and price control which undermined the acceptability of British rule among the mass of Baganda.

There was a further crisis in relations between the British and the Baganda in the mid-1950s. It was quite clear that the relationship between Buganda and the emerging state of Uganda was similarly unresolved in 1962, the year of independence from Britain. It remained so until Milton Obote and Idi Amin abolished the kingdom by force in 1966 (though the issue was not put to rest even by that action). Meanwhile, twenty years earlier, the shrinking limits of British power were already visible, even before the disturbances of January 1945 broadcast them still more widely for all to see.

---

1. See Chapter 3.
2. C.Harwich to Rita Hinden, 26 August 1945, Rhodes House FCB Box 125, file 2.
3. D.S.K.Musoke, *Buganda Nyafe*, 1944: in Low, *The Mind of Buganda*, 1971, p.119.
4. This is to be found in Rhodes House, Oxford. Specific references follow.
5. Reported in *Uganda Herald*, 5 June 1940 and 24 July 1940.
6. Mitchell, Diary, 15 September 1939.
7. Kivu to Hinden, 2 November 1943, Rhodes House FCB Box 125 file 1.
8. Hailey quoted in Apter, *The Political Kingdom*, 1961, p.205.
9. Kivu to the Chief Secretary, 17 May 1940, Rhodes House FCB Box 125 file 1.
10. C.Harwich to Hinden, 26 August 1945.
11. L.M.Boyd, 'Civil Disturbances, 1949', secret memorandum, para.9, PRO CO 537/4679.
12. Maindi to Hinden, 4 July 1945, Rhodes House FCB Box 125 file 1.
13. L.M.Boyd, 'Civil Disturbances, 1949', para. 12.
14. *ibid.* para. 11.
15. Bishop Stuart to the Archbishop of Canterbury, 30 October 1943, Rhodes House FCB Box 125 file 1.
16. Report, *Uganda Herald*, 25 November 1942.
17. G.C.Turner to Gater, 14 February 1945, Turner Correspondence, Rhodes House MSS Afr.s.643.
18. Kivu to Fabian Colonial Bureau, 22 June 1944, Rhodes House FCB Box 125 file 1.
19. Kivu to Secretary of State, 19 September 1944, Rhodes House FCB Box 125 file 1.

20. P.L.Musoke to Hinden, 9 May 1944, Rhodes House FCB Box 125 file 1.

21. Maindi to Hinden, 23 May 1945, Rhodes House FCB Box 125 file 1.

22. P.L.Musoke to Hinden, 9 May 1944, Rhodes House FCB Box 125 file 1.

23. D.S.K.Musoke, *Buganda Nyafe*, in Low, *The Mind of Buganda*, 1971, p 124.

24. Kivu to Hinden, 2 November 1943, Rhodes House FCB Box 125 file 1.

25. L.M.Boyd, 'Civil Disturbances, 1949', para. 14.

26. Anonymous report, 'Background to Buganda', undated, p.2, PRO WO 276/73.

27. D.N.Newbold to C.W.M.Cox, 31 July 1944, in K.D.D.Henderson, *The Making of the Modern Sudan*, 1953, p.393.

28. Maindi to Hinden, 15 September 1945, Rhodes House FCB Box 125 file 1.

29. Quoted in 'Report of the sub-committee of the Lukiiko which was set up to look into the recommendations made by the Hancock committee', no date, .47; in Sir W.K.Hancock Buganda Papers, File 5, Institute of Commonwealth Studies.

30. Dundas to Dawe, 7 September 1943, PRO CO 536/209/40100/3/1943.

31. Kabaka to the Lukiiko, 23 October 1944, quoted in Temple-Perkins, *Such is the Burden*, 1946, p.36.

32. *ibid.*

33. Maindi to Hinden, 14 April 1945, Rhodes House FCB Box 125 file 1.

34. Kive to 'The British Imperial Government', 2 November 1943, Rhodes House FCB Box 125 file 1.

35. Bird, 'Background to the Riots', Bird Papers.

36. Turner to Marjery Perham, 6 July 1945, Turner Correspondence.

37 Buganda Papers, File 5 p.1.

38. Turner to Marjery Perham, 6 July 1945, Turner Correspondence.

39. Turner to Marjery Perham, 6 July 1945, Turner Correspondence.

40. Harwich to Hinden, 26 August 1945, Rhodes House FCB Box 120 file 2.

41. 'Background to Buganda', p.1. PRO WO 276/73.

42. Sir Arthur Dawe, 19 January 1939, quoted in John Flint, 'Planned Decolonisation and its Failure in British Africa', *African Affairs*, vol 82, no. 328, July 1983, p.395.

43. Dundas to Dawe, 7 September 1943, PRO CO 536/209/40100/3/1943.

44. Newbold to Turner, 17 September 1944, in Henderson, 'The Making of the Modern Sudan', 1953, p.406.

45. Bird, 'Background to the Riots'.

46. Boyd, 'Civil Disturbances', para. 13.

47. Hailey, quoted in Flint, 'Planned Decolonisation', *loc.cit.*, p.400.

48. Bird, 'Background to the Riots'.

12
The Disturbances of January 1945[1]

The events

In January 1945, strikes occurred and rioting broke out in many of the towns of Uganda. The conventional wisdom holds that the causes of these disturbances were political: that their origins and course can only be understood by reference to the factional ambitions of a limited number of politically active Baganda. This 'conspiracy theory' had two main contemporary sources: first, Governor John Hall, who formulated and expressed such an interpretation during the troubles themselves; and later Chief Justice Norman Whitley, who chaired the Commission of Inquiry and whose Report was published in mid-July 1945. We will have cause to dismember much of Whitley's deeply flawed interpretation of what happened.

In the whole of Uganda's colonial history after the establishment of British power, only the subsequent 1949 riots exceeded the January 1945 disturbances in dramatic content and scale of protest. Yet neither the episode nor the official report on it has received the sustained treatment each deserves. To a considerable extent, historians of colonial Uganda have been content to accept the official interpretation. The suppression of the disturbances led British officials at the time to conclude that fundamentally all was well. And this apparent success seems subsequently to have prevented historians from giving sufficient attention to an episode which reveals in sharp relief a British colonial state in crisis.

The disturbances of January 1945 were the most vivid manifestation of the impact of the Second World War on Uganda. Their origins, the colonial state's response to them, and the official interpretation of what took place, all provide clear evidence of the Protectorate government's dwindling grasp of reality, and of power. By this time – the last months of the wartime mobilisation of men, money and materials – the British colonial state was severely undermanned and overworked. Governing Buganda was proving very difficult; and British failure to exercise effective 'control' over imports and prices was causing widespread economic hardship and grounds for popular grievance. The events of January 1945 may therefore be seen as a watershed for colonialism in Uganda, by virtue of what they exposed: not only the impoverishment and frustration of African consumers but also the impoverishment of the political resources of the British colonial state.

The unrest may be said to have progressed through three phases (for which Whitley's Report may serve, at this stage, as a record of main events). The first phase was characterised by relatively minor and orderly strikes at three locations in Buganda. First, on 5 January there was a strike among Public Works Department (PWD) labour in Masaka. Then on 8 and 9 January came further small strikes there among PWD, township, and factory workers; and in Entebbe there was a strike by PWD and township labour. These strikes persisted for some days, with some reported intimidation of workers, until a grant of increased wages led to a settlement in both towns. Meanwhile, in the second week of January, Kampala experienced minor, non-violent, strikes among PWD and township employees and among workers of the E.A.Tobacco Company.

The second phase consisted of a subsequent week of strikes, and disturbances accompanied by violence, both in Buganda and beyond. From Monday 15 January, Kampala and its environs experienced widespread strikes. Clerical, skilled and unskilled workers in every government department went on strike, as did Post Office workers. Communications suffered further as telegraph wires were cut and the railway service was disrupted by both strikes and sabotage. Strikes affected hospitals and threatened water and power services; and there was a strike among native government police in Buganda. Government agencies were not the only places to be affected. Shops closed and businesses were brought to a standstill. Work was held up on getting ginneries into working order, and this was to delay by two weeks the opening of the cotton-processing season. Houseboys went on strike; bus drivers abandoned their buses; food supplies were intercepted at roadblocks; and Indian premises were looted. On 16 January, printers of the *Uganda Herald* refused to work, reducing the following day's edition to a single-sheet summary under the somewhat plaintive headline 'Widespread Strikes in Kampala...'.

Violence accompanied the strikes during this week-long phase. The strikes in Kampala began quite peacefully but intimidation led to violence. On Tuesday 16, there was much disturbance and violence: large crowds formed, shops and cars were attacked, Indians were assaulted and police stoned. From Wednesday 17 serious trouble began outside Kampala, indeed outside Buganda, in Jinja, Iganga, Mbale and Tororo. The Jinja unrest began with a strike at the BAT factory and here too there were roadblocks, disruption of hospitals, and sabotage of the railway.

The British administration in Uganda appears to have been taken by surprise. Its initial, though not immediate, response was to attempt to restore order by force. When it was clear that the police could not cope, army reinforcements were summoned. Troops were called to the Koja camp for Polish refugees, 40 miles from Kampala on the shore of Lake Victoria. Here, a crowd of government employees, estimated at over 2000, held up a milk lorry outside the camp. When the KAR came to release it, clashes resulted in four rioters being killed and eleven injured. During the week there was further trouble in Buganda: at the Uganda Sugar Factory, Lugazi; at St Mary's Mission, Kisubi; at Mubende, where working hospital staff were attacked; and at Masaka, where there was more rioting and blocking of roads, and where Indians, coffee-buyers and cotton-ginnery workers were attacked or threatened. Towards the end of this disturbed week, most troubles seem to have been in Kampala, but on Saturday 20 January two rioters were shot and wounded by police in Mbarara, Ankole. On the following day there was a further riot on Buganda's border with Busoga. Shops in rural areas were looted.

Once order was being restored, by force where necessary, the authorities turned to exhortation, propaganda, and even dialogue.

Governor Hall, absent from Entebbe at the outset, did not issue an official proclamation until Saturday 20 January when he told the strikers to return to work and promised to look into their grievances. Meanwhile the Kabaka, who co-operated closely with Hall throughout the troubles (he and Hall met on the Sunday to agree to a common response) received spokesmen for the strikers.[2] Their representatives made three demands, of which we may term one 'political' and two 'economic'. They demanded changes in the Kabaka's ministry, increased rates of pay for workers, and better prices for crops for farmers.[3]

In the third phase, during the course of the following week, the violence subsided and there was a general return to work. Kampala was quiet over the weekend of 20 and 21 January, and on Monday 22 there was a much improved attendance at work. Then, on Tuesday 23, events took place at the Kabaka's residence which were to attract much comment. Indeed, they represent the centrepiece of the subsequent conspiracy theory. On this day, a crowd of around 500 demanded the removal of Kulubya from the Buganda government ministry. On the news spreading that he had already resigned the crowd, apparently satisfied, dispersed. There were no disturbances in Kampala after 23 January. And the next day Wamala, the Katikkiro aligned with the anti-Kulubya faction, was heard to conclude that in forcing Kulubya's resignation they had achieved their objective. Meanwhile, the *Uganda Herald* could report 'Strike Situation Easier'. It later recorded that local labour troubles ended on that Wednesday, 24 January. Further afield, strikes in Masaka and at the BAT factory in Jinja continued into the later part of the week, when there were also small strikes in Gulu and Lira in the north. The last strikes occurred on 6 and 7 February, in Toro.

Nine men died during the disturbances. One Indian was killed when a mob attacked his lorry outside Kampala. There were eight dead and fourteen wounded among the rioters. Four were killed in the Koja incident. A Mutoro was shot in Kampala on 16 January after a large crowd attacked Indian houses; and the next day a Banyarwanda was killed at the site of the Kawanda agricultural station after a crowd attacked non-striking workers. On the same day, a

Congolese was shot when a mob tried to intimidate hospital workers at Namirembe, Kampala; and finally a Mutoro was shot in Masaka on 19 January when a mob attacked a police constable.

The conspiracy theory and its flaws

What was the cause of the disturbances – or, perhaps, what was not? The formulation of the conspiracy theory which came to be the official answer to this question can be seen to evolve in successive confidential telegrams from Uganda to the Colonial Office. First, Hall's deputy reported that 'the manner in which the situation developed suggests organised instigation'.[4] Hall himself then imputed a political motivation, when he added that 'the strike is the result of careful and widespread organisation which had primarily a political purpose aimed at paralysing government and other essential services'.[5]

It was on the evening of Tuesday 23 that Hall gave the first public expression of his view, in the second of his Kampala broadcasts. He asserted then that the main object of the organisers of the strike was to put pressure on the Kabaka to change the Buganda government. This was 'the hidden motive which undoubtedly inspired them (the strikes) and for which they were organised and planned'.[6] A month later, Hall told the Lukiiko that the disturbances were prearranged, that the instigators sought office for themselves and their nominees, making fantastic promises to the mass of people in order to gain their support. Such activity, he stressed, was not merely political, it was treasonable – this being wartime – 'and there is no place for treachery in Buganda'.[7] Hall subsequently told his Legislative Council that the disturbances were caused by a 'small disaffected and self-seeking minority'.[8]

For the mature version of the conspiracy theory we must turn back to Chief Justice Whitley's Report. In the seventh of his 88 paragraphs he offered his verdict: 'It early became evident that the origins of the disturbances were political rather than economic'. Whitley claimed that the conspiracy rested on the calling of a general strike – for which 'D- Day' was Monday 15 January – to paralyse all public services and lead to chaos. The aim was to provide the opportunity for a political faction to seize power and patronage in the Kabaka's government, replace the Kabaka, and go on to shake off British control. The background was one of intrigue, factionalism, planning, and rumour-mongering, aimed at discrediting both the Protectorate government and the incumbent Buganda government.

There are three main grounds for rejecting this official, and long respected, version of events. First, the evidence for it is extremely thin; secondly, it ignores facts which it cannot easily accommodate; and thirdly it distorts the allegedly crucial events of Tuesday 23 January.

First, the evidence: how did Whitley try to substantiate his interpretation? Most of his evidence lay in paragraph 18 of the report. This paragraph presented, it was claimed, 'only a few chosen from a great number of items of evidence which, taken together, indicate conclusively ... a political origin' of the disturbances. When examined closely however, fifteen of the eighteen pieces of 'evidence' assembled at this point in the report look anything but conclusive. Eight describe the background in Buganda of criticism of British rule and of the native government; another refers to the coincidental timing of the strikes; three are instances of intimidation (though no date can be deduced from two of them, nor is a political motive revealed in any); two more are instances of agitation, both occurring outside Buganda and before 15 January; and the remaining item seeks to incriminate Ignatius Musazi – through his having been at school in England during the General Strike of 1926, nearly twenty years earlier.

If 'evidence' such as this is indeed unconvincing, the remaining three items in paragraph 18 make it easier for us to understand, though not endorse, Whitley's conclusion. First, witnesses testified that such known agitators as Musazi (another was James Kivu) travelled extensively by car in Buganda and Busoga at the height of the troubles to address workers. Kivu, like Musazi, was one of a 'gang of four' subsequently arrested and deported. Meetings held in Kampala towards the end of the 'first phase' were presented as evidence that there was prior warning and promotion of strikes. The remaining two points focus on the events of Tuesday 23 January at the Kabaka's residence: the apparent satisfaction of the crowd on hearing of the fall of Kulubya, and the subsequent comment by Wamala, referred to above. Hall had earlier assumed Kulubya's pivotal significance. In this respect as in others, Whitley's interpretation and deductions owed much to Hall's.

In sum, however, the agents of the British colonial state had very little evidence for their political conspiracy theory. Whitley himself admitted that it did not amount to much; and that his views were 'founded on inferences from facts ... and a variegated assortment of indirect evidence' (1945: para.23). As for the plotters' meetings, 'there is nothing definite' (1945: para.24). He had insufficient evidence against 'the real heads who plotted the whole affair' – either for criminal proceedings 'or indeed to ascertain definitely who they were' (1945: para.54). This was because 'those who are in the know are either in the plot or are afraid to speak' (1945: para.23). The 'gang of four', and Wamala, were not tried in the courts but detained and deported under emergency powers. The absence of any evidence of conspiracy was presented as proof of its existence.

Hall and Whitley repeatedly claimed that intimidation took place during the disturbances and alleged that such pressure had a political motive. The English-language press agreed, but only partially. For example, the Kampala correspondent of *The East African Standard* maintained on 17 January, when the strike was at its height, that '90% of native employees have no desire to leave work'. Although the fact that only 9 out of a total of 347 eventual convictions were for intimidation raises some doubt as to its scale, a more important question remains.[9] Was the ulterior purpose of intimidation political, as Hall and Whitley claimed, or economic?

Neither newspaper identified a political element in any orchestration of the disturbances. In fact each at the time assumed that economic grievances were the underlying cause. On 24 January, 'Sundowner' in the *Uganda Herald* assumed that the original dispute was about pay, and that trouble began with the involvement of what he termed the 'rag-tag and bob-tail of Kampala's unemployables'. While observing that there was 'obviously a well organised attempt to dislocate the normal life of the country', *The East African Standard* paid only qualified lip-service to the official conspiracy theory. 'We are told', it recorded, 'that there was a political objective inspiring the strikers, apart from the financial hardships against which most of the strikers had been agitating'.[10]

Whitley was again short of evidence when he tried to sustain various claims concerning the inception of the strikes. On the one hand, he argued that there were months of planning for a co-ordinated outbreak of strike action (1945: para.29). On the other hand, he laid great stress on the role of activists touring the protectorate in efforts to spread strikes by direct agitation (1945: para.36). He offered no evidence for the former claim. The latter breaks down on a glance at the map. The suggestion of a spreading effect fails to account for trouble in Mbale preceding trouble in Iganga, or the trouble in Jinja preceding that in Lugazi. It is true that trouble in relatively distant Mbarara was relatively late, but this case raises other major questions. How could the incitement of unrest in Mbarara, in Ankole, put pressure on the Kabaka of Buganda? And how could the BAT strike in Jinja, across the Nile and again beyond the boundaries of Buganda, apply such pressure? Finally, how convincing is the conspiracy theory in the light of an almost complete absence of reports of *political* demands being made by strikers, anywhere in the protectorate?

A second major flaw in the conspiracy theory is that it ignored facts, such as these, which it could not accommodate. In laying stress on two dates – Monday 15 January as 'D-Day' for the general strike; and Tuesday 23 January as the day of Kulubya's resignation – it left two particular questions unasked and unanswered. First, how are we to account for the strikes which occurred, and were settled, before that Monday? Secondly, how are we to account for the strikes which continued, or in some cases began, after that Tuesday?

Of the earlier strikes, Whitley confessed: 'Why there were strikes in Masaka and Entebbe . . . is not quite clear'. He suggested rather fancifully that they might have been 'rehearsals or tryouts' but he himself accepted that this was 'mere speculation' (1945: para.36). He offered no evidence that these strikes were accompanied by political demands, nor that anything other than a concession on pay ended them. Yet he deduced nothing from the fact that the strikes 'quickly ceased on the 15th when they (the strikers) were given an increase in wages' (1945: para.35). Although predisposed towards other suggestions of co-ordination, he declined to link these earlier strikes with the later ones of 'the second phase'. Yet it seems reasonable to suppose that the success of a strike among PWD and township employees in Entebbe would encourage fellow workers in neighbouring Kampala. Whitley expressed some regret at the speedy settlement of the Entebbe dispute; yet it is hard to see how he could do so without implying – even acknowledging – a link between that successful strike action, for higher pay, and subsequent similar action elsewhere.

Whitley's omissions go further. Though there was a general return to work by the morning of Wednesday 24 January, two relatively serious strikes, in Masaka and at the BAT factory in Jinja, continued beyond that date, while a number of smaller strikes began only afterwards. No explanation can be found for any of these occurrences in Whitley's report. There was merely one later official comment to the effect that a 'few sporadic outbreaks in distant parts of the country ... were probably somewhat behind schedule in receiving their instructions from the strike organisers' (Labour Report 1945: para.16). Even this blend of fantasy and speculation did not attempt to establish any possible relationship between strikes in Gulu and Lira and political conspiracy in Buganda.

Thirdly, the conspiracy theory abused evidence in relation to the events of Tuesday 23 January, its focal point. Whitley's view, that this episode brought an end to the strikes and disturbances, can be invalidated in two ways. First, there was a considerable return to work *before* the fall of Kulubya on that day. Hall reported a limited return to work even before the end of the previous week.[11] Then on that weekend came two appeals for a return to work: his own and, particularly awkward for conspiracy theorists, a qualified appeal from the representatives of the strikers themselves after their meeting with the Kabaka.[12] There was indeed a return to work on Monday 22 January partly, it may be assumed, in response to one or other of these appeals. On that day, the report itself observed, 'those who had left work began to return' (Whitley 1945: para.48). The strike in Mbale was 'practically over as nearly everyone' was back at work.[13] And an independent estimate of work attendance levels on

Tuesday 23 – before there was any political triumph to celebrate – was 45 per cent among skilled workers and 50 per cent among unskilled.[14]

Nor can the accelerated return to work by the morning of Wednesday 24 simply be attributed to the fall of Kulubya on the previous day. It followed reassurances (rather than concessions) promised by the Kabaka. On that same Tuesday, these reassurances were accepted by a majority of the crowd assembled at his residence. This majority then dispersed, having also been addressed by two of the strike leaders, and all this occurred *before* news of Kulubya's resignation had become known. Whitley's resting of his case on this political demand and its satisfaction was thus unsound (1945: para.47). He ignored the fact that it was only a minority, about a quarter, of the original crowd which involved itself in the call for Kulubya's departure; and the fact that the Kabaka's reassurances had earlier been well received by the majority of those present. Moreover, the fall of Kulubya fails to match alleged plans to overthrow both Buganda and Protectorate governments.

The eventual return to normality is likely to have had causes different from, and simpler than, those ascribed by conspiracy theorists. First there was the effective suppression of violence and disturbance by security forces during the previous week. Then came the reassurances made by both the Kabaka and Governor Hall. African workers were perhaps prudent, in the absence of trades unions and strike pay, and at risk of losing their jobs, to rely on such promises. The timing of this normalisation needs to be stressed. We have noted Whitley's pronouncement that there were no more disturbances in Kampala after 23 January, the second Tuesday. This is true, but it is true also that there had been no disturbances in Kampala for some days beforehand. The report acknowledged that the previous Saturday was quiet, and 'nothing of note happened in Kampala an Sunday 21' (Whitley 1945: para.48). Nowhere did either Hall or Whitley mention any trouble on Monday 22. Put in this perspective, Whitley's point about the lack of disturbances after the events of Tuesday 23 loses its significance.

One is bound to conclude that Whitley began with a theory –

Hall's – and sought in his report to prove it. This was the view of at least one of the participants at the time. 'The governor had made his judgement before appointing the Commission of Inquiry', wrote Maindi of UAMDA, 'so the Commissioner started his inquiry biased'.[15] A more detached observer, British Labour politician, Arthur Creech Jones, charged Whitley with having produced 'no clear analysis' but rather 'just the kind of report which would come from a worthy Britisher in a country he did not particularly well know.... Somehow it never gets to the heart of the problem'.[16] Sir Keith Hancock wrote subsequently of Whitley that 'he seems rather daring in some of his inferences from the evidence'.[17] We need not rely alone however on such contemporary or near-contemporary dismissals. The conspiracy theory remains inconsistent with most of the material marshalled in the report which was intended to substantiate it. Both the report and the conspiracy theory are discredited by their own internal contradictions.

Re-appraisal

We need therefore to look elsewhere for the explanation. Political infighting in Buganda will not do. We have to recognise instead the central importance of local wartime economic factors in the events of January 1945. And we should see the disturbances as evidence of a profound crisis in British colonialism in Uganda at that time, with the official report itself representing one of the symptoms of that crisis.

The Whitley Report and its conspiracy theory either ignored or dismissed important evidence on the state of the economy in Uganda in January 1945. We have already examined the failure of measures designed to control imports and prices. Africans experienced a steep rise in their cost of living, especially in the towns and on the plantations, as a result of wartime conditions and the inability of government to counter them. The annual Blue Books show that some prices at Mombasa for imported cotton piece-goods, much sought after by African consumers, rose by as much as six times during the war years. Retail prices in Uganda had already risen by up to 60 per cent during the first two years – that is, before Japan's entry into the war drastically reduced supply (Labour Report 1941: para.6). By 1945, consumers in Uganda were paying 13.35 shillings for cotton goods which had cost 4.35 shillings in 1941. This was a threefold increase over four years, and yet was a controlled price which had been authorised as being justified (Whitley 1945: para.31). In the event, cloth became 'almost beyond the purchasing power of the poor'.[18]

Prices of other items, recorded in annual Labour Reports and Blue Books, tell a similar story. By the end of 1941 drugs and medicines had risen by 15 per cent, and shoes by 60 per cent.[19] The price of imported bicycles nearly doubled, and that of imported lamps and lanterns more than doubled, between 1939 and 1944; and there was a six-fold increase in the retail price of cooking pots in Kampala during the same period.[20] Hoes became difficult to obtain at controlled prices.[21] Food was perhaps less of a problem. Many Africans grew their own, and the retail prices rose less sharply than for manufactured imports. Yet green bananas (matooke), a staple, rose in price in Kampala from around 1 shilling a bunch to around 1/50 a bunch between 1940 and 1944, according to official figures, while one contemporary estimate was that the increase was as high as 80 per cent.[22] Each rise contributed further to the problem of dwindling purchasing power.

Officially recorded or permitted prices, such as those mentioned above, disguised the facts by underestimating them. The existence of the black market makes it impossible to determine exactly the level of prices paid, although prosecutions reveal some illegal profit margins and thus provide some measure. Conspiracy theorists admitted this factor. Whitley conceded that 'black-marketing undoubtedly exists'. His report acknowledged that 'the economic factor is present and applies fairly equally throughout the Protectorate, though the town-dwellers are the more hard-hit.... There has undoubtedly been a substantial all-round increase in the cost of living' (Whitley 1945: para.31). Hall went further. During the disturbances he acknowledged that the 'high cost of living and above all the greatly increased cost of essential piece goods, *acute shortage of which has operated to defeat price control,* have imposed special hardship on the poorer elements of the African and Asian population and created mounting discontent'.[23]

Nonetheless, officials seem for the most part to have underestimated the degree of price rises. They calculated that the cost of living rose one and a half times between 1939 and 1945 (Annual Report 1946: 11). What appears to be a closer contemporary estimate was given by the prominent Indian H.K.Jaffer: he maintained that there had been an overall three-fold increase during the war years up to late 1944.[24] Official cost of living indices underestimated inflation because their calculations used only listed prices. In fact, as Timothy Oberst has written, 'the state was helpless in the face of powerful economic forces' in circumstances such as these (1988: 120).

On the wages side, the attitude of the Protectorate government lacked any consistency. It was acknowledged that wages were too low. Yet Governor Hall did not accept that a fall in 'real' wages might in fact have caused the disturbances, even when he complained that those involved in strike action had not first enquired whether their wage grievances were being investigated. The timing of the return to work suggests that it was reassurances on wages, included in co-ordinated statements by the Kabaka and Governor Hall on Tuesday 23 January, which helped to accelerate the already considerable return to work on the following day. Even so, the Protectorate government denied that such reassurance 'had been in any way influenced by the strike or disorders'.[25]

Instead, the British administration maintained that remedial action on wages was already being undertaken before the disturbances. There was some truth in this. Hall had set up an Advisory Board on minimum wages just before the strikes began. And a government committee on war bonus – supplementary payments to reflect the increase in the wartime cost of living – had actually completed its investigations, concluding that increases in war bonus would be 'proper, justified and necessary' (Whitley 1945: para.70). But its findings did not appear to inform official evaluations of the disturbances; and its report, completed by 10 January 1945, had not been acted on, or even officially made public.

War bonus had earlier been paid to Africans employed by government. The first time was in 1943, when the maximum increase, for the lowest paid in Kampala, amounted to 20 per cent. There was a further increase in 1944, averaging 10 per cent in the lower paid posts. Pressure seems to have built up prior to each of these awards, and to have prompted them. Hall later wrote, of the 1944 award, that the increases had had a 'generally mollifying effect'.[26] It was demands for further increases, spurred by the publication of new Kenya rates in 1944, which led to the setting up of the new war bonus enquiry in October 1944 and thus to the 10 January 1945 findings. For example, the Buganda civil servants appealed to the Lukiiko for a further war bonus in October 1944; and in December 1944 tailors tried to organise themselves in pursuit of higher pay via the vernacular press.

The cost of living was the issue at the very heart of the strikes – but this conclusion was never (publicly) drawn by the British. In the event, new rates of war bonus were introduced, immediately after the disturbances; and the various measures on wages, adopted both beforehand and afterwards, indicate that the British authorities had some capacity for necessary remedial action. But even when the Protectorate government noted that there *was* hardship, owing to the high cost of living, it did not admit that this was instrumental in causing the disturbances. A public announcement close to 10 January, to the effect that a significant increase of war bonus was imminent, might well have prevented them. K.B. Maindi suggested as much at the time. He claimed that rumours spread that wages were about to be increased. Wage rises were known to have been recommended by the government's committee on 10 January; and it is notable that the main strikes began after the failure of the implementation of this expected wage rise.[27] The money was available: the Protectorate government in Uganda had 'never ... been so well supported by monetary reserves'.[28] It was only held back, it seems, by its fears of inflation.

It was not just in government employment that real wages had dropped. The first two years of war witnessed almost no changes in general wage levels – unlike price levels. By 1942, some upward movement was being reported, with a number of larger commercial undertakings awarding increases of between 5 and 33 per cent (Labour Report 1942: para.6). Yet in 1943, the payment of war bonus outside government service was still the exception rather than the rule. It was not given before 1945 in, for example, the tobacco factories or the sugar plantations – both of which were centres of unrest in January 1945. On the other hand, bonus payments of 20 per cent were normal in cotton-ginning, with 50 per cent paid in parts of Buganda because of labour shortage there (Labour Report 1945: para.7). Indeed, a simple demand and supply mechanism seems to have operated: wages rose when labour was scarce. By 1944, when labour was 'generally in short supply' and shortages were 'acute at times', Africans who were willing to work could successfully demand better pay and conditions (Labour Report 1944: para.3). Nowhere, however, did wages keep pace with prices. This was despite the fact that businesses like the Uganda Company were enjoying annual increases in their wartime profits.

Moreover, by denying the significance of prices and wages, the Protectorate government denied Uganda's own recent experience of labour unrest – including those recorded in its own annual Labour Reports. We can sketch a revealing picture of earlier wartime strikes and riots, less well known than those of January 1945. At least two of the main centres of labour unrest in 1945 had already been trouble spots: Kampala's PWD, and the Lugazi sugar plantation. PWD and township labour in Kampala went on strike in 1940 over hours of work, and again over hours and food rations (in effect, pay) in 1944. In the latter case they were successful. There were reports in the press of two riots involving immigrant labour in 1940, and a further 'alleged serious riot' at Lugazi in 1941.[29] In the former year, the Buganda Resident had written to both the Provincial Medical Officer and the Inspector of Labour about 'the very unsatisfactory state of affairs' on these estates of the Uganda Sugar Factory, noting the 'large number of desertions' from the work force there, and specifically criticising the low level of housing, sanitation and food as well as the poor wages.[30] It was after another strike and riot at Lugazi in 1942, over hours and living conditions, that the Labour Advisory Committee was instructed to investigate the problems associated with immigrant labour. By now, there was expression of public concern. At the end of 1942, reference was made in the Legislative Council to 'the serious labour troubles which we have had with us for so long but have done so little to control'.[31]

There were other precursors of the 1945 labour troubles. In 1944 there was a further strike at Lugazi over food provision (Labour Report 1944: para.16). In 1943 there were strikes for increased pay at workshops of the Uganda Industrial Committee, and at the Yellow Fever Research Institute, Entebbe, accompanied by 'unrest and murmurings accentuated by grievous shortage of food and piece-goods and, of course, extreme black-marketeering'.[32] By 1944, there was a marked increase in labour unrest. In at least three out of the five main 1944 strikes the issue was wages or food provision (Labour Report 1944: para.16). The rise in the cost of living was certainly becoming increasingly burdensome. In the light of the evidence it is reasonable to see the disturbances of January 1945 as the culmination of years of dissatisfaction over real wages – rather than as a singular act of political conspiracy.

Against this background indeed, analysis of January 1945 should focus on two, related, questions: what demands were made by workers on strike? And what brought strike action to an end? All sources agree that demands for increased wages accompanied the strikes. It is unfortunate that the precise nature of these demands is lost in the hyperbole of critical contemporary observers. The Protectorate government dismissed the demands for increase in wages as 'preposterously high'.[33] To Whitley they appeared 'fantastic' (1945: para.18). In this respect, the English-language press agreed. The *Uganda Herald* wrote on 24 January of 'utterly exorbitant demands', and five days earlier *The East African Standard* referred to the 'ridiculous sums' being discussed. Instances of unrest cited in the Whitley Report partly sustain the significance of the wages issue, but we are not given figures. So, cattle-traders in Mbarara were aware that the Baganda were 'rebelling ... in order to get higher wages' (Whitley 1945: 19). And as we have seen, one of three demands put to the Kabaka by strikers' representatives during the troubles was for 'increased rates of pay'.

On one occasion we are told exactly the amount of wage increase being demanded. Workers with the Kampala Township Authority and PWD were seeking a minimum wage of 45 shillings a month.[34] There are no grounds for assuming that this was typical, but it is significant that these were men who had been on strike previously, and were at the heart of events in January 1945, following the example of their Entebbe counterparts. At this time, top rates for unskilled African labour in PWD employment were around 21 shillings, and in other government work around 28 shillings. An increase from the latter figure to the full 45 shillings would have amounted to a rise of about 60 per cent. In the light of the prevailing rise in the cost of living, and in view of the subsequent grant of war bonus increases, some of these figures might appear in retrospect rather less than 'preposterous', 'fantastic', 'exorbitant' or 'ridiculous'.

Figures are as elusive when we turn to the settlement of the strikes, but the implications are clear. Strikes in January 1945 were settled by the granting of wage increases. Returns to work were generally brought about by the promise of improvements in pay. Then further strikes spread as a result of such successes and concessions. The strike among Entebbe township and PWD labourers which began on 8/9 January 'quickly ceased on the 15th when they were given an increase in wages which the government considered justified' (Whitley 1945: para.35). Whitley doggedly deduced nothing from the fact that a strike about wages was settled by a wage increase. Hall, too, was reluctant to acknowledge links of this kind. On the one hand, on 25 January he did urge the immediate publication of new war bonus details – on the telling grounds that the workers had only given up their strikes and returned to work in the anticipation of such increases. They must be paid now, he urged, 'if recrudescence of trouble is to be avoided'.[35] Yet elsewhere the governor persisted in attributing trouble to political conspiracy. Whitley's regret that the substantial Entebbe pay award had been made too promptly suggests a spreading effect rather than pre-planned action. Strikes had begun in Mbale following news of strikes in Kampala.

It is perhaps symbolic that the only civilian who lost his life as victim of the disturbances was an Indian. The position of Indians as retailers was especially resented by Africans at a time of rising prices. It was not necessary for Hall to specify Indian ownership when he referred to the 'looting of isolated shops in rural areas'.[36] A gathering outside Indian shops on the Masaka road led to prosecutions for riotous assembly. Attacks on Indians and Indian shops were common enough to be described by Hall as 'typical'.[37] Indians were not only retailers. Elizabeth Perkins has observed that Indians came under attack as employers, too. In the Masaka road incident, servants were demanding higher wages of Indians (1972: 20). It can be argued that attacks on Indians during the strikes are more consistent with an 'economic' than with a 'political' interpretation of their origin and purpose.

Conclusion

We may conclude that economic grievances in towns and among labourers on plantations lay at the heart of the strikers' interests and largely explain the origin, the spread and the settlement of the strike movement in January 1945. Although higher pay to cotton farmers was, as we have seen, among the strikers' demands, little or no evidence is marshalled by those who would give the 1945 disturbances a strong rural dimension (and thus make them resemble those of 1949). Strikes spread from town to town by example – and through the 'domino effect' of success – as much as by any intimidation. The main shared grievance was the fall in real wages brought on by wartime conditions and the colonial government's failure to control imports and prices.

This conclusion from the available evidence was widely expressed at the time, if avoided by Hall and Whitley. Maindi insisted that 'the causes were economic, higher wages, pure and simple'.[38] Strangely, some official voices provided an echo of assent. The military authorities attributed the strikes to 'wages dissatisfaction'.[39] Orde-Browne, who had been studying labour conditions in Uganda at the time of the disturbances, subsequently stated that 'the disorders began with a strike over pay rates' (1946: para.339). Sir Keith Hancock was later to ask, of Whitley's report, 'Can you so easily play down the price-wage situation?'[40]

What part did politics play? Orde-Browne's contemporary suggestion is telling. He wrote, 'I was under the impression that the beginning of the strike had been action by PWD employees at Entebbe, and that this had been seized upon as a pretext by the agitators for their political aims'.[41] It is just such a picture which emerges from the remainder of the contemporary evidence too. Into a social and economic crisis stepped political opportunism. Political activists in Buganda seized their chance to achieve their long-cherished goal: the overthrow of Kulubya. 'They thus used labour discontent as a political weapon', as Hall himself said in his 23 January broadcast.[42] Maindi claimed that 'nobody knew what the next day would bring, but as the culminating action turned out to be political, it seemed as if it was planned so'.[43] Another African observer wrote, 'We have had a widespread strike which started with labour in the Protectorate government, and ended up politically'.[44]

The 'conspiracy theory' of Hall and Whitley therefore stood contemporary evidence on its head, by focussing on Baganda politicians rather than on economic problems among the mass of Africans. Why was this interpretation, as it were, the wrong way round? There are several possible explanations. First, both Hall and Whitley were newcomers to Buganda. Their verdicts could be attributed partly to ignorance. Hall had only just arrived in the country as governor. Whitley frankly admitted that 'prior to sitting as Commissioner I knew nothing whatsoever of the internal domestic politics of the Buganda Kingdom'(1945: para.4). Secondly, they were nervous; and ignorance reinforced their shared sense of insecurity. The British administration was over-stretched. There was a war on: disturbance could be, and was, interpreted as subversion or even treason. As Oberst has written: 'In a colonial context ... any strike inherently assumed a political dimension' (1988: 123). Challenge to order was the nightmare of an undermanned colonial state, and concern for future security played a large part in the recommendations of former Major N. H. P. Whitley's report.

Thirdly, there may have been an additional, if perhaps contradictory, element of self-delusion. 'The vast majority ... realise that they are wisely and justly governed', wrote Whitley of Uganda's Africans, who were variously described as 'happy and contented ... well fed and cheerful' (1945: paras.86, 87). For British officials, 'conspiracy theory' was preferable to admitting to themselves, or to the

Colonial Office, that there was anything fundamentally wrong in Uganda or that there existed problems in the Protectorate which were beyond the capacity of the colonial state to solve. Its presence and legitimacy were at stake. Scapegoats were required.

Yet ignorance, nervousness, or self-delusion do not rule out a further possibility. It seems that the political opportunism of certain Baganda was matched by an uncharacteristic political opportunism on the part of the British colonial state itself. For the British authorities now seized their chance to rid themselves of known trouble-makers – albeit briefly, in cases such as Musazi's, noted earlier – in a purge which began in the aftermath of the disturbances and extended, as we shall see, into most of the rest of the year. This implies political calculation on the part of the colonial state, following the unnerving events of January 1945. It also implies an element of deliberate distortion in the propagation of the view that Baganda troublemakers, rather than the intractable economic and social consequences of war, were responsible for the disturbances.

In one final respect, furthermore, Whitley's report served only poorly to substantiate the Ganda conspiracy theory which inspired it. Whitley observed, in apparent contradiction of this interpretation, that 'the great majority of the rioters ... were not Baganda but labourers and unemployed from outside Buganda' (1945: para.60). He gave no precise figures, but the comparative absence of Baganda from the casualties offers some limited reinforcement of his statement. Who were the activists in the strikes and disturbances? Our detailed knowledge of the 347 court convictions is patchy, but we are told that in some 'typical' cases of 'riot' and 'carrying sticks', 17 out of 31 convicted were Baganda; and that among government labourers convicted following the Koja camp incident there were 15 Baganda and 8 Banyarwanda (out of 37).[45] Roughly half and half: such figures do little to confirm a political conspiracy, but more to show that economic grievances arising out of the war affected all the groups represented in the mixed labour forces of the plantations, and in the mixed populations of towns, in and around Buganda.

In sum, the disturbances of January 1945 demonstrated the British colonial state's inability to sustain import levels and control price levels on behalf of the African as consumer, and its inability to anticipate the ensuing political crisis. [And in Buganda they took place in the context of that other very sensitive 'economic' issue – land.] The colonial state's shortcomings were evident elsewhere too: in the interpretation of the episode which it made public; and in its handling of the general crisis (after the suppression of the disturbances), which is the subject of a later chapter.[46] January 1945 called into question – by Africans if not by British officials – the reputation and competence of the colonial state. Furthermore, it can be argued that it was this questioning and new consciousness which provided the real 'turning-point in Africa', rather than merely what was happening within the Colonial Office in London at this time (Pearce 1982: *passim*). It is not surprising, of course, that a remote and understaffed equatorial protectorate, dependent on vulnerable links with the global economy, should struggle to function effectively in a context of world war. This is not the point. As far as ever-increasing numbers of African subjects were concerned, Britain's waning ability to govern Uganda was being exposed.

1. An earlier version of this chapter was published in *African Affairs*, 91, no.365, October 1992.
2. Hall to Secretary of State, 22 January 1945, 'Labour Strikes and Disturbances', PRO CO. 536/215/40339/1/1945. Correspondence cited in the rest of this chapter is to be found in this file, unless otherwise stated..
3. Reported in *Uganda Herald*, 24 January 1945.
4. Governor's Deputy to Secretary of State, 17 January 1945.
5. Hall to Secretary of State, 20 January 1945.
6. Emergency Communique No 5, in PRO CO 536/215/40339/1/1945.
7. Text carried in *Uganda Herald*, 7 March 1945.
8. Hall to the Legislative Council, 4 December 1945.
9. Hall to Secretary of State, 27 February, 9 April, 1945.
10. *East African Standard*, 19, 26, January 1945.
11. Hall to Secretary of State, 20 January 1945.
12. Hall to Secretary of State, 22 January 1945.
13. Elliott, Mbale Diary, 22 January 1945.

14. *East African Standard*, 26 January 1945.

15. K.B.Maindi to Rita Hinden, 29 July 1945 RH FCB Box 127 file 1.

16. A.Creech Jones to Rita Hinden, 29 July 1945, RH FCB Box 127 file 1.

17. Buganda Papers, File 5, p.1, Sir W.K.Hancock Papers, Institute of Commonwealth Studies

18. A.W.Turner-Russell, letter, *Uganda Herald*, 7 February 1945.

19. *Labour Reports* for 1940 and 1941. Later reports did not provide comparable figures.

20. *Blue Books*, 1939 and 1944.

21. Agriculture Department Annual Report, 1944-45, foreword.

22. *Blue Books* for 1940 and 1944; also C.Harwich, 'Notes on 1945' in RH FCB Box 127 file 1.

23. Hall to Secretary of State, 28 January 1945. My italics. Also see Chapter 10 for fuller coverage of the black market and the failure of price control.

24. Quoted in Engholm, 'Immigrant influences', 1968, p.361.

25. Hall to Secretary of State, 26, 22, January 1945.

26. Hall to Secretary of State, 28 January 1945.

27. Maindi to Hinden, 15 September 1945, RH FCB Box 125 file 1.

28. Acting Chief Secretary to the Legislative Council, 18 December 1944.

29. *Uganda Herald*, 3 April, 24 July 1940; 29 March 1941.

30. Uganda Protectorate Secretarial Minute Paper R 308/1, 4 June 1940, Uganda National Archive, Entebbe.

31. R.G.Dakin to the Legislative Council, 14 December 1942.

32. C.Harwich, 'Notes on 1945', RH FCB Box 127 file 1.

33. Governor's Deputy to Secretary of State, 17 January 1945.

34. Rev.A.M.Williams to Rev.H.D.Hopper, 20 January 1945, PRO CO 536/215/40339/1/1945.

35. Hall to Secretary of State, 25 January 1945.

36. Hall to Secretary of State, 22 January 1945.

37. Hall to Secretary of State, 27 February 1945.

38. Maindi to Hinden, 15 September 1945, RH FCB Box 127 file 1.

39. GOC to War Office, 18 January 1945, PRO CO 536/215/40339/1/1945.

40. Buganda Papers File 5, p.1.

41. CO minute, 10 September 1946, CO 822/130/2.

42. Hall to Secretary of State, 28 January 1945.

43. Maindi to Hinden, 15 September 1945, RH FCB Box 127 file 1.

44 Kalule Sempa to Rev.Canon H.M.Grace, 22 February 1945, PRO CO 536/215/40339/1/1945.

45. Hall to Secretary of State, 27 February, 9 April, 1945.

46. See Chapter 14.

13

The Return of Uganda's Soldiers

Introduction

Around 77,000 Ugandan Africans were enlisted in the armed forces of Britain during the course of the Second World War.[1] These were men most of whom, as we noted earlier, would probably never have left the protectorate during the course of their lives, in normal circumstances. Subsequently the great majority returned to civilian life in Uganda during the twelve months following victory over Japan, in August 1945. Before we look at the official reaction and response to the troubles of January 1945, and more generally at the delusions of the colonial state in the late 1940s, we should consider the significance of this wartime experience of the 'askaris' and of their return home.

This question has tended to receive less attention than it deserves as an episode which offers us a clear and well documented insight into the reality of life on the ground when Britain was governing Uganda. In particular, a central ingredient in the story has been wholly neglected: the agency of British colonial administrators. We should look at their response to, and handling of, what appeared to them in 1945-46 to be a large and alarming problem. As students of the past we need, now, to match the keen attention which was given to the matter by British officials then. Also we should ask: was the reabsorption as smooth and efficient as was claimed at the time? If so, what credit could the colonial state claim for this outcome? Much of interest can be learnt both from the Protectorate government's perception of the problem, and from assessing its competence in handling it.

We shall see that, in its own particular way, the return of the askaris explored the limits of power of the British in Uganda. There is little evidence here of an all-powerful colonial state, confident in the wake of triumph over Nazism and that particular threat to the Empire. The opposite is the case. In general its personnel proved to be anxious – over-anxious – and its measures ineffectual. There was no contradiction here, because to a very great extent the askaris eventually settled themselves back into civilian life without disruption.

As has been assumed, there was a political dimension to this process of re-absorption; but it was not for the most part the one which has previously been accepted. Any special association of the returned soldiers with 'African nationalism' is to a large extent fruitless in the case of Uganda, as well as self-limiting – a teleological concern which has diverted scholars from more rewarding lines of enquiry. There is little to suggest that the askaris returned to Uganda intoxicated by political ideas which challenged the colonial state. Rather, their wartime experience had an impact on Uganda's soldiers which was not directly political but, as it were, material. They returned to a Uganda where prospects for employment were poor and opportunities for entrepreneurs were restricted. There were also few opportunities for consumption, with acute shortages of imported goods: insufficient (or too costly) for them, just as they were for Africans who had stayed at home. The colonial state was increasingly conscious of the fundamental need to satisfy all its subjects – and above all the returning soldiers – in economic and material terms, but it proved unable to do so. At the economic level of collaboration, it was failing. Apart from a small minority of disaffected former soldiers, if the ex-servicemen as a whole made a political impact in Uganda in the later 1940s, they did so by adding the frustration of their own expectations to a pre-existing and general accumulation of *material* grievance among Africans, which was eroding their collective acquiescence in British colonial rule.

Apprehension

When British officials in Uganda at the time contemplated the imminent return of the askaris, they mainly dwelt on two themes, each of which concerned standard of living rather than political ideology. They recognised, first, that enlisted Africans enjoyed a higher material and physical prosperity than they had previously experienced. After all, the prospect of such relative well-being had helped to stimulate recruitment initially. The problem now lay in the fact that such a material quality of life would be hard to find – that is, impossible for colonial authorities to replicate – on their return to village life in Uganda. Not 'for many years to come', wrote Mitchell in 1945, could a discharged soldier expect 'to receive a minimum wage of 48/- per month together with a high standard of feeding, clothing and housing provided free of charge'.[2] After visiting Kigezi district in 1947, Elspeth Huxley wrote, rather more exuberantly, that 'the local millionaires are the ex-soldiers, who were paid fabulous sums while serving, and when they left presented with a fortune that passed the wildest dreams of the richest cultivator' (1948: 215). As Mitchell observed, it was not indeed merely a matter of regular, relatively well paid, employment. Many contemporaries testified to the degree of physical well-being which recruits experienced after they joined up, arising from routine medical attention and a better diet. If man is what he eats, these men were going to be dissatisfied on their return home.

Secondly, active service was seen by some to be an exciting adventure, by comparison with which village life might prove intolerably dull. One official predicted that within a few months returning 'askaris' would be bored 'with the uneventful placidity and stagnation of the village in the bush'.[3] The post of Development and Welfare Secretary was created in Uganda in 1944 'to banish dullness, ignorance and superstitious fear from African rural life and to introduce new elements of activity and happiness there'.[4] Colonialism is not commonly associated with the pursuit of happiness. This was indeed an ambitious goal. But it made good sense; and it is revealing that the committee charged with making proposals for post-war development concerned itself with the 'civil reinstatement, absorption and contentment of ex-soldiers'.[5] Would returned Africans be content? The official responsible for inter-territorial training schemes, P.E.Williams, made a worrying forecast. He expected that rural home life for African ex-servicemen would soon pall. They would be unprepared for the amount of hard work required for a civilian to attain the higher standard of living enjoyed in the army – were this, despite Mitchell's forecast noted above, even achievable. Discontent would ensue. 'I fear that the African will not consider that his own lack of effort is the root of the trouble, but he will blame others'.[6]

The Uganda National Archive houses evidence of a third official theme, or preoccupation: the fear of truculence. As early as August 1943, Governor Dundas was describing for London how askaris on leave were behaving. They were 'on the whole well behaved' he acknowledged, but 'close observation' of 'attitudes and tendencies' was now required, to gain 'some indication of what to expect when it comes to demobilisation'.[7] He duly sought information from across the protectorate, on a regular basis. Subsequent reports should have reassured him. Outside Buganda, apart from three former askaris who had 'started a reign of terror' in Karamoja, comprising extortion, assaulting chiefs, and stealing goats (resulting in sentences of up to one and a half years' hard labour), there were no specific incidents to report. And what is noteworthy about the first report from within Buganda is the seeming triviality of its content. There was some 'swagger and bravado' amidst the otherwise 'reasonably good' behaviour. One soldier declared that no chief – not even the Kabaka – had any jurisdiction over him when he was on leave; and another walked out of a cinema while the National Anthem was being played. Alarming! Six months later, the Resident referred to a 'natural inclination on the part of the soldiers to question at times the orders of the less intelligent sub-chiefs'. But Dundas was informed that behaviour in general was still satisfactory; and we may anyway note again that the authority of many chiefs (some of them very senior) in the kingdom by 1944 was already wearing thin among Baganda who had not left their homes to go to war.

Overall, however, most contemporary official expressions of concern in Uganda are notable for stressing the likely material complaints of returned askaris, rather than any expected new political aspirations among them. But some other contemporaries did fear an ideological transformation. Among these was Governor Jackson of Tanganyika, who spoke of 'these restless and far travelled thousands' who would lose their 'awe' of the white man.[8] Similarly, 'Sundowner' in the *Uganda Herald* predicted that 'the returned soldier will be an entirely different person from his stay-at-home brother'.[9] A British Fabian pamphlet imagined a 'deep social and psychological dislocation' that African servicemen would be experiencing.[10] G.C.Turner, Principal of Makerere, also believed 'the war is doing what some people fear: it is putting ideas into the African's head'.[11] Fearful expectations, however, are not evidence for what eventually took place.

We find here an understandable concern among British officials that former soldiers, once demobilised, would not be easily reabsorbed into the local economy. While in Britain unemployment was essentially a social and economic problem, in a colonial state such as Uganda it could swiftly assume a more serious political dimension. Consent, order itself, would be threatened. It was far easier to demobilise than to employ – though even the former task exposed a level of administrative inadequacy.

Official measures
The major process of formal demobilisation was handled at an inter-territorial level, as a combined military-civilian operation. The army was responsible for returning each ex-serviceman to his district, after which the provincial administration took over. Thousands of askaris dispersed through the Kampala railhead were greeted, by the protectorate agent, with tea, buns and cigarettes. Away from these relaxed scenes, though, there was anxiety. An organisation had to be set up 'in one working day' to handle the large batches of soldiers returning to Buganda, as 'it was decided at the outset that at whatever cost these men must not be kept waiting for their pay' (Annual Reports 1939-46: 3).

The next stage, re-absorption, was rightly seen as the greater challenge facing officials. It was always the government's intention that soldiers should return to their villages, so everything was done to encourage a 'back to the land' movement. All propaganda stressed the primary importance to Uganda of agriculture. A leaflet issued to African soldiers in mid-1945 said – by way of instruction, prediction or exhortation – 'Agriculture is the wealth of East Africa and the majority of you will return to agriculture.... Good agriculture is skilled work, which brings credit on the man who works with his brain as well as his hands'.[12]

Whatever the effectiveness of such propaganda, it was recognised that there were men who would not be content to return to the land and who would demand non-agricultural jobs.[13] The government's main contribution towards re-absorption thus took the form of providing training. The Kampala and Elgon (Mbale) Technical Schools offered two year 'class A' courses for builders, carpenters, tailors, turners, plumbers, mechanics, electricians and the like. Elsewhere, in the widely scattered locations of Bombo and Tororo, Soroti and Lira, Arua and Fort Portal, there were twelve-month 'class B' courses for men expected to return to their villages and to practise as cobblers, bricklayers or blacksmiths. There were also specialist training centres, adapted or newly set up, for various professions: three for medical assistants, three for agriculturists, two for teachers. A number of ex-servicemen also trained for admission into the police and prisons services.[14] The administration eventually laid aside considerable sums in its estimates for 1945 and 1946 for re-absorption expenditure – on buildings and equipment, allowances and rations.[15]

Yet a further fear was that these measures, however impressive they appeared on paper, and however costly they were to prove to sustain, would not be enough; that there would be a gap between government provision and the aspirations of the mass of askaris. The financial secretary asked: 'How many ex-soldiers will require training, or rather will want training?' He went on to suggest that 'undertakings' and 'commitments' given to soldiers would be difficult to fulfil.[16] The questionnaire given to every demobilised soldier, which invited responses on their training and job aspirations, seems indeed to have been interpreted by many soldiers as a promise that such opportunities were guaranteed. A survey of askaris of Teso origin revealed that 30 per cent would be happy to remain in the army; only 10 per cent wanted to return to the land; and between 40 per cent and 50 per cent 'expected' to get jobs in government service on discharge.[17]

But (except in agriculture) there was not enough training, and not enough jobs. The capacity of the training courses was tiny in comparison with the overall numbers. The Elgon Technical School, the main centre for ex-soldiers, could accommodate just 80 men. The total capacity of all the 'class B' centres was 1035, while the three medical training centres could only take a maximum of 50 each. And despite their anxieties, the Ugandan authorities had been slow in setting up their training programmes. In 1943, Dundas was describing the problem of returning soldiers as 'distant'.[18] The Uganda Civil Reabsorption Officer spent months in 1945 finding office space and equipment, and liaising with Kenya and the districts. He was not ready to operate until the end of October. Statistics were not kept until after July 1945, by which time around 17,000 soldiers had already returned.[19] Nor was training provision integrated with development programmes. It was insufficient to meet demand and was scarcely the 'comprehensive programme' that Governor Hall called it.[20]

The training itself stumbled first on askari illiteracy. The majority of applicants for 'A courses' in the Technical Schools were incapable of reading a foot-rule.[21] 90 per cent of the soldiers were said to be illiterate.[22] The questionnaires given to demobilised soldiers advised those who could not write to ask their officers to complete the forms for them. In the event, returned questionnaires were frequently indecipherable. An earlier official training scheme, initiated during the war, had similarly floundered. When the government in 1942 proposed the training of twenty-five Ugandans as operators in the cotton textile industry, 'they were found to be not satisfactory workers and some were incapable of learning' and so they were discharged.[23] We witness here no attempt by colonial rulers to deprive African subjects of the opportunity to advance, but a sorry recognition of the inadequacy of previous basic educational provision in the protectorate.

For the administration, training at the end of the war included 'the development of character and sense of responsibility' among the askaris.[24] Therefore it must have been a disappointment to officials to find that many ex-servicemen apparently attended courses only in order to benefit from the free issue of rations, allowances and blankets. The courses regarded by the administration as the most important were those in which demobilised soldiers showed least interest: agriculture courses. Even announcement of their launch had been somewhat apologetic: 'It is not thought that many ex-soldier tradesmen will wish to undergo courses in better methods of agriculture, but for those who do so wish training will be available'.[25] During 1946 and 1947, a total of 1367 ex-soldiers were trained in agriculture; yet course capacity in 1947 alone was 1800. As for ex-soldiers finding employment, the administration had to admit that far more did so independently of government agency than through it.

Governor Mitchell had anticipated as early as 1940 that there could be acute unemployment, 'especially amongst motor-drivers, hospital orderlies and the whole class of better-paid Africans in the forces'.[26] He had had no reason to change his mind by June 1945 when he was predicting an imminent 'serious problem of unemployment for certain classes of returned soldiers'.[27] He drew attention in particular to 'those who consider themselves lorry-drivers'. These were thought likely to be a problem in Uganda, because they were already associated with agitation. As one contemporary put it, 'Even before the war, the African driver was undisciplined and troublesome'.[28] From its foundation, the Uganda African Motor Drivers' Association had shown its capacity for organisation and its ability to provide a political platform – so it did not need its members' war service to accomplish that. Over 7000 lorry drivers from Uganda then served in the army during the war, with 2888 from the Mengo district of Buganda alone.[29] As an official report put it, 'It has been made clear to ex-soldiers that only an extremely small proportion of these drivers was likely to obtain civilian employment as such'.[30] For many, there were to be additional grounds for frustration: of the 1084 ex-army drivers who presented themselves for civilian driving tests in Kampala, 571 failed.[31] Only 308 of the 2888 were known both to have passed and to have found civilian employment by the end of 1946. The 97 ex-military lorries (and 48 motorbikes) which had been made officially available for purchase by former army drivers by the end of 1946 could not have satisfied demand.[32]

There was a further, alarming, dimension here: the pursuit of job opportunities for returned soldiers raised the Indian question. Was it now time for Indians to be replaced by Africans? The potential enhancement of job prospects for returned askaris was presented as a justification for the introduction of Indian Immigration control in 1945. An official memorandum of June 1945, when the main demobilisation was getting under way, put it as follows: 'Places in the country's economy have to be kept for them [askaris], and many will have served in India and will feel that they are as capable as the Indian now in trade and craft. The Asian population of East Africa served an essential and valuable purpose at the start.... Today, those functions belong to the past or can be performed by Africans whom it is our duty to train and guide for just such purposes'.[33] Elspeth Huxley added her own note of urgency on this score. 'African askaris, returning now in 10s of 1000s, look with some resentment on Indian traders, clerks and skilled men, who occupy jobs which they increasingly feel should rightly be theirs'.[34] She recognised the frustration felt by an African ex-soldier who was anxious to invest a gratuity in a bus and start a business but was unable to do so.

July 1950 provides another insight into the Indian question. The Uganda government received a petition from one S.Lutu, a former askari. His application for a licence to operate a bus took the form of a protest. 'Most of the important routes in Uganda have gone to Indians, both of the Uganda Transport Company and the Eastern Province Bus Company.' he wrote. Instancing apparently a political consciousness, too, heightened by war service and now applied to his grievance over employment opportunities, he went on: 'We the ex-military service men do not receive due consideration. We who fought for the liberty of the whole world should be among the first to reap the fruits of peace.'[35] The previous year, a petition from three Africans in Busoga ranged more widely still. 'Indians should quit smaller towns ... Some must go to India,' it proclaimed. 'Every kind of trade that we ask for' it went on, 'is said to have been already acquired by the Indian.'[36] There is no indication as to whether any of these supplicants, other than Lutu, were themselves former servicemen. What is clear, however, is that in the immediate aftermath of war there were heightened expectations, and tension between Indian and African, which were fuelled by the aspirations of former askaris. The long-established Indian grip remained tight, however, and African resentment continued through the later 1940s and beyond.

There was a further great preoccupation of East African governments. As well as unemployment, they were anxious about inflation. Some measures were introduced to try to reduce the inflationary spending-power of the demobilised soldier. He was paid in two ways. On arrival at his district headquarters, he received 56 days' pay plus an overseas service increment. It had been agreed that 'payments due to the discharged ex-soldier shall be made as near as possible to his home in order to avoid dissipation'.[37] War gratuity and clothing allowance, however, were paid into a post office savings bank account on his behalf. This racially discriminatory device – European and Indians received all payments directly – was undertaken in the knowledge of the shortage of consumer goods, and in order to avoid worsening the existing inflation. It did not work. It was soon admitted that the average ex-soldier withdrew his money quickly, and that a proportion of the money was spent 'unwisely'.[38]

Attempts to get soldiers to save rather than spend had begun during the war, when slips urging them to do so were put into the pay-books of soldiers on leave. On demobilisation they were again urged to save and not to give money to, for example, any trading societies being set up by other ex-servicemen until such societies had been officially recognised. Governor Hall considered that some of the £1 million of war gratuities and back pay that was in the hands of demobilised soldiers might sensibly be spent on co-operative schemes.[39] But Ganda entrepreneurs of questionable prospects and reliability attracted funds so easily that the Kabaka was moved to issue cautionary advice for those with money to invest.[40]

Overall, in anticipation of the return of the askaris, the nervousness of the British administration was at times acute. They would, it was feared, expect a high standard of living, yet be unable to secure jobs of their choice; have to return to village life yet want to escape from it; and feed an inflation which could, in turn, intensify their grievances. The Resident, Buganda, expressed to the Lukiiko his 'concern' about the imminent return of askaris, and urged chiefs actively to reabsorb them.[41] Official and unofficial nervousness fed each other. As Mitchell observed in June 1945, 'A part, at any rate, of the non-native population, including some Europeans, has already got itself into a state of alarm about returned soldiers'.[42] A.W. Turner-Russell was perhaps one such. Manager of a plantation 60 miles from Kampala, he claimed in early 1946 that in 15 years he had never previously felt 'such an atmosphere of mistrust, suspicion and no confidence in the British as well as the African governments'. In Buganda, he added, there was 'a seething pot of strife only waiting the opportunity of expressing itself: this I feel may be when the men folk return from the army'.[43]

Returning askaris were clearly regarded as a menacing prospect in 1944 when consideration was being given to the future role of the government technical schools. It was considered 'undesirable to accommodate in close proximity young pupils enrolled for civil training, and older returned soldiers who had not previously belonged to the school and whose influence might frequently be far from beneficial'.[44] In the event, ex-soldiers were indeed confined to a single wing of the Kampala Technical School. A.P. Elliott of Makerere anticipated strained race relations: 'Africans who served alongside British troops seem to have found a more comradely attitude ... while here in the colonies every white man occupies a niche in the social and official hierarchy' – and Indians, too, he might have added.[45] A committee of officials and unofficials had agreed in 1944 that in the transitional period between demobilisation and re-absorption, Uganda could expect 'some boisterousness, some flouting of traditional authority, some increase in crime, and some spasmodic violence from malcontent unemployables'.[46]

What was to be done? The military was again turned to for reassurance. Mitchell, now governor of Kenya, felt in mid-1945 that 'a small British garrison', two battalions of regular British troops, would inspire confidence; and, if stationed in the Kenya Highlands, could be easily deployed.[47] Meanwhile, steps should be taken to remove any supplies and stacks of arms and ammunition which could fall into the wrong hands. Publicly, Hall merely described demobilisation as 'a testing problem'.[48] Privately, he admitted it was a 'cause for anxiety' ... and other officials were confessing that the Protectorate government was 'faced with a demobilising programme which it is feared may be on a more intensive scale than they can efficiently manage'.[49] In October 1945, all the East African governors viewed 'with some concern the possibility of disturbances occurring in their territories when demobilisation has taken place' – this, in addition to 'the continuous political tension in Buganda'.[50] Hall had already insisted, partly 'in view of the possible return of certain demobilised soldiers' in late 1945, that troops should be held in readiness at least until the end of the year.[51]

Assessment

In the event, what did the return of the askaris amount to? How well founded were British fears? How, if at all, did former service men make governing Uganda still more difficult?

Kabwegyere insists that African soldiers 'learned of their plight under colonial domination' while on war service (1974: 252). For a number this was no doubt the case. Ironically, however, the example which he cites to illustrate his point, the pamphlet written in 1944 by a serving Muganda soldier, R.H. Kakembo, in fact tends to undermine it. For beneath the vocabulary of 'fighting for democracy', and beyond a ritualistic reference to the Atlantic Charter, lies Kakembo's primary concern: the kind of life the demobilised serviceman could expect to lead afterwards. Will he 'be satisfied to go back home to his village and live in the same dull conditions that he lived in before the war?' Kakembo asks; and he quotes the responses of men back from leave in their villages, including their criticism of 'neglect' and 'backwardness'. His advice to the colonial administration is that it should start to create jobs and provide support for Africans seeking employment in trading companies and co-operatives. His request, indeed, is not for *less* colonialism but for *more*: more development, more education, and an improved standard of living. Kakembo would welcome 'democracy', beginning locally, but meanwhile he fully accepts the British presence and British initiative as the only means of providing his fellow Africans with jobs, a high standard of living, and an escape from rural backwardness (1946: *passim*).

Even so, a number of the more critical Baganda of the period had indeed served in the army – and were among those earliest 'demobilised'. Spartas Mukasa, a prominent figure in the Bataka Party served in the Kenya African Rifles. D.K. Sekkuma complained at being conscripted for war service while away from his home, although he was apparently a free man by early 1944.[52] S.K. Kisingiri, one of the deportees of late 1945, claimed to have volunteered for service and to have been discharged after two years on medical grounds.[53] James Kivu, by 1945 a veteran critic of British authority, had served with the armed forces in the *First* World War. And Kakembo himself is a further example of a former askari who subsequently clashed with civilian authority in Uganda. Though the menace of his pamphlet has been exaggerated – Kabwegyere sees in the pamphlet a radicalism which is not there (1974: 315-6) – his subsequent movements are of interest. After demobilisation he found employment with the Buganda government. He then branched out and was involved in the formation of an ex-soldiers' trading company which became financially and legally suspect. Kakembo himself was said to have been 'unreasonable and obstinate' over the company's operations, making false claims in appeals for funds in the local press.[54]

There is also more circumstantial evidence for askari involvement in opposition and protest. 1946 was a relatively quiet year in Buganda, while 1947 saw a return to dissident activity. This lull coincided with the period of some months during which returned askaris were widely expected to be at home, in their villages, enjoying their leisure and spending-power. Few sought employment in 1946: ex-servicemen were not required to pay poll tax in the first year after demobilisation, and there were still shortages of imported consumer goods to buy. Applications for training courses tell a similar story: only 120 by March 1945, but 3800 – far more than the total places available – by December.[55] The high failure rate in the courses themselves could have led to disappointment, frustration and antagonism. An official report commented on the 'comparatively low percentage of completed courses and issue of final certificates' and added that one out of eight of those accepted onto courses had to be dismissed for misconduct or desertion, laziness or lack of interest.[56]

Taken as a whole, however, such material does not validate the British officials' nightmare vision. On balance, the weight of the available evidence favours the view that the askaris were generally reabsorbed without major disturbance. The silence of the official reports on the troubles of 1945 and 1949 supports this conclusion. Whitley, quick to identify and accuse trouble-makers and agitators, was not shaken from his (mistaken) assumption that demobilisation had not even begun by January 1945. But evidence of any pivotal involvement by ex-soldiers in those troubles eluded even his search for scapegoats (1945: para.74). There is no doubt that demobilisation was complete by 1949, but Kingdon made no reference to the return of the askaris in his more diligent quest for the origins of these later disturbances. Even when he singled out leaders of the troubles and considered their backgrounds, again there was no reference to war service – notably in the case of Spartas Mukasa, who was described as a former school-teacher rather than as a former soldier (1950: para.412). War experience may of course have been a factor – if only a supplementary one in the case of men who were already critical of colonial rule before their service. We might, furthermore, expect the Resident of Buganda to have made some reference to the askaris if they had been prominent, but Boyd was silent in his secret memorandum, 'Civil Disturbances'. So too was the Muganda commentator, E.M.K. Mulira, in 'Troubled Uganda'.

Such silence is instructive. And some explicit official observations of the period may explain it and confirm that officials had worried unnecessarily. The first report on re-absorption expressed gratitude to 'the African soldier, who, generally speaking, brought an invaluable sense of discipline and co-operation with him on his return'; and this view is not contradicted in the follow-up report.[57] The Annual Report of 1946 concluded that 'the influence of these returning servicemen has been for the good'. The unofficial European voice expressed the same view, acknowledging that the worst apprehensions had not been borne out, and that askaris clearly benefited from the discipline and self-respect they had acquired in the forces. They were, in short, 'a force for good'.[58]

The most unexpected, and thus perhaps most persuasive, com-

ment was that of the military itself. In late 1945, the army considered that 'the steadying influence of released askaris' would contribute
to peace in Buganda.[59] In the event, elsewhere in the Northern and
Western Provinces returning soldiers 'on the whole' were 'prepared to
accept the authority of their clan heads and tribal chiefs and to revert to
their former place in the social organisation of the clan or tribe' (Annual
Reports 1939-46: 70). An early view from the Eastern Province was
that soldiers were reabsorbed 'without disturbance, and the great majority appear to have settled down well, most returning to the land'.[60] A
subsequent verdict ironically laments just how smoothly reabsorption
had taken place there. 'It had been hoped that the return to civil life of
tens of thousands of soldiers, whose mental horizon had been widened
by their experiences in many parts of the world, and who had learned
that hard work coupled with a proper diet improved their physique and
consequently their output capacity, would act as the proverbial leaven
on the rest of the population. That hope has proved vain' (Annual Reports 1939-46: 54).

The government's anxieties thus proved to be exaggerated. If
askaris did contribute to trouble and tension in the later 1940s, or
achieve political prominence later, they did so neither in sufficient
numbers to catch the eye of contemporaries nor merely because they
were former soldiers. There are too many variables other than war
service, such as personality or occupation, for firm conclusions. For
his part, Eugene Schleh has persuasively argued that the return of
Uganda's askaris had little political importance. In his assessment,
there was only one politically significant ex-servicemen's organisation in Uganda after the Second World War. This was the *Kawonawo*
group, which was rooted in the Ganda rural areas and included 18,000
former serving Baganda soldiers. However, Schleh points out, this
group did not adopt 'a national outlook'. And its political activity
began only in the later 1950s when it provided support for the Kabaka
in Buganda's effort to secure its future in an independent Uganda.
Schleh concludes that war service represented only one of several
forms of exposure to what he calls 'modernising influences' (1968:
220).

There were grounds enough for grievance and complaint within

Uganda, in Buganda especially, among Africans who had stayed at home, to explain the mood of the late 1940s. In 1946, moreover, Orde-Browne detected 'a general trend towards lawlessness' – which he attributed to the acute shortage of goods to buy (1946: para.41). It seems that acquiescence was breaking down within Uganda. At the same time, returned soldiers, too, were prospective and frustrated consumers, and ones who had recently enjoyed abnormally rich material comforts. One British official in Uganda in mid-1946 went so far as to claim that 'in our present economy crime is a necessity'; but although Harwich wrote about demobilisation as well as delinquency, he did not relate the one to the other.[61]

Political ideas were an abstraction, but the comparison between life in the forces and life back in Uganda was tangible. Dundas had perceived in 1942, 'Even the stay-at-home African has had liberty and equality of opportunity dinned into his ears, day in and day out'.[62] For the ex-askari, as for the stay-at-home African, it was his daily experience, rather than any new ideological perspective, which led to the disturbances and the political tensions of the end-of-war period.

How well did the British administration handle the whole operation of demobilisation and re-absorption? As was perennially the case with Banyarwanda immigration, the government could not even record, let alone influence, the employment potential and movements of the great mass of demobilised soldiers. Just as nothing could be done about the soldiers' impact, while on service, on labour shortage and inflation in Uganda, so little could be done officially, once they returned, to integrate them into ambitious schemes of post-war development. The main effect of their return seems to have been to intensify what we might term the crisis of shortages. A further result was to place still greater strain on a range of government departments already severely over-stretched during the Second World War by the widening gap between duties and manpower. In these respects therefore, returning askaris did make governing Uganda even more difficult than before.

In 1944 all the East African governments had recognised 'the closest relationship between demobilisation, re-absorption and development – three aspects of a single activity which will require single direction'.[63] But the case of Uganda shows that in practice there was more competition than integration in the planning of expenditure. There were neither the staff nor the materials for all desired projects to go ahead. Meanwhile, the 6-year Development Plan drawn up for Uganda by Worthington in 1946 made only a single passing reference to the returned askaris (1946: para.171). In short, in Uganda we do not observe a prior incorporation into the development programme of the former askaris; rather, we see the programme being adapted hastily and piecemeal in an attempt to accommodate and occupy the askaris.

We may conclude that the askaris played no particular part as a group in the political activity of the later 1940s in Uganda. Specifically, Ignatius Musazi's later assessment of 'the ex-servicemen's political consciousness and organisational ability as indispensable to the general strike of January 1945' looks at best questionable (1966: 18-22). We need not doubt that some ex-servicemen, deserters among them, played some part in the troubles – but Musazi's account is generally emotional and ideological, colourful, and distorted. The political importance of the Ugandan askaris lies elsewhere.

The return of these soldiers provides a micro-study of the scale of the challenges faced by those who governed Uganda at that time. Above all, such a study reveals the colonial state's inability, just after the war, to guarantee a material standard of living or adequate employment opportunities for its African subjects – whether returned soldiers or not – sufficient to guarantee their continued acquiescence in British colonial rule. [By contrast, given a new Labour government committed to a welfare state, the mass of the British people at home were far readier to tolerate their own austerity than were the mass of African subjects in a British colonial dependency.] It is an episode marked not by arbitrary or ruthless government but by official inadequacy – and by a dependence, ultimately, on the consent of the askaris to be reabsorbed, or to reabsorb themselves, into civilian life.

So we are again confronted by a Tolstoyan image, of the 'swarm-life' of mankind. Seventy thousand Ugandan soldiers went off to war; and then (for the most part) they returned home. The British colonial state in Uganda seems to have taken only a minor role in this great drama, beyond a sub-plot of nervous apprehension interrupted by occasional flurries of largely inconsequential activity.

---

1. Civil Reabsorption Progress Reports, December 1946, March 1948, Foreign and Commonwealth Office. Library. Subsequently referred to as CRPR, 1946 and CRPR, 1948.
2. P.E.Mitchell, 'Note on Civil Security in East Africa after the War', June 1945, PRO CO 822 113/3.
3. Harwich to Hinden, 26 August 1945, RH FCB Box 125 file 2.
4. Acting Chief Secretary to the Legislative Council, 18 December 1944.
5. Standing Finance Committee and Development and Welfare Committee Joint Report, 'Postwar Development', 1944, Appendix E. My italics.
6. P.E.Williams, Director of Training, Memorandum to the East Africa Governors' Conference, undated (1945), PRO CO 822/118/5.
7. Governor to Colonial Secretary, 9 August 1943, F 78/85/1, Uganda National Archive, Entebbe.
8. Sir W.Jackson, 'Notes on Postwar Development in East Africa', undated (1943), PRO CO 822/108/20.
9. *Uganda Herald*, 21 March 1945.
10. 'Demobilisation, Housing and Labour in Africa', 1944.
11. Foreword to Kakembo 'An African Soldier Speaks', October 1944, draft, PRO CO 822/118/4.
12. 'Manpower, Demobilisation and Reabsorption', report, Nairobi 1945, Appendix II.
13. 'Postwar Development', 1944, Appendix E.
14. CRPR, 1946, pp.8-10.
15. Hall to Secretary of State, 23 November 1945, PRO CO 536/212/40100/1945.
16. Financial Secretary to the Legislative Council, 4 December 1945.
17. Harwich to Hinden, 1 October 1945, RH FCB Box 125 file 2.
18. Dundas to Dawe, 7 September 1943, PRO CO 536/209/40100/3/43.
19. CRPR, 1946, p.1.
20. Hall to the Legislative Council, 4 December 1945.
21. CRPR, 1948, p.17.

22. Official Note, *Uganda Herald*, 3 July 1947.
23. Chief Secretary to Jardine, Matheson and Company, Kampala, 15 January 1942, F 23/307, Uganda National Archive, Entebbe.
24. CRPR, 1946, p.11.
25. Joint Report, 'Postwar Development', 1944, Appendix E.
26. Memorandum for the East Africa Governors' Conference, 30 December 1940, PRO CO 962/15.
27. 'Note on Civil Security in East Africa after the War'.
28. Harwich to Hinden, 1 October 1945, RH FCB Box 125 file 2.
29. CRPR, 1948, p.28.
30. CRPR, 1946, pp.14-15.
31. CRPR, 1948, p.28.
32. CRPR, 1946, p.6.
33. 'Immigration Policy', produced by the Uganda Government for the East Africa Governors' Conference, June 1945, PRO CO 822/113/2.
34. *The Times*, 25 March 1946.
35. Sent to the Secretary of the Transport Board, Kampala, 26 July 1950, R 156/132, Uganda National Archive, Entebbe.
36. June 1949, R 157/51, Uganda National Archive, Entebbe.
37. Agreed at the East Africa Manpower Conference, November 1943: see 'Progress Report on Demobilisation', 1944, para.2.
38. CRPR, 1946, p.3.
39. Hall to the Legislative Council, 18 June 1945, quoted in *Uganda Herald*, 20 June 1945.
40. Kabaka to the Buganda Lukiiko, 3 September 1945, quoted in *Uganda Herald*, 5 September 1945.
41. Report on Lukiiko proceedings, *Uganda Herald*, 20 March 1946.
42. Mitchell, 'Note on Civil Security in East Africa after the War'.
43. Turner-Russell to Rita Hinden, 1 April 1946, RH FCB Box 125 file 2.
44. 'Report of the Technical Training Committee', November 1944, in J. Sykes, 'Uganda Education', RH MSS. Afr.s.716.
45. Elliott to Hinden, 17 December 1946, RH FCB Box 125 file 2.
46. 'Postwar Development', 1944, Appendix B.
47. Mitchell, 'Note on Civil Security in East Africa after the War'.
48. Hall to the Legislative Council, 4 December 1945.
49. Quoted by Lt.-Col. Wilson, 'Report of Internal Security Situation in Uganda', 6 September 1945, PRO WO 276/73.
50. Brigadier Williams to H.Q. N/S Area Command, 23 October 1945, PRO WO 276/74.

51. Major P.C.O'Brien, 'Political Situation in Uganda', 7 July 1945, PRO WO 276/73.
52. Sekkuma to the Fabian Colonial Bureau, 28 January 1944, RH FCB Box 125 file 1.
53. Kisingiri to Secretary of State, 10 October 1945, RH FCB Box 125 file 1.
54. Hall to Creasy, Colonial Office, 10 October 1945, PRO CO 822/118/4.
55. CRPR, 1946, p.6.
56. CRPR, 1946, p.25.
57. CRPR, 1946, p.1.
58. Editorial, *Uganda Herald*, 7 February 1948.
59. Anonymous, 'Background to Buganda', undated (late 1945), PRO WO 276/73.
60. Childs-Clarke, 'Report on Eastern Province for 1946', para.2.
61. Harwich to Hinden, 4 August 1946, RH FCB Box 125 file 2.
62. Dundas, 'Postwar Attitude toward Social and Administrative Policy in Africa', 21 April, 1942, quoted in Kabwegyere, 1974, p.210.
63. 'Progress Report on Demobilisation', 1944, para.3.

14
1945-1949 : Reaction and Delusion

Purge

From the time of Lugard's arrival and the declaration of the protectorate, the first requirement of the British authorities in Uganda was order. Only on such a basis could a superstructure of law be constructed, and could steps be taken to make the territory pay for itself. Without order there could be no colonial state. But in 1945, the year after its fiftieth anniversary, the Uganda Protectorate experienced disorders on an unprecedented scale. The outbreak of strikes and violence took the British colonial state by surprise. During the later 1940s, its responses to those disturbances – even more than its response to the return of the askaris – would provide a further illustration of the British administration's limited power and competence in governing Uganda. Its initial response was repression and prosecution, as part of a police and military action sustained for more than a year. This was accompanied in Buganda by a British purge of African chiefs. But the negative path of repression, coercion and purge led nowhere.

There were also to be some positive post-war policy initiatives, certainly. But here the government's approach, while well enough intentioned, was unimaginatively anachronistic. In as much as it amounted to a form of 'enlightened despotism', it shared self-limiting characteristics with its eighteenth century European antecedents. Thus plans drawn up by British policy-makers allegedly pursued the common good; but they were imposed from above by the British state on African society, and imposed without consultation. Instead, the British put their faith in a major public relations exercise. Like its predecessors in Europe, this particular regime was in fact in no position to be 'despotic'.

Propaganda proved to be no substitute for dialogue. British officials failed to recognise fully the concerns of African consumers, and the aspirations of African entrepreneurs, accentuated by the Second World War. Their political response was inadequate. And the price of their myopia was the still greater crisis of 1949, which, as we shall see, further discredited them. On this occasion, ironically, the Ganda chiefly hierarchy proved 'loyal' – but powerless. This time, political collaboration, too, was in tatters. 1949 seemed to show that British power in the aftermath of war was circumscribed above all by a nervous narrowness of vision, and a lack of shrewd political realism. The Protectorate government entered the next decade, its last, as the agent of lame-duck colonialism.

Meanwhile, the suppression of the earlier disturbances in 1945 hardly deserved Whitley's description as 'magnificent' (1945: para.62). As he himself recorded, on 15 January, when the serious widespread strike action began, the police were 'everywhere hopelessly outnumbered' in Kampala (1945: para.39). In Uganda as a whole at this time there was just one policeman for every 3500 of population, the lowest ratio for anywhere in British East Africa. This was in itself a reflection of routine government by consent. In January 1945, a large part of this small force was absent with the governor in Karamoja. By noon on 15 January it was clear that those who remained would require assistance. Two hundred men were summoned from the Infantry Training Centre at Jinja, fifty miles away. Some of these arrived that evening but others were delayed till Tuesday 16 January, by mechanical trouble. On that day, 110 European and 48 Asian special constables were enrolled. This manpower then had to be reinforced from Kenya. By the evening of 18 January, armoured cars from Nanyuki had begun to arrive in Kampala. By Saturday 20 January, order in Kampala was restored, but the disturbances had stretched the means of control within Uganda to the limit and reduced the British authorities to measures of hasty improvisation.

The original feebleness of this response was soon outweighed by the colonial state's subsequent excesses. Its punitive measures were heavy-handed enough to alarm the Colonial Office. There were 558 prosecutions. Of the 347 convictions, 268 were for 'riot' and another 53 for 'assault'.[1] These figures seemed high for disturbances typified more by strikes and demonstrations than by sustained violence. The Colonial Office had to explain to Parliament and to the British press why so many were prosecuted and why their sentences were so severe. Wamala, Prince Suna, and four others were deported. Of the 347 convicted in the courts, 182 received sentences of nine months or more. Responding in mid-February to the news that 305 men were then in custody awaiting trial, Andrew Cohen at the Colonial Office in London feared that publication of this figure would 'give rise to serious concern'.[2] He proposed that Governor Hall be urged to process cases quickly and told of the undesirability of filling Uganda's prisons in this way. At the end of May, Cohen was still admitting the awkwardness of revealing the whole truth about the number of arrests and the severity of the sentences. He suggested that details be withheld until the report being drawn up by Whitley was available, to offer a justification for the figures.[3]

At least one contemporary in London thus recognised that the Protectorate government's measures were excessive. Were such measures evidence of confidence and strength, or of nervousness and weakness? They bore the clear hallmarks of the latter. The British response seems alarmist and even vengeful. It was the work of an administration embarrassed alike by having been caught unprepared and by having to explain itself thereafter to its metropolitan masters.

The prosecution of those arrested at the time of the disturbances was followed by a purge of the Ganda ruling hierarchy. This too appears to have placed revenge before dialogue and the defusing of unrest, and deserves more attention than it has received. In a sense, the British in Uganda now tried to turn the clock back, to the period before the Second World War when the Buganda government was in the hands of the two 'loyal' ministers, Nsibirwa and Kulubya. The most conspicuous single step in the purge was therefore the reappointment of Nsibirwa as Katikkiro, in the wake of Wamala's removal. Just as significant, and provocative, was the appointment of Kulubya, who had been the prime target of disaffected Baganda in January 1945, to the compensation committee set up to assess damage and loss caused by the disturbances.[4]

The general purpose of the purge was to cleanse Buganda of 'disloyal' influences, which in British official eyes the disturbances had served to identify. A largely neglected aspect of Whitley's report is the very first of his recommendations: that in future, chiefs should be selected more carefully and that, if they should prove 'lazy', 'disloyal' or 'incompetent', they should be swiftly removed (1945: para.74). The Protectorate government acted on this advice. Just a month after its publication, two deputy ministers associated with Wamala, two saza chiefs (both previously petitioners against Kulubya), and ten gombolola chiefs were forced to resign and were replaced (Boyd 1949: para.21).

Specifically, the purge was intended at last to make possible the passing of the 'Law to Empower the Kabaka to Acquire Land for Purposes Beneficial to the Nation' – specifically, the land at Makerere and Kawanda. During the previous year, the British authorities had repeatedly underestimated the significance of this land question. *Buganda Nyafe,* which should have been taken seriously, was still being dismissed by Whitley as a pernicious work of subversion in June 1945. Nonetheless, Governor Hall recognised that the land bill would not become law unless its opponents in the Buganda Ministry and the Lukiiko were removed or at least overawed.

The logic of what Hall was doing was evident, not least to the acting president of the Uganda African Motor Drivers' Association. K.B. Maindi saw that the Kabaka was being persuaded to dismiss and appoint ministers and chiefs in order to get a compliant Lukiiko to pass the land bill. In particular, he argued, Wamala had been removed because of his opposition to the bill, after which Nsibirwa was re-appointed 'for nothing but because he can help the Government to amend the 1900 Agreement to have our land alienated'.[5] In the absence of alternative legitimate political channels, men like Maindi in the UAMDA concerned themselves with a broad range of economic and political issues. Maindi himself was an energetic and persuasive campaigner – on issues as diverse as the compulsory innoculation of African cattle against rinderpest, and the closing down by the Kabaka of a co-operative printing press in 1945.[6] He was an informed and articulate spokesman for an organisation enjoying considerable popular backing as Uganda's first officially registered trade union. And though it was not disinterested, his analysis of events, revealed in correspondence with the Aborigines' Protection Society, the Anti-Slavery Society and, above all, the Fabian Society, throws at least as much light on the situation in Uganda around 1945 as does, for example, Whitley's report.

Meanwhile, as the new Katikkiro tried to reassure the Baganda through statements in the press, the purge proceeded. New appointments were made of potentially 'loyal' chiefs. The landowner Kitamirike is an example of one who gained this reward for his compliance. His land was required for the Cotton Research Station. When he agreed to sell he was made a saza chief, thus gaining entry into the Lukiiko. Overall, Hall was delighted. 'The purge of the Kabaka's government has gone off so well', he wrote to the military authorities in Nanyuki, at the end of August.[7] Almost at once this 'wholesale removal of senior chiefs in Buganda' achieved its immediate purpose.[8] The Lukiiko passed the land bill on 4 September 1945. Or, as Mulira wrote, Nsibirwa passed it.[9]

The purge did nothing to dispel widespread criticism of the land bill, however. And the Protectorate government, which had recently reinstalled Nsibirwa to restore its influence in the kingdom and to secure the passing of the land bill, proved unable to protect him from its opponents. The following day, on his way to Namirembe Cathedral, Nsibirwa was murdered. G.W. Senkatuka, who had recently been released from a detention incurred during the disturbances, was found guilty of his murder. Evidence was heard during the trial that he had been particularly angered by the Lukiiko's submissiveness on the land question.[10] He was sentenced to death. By contrast, the murdered Nsibirwa was lauded in the official British *Gazette* as a 'great and fearless patriot' and a 'great and wise Katikkiro'.[11] But this could not conceal a degree of British responsibility for his death. Temple-Perkins, Resident of Buganda until June 1945, had urged Hall and his own successor as Resident not to reappoint Nsibirwa, because of his record in the 1941 Namasole affair (1946: 141). A Muganda critic wrote to Hall in May that 'the appointment of the present nominee is highly objectionable to the public'.[12] Maindi was to add more harshly that 'this present Governor is a man who never listens to the people and as a result he, so to speak, caused the death of our late Katikkiro'.[13]

From the British colonial authorities' point of view, however, there seemed to be cause for satisfaction. The bill had been passed. They found an acceptable successor to Nsibirwa as Katikkiro in the person of Kawalya Kagwa, son of Sir Apolo Kagwa. Nsibirwa's murder also gave the British authorities the opportunity to complete their purge. In the words of the Kabaka, in whose name it was carried out, 'the act of murdering Nsibirwa was the crime of a single man but the plotting of the outrage is the conspiracy of many'.[14] A number of additional Baganda were now taken into custody, including 'several of the chiefs', the Kabaka explained, 'who were recently retired owing to their attitude during the January disturbances'. Fourteen Baganda were deported: two, including a former deputy Katikkiro, to the Seychelles; the remainder, including the author of *Buganda Nyafe* and a number of former gombolola chiefs, to Kitgum in the far north of Uganda. These men were known opponents of the Makerere extension: one, Shem Spire, was son of one of the Baganda landowners concerned. Six more gombolola chiefs were forced to retire. There were no visible repercussions in the wake of these dramatic events. [We may note, here, that pensions were paid by the government, even to chiefs sacked for their role in the disturbances.[15] Such acts of compensation appear as an indicative counterbalance to the purge itself.] British officials could conclude that 'the country has been purged thoroughly of an active disturbing element'.[16]

The purge lacked political vision, however, or any part in a long-term strategy for the protectorate. It was little more than a sudden, arbitrary and short-sighted reversal of Dundas's 1944 reforms. As Pratt puts it, 'the riots of 1945 were taken as proof that the older pattern of rule should be re-established' (1960: 280). The protectorate agents based in Masaka and Mubende now became, in addition, 'Assistant Residents'. This reintroduced a three-district Buganda and the closer supervision of chiefs' work which Dundas had sought to remove. Whitley had advocated such a step, arguing that 'the personal contacts of administrative officers with chiefs and with the people which used to exist in Buganda should not only be restored but be increased' (1945: para.74). Baganda such as Maindi saw things differently, regretting that 'a reversal to the old order was resorted to'.[17] And Maindi noted the irony in having a Resident now not merely advising the Kabaka, as had been proposed, but acting in a 'dictatorial' manner, such as determining afresh who should be chiefs.

In forcing through the purge of chiefs in Buganda after the disturbances of January 1945, the British authorities in Uganda certainly appeared to be acting both unconstitutionally and extra-judicially. Maindi presented the exile of detainees as a violation of the 1900 Agreement, since the Lukiiko had not been consulted. This charge is given weight by Temple-Perkins's testimony. Whereas Governor Hall announced that the deportations took place with the full consent of the Kabaka and the Lukiiko, Temple-Perkins wrote later that this was not true (1946:116). He maintained that both he and the Kabaka had protested, but in vain. Moreover, when Nsibirwa was reappointed Katikkiro, he was forced on a Lukiiko which had rejected him in 1941. Finally, the whole Ganda constitutional question was put into perspective in 1946 by the new Resident in an address to the Lukiiko. He chose to stress the *limitations* which the 1900 Agreement placed on Buganda's autonomy. 'There are some Baganda', he said, 'who foolishly think that the agreement gives them independence from British guidance and supervision'. He advised his audience to 'trust in the Protectorate government .... We are anxious to help you advance'.[18] But this was delusion: by now, trust was in short supply.

Meanwhile, chiefs were dismissed and deported without benefit of trial. One critic, P.L. Musoke, complained that deportations after January 1945 were based on 'unfounded and untrue information', without cases being heard in the law courts. The British merely 'rely upon what the few chiefs say who mislead them'.[19] The January disturbances occurred while wartime legislation was in force, so its removal made things more difficult for the prosecution. Indeed, one of Hall's 'causes for anxiety' by September 1945 was the fact that 'the end of the war and the relaxing of the Defence regulations has made it far more difficult legally to detain political suspects'.[20] Maindi protested that people were again deported, after September, on only the word of 'unreliable' chiefs. An example is the case of S.K. Kisingiri, an influential Muganda landowner sentenced to exile in the Seychelles. He complained that no-one had identified his accusers or their charges against him. 'I realise the necessity for wartime legislation', he wrote, but 'that legislation was tolerated only as a temporary measure in time of national emergency'.[21] He protested his innocence in vain.

Some British officials were clearly disturbed by what happened in 1945. Temple-Perkins did not know which chiefs to trust. His staff deserted him and he felt himself under threat. 'For months 1 had incessant anxiety', he wrote later. 'I arranged for a police guard, and kept the flag flying, and had my meals with friends'(1946: 115). Remarkably, these are the words of a Resident of Buganda, the official appointed by the governor to oversee and manage the affairs of the most important province in the Uganda Protectorate. And they refer to a period just after the apparently successful crushing of allegedly unrepresentative elements, among a people of whom, it was claimed, 'the vast majority realise that they are wisely and justly governed' (Whitley 1945: para.67).

Governor Hall, too, was anxious, but he was also determined and assertive. His anxieties after the troubles related to the possible consequences of the decisive purge he intended in Buganda. War Office records reveal how apprehensive he was. In the first week of July, Major P.L.O'Brien of Northern Area, East Africa Command, visited Uganda. In a confidential report on 'The Political Situation in Uganda', he referred to an interview with the governor.

> His Excellency explained that there are now so many elements disloyal to the British Government both among the senior saza chiefs and in the Native Government itself that he has decided to take strong action and have the disloyal elements removed and the Buganda Native Government cleaned up. In order to do this he is having loyal Baganda appointed to high posts in the Native Lukiko and giving them full support in clearing out the disloyal element. H.E. said that

these changes will take place within the next six weeks and he himself considered that there was at least a 50% or even greater chance of trouble during that period. When questioned on the desirability of maintaining a military force in readiness until say the end of the year, he stated that on no account should any precautions be relaxed for the next 6 weeks; after that he would like to review the situation again. Certain of his senior officials, when approached on this subject, were quite definitely of the same opinion.[22]

We see here that the British authorities had been losing their grip on Baganda affairs for so long – and, as January disclosed, to such an extent – that, when an attempt to tighten that grip was decided upon, it lacked all political subtlety and appeared likely to require military endorsement.

Hall's concerns were not restricted to that six-week period. A KAR company had already arrived in Kampala, to be available in the event of renewed civil disturbances. And it had already been decided, when this battalion was selected, that no Baganda personnel should accompany it. By the end of August, and the end of this phase of the purge, Hall was content for a squadron of armoured cars to leave Uganda, but he was reassured to know that an infantry company of KAR would remain at Jinja. When Nsibirwa was murdered, Hall at once called both this company and a troop of armoured cars to Kampala from Jinja. A week after the murder, Lt Col Wilson recorded 'a distinct possibility of further trouble. From H.E. downwards all are emphatic that the Internal Security Company must remain for the present at Kampala. Kampala is regarded as a particular danger spot. The African lesser intelligentsia comprising such people as schoolmasters are regarded as possible troublemakers'.[23] Lesser intelligentsia or not, it is striking that the possible dissent of, among others, some schoolmasters – or even former schoolmasters such as Ignatius Musazi who had taught at Budo from 1928-1933 – could require not only an infantry company but also, as Wilson proposed, the retention of a squadron of armoured cars in Uganda for an indefinite period.

Despite the heavy-handedness of British policy at this time, acute apprehension among officials in Uganda was the norm by 1945. On

21 April C.R.S.Pitman, Director, Security Intelligence, Kampala, wrote a note to the Security Liaison Officer attached to the East African Governors' Conference in Nairobi. Its subject matter is a remarkable illustration of the extent of official nervousness in the wake of the January disturbances. Baldly heading his note 'THREAT-ENED STRIKE OF TOWNSHIP LABOUR', Pitman proceeded to re-port that 'there were slight murmurings on the subject of a strike amongst the Township labour, amounting to about 100 individuals, on 14th April'.[24] This local labour problem, we learn, concerned uncertainty about war bonus back-pay for casual labourers. One morning when assembling for work, Pitman wrote, the workers were 'definitely sullen and non-co-operative'. He went on to acknowledge however that 'these Africans' proved in the end to have been 'per-fectly reasonable in their behaviour'. Nevertheless, Pitman saw fit to post a lengthy report to Nairobi. Even such 'slight murmurings' alarmed security personnel in 1945.

Acknowledged dependence on the army extended into 1946. Buganda, where there were substantial issues unresolved, remained the area causing most concern. The limitations of the Buganda Na-tive Police as a force for keeping order had been visible in January 1945 and noted by Whitley in his Report. Land was the problem which would not go away, and could not be tackled further by the Protectorate government without a military insurance policy. In Janu-ary 1946, Hall told H.Q. Northern Area that he wanted to retain armoured cars at Jinja, even though the army wanted them back in Kenya, until he had completed the acquisition of additional land for Makerere College. The army agreed to leave a squadron of armoured cars in Uganda at least until the end of April, when unrest was an-ticipated in relation not only to Makerere land but also to the hang-ing of Nsibirwa's killer, Senkatuka.[25]

Constitutional change

The Protectorate government in Uganda, shaken in January 1945, leaned for the next 15 months on the crutches of military force. In the wake of the disturbances, it failed to launch any political initiative adequate to redress Ganda grievances. Instead, it announced two

constitutional changes which were an inadequate substitute for political vision and initiative. For the Baganda especially, they proved
irrelevant, provocative, or inadequate. We will consider them in turn:
first the admission of Africans to the Protectorate government's
Legislative Council, and secondly the introduction of elections to the
Buganda Lukiiko.

The question of African representation on the Legislative Council had been raised indirectly in 1942, as the result of pressure not
from Africans but from Europeans and Indians. They requested then
that the number of unofficials in the Legislative Council should be
increased from four to six. The Colonial Office refused, on the grounds
that such a move would raise the awkward question of African representation. In 1944, Dundas was again under pressure to act, because Kenya was setting a precedent by nominating the first African
to the Kenyan Legislative Council. Dundas and the Colonial Office
were both reluctant to follow this lead in Uganda. Dundas had recently said that he would find it 'extremely difficult' to nominate an
African capable of, or interested in, representing the interests 'of any
appreciable portion of the African population of Uganda'.[26] The
Colonial Office sympathised. 'It is by no means certain either that
Africans want it or that the time is yet ripe for it', wrote one official.[27] But on this occasion, external pressure proved irresistible.
Within a year, with British policy in Uganda being questioned in the
House of Commons, three Africans were appointed.

British officials had anticipated that whenever it was decided to
appoint Africans to the Uganda Legislative Council, the Baganda
would object. On the one hand, Ganda ministers were opposed to
their kingdom's participation in the protectorate's legislature because,
in the words of A.H.Cox, the war-time Resident, 'none of their na-
tionals could be part of a *protectorate* organisation which might have
power over the *Native* Government'.[28] Even hesitant steps towards
more representative institutions at the centre of the British colonial
state in Uganda were an uncomfortable reminder to the Baganda that
they, too, were a part of that wider entity. On the other hand, if the
Baganda were to be given a place on the Legislative Council, during
this time of division and faction within the kingdom itself, which

Muganda if any could speak for the people as a whole? This British apprehension was well founded. A minister of the Buganda government was now nominated as one of the three African members of the council. But the selection of the newly installed Katikkiro, Kawalya Kagwa, as Buganda's member only provoked Ganda critics of the British administration. They were particularly outraged when Kagwa announced in 1946 that 'In this country of Buganda we as a people have no fundamental or widespread grievance' (Temple-Perkins 1946: 129). There was more at stake, however, than the further straining of relations between the British and the Baganda. Dundas had referred in 1944 to 'some incompatibility in principle between the system of Indirect Rule, and direct Native participation in the government of the protectorate'.[29] He was right. The questions which had haunted both Mitchell and Dundas remained. How should indirect rule evolve? How could Buganda be merged with the rest of the protectorate? There existed no blueprint. And in practice, the appointment of three Africans to the protectorate's Legislative Council in 1945 did more to highlight this constitutional dilemma than to solve it.[30]

The second constitutional change of 1945 was, by contrast, concerned specifically with Buganda. Its immediate purpose, Governor Hall conceded, was to meet a local political demand.[31] It was not designed to ease Buganda's incorporation into the protectorate as a whole, and indeed it had little congruity with the Legislative Council measure. It brought elections and a degree of representation to the workings of the Buganda Lukiiko. This was to be a half-hearted reform, however, and it only won the Baganda's half-hearted response. The Lukiiko comprised 89 members, of whom 60 were formerly notables chosen by the Kabaka. Of these, 31 were now to be elected. The new members, elected 'by a very indirect electoral system', first took their places in March 1946 (Apter 1961: 231). The miruka (parish) level elections aroused little interest. Taxpayers did not all exercise their right to vote. Outspoken elected members were described in the 1950 Annual Report on Buganda as representing but a fraction of the electorate, 'such was the lack of interest in the elections shown by the Ordinary Muganda'.[32] British officials regretted criticisms voiced by the newly elected members. But as Apter has written, these representative members in the Lukiiko 'were acting as politicians. Without anyone to guide them, they were reaching out into the areas which they represented, trying to establish their leadership' (1961: 243).

There was inevitable Ganda frustration at the slow pace of change, among that 'emerging class' identified by Lord Hailey.[33] The figure of 31 was raised to 36 in 1947, but for Baganda who sought an overall elected majority in the Lukiiko, none of these measures was enough. In 1944, Dundas had urged the Kabaka 'to include adequate representation of the people, both peasants and the professional classes' in the Lukiiko.[34] He had not managed to achieve any such change, and only heightened expectations which were then disappointed subsequently. In May 1945, Governor Hall was being asked by local campaigners for all the 60 Lukiiko seats to be given to 'the people'.[35] There was an urgency about this question at this time. Only through elections to all 60 seats was there a possibility of blocking the land bill. First the UAMDA and then the Bataka Party took up the cause of the 60 seats. The partial reform of 1945/46 did not satisfy but rather stimulated the appetite for constitutional change in Buganda.[36]

Grievances
Between 1945 and 1949, the Protectorate government allowed four years to elapse during which it concentrated myopically on its own plans for the future. It failed to grasp the political initiative in Buganda, or elsewhere in Uganda, by trying to satisfy present African grievances. British plans included a hydro-electric installation on the river Nile near Jinja; a cement factory at Tororo; the extension of the railway westwards to Kasese; and a textile factory at Jinja. This vision promised long term development but neglected immediate African priorities arising from, or reinforced by, the Second World War. The war confirmed the racially exclusive arrangements for the processing and disposal of cash crops and led to the setting up of the Cotton Fund and its coffee equivalent which denied African farmers a proportion of their purchasing power. Especially in the world of the black market, it intensified hostility to Indians. The war promoted

only limited Africanisation, discussed below. It resurrected, too, the possibility of 'closer union' with Kenya, which was felt to threaten all Africans, not only landowners, and which remained an issue at least until the birth of the East Africa High Commission in 1948. Also, wartime campaigns ushered in an overdose of government interventionism, which remained a characteristic of these post-war years. But this catalogue of African concerns, augmented by wartime experience, remained largely ignored. Meanwhile, British paternalism served to block some avenues of African enterprise: thus the Resident of Buganda, while approving of co-operatives in general, declined in 1945 to support co-operatives 'whose sole purpose is the personal gain of the promoters and whose activities are limited to robbing the producers'.[37]

Although, as we saw in the last chapter, the Second World War seems not in general to have turned Uganda's African servicemen into opponents of colonial rule, the conflict did provide critics with a glossary for complaint. James Kivu charged the British government with 'racial dictatorship', in place of any liberty other than 'liberty to obey your rules and regulations'. 'We have joined arms in fighting for liberty and freedom against dictators,' he wrote in 1944 during pressure on the Lukiiko to pass the land bill, 'and are at the same time being forced into submission by dictatorial enforcement'.[38] Mindful of the propaganda used by authorities to summon troops, G.W. Lwere wrote, after the 1945 disturbances, 'it was a betrayal of our fighting men if we persuaded them to go to fight for democracy only to come back and find our government autocratic, in which case they would have sacrificed their blood for nothing'.[39] Another UAMDA spokesman told Rita Hinden: 'Our people went to war against a common enemy under the British Flag and fought. Now we are being treated like slaves'.[40]

The further troubles of 1949 were evidence of the British lack of success in dealing with the repercussions of the Second World War, and of their failure to respond to the accumulating grievances of aspiring sections of African society in the post-war period. And not only in Buganda. Arthur Creech Jones was presented with a memorandum on his visit to Tororo in Eastern Province in 1946 which listed complaints about prices paid to farmers for export crops, about African pay, and about Indians.[41] Officials seem to have been locked into a narrow pre-war perception of the two categories of chiefs and peasants which excluded recognition of the interests of a new, more varied, generation of Africans. Aspiring entrepreneurs challenged the barriers to the processing and free disposal of primary produce. In 1944, the Baganda Growers' Co-operative Union tried to avoid selling their coffee to the established buying pools and to make their own use of a grinder's machine. They were officially barred in both attempts. Restrictions on the ginning and free disposal of cotton after the war frustrated an even greater number of enterprising Africans in Uganda. Kingdon's report on the 1949 disturbances provides a measure of the weight of this matter by devoting 37 paragraphs to it.[42] And innumerable peasant producers of both coffee and cotton were increasingly concerned with the persistence of the Funds. These continued to amass huge sums for potential government spending by restricting prices paid to farmers – though this money represented the reward for their work, and their purchasing power as consumers. When elections of unofficials to the Lukiiko began in Buganda, it was small businessmen and farmers who were chosen to voice grievances such as these.

There were other aggrieved Africans, amongst those whom the Colonial Office now recognised as 'a strong and growing middle-class of wealth and education in Uganda'.[43] The war provided some new employment opportunities for educated Africans in government occupations, as Europeans left for military service. But limited promotion could feed frustration. By 1941 and 1942 African members of the Agricultural Department 'had to take a much greater share of the field work' than they had done previously.[44] But as we can see in the parallel case of the Medical Department, there were ceilings on advancement. African Assistant Medical Officers acted increasingly as District Medical Officers during the war, carrying out most of the routine duties formerly assigned to Europeans, only to discover that they were not entitled to equal rates of pay, and that a 'colour bar' blocked their career prospects.[45] The war also saw an expansion of the Land and Surveys Department; but when an African graduate of the Makerere Land Survey course tried to operate privately rather than work for government he was forbidden to practise.[46] The educated class included other professionals who could be disaffected, such as African teachers, and journalists on the vernacular newspapers.

We have already met examples of the war and immediate postwar period having produced a general increase in racial consciousness, too. There was a suspicion of Europeans, whether in the administration, in commerce or in Kenya. Not all critics matched the language of C.S. Mulumba, writing in 1948. 'We scorn you like the droppings in a privy', he wrote. 'You English are liars, thieves, drunkards, idlers, who drain away the money of the black folk' (quoted in Kingdon 1950: para.370). But as measured a critic as E.M.K. Mulira regretted the general refusal of the European to recognise the black man's capabilities (1950: 41). A typical case may be that of H.J. Southam, a European technician who went to Uganda on contract after the Second World War to work on the railway extension. He neatly encapsulated what was probably an endemic attitude. 'The first thing I learned', he wrote, 'was to treat the natives fairly but not as equals' (1961:15). Little had changed by the time John Gunther visited Uganda in 1952-53 and reported that 'few private mixed parties take place, and the old-style British still refuse any social contact with negroes, except at official functions' (1955: 417).

Of still greater significance was the rising hostility to Indians. Cotton producers sold their cotton to Indian ginneries, where they were convinced they were cheated; and in due course they might well purchase consumer goods from an Indian retailer. Kingdon quotes an example of African opinion on this issue. 'All imported materials arrive here already bought by Indian millionaires, who sell them to other Indians, who sell them to a third party – Indians. The latter then sell them to Africans. The result is thieving' (1950: para.68). 'Indians have overwhelmed trade business', Creech Jones had been told in Tororo, and the British were thus urged to confine Indians to main towns. A Cotton Commission Report claimed that there was Indian malpractice in the industry in late 1948. It noted 'widespread cheating by Indian cotton buyers', adding that this was having 'a disastrous effect upon the relations between the African and Asian races in Uganda'.[47] The report thus seemed to give official sanction to existing attitudes, and may even have contributed to the further violence against Indians in 1949.

The British colonial state was now confronted with the consequences of the particular racial pattern – the 'three-tier system', the hierarchy of European, Indian and African – that it had helped to establish and which for some time had served it well enough. There was by the later 1940s a swell of articulated opposition to the privileged position of Europeans and Indians in Uganda. An African resident of Kampala wrote, in the immediate aftermath of the 1945 disturbances, 'I am afraid Buganda may become totally estranged to the whites'.[48] In 1946, Hall could claim that 'we have still in Uganda friendship and harmony between the different races'; but he added, with greater realism if understatement, 'we are, 1 think, in some danger of losing that very precious thing'.[49]

Perhaps resentment was greatest among those who perceived themselves as victims: Ganda chiefs deposed by European authority in 1945, or businessmen who had failed in occupations largely defined by race. A good example of the failed entrepreneur is D.K. Sekkuma, a frustrated Muganda businessman who periodically lobbied the local press and the Kabaka in Uganda – and, like a number of his contemporaries, the Fabians, the Labour Party and the Colonial Secretary in England. He wrote on behalf of such organisations as 'The League of Uganda Citizens and Labour Party' and 'The African Brewers and Sellers Company'. Behind his references to Thomas More and the Atlantic Charter, coupled with offensive language which twice led to prison sentences, lay a deeply felt grievance about restrictions on African trading.[50] For such traders in the later war years and after, failure was the more painful in view of all the apparent possibilities. As Apter neatly remarks, 'the greater the number of Africans in trade, the more there were with grievances' (1961: 240).

1949 and beyond: an assessment

Thus British political initiatives in Buganda in early 1945 did not centre on defusing conflict by redressing grievances among the mass of Africans, but on bolstering a regime which increasingly lacked popular consent within the kingdom. The July 1945 purge (and replacement) of chiefs in Buganda was devoted to the restoration and maintenance of order, following the disturbances of January. It sought to secure what an official in London had described as 'adequate essential control'.[51] This was to be on the basis of a renewed relationship between British authority and collaborating Baganda chiefs, reconstituted since January by a process of dismissal and appointment. Events were to prove that it was far too late for such a strategy to succeed, except superficially and in the short term.

Indeed, the years 1945 to 1949 were to witness a further collapse of collaboration in Buganda. To be of use, collaborators had to be mediators. As Ronald Robinson wrote: 'The irony of collaborative systems lay in the fact that although the white invaders could exert leverage on ruling elites they could not do without their mediation. Collaborators had to perform one set of functions in the external or "modern sector" yet square them with another and more crucial set in the indigenous society' (1972: 121,122). By 1945, the strains in this system of maintaining control in Buganda were on an unprecedented scale. The exercise of 'mediation' was no longer possible. The interests and aspirations of the two groups with whom collaborating chiefs had to deal – on the one hand British officials, and on the other hand a Ganda society increasingly aggrieved and politicised – had begun to diverge into unavoidable confrontation. At the end of 1946, A.P. Elliott of Makerere described Uganda as 'quiescent at the moment [but] there is plenty of underground discontent in Buganda still and its roots go right down into the nature of a political and economic situation which will change much more slowly than the thinking of the people who live in it'. And, he added, first among reasons for discontent was 'the creaking machinery of indirect rule'.[52]

Why could Ganda chiefs no longer mediate? They were neither hereditary nor necessarily local. In Buganda, they frequently had no previous connection with their area of responsibility, being promoted from one area to another. Kingdon noted that 'the people owe no special loyalty to, and have no affection for, the individual who happens, at the moment, to be their immediate ruler' (1950: para.37). In 1946 came this typical cry: 'All the chiefs in Buganda pass all new laws unanimously in the Lukiiko against the will of the majority of the public'.[53] Apter has offered a contrasting portrait, of someone whom such a critic as this might have accepted as a chief in the 1945 to 1949 period: 'He has fought against inroads by the Protectorate government and against Closer Union. He has engaged in constant battles against traitors from within, such as Nsibirwa and Kulubya. Despoilers lie in wait for him to take away his land, often under the pretext of good causes, such as in the Makerere affair' and so on (1961: 256). But since the 1945 purge such a man as this tended no longer to be a chief.

The events of 1949 showed the futility of the British strategy of placing confidence in chiefs of their own choice who could not win general respect and consent in Buganda. Four years of further tension gave way to an outburst of protest. There was a complete breakdown of order in Buganda in 1949, despite the laborious attempts of British officials to rebuild an effective collaboration through such Ganda chiefs since 1945. On 27 April 1949, the whole of Buganda was designated a 'disturbed area' (Kingdon 1950: para.186). The disturbances were on an even greater scale than those of 1945. There were strikes, intimidation, riots, looting, hijacking of vehicles, violence against persons and property, and illegal gatherings of crowds of up to 8000 people. Kampala was a centre of unrest but the protest was Buganda-wide and farmers this time played a far more prominent role than in 1945. There were over 400 cases of arson. The security forces were again called in to restore order although, as the editor of the *Uganda Herald* observed, 'troops and police cannot deal with the political troubles that face Buganda'.[54] There were just 8 fatal casualties, but the number of arrests reached 2000, four times the 1945 figure.

1949 gave proof that chiefs could no longer provide what Pratt has defined as 'that minimum of local support which is needed if colonial rule is not openly to rest on superior power' (1960: 281). The irrelevance of the British administration's focus on collaborating chiefs was laid bare. This time, unlike 1945, the Baganda chiefs remained 'loyal' – but they were quite unable to maintain order. It was clear to the Resident 'that the Buganda government's administrative control over large areas had completely broken down' (Boyd

1949: part II). Ganda rejection of the regime installed in the kingdom after the 1945 disturbances was explicit and uncompromising. Three specifically political demands of 1949 challenged the Native Government, and posed the question: who should be governing Buganda? The first demand called for the people to elect their own chiefs; the second, for a substantial elected unofficial majority in the Lukiiko, which had been so long a chiefs' body; and the third, for the dismissal of the present Buganda Government, not only ministers but chiefs too. These protests were clearly anti-British as well. It seems insufficient to regard them, as Gertzel does, as local activity directed 'not against the Protectorate government but against the Lukiiko' (1976: 69). Buganda held a central place – geographically, economically, politically – in the protectorate. Grievances relating to the processing of crops and the Funds ultimately concerned British, not Ganda, authorities. And the regime being challenged in Buganda was the British colonial state's deliberately and painfully constructed creature.

The response of the Protectorate government to the riots of 1949 was so politically impoverished that it acts as a fittingly symbolic postscript. Governor Hall's explanation of these disturbances of unprecedented scale was trivial and fanciful. He blamed the personal wickedness of his political opponents – 'a comparatively few evil and self-seeking men' – for the troubles (Apter 1961: 260). And he blamed communist penetration, even though Kingdon found 'no evidence that the disturbances were actually communist-inspired' and concluded that 'there is no evidence whatever of communist activities in Buganda' (1950: para.411). Hall refused even now, despite the scale of disturbances, to acknowledge a widespread problem of grievance and disaffection. 'The great mass of the Baganda' were too sensible to be deceived by lies and slanders, he went on to claim. Victim perhaps of a shared delusion, the Kabaka meanwhile was dismissing his opponents as 'pests' and 'traitors'.[55]

It is ironic that the Public Relations and Social Welfare Department of the Protectorate government (PRSWD), established in late 1946, should have published its first annual report in that most troubled year, 1949. Successor to the Information Office set up in 1939, it attempted by newspapers and communiques, mobile cinemas and demonstration teams, to serve as 'a channel of information between the Government and the people, and to popularise and promote all measures directed to the social progress and material welfare of the people'.[56] The strategic purpose was in fact, from the outset, defensive. Back in January 1945, the Chief Secretary had sent a memorandum to all government departments, urging them to keep 'the African' informed and 'supplied with full explanations of measures that government is taking affecting the African population, *so as to anticipate wherever possible misunderstanding or false rumour*'.[57] However, the events of 1949 offered a most vivid illustration of the shortcomings of post-war British policy in general and of this department's irrelevance in particular.

Hall's analysis of the department's task, at its birth, had included these words (recorded in its first annual report):

> ...ignorance by the people of what their Government is doing or attempting to do for them, and for what object, and ignorance by the Government of what the people are wanting, saying and thinking, create misunderstanding, suspicion and discontent which, starting as mere grit on the wheels, can, if neglected, become a large-sized spanner in the works. In almost every case they are avoidable.[58]

As a text for the history of Uganda in the late 1940s, the first part of this analysis is heavily laden with dramatic irony. Although lip service was also paid to the need to listen to 'the people', it remained the Protectorate government's stubborn assumption that all would be well if officials and chiefs explained everything to their subjects. But this belief in a colonial harmony, founded on clear explanation of policies devised in London or Entebbe, ignored the fact that there were economic and political issues at stake which were more serious than those which any public relations exercise could possibly contain. The Protectorate government *ignored*, as Hall had put it, 'what the people are wanting'. He himself did not appear to accept that it is *more* important for a government to understand the people than for a people to understand its government.

In some respects, Governor Hall had been preoccupied with official ignorance for some time. But his preoccupation had not been with 'what the people are wanting' but with what his opponents might be plotting. 'The civil intelligence service', he told the army in 1945, 'gets far too little real information in this land of intrigue, fear and house-burning'.[59] In due course, D.K. Sekkuma was to complain about an extension of intelligence gathering, and of 'added personnel for the purpose of sneaking about and stalking every nook of the country to spy on the people'.[60] Yet the British and Ganda authorities still had to be rescued by troops in 1949.

Although Hall appeared to advocate a two-way process of communication through the PRSWD, the Protectorate government failed to provide adequate channels for the articulation of African grievances in Uganda. As a result, and to its embarrassment, it failed to conceal its post-war shortcomings from the wider world. The Uganda African Motor Drivers' Association's wide-ranging appeals to the Protectorate government were regularly rejected. The UAMDA's president was told that 'Government is not prepared to take cognisance of representations from your association on matters which are not germane to its objects'.[61] But when Kivu had adopted the authorised channels via the Native Government to the Resident, the latter had merely replied, 'your objections have been noted'.[62]

Critics thus frustrated in Uganda – though left free by the authorities to carry on correspondence whether at home or abroad – sought sympathy overseas, especially after the Second World War. The Bataka Party sent C.S. Mulumba abroad, to appeal to the British Government and to the United Nations via the USSR's Mr Gromyko. And Musazi flew to Britain on behalf of the Uganda African Farmers' Union in December 1948. Meanwhile there was the regular correspondence, with the Fabian Colonial Bureau, by leaders of the UAMDA as well as other disaffected Ugandan Africans. As a result of this, the Fabians requested a second commission of inquiry into the 1945 disturbances. The Protectorate government's bluff was being called. Its African critics in Uganda would not be silent, and they succeeded throughout the late 1940s in taking abroad complaints which the local British administration in Uganda either refused to recognise or sought to suppress.

When the British authorities resorted to coercion, the concentration of force restored their belief in 'the value of an efficient military body in quelling disturbances'.[63] But the Protectorate government lacked both the will and the means – not to mention the support from Britain – to run a police state. In fact, it could be argued that in one respect they were too lenient in dealing with their critics: several detainees of 1945, such as Musazi and the saza chief Bazongere, were soon released, only to return to active politics in Buganda in 1946 and to continue their opposition to the British administration and the Buganda establishment. If Senkatuka had been detained longer after January 1945, he would not have been free to murder Nsibirwa in September of that year.

Force meanwhile alienated those, especially Baganda, against whom it was used. Maindi wrote in March 1945 that 'the present governor, with his experience of Arab tribes, is causing great suspicion and resentment because of the measures he has taken. Although they are fit for the rebellious Arabs, they are not fit for application here. We are not Arabs but Baganda'.[64] Half-baked coercion did not work. Moreover, the deportations of 1945 contributed to the emergence of the Bataka Party from 1946.[65] The party 'became the collecting bag for all those who had complaints against the government' (Mulira 1950: 37). It played a major role in the period leading to the 1949 disturbances. Repression was no substitute for policy.

And purge was no substitute for politics. The collaboration on which the British colonial state had depended now malfunctioned at every level, in Buganda especially. In the short term, the purge of chiefs in Buganda seemed to work: Boyd, later Resident, could claim that the year 1946 was one of 'peaceful progress and consolidation' in which 'agitation over the Lukiiko Land Law slowly subsided' (1949: para.25). In 1949, the chiefs remained 'loyal'. But the British were merely propping up an unpopular regime. As we have seen, in the later 1940s the British could not effectively exercise their authority, nor even in 1949 sustain order, through chiefs who were incapable of performing a mediating role. Meanwhile, the acquiescence of the mass of Baganda in colonial rule was still being put to the test. The Cotton and Coffee funds materially affected them all as producer-consumers; and to their grievances were now added the accumulating frustrations of aspiring entrepreneurs.

In the aftermath of 1945, the British colonial state seems to have been limited most by the poverty of its own imagination. British officials were trapped in a perception of Baganda as either 'loyal' or 'disloyal': an understandable categorisation during the war, but gravely inadequate thereafter. Yet we should remember that colonial officials were sent out to administer, not trained to govern. British officials in Uganda were not equipped with the political skill to engage their subjects in Britain's post-war endeavours. Cranford Pratt wrote that, when it abandoned the Dundas reforms in Buganda, the Protectorate government 'offered little in their place' (1960: 289). This is an understatement; nothing was offered which could win the consent of disaffected Baganda in the post-war years.

Delusion was the dominant characteristic of the official mind in Uganda in the later 1940s. Whitley had termed the January 1945 disturbances 'a blessing in disguise' for having revealed shortcomings of administration, and the murder of Nsibirwa a further 'blessing', because it provided further excuse to attack 'the political virus' in Buganda (1945: para.87). But in 1945 and again in 1949, official analyses of serious disorder took account of everything except the facts. These included not only well publicised and widespread political and economic grievances, but also the later 1940s erosion of acquiescence in British colonial rule in its by now conventional form. In the aftermath of 1945, reaction, opportunism and arbitrariness undermined rather than consolidated British authority. It is easier to account for a degree of administrative blindness prior to 1945 than to do so for the subsequent period, especially because 1945 provided such a stark and admonitory illustration of the consequences of official complacency and delusion. The late 1940s were, for the British governing Uganda, years of flawed political judgement, misguided priorities, and a waste of the opportunity to exercise in its own interests such power as it possessed.

---

1. Hall to Secretary of State, 27 February 1945, 9 April 1945, PRO CO 536/215/40339/1/1945.

2. Cohen, minute, 19 February 1945, PRO CO 536/215/40339/1/1945.

3. Cohen, minute, 30 April, 1945, PRO CO 536/215/40339/1/1945.

4. *Uganda Gazette*, 10 August 1945.

5. Maindi to Hinden, 9 July 1945, RH FCB Box 125 file 1. The Maindi correspondence used in this chapter is located in this file, unless otherwise stated .

6. *ibid.*

7. Hall to Major-General C.C.Fowkes, 24 August 1945, PRO WO 276/73.

8. Harwich to Hinden, 26 August 1945, RH FCB Box 125 file 2.

9. 'Troubled Uganda', proof copy, p.26, RH FCB Box 33 file 3.

10. Report, *Uganda Herald*, 17 October 1945.

11. *Uganda Gazette*, 6 September 1945.

12. G.W.Lwere, Secretary of 'The Amalgamated Associations', to Hall, 16 May 1945, RH FCB Box 125 file 1.

13. Maindi to the Fabian Colonial Bureau, 3 November 1945.

14. Kabaka to the Buganda Lukiiko, reported in the *Uganda H*erald, 12 September 1945.

15. Chief Secretary's Office, report, 17 March 1952, R 156/191, Uganda National Archive, Entebbe.

16. War Office report, 'Background to Uganda', PRO WO 276/73.

17. Maindi to Hinden, 14 April 1945.

18. Report, *Uganda Herald*, 20 March 1946.

19. Musoke, President of the Buganda branch of UAMDA, to Hinden, 4 June 1945, RH FCB Box 125 file 1.

20. Hall's views were quoted by Lt-Col Wilson in 'Report of Internal Security Situation in Uganda', 6 September 1945, PRO WO 276/73.

21. S.K.Kisingiri, from Luzira Prison, to Secretary of State, 10 October 1945, RH FCB Box 125 file 1.

22. 'The Political Situation in Uganda', 7 July 1945, PRO WO 276/73.

23. Lt.Col Wilson to H.Q. N.Area, 12 September 1945, PRO WO 276/73.

24. C.R.S.Pitman to Security Liaison Officer, Nairobi, 21 April 1945, PRO WO 276/73.

25. Lt Col Fenner, secret memorandum, 'Unrest Uganda', 18 January 1946, PRO WO 276/73.

26. Undated memorandum, late 1943, on revised CO proposals for Closer Union, PRO CO 822/108/20.

27. Gater to Dundas, 9 December 1944, PRO CO 536/211/40020/6/1944.

28. Quoted by Dundas in his letter to Gater, 12 June 1944, PRO CO 536/211/40020/6/1944. My italics.

29. Dundas to Gater, 12 June 1944, PRO CO 536/211/40020/6/1944.

30. The three Africans were all officials: Kawalya Kagwa, as Katikkiro of Buganda, along with a Katikkiro to 'represent' Western Province and a Secretary-General to 'represent' Eastern Province.

31. Hall to the Legislative Council, 4 December 1945.

32. Kingdom of Buganda Annual Report, 1950, quoted in Apter, *The Political Kingdom*, p.243.

33. Reference was made in Chapter 3 to Hailey's analysis in *Native Administration*, 1944, p.188.

34. Dundas to the Buganda Lukiiko, reported in *Uganda Herald*, 4 October 1944.

35. For example, Lwere to Governor, 16 May 1945, RH FCB Box 125 file 1.

36. For a fuller discussion of Ganda politics in this period, see Apter, *The Political Kingdom*, chapters 11 and 12, *passim*.

37. Resident, Buganda, to Chief Secretary, 29 March 1945, Uganda Protectorate Secretarial Minute Paper, R 147/1, Uganda National Archive, Entebbe.

38. Kivu to The Imperial British Government, 2 November 1943; and to the Fabian Colonial Bureau, 22 June 1944, RH FCB Box 125 file 1.

39. Lwere to the Kabaka, 15 March 1945, RH FCB Box 125 file 1.

40. Kiwanuka, vice-president of UAMDA, to Hinden, 14 May 1945, RH FCB Box 125 file 1.

41. Report, *Uganda Herald*, 28 August 1946.

42. Kingdon D. (1950), *Report of the Commission of Inquiry into the Disturbances in Uganda during April 1949*, Entebbe.

43. Beckett, minute, undated, PRO CO 536/208/40099/42.

44. Agriculture Department Annual Report, 1941-42, p.2.

45. Turner-Russell to Hinden, 1 April 1946, RH FCB Box 125 file 2.

46. Zuima to Secretary of State, 25 October 1944, RH FCB Box 125 file 1.

47. Report of the Cotton Industry Commission, 1948, para.70.

48. K.Sempa to Canon Grace, 22 February 1945, PRO CO 536/215/40339/ 1/1945.

49. Hall to the Legislative Council, reported in *Uganda Herald*, 4 December 1946.

50. Sekkuma's correspondence is located in Rhodes House, FCB Box 125 files 1 and 2, and Box 127 file 1.

51. Beckett, minute, undated (late 1942), PRO CO 536/208/40099/42.

52. Elliott to Hinden, 17 February 1946, RH FCB Box 125 file 2.

53. Yake, letter to *Uganda Herald*, 18 September 1946 .

54. *Uganda Herald*, 10 May 1949.

55. Reported in emergency edition of the *Uganda Herald*, 30 April 1949.

314 *Governing Uganda*

56. Annual Report of the Public Relations and Social Welfare Department, 1947-48.
57. Circular memorandum dated 23 January 1945, F 78/37/7, Uganda National Archive, Entebbe. My italics.
58. Hall to the Legislative Council, 3 December 1946.
59. Quoted in Lt Col Wilson, 'Report of Internal Security Situation in Uganda'.
60. Sekkuma to the Fabian Colonial Bureau, 25 July 1947, RH FCB Box 125 file 2.
61. Chief Secretary to Kivu, 18 November 1940, RH FCB Box 125 file 1.
62. Resident to Kivu, 15 April 1940, RH FCB Box 125 file 1.
63. 'Background to Uganda', PRO WO 276/73. The emphasis, on 'over' and 'at', is original.
64. Maindi to the Anti-Slavery Society and Fabian Colonial Bureau, 17 March 1945.
65. For an analysis of the emergence of the Bataka Party at this time, see Apter, *The Political Kingdom*, pp.248-250.

15

The 1950s: Cul-de-sac Colonialism and the Colonial Legacy

Half a century of colonial rule: a review

At the beginning of the twentieth century, Joseph Chamberlain forecast a period of ascendancy for the British Empire. Yet things seemed bad. 'At the present moment, the Empire is being attacked on all sides and, in our isolation, we must look to ourselves', observed the Colonial Secretary. But he could see the way ahead: 'The days are for great empires and not for little states', he added. As he had said five years earlier, much depended on Britain's own resolve: 'If Greater Britain remains united, no empire in the world can ever surpass it in area, population, in wealth, or in the diversity of its resources'.[1] In such a way, as Robinson and Gallagher remarked, did Joseph Chamberlain 'set a new value on the possession of territory' (1961: 396).

Chamberlain's imperial vision was not in fact widely shared at the time, nor did it have much effect on the acquisition of African territory during the period of partition. But one could argue that the aspiration was broadly vindicated in the case of Uganda, during the Second World War. As we have seen, the British colonial state there was summoned to do what it could to serve the global war effort between 1940 and 1945; and it did mobilise a considerable proportion of the protectorate's resources. This amounted to a contribution to the Empire which Joseph Chamberlain's successor as Secretary of State could describe as 'noble and valuable'.[2]

This study has not sought to deny the power of the British colonial state, but rather to measure it; not to belittle its impact on African society, but rather to show that governing Uganda was always problematical and that Africans played a huge part in shaping events during the colonial period. During the Second World War, the campaigns to recruit men, to raise revenue, and to produce food and other exportable raw materials, all had to consider the elasticity of African acquiescence. Local British officials enjoyed no simple freedom to 'exploit'. They had to estimate the extent to which unwelcome policies would be tolerated without significant protest and disturbance; and the extent to which the authority of co-operative African chiefs, acting on their behalf, could be laid open to popular challenge and the risk of rejection. Before the Second World War, the Protectorate government in Uganda had scarcely been tested. It had had little practice in making such fine political calculations; and, as we have seen, it proved unable during the war to prevent either disorder or hostility to chiefs as the agents of British colonial rule. After the war, this government was, as Wrigley remarks, certainly *not* 'sufficiently powerful to have its policies acquiesced in without popular questioning' (1959: 72).

The war made heavier demands than ever before on Britain's undermanned overseas possessions. In Uganda, broadly collaborative relationships with its African subjects had previously sustained a colonial state which – as we have seen repeatedly – was very far from 'absolute'. These economic and political relationships now became very seriously undermined. The state failed as a provider of goods. A marked decline in African consumers' purchasing power discredited an alien authority which tried and failed to establish effective wartime control over imports and prices. Alongside the highly sensitive local land issue, this led to the disturbances of January 1945. Secondly, the British so mishandled Buganda that political as well as economic collaboration came under the severest strain there, to the point of collapse. Furthermore, while the Second World War resurrected the most sensitive issues of old – such as land, East African 'closer union', and the place of Indians in Uganda – it also added others no less sensitive, like the Cotton and Coffee Funds. Whatever the considerations which had made for African acquiescence in British colonial rule before the war, they came to be heavily outweighed by issues like these which arose out of it.

When the war ended, the British administration in Uganda found itself caught between imperial priorities redefined in London and invigorated African demands in Uganda, especially in Buganda. A new consciousness among Africans in Uganda did not in most cases depend, as Sithole would lead us to conclude, on askaris' experience overseas of white men proving as weak and vulnerable as any other, when at war (1968: 157-163). Adu Boahen reminds us that Africans already had a clear-headed understanding of colonial rule (1987: 63). Moreover, it was the Africans left behind in Uganda who experienced the demanding colonial interventions of the mobilisation programmes, and the colonial power's failure to protect them from the economic repercussions of global war. It was primarily these Africans, too, who participated in strikes and disturbances in 1945 and subsequently witnessed the combination of vulnerability and vindictiveness which characterised the British colonial state's response to them. The Second World War enhanced African political consciousness in Uganda, less by sending soldiers away to fight (or by the promulgation of the Atlantic Charter) than by discrediting British authority on the ground. By the end of the war period, the interests of rulers and ruled, which for much of the 1920s and 1930s had been at least reconcilable where they were not shared, appear broadly to have entered a phase of irreversible divergence. Africans now had aspirations of their own. By the end of the war, African opinion replaced that of the European expatriates as the major local pressure on the Protectorate government – which first ignored it and then proved incapable of satisfying it.

In some other respects, however, the Second World War brought little change. Thus the pattern of African production in Uganda was modified rather than transformed – for example by the increased emphasis on tobacco, the shift towards coffee, and the spread of maize cultivation which British officials found so difficult to contain. And in the absence of significant wartime industrialisation, there was no significant urbanisation either. While Nairobi's population nearly doubled during the war period, the population of Kampala in 1948, an estimated 22,100, showed scarcely a 50 per cent increase on what it had been in 1911/12 – that is, before the *First* World War (Low and Smith 1976: 582)).

The Second World War was thus a period of continuity as well as change. And this continuity is well illustrated by one final symbolic example from the war period. In March 1943, the Protectorate government introduced a specific form of prohibition. It banned the manufacture, sale, consumption and possession of *waragi*, defined in the ordinance as 'any native spirituous liquor'.[3] Drunkenness was clearly no aid to the war effort and, it was believed, was corrupting African morals. But how was this measure to be enforced? The police were given powers of search; but they were far too few to have any impact. Nor could the quality of police manpower be relied upon: by the early part of 1946, 'recruiting was at its lowest ebb and some candidates had to be accepted who did not even approximate to the already lowered standard' (Annual Report 1946: 75). This law was an ass, since it was clearly unenforceable. A year after its introduction, the claim was made that '90% of the labour trouble is attributable to the spirituous liquors'.[4] At the end of the war, excessive drinking by Africans was assumed to be contributing to the rise in crime, too. So there were renewed calls for the stamping out of *waragi*. But prohibition, whether partial or total, had already been shown to be quite beyond the powers of the local British administration to enforce. In this respect, as in so many others for the British colonial state, continuity during the period of the Second World War resided primarily in its own limited effectiveness.

And yet the exhausted and exposed colonial state survived. How did it come through the crisis? First, it was never directly challenged. Though it faced some impassable obstacles in its attempts to maximise and control the wartime mobilisation of resources, even the disturbances of January 1945 were a spontaneous outburst of protest rather than an attempt to overthrow colonial rule. Secondly, Britain retained the means of coercion. After all, with its allies it had *won* the Second World War. With its prestige and its empire largely intact, it still had the means *in extremis* to send to Uganda troops from outside – as indeed it did from Kenya in both 1945 and 1949. Thirdly, the Protectorate government eventually made some concessions to African demands: for example, in allowing African co-operatives to engage in cotton ginning and coffee-curing. But as the British colonial state in Uganda sought now to reconstruct itself – or at least to reconstruct its legitimacy and acceptability – it was to do so in a new and wider context, a context in which colonialism, whatever measures it adopted, was having to come to terms with its own mortality.

The new context: decolonisation

At the dawn of the 1950s, the British still appeared to be in control of events, or at least of long-term planning and policy for the protectorate. And at the same time the role of Uganda's Africans appeared to be one of responding and reacting. There is only the most fragile evidence, at this point especially, of any significant protectorate-wide nationalist movement.

But there was a flaw in the British position. Both before the war, in 1938, and during it, in 1943, eventual self-government for Britain's colonial dependencies had been clearly articulated in London as government policy. Now, in the aftermath of the Second World War, events themselves brought that previously distant prospect ever nearer. Britain had been severely weakened by a conflict which saw the emergence of two potential 'super powers', the USA and the USSR, each committed to an anti-colonial posture, as was, of course, the new United Nations. Britain's own Labour Government had no taste for perpetuating empire, except perhaps in the short-term to help solve major domestic economic and financial problems. We may note that the Tanganyika groundnut scheme of the later 1940s spectacularly failed to deliver in this respect, and remains to this day an East African object lesson – not always learnt – on how not to pursue 'development' objectives. And events elsewhere in Britain's empire pointed the way. India gained its independence in 1947 – having previously been not merely 'the jewel in the crown' of the empire but, it will be recalled, the major strategic consideration in Uganda's being claimed as a British protectorate in the 1890s. Still more telling perhaps were post-war developments in British West Africa.

Far away in landlocked equatorial Uganda, however, colonial rulers were as yet less ready to accept that responsibility might shortly be relinquished and that their days of governing Uganda were numbered. It was by no means obvious here that power would shortly be devolved to African majorities. There were clearly doubts, even in the Labour government of the day, as to whether these East Africans were 'ready' to move towards full independence. Thus on a visit to Uganda in 1946, Arthur Creech Jones told the Buganda Lukiiko that they were still proceeding 'along the road towards civilisation'; there was no mention of the road to independence.[5] That such language was still used by British authorities at this time is in retrospect remarkable. And local officials had their own variations. Thus three years later in November 1949, shortly after the major Buganda riots, the Resident, L.M.Boyd, was still referring to Uganda as the 'Little Black Baby' deposited on John Bull's doorstep – half a century after the cartoon depicting this scene had appeared in Punch – and speaking of its 'little pranks and occasional little kicks at its ayah's shins, now that it is beginning to find its feet'.[6]

But much was to change in 1952 with the arrival of Andrew Cohen as governor. His agenda was to leave British officials in the protectorate in no doubt as to the course that Uganda was taking (had any failed to note the significance, a year earlier, of Kwame Nkrumah being appointed Leader of Government Business in another tropical British colonial dependency, the Gold Coast). Previous contradictions contained within British ruling attitudes had been inadvertently revealed by Rees Williams, Under Secretary of State for the Colonies, during a visit to Uganda in 1948. Addressing a meeting in Jinja, he had said: 'Many people pretend to talk on behalf of the African but they do not really know what the African *wants*. I have come out here as one of the King's Ministers to see the people of Uganda and to find out what are their *needs*'.[7] But 'wants' and 'needs' are not the same thing, especially when they are defined by different parties. It is curious to note that Arthur Creech Jones, Rees Williams's Colonial Secretary at the time, had acknowledged by this time that 'the days are passing when policies can be made independent of the colonial peoples'.[8] But neither his Under Secretary, nor British officials in Uganda who were accountable to him, yet acted on his dictum.

Though African interests and opinions were now the criteria by which any British policy, and its prospects for success, had to be judged, it was Cohen rather than 'the colonial peoples' in Uganda who propelled the protectorate towards independence in the 1950s. British metropolitan initiative was more of a cause than surging 'nationalism'. African political aspirations in Uganda at this time remained complex and diverse, which tends to lend weight to Ronald Robinson's more general, trenchant, observation that 'whatever persuaded the British Empire [in 1947] to plan its own demise in tropical Africa, it was not fear of black African freedom fighters' (1980: 52). Cohen set out to accelerate Uganda's progress towards self-rule. He sought, as he did so, a formula for a viable post-colonial African state. In the former endeavour he was successful – independence followed, in 1962. But in the latter he failed – civil wars and coups overshadowed the first independence generation.

Cohen's failure to find the formula could not necessarily have been foreseen, if only because at any given moment there was great uncertainty as to how much time he had to work in. But the mid to late 1950s were to provide further and conclusive evidence that since the Second World War African impetus and not British colonial will was the *ultimate* arbiter of the direction that Uganda would take. Cohen's venture in fact brought back to prominence divisions within the territory – each of which long pre-dated the start of British colonial rule just sixty years earlier. It served, too, to illustrate the enormous challenge to be faced by any government in Uganda (even one trying to function decades after independence): how to contain centrifugal tendencies and to forge a viable state.

The districts: towards a post-colonial constitution?
There were broadly three levels of administrative reference in Uganda when Cohen arrived in January 1952. There was the central government, located in Entebbe. There was, secondly, a provincial level, at which African provincial councils to the west, north and east of Buganda were the recent brainchild of his predecessor John Hall in 1949. And there were, thirdly, the districts, which themselves comprised layers of activity, from county to parish level. A number of districts enjoyed a firmly rooted historic identity, and even political authority.

By the 1930s, the districts were well established as territorial units, for which British district officers were severally responsible. The piecemeal superimposition of colonial rule could initially fuse only crudely with the complexities of existing social identities, of whatever longevity. But British administrators did what they could to adapt colonial to pre-colonial patterns, in order to make their own administration as easy and as cheap as possible. Thomas and Scott, administrators themselves, declared with some pride, in 1935, that although 'there has been no rigid standardisation, in every district it has been found practicable to fit the elements of pre-existing society into a uniform framework with the minimum distortion in either'. The appointment of chiefs by the British recognised instances where 'the hereditary principle has long-standing validity'. The upshot was, now the era of the use of Baganda agents was past, that 'about every chief today is of the same tribe, and often the same tribal subdivision, as his subjects'. These men were expected in time 'to become more consciously the interpreters of the aspirations of their people' (1935: 83,84). Of course, Thomas and Scott could foresee neither the erosion of chiefly authority over the next couple of decades nor the triumph of the elective principle. They were right, however, to imply that by recognising and institutionalising the district in this particular way the British were enhancing the durability of a kind of localism. While this practice was 'divisive' in the limited sense of perpetuating existing divisions, critics of the alleged 'divide and rule' machinations of colonial rule have probably not considered whether there were any available short-term alternatives to the convenience of appointing chiefs who were men of local, that is local tribal, standing.

Indeed, the Entebbe archive houses evidence of the extent to which an embryonic elective principle was in fact being incorporated into the protectorate's political culture, in some areas, even before the Second World War. A report on the appointment of chiefs in Eastern Province in the late 1930s records 'selection approved by the people'; 'the people are unanimous in their choice'; and again 'he is the choice of both the district lukiiko and of the people'. Another chief was 'voted by the clan'; and so on.[9] Such instances may not be typical – there could also be political interference, with chosen chiefs regarded as unsuitable being replaced – but they do represent part of the overall picture. In the eastern district of Budama, chiefs of local origin were being appointed for the first time in 1938, to replace 'government agents'. The provincial commissioner reported that 'the natives of Budama have recently become most tribe-conscious'. There were complications here, however: each of the three counties of the district had heterogeneous populations. In one of these counties, where most inhabitants were Bagwe, a Mugwe was duly chosen/appointed as chief; but a minority, the Basamia, sought a district of their own under a man of their own. The British obliged in this case only to the extent of recognising a Musamia as a chief at county level.[10] This was British colonial rule in its heyday: not trampling 'absolutely' over district-based sensibilities, but trying to locate and install personnel who, in all the numerous localities of the protectorate, might act as their agents in the (as yet) limited tasks of minimal government, which scarcely at this stage went beyond the maintenance of order and the collection of taxes.

The later 1940s saw further developments in the districts, in the wake of the war. At this time there was a cautious attempt, from above, to formally democratise the African local governments. A 1949 ordinance, confirming the (tribal) district as the heart of local government, gave all district councils corporate powers, albeit under the chiefs. But subsequently, in the 1955 ordinance, councils themselves became (outside Buganda) the district administration – even if subject to Protectorate government approval (Burke 1964: 38-40). Councils became a focus for political activity and thus stirred political consciousness at the district level (Gertzel 1976: 82-83). Old divisions in the districts re-surfaced: religious differences found a new form, while widespread resentment of the privileged position of Indians had the makings of a territory-wide issue. But these embryonic African district governments had little taste for merging themselves in Hall's projected *provincial* councils (Gertzel 1976: 70). By now, identification with the district had a life of its own.

Cohen, too, was to give his attention first to the districts. If this focus was understandable, so too was his complementary marginalising of the province as an intermediate level. More than Hall, what he had in mind was a unitary state in which districts would engage with the centre. By contrast, it was felt that four large provinces (including Buganda) would draw Uganda towards a looser-knit, federalist, constitutional order. Thus a succession of district-based initiatives marked Cohen's governorship, from his implementing the recommendations of the Wallis Report in 1952 (in the 1955 ordinance referred to above) to his setting up the Wild Committee in 1958.[11] The fruit of these initiatives was the further animation of district political life. To an extent, this is what Cohen wanted – but there was to be, in the longer term, an ironic unintended down side. Even in 1952 Wallis reported that the local chiefs wanted to achieve for their districts the status of a native state *à la* Buganda, rather than to find an appropriate place in a unitary Uganda (Gertzel 1976: 79). As for people in the districts at that time, Wallis found that in general, apart from migrant labourers, they had neither awareness of, nor interest in, the protectorate beyond their district borders.

Yet the raising of local consciousness could in time have a variety of significant political repercussions. It could, for example, arouse a *suspicion* of the centre – and in particular of whatever constitutional position Buganda might enjoy in the future. Conversely, perhaps rather later, it could stimulate an appetite for *access*, on behalf of the district, to the economic power and wealth that an Africanised central government promised. This latter perception by districts, of the state as an agency for satisfying local/tribal expectations rather than promoting territory-wide benefit, was subsequently to prove all but fatal to the well-being of Uganda as an independent African state. As Fred Burke already dryly observed, just after independence, 'not a few representatives to Uganda's National Assembly are inclined to regard themselves (and, just as important, are regarded by their fellow tribesmen) as district-tribal ambassadors' (1964: 229).

What Cohen did not, and in the limited time available to him probably could not, achieve was an erosion of localism, a submerging of district-tribal identities in his pursuit of a united and national Uganda. Perhaps it was a logical impossibility: any attempt to heighten the self-consciousness of the districts already established in the protectorate was likely to make the forging of national consciousness more, rather than less, difficult. So when the District Councils Ordinance of 1955 gave African district councils 'a good deal more power and patronage than they previously enjoyed', it followed that the council assumed increased importance everywhere. This enhanced position and the increased political activity at that level 'increased the sense of district identity' (Gertzel 1976: 86,88). And this development was taking place just a very few years before Uganda was to achieve full political independence from Britain.

It did not much matter that some of these councils were despised by British officials who, in the 1950s, had to work with them. B.L. Jacobs in Lango realised at the time that the district council elections of 1955 were 'a considerable leap' but he despaired at the prospect of authority being passed to it. He sadly concluded, from the poor level of debate and behaviour, that there was more to democracy than the franchise. And he saw the district council as the enemy of progress towards a Ugandan consciousness, preoccupied as it was with local concerns and its own identity.[12] But the 'men on the spot' like Jacobs could only regret; they could not undo what had been done. And the roots of potential centrifugalism took firmer hold.

Shortly after he left Uganda in 1957, Andrew Cohen offered a retrospective description of district work in the protectorate during his governorship. It was characterised by variety, he wrote, and by obstacles. In Karamoja, the initiative in attempting to save the land 'comes almost entirely from the British officers. It is an uphill task, for the people are intensely resistant to change and inclined to violence if pressed too far'. Bugisu, by contrast, was 'affected by politics. The DC was often heavily involved in them [and] had the delicate task of holding the ring between different factions' (Cohen 1959: 67,70). In such circumstances, the British officer's ignorance of complex local issues could, as ever, be exploited. Cohen concluded that one of the main functions of the district officer was diplomacy. He explained: plans and programmes 'cannot be forced on the people. If they are to be effective, the people must be persuaded to accept them, and the process of persuasion may take weeks or even months' (1959: 72). Sentiments such as these prefigured those of Cohen's successor, Yoweri Museveni, some thirty years later in independent Uganda. They are the more convincing for coming from a man who believed in the efficacy of British colonial initiative and action. Overall, though, they do not convey a picture of a British colonial state entirely in control of the destiny of Uganda.

Who, indeed, was exploiting whom? Cohen himself had famously been the victim of political satire. On his arrival in Uganda in 1952 he was invited to a lavish party given by I.K.Musazi. Cohen and his wife gladly applauded a troupe of dancing girls – quite unaware that they had been singing (in Luganda) 'Governor Hall stole our cotton'.[13] Such an anecdote reinforces a serious theme. In a wide survey of British colonial administration, referring mainly to the inter-war period, Michael Crowder stressed the general *ignorance* of district officers, and showed how local African intermediaries 'invariably exploited' this (1970: 348). Crowder's observation is in turn reminiscent of the even more belittling image of the local agent of the inter-war British Empire offered by George Orwell, from personal experience in Burma. In his essay, 'Shooting an Elephant', he wrote of 'the hollowness, the futility of the white man's dominion. It is the condition of his rule that he shall spend his life in trying to impress "the natives" and so in every crisis he has got to do what the "natives" expect of him'. Orwell's own conclusion was concise and bleak: 'When the white man turns tyrant it is his own freedom that he destroys' (1970 vol.1: 269). Just as the *intendants* of Louis XIV's French 'absolutism' are now recognised to have been few in number, overworked, and prey to local influences, so we must acknowledge the limited potential of local officers in a British colonial state such as Uganda. Opportunities for arbitrary decisions may have been numerous; but there was little scope for tyranny here.

Yet in the 1950s district officers were free to go about their business in Uganda and, so far from living in fear of political challenge, let alone violence, to enjoy themselves. Recently published recollections of expatriates who worked in government service in the protectorate in the 1950s all testify to what was, for them at any rate, a largely care-free 'golden era'. Whether or not they had received adequate training in post-war England, they relished the challenges they faced. Thus W.L. Bell recalls arriving in Uganda in 1947. 'I was twenty-seven, [and] had no degree (or any other recognised qualification).... Of Africa, the African, the language, the customs, the role of a District Officer, I still knew nothing. It was with high expectation that I received marching orders to Gulu' (Brown 1996: 103,106) What is typical in this memoir, of the late 1940s, is not so much the absence of any training as the enthusiasm and self-confidence with which Bell approached his posting. There was no sense of insecurity.

When another district commissioner arrived in Ankole in 1955, he wrote: 'No one is armed in the conventional sense and, I am told, we certainly neither need nor have escorts'. Four years later this same official was in Masaka, responsible with just one expatriate colleague, and 'a hundred or so' policemen, for law and order in a district of 400,000 people spread over nearly 4000 square miles (Forward 1999: 31, 83). Meanwhile, in the north at Kitgum, Acting District Commissioner H.J.B. Allen could write home, in 1957, 'it is desperately hard work, but enormous fun'.[14] The evidence suggests that these were not the agents of an intolerable rule: there was not a great deal for Africans to have to tolerate. Another senior colonial official, William Ryrie, wrote of the late 1950s, 'There was hardly any sign of resistance to British rule' – despite there being no certainty yet of an imminent British departure. Independence was still thought to be anything from 15 to 25 years away (Brown 1996: 350). In the meantime, British officers remained in post: 'sitting among the villagers and listening – listening for hours at a time' (Furse 1962: 263). Not only listening – recommendations by local councils still had to be approved, or not, by higher colonial authority – but listening still: such was the reality in the 1950s of supervising the districts, the administrative units on which British government was founded and with which Africans most strongly identified.

The other two dimensions of Cohen's three-pronged political and constitutional initiative need less detailed attention here, but they do require some evaluation. There was nothing theoretically inconsistent with his district-centred proposals in either. He moved, first, to increase African participation in central government. He subsequently sought to democratise institutions within Buganda.

The former policy faced huge obstacles. Changes at the centre could never match those in the districts, either in tempo or in the degree of interest and commitment they aroused. It was not until 1956 that there were as many as 30 African unofficials in the Legislative Council, and they numbered no more than half of the total, the others being representatives of the European and Indian communities. And it was not until 1958 that the first direct elections for the Legislative Council were held – with independence, as we know now, only four years away. Moreover, Uganda-wide political parties had not had time to establish any trans-local loyalties and vision. I.K. Musazi and Abu Mayanja had toured the districts on behalf of the fledgling Uganda National Congress in 1952 and 1953 but were unable to inspire mass mobilisation on national issues (Gertzel 1976: 80).

By 1957, when he left Uganda, Cohen's strategy for a unitary state based on the districts had all but collapsed. And by this time too, Buganda, far from proceeding steadily towards integration with the rest of Uganda, was in the grip of a neo-traditionalism which threatened to detach it completely from the territorial entity with which it had been peculiarly, and increasingly uneasily, associated. Cohen's policy of democratising Ganda institutions was overwhelmed by the so-called Kabaka Crisis of 1953-55 which torpedoed his ingenious strategy.

What can be learnt from this extraordinary sequence of events? The crisis was not, to be fair, entirely the governor's fault. One could even assert that, given Buganda's pre-colonial history and then its unique status under British colonial rule, the acceleration of Uganda towards independence was bound to cause some kind of structural crisis concerning the kingdom. That said, the drama arose out of issues at least partly caused by contemporary official British incompetence.

The first of these was renewed uncertainty about Britain's long-term strategy for East Africa. Against the background of a European-dominated federation being imposed on Britain's Central African territories, Secretary of State Oliver Lyttleton spoke in June 1953 of the possibility 'of still larger measures of unification, and possibly still larger measures of federation of the whole East African territories'(Low 1971: 108). That was enough, as Kabaka Mutesa II later put it, 'to bring all Baganda anxiety frothing to the surface' (1967: 118). The Lukiiko protested; and the Kabaka requested that responsibility for Buganda in Britain should be transferred from the Colonial Office to the Foreign Office, as a guarantee that in future Buganda's interests at least would be independently safeguarded.

The second issue concerned a more immediate prospect: that of Buganda's fuller incorporation into the Uganda Protectorate, as a step in the latter's constitutional evolution towards self-government. Governor Cohen announced in August 1953 that Uganda's Legislative Council was to be further strengthened and democratised by the election of 14 African representatives. Of these, 3 would be Baganda; and the 14 would be matched by 7 Europeans and 7 Indians. There were African objections to the further institutionalisation of a disproportionate multiracialism in Uganda. But the even greater issue for the Baganda was the prospect that in future the 'Baganda would at best simply be part of a unitary state along with its neighbours' – who might be able to line up against them (Low 1971: 109-110). The Kabaka and the Lukiiko, which since March 1953 was more broadly representative of Ganda opinion than before, refused to co-operate with Cohen's proposal. Cohen's discussions with Mutesa ended in deadlock; and on 30 November 1953 the governor deported the Kabaka to Britain.

At first sight, the year 1953 therefore presented the British, in London and in Entebbe, as masters of Uganda's destiny: formulating policies, and not flinching from dismissing the ruler of Uganda's most prominent African people. But what happened next? At once, as the professor of history at Makerere at the time relates, 'the heavy-handed intervention of the Protectorate government in Buganda's affairs rallied all sections of the people and made the Kabaka once more the focus of Baganda loyalties' (Ingham 1962: 417). And in due course, two years later, the Kabaka made a triumphal return. By this time, the British had had to make concessions on both the main issues. They pledged that East African federation would not be imposed without the consent of the people of Uganda (Ingham 1962: 417). And meanwhile, on the question of multiracialism within

Uganda, Lyttleton announced that Uganda's future – as its past had been – was to be as 'primarily an African country'.[15]

This restoration of British-Baganda relations, which preceded the Kabaka's return and entailed a new formula for Buganda's co-existence with the protectorate, owed little directly to the metropolitan British government. It arose from prolonged discussions between Governor Cohen and leading Baganda in Kampala, during Mutesa's exile. The most extraordinary feature of these Namirembe Conferences was that their course, between July and September 1954, was entrusted to a neutral and unofficial third party, Sir Keith Hancock, the Australian academic who at that time was Director of the Institute of Commonwealth Studies at London University. Low writes that 'it is difficult to think of any other occasion on which a British governor sat down with a locally elected committee under an independent chairman to discuss constitutional reforms in his territory' (1971: 124).

The outcome of the discussions included, in 1955, a replacement of the 1900 Agreement. The Kabaka agreed to accept, as Cohen wished, a more representative government in Buganda, and to function from then on as a constitutional monarch. And yet at the same time, Buganda took on more governmental responsibilities from central government, in areas such as education and agriculture. This revised Agreement therefore achieved, in effect, a fuller form of internal self-government for Buganda than it had previously enjoyed. The Kabaka might have surrendered his autocracy, but he nevertheless achieved greater practical autonomy for the kingdom of Buganda within the protectorate. This arrangement was thus a setback for Cohen's policy, enunciated only two years earlier, that 'the future of Uganda must lie in a *unitary* form of central government on parliamentary lines covering the whole country' (Low 1971: 105. My italics). From 1955, as Cherry Gertzel has written, 'Buganda's relationship with the centre much more closely approximated to a federal position. To this extent the principle of a unitary state had been significantly modified' (1976: 75). Indeed, subsequently it was decided in 1961 that while Uganda should for the most part be a unitary state, Buganda's relations with the central government should be upon a federal basis.

In short, the Kabaka Crisis of 1953-55 was further evidence that the British could no longer manage political collaboration within Buganda as effectively as they had once done, before the Second World War. The 1949 riots had revealed the short-sightedness of reliance on unpopular ministers and chiefs; and anyway, during the early 1950s, as D.A. Low remarks, 'the props of overgrown chiefly authority were patently buckling'. As he also shows, the emergence of populism in Buganda led to a shift in the *locus* of power within the kingdom in the mid 1950s, 'away from the chiefs as such, to the people and those in whom they chose to repose their confidence' (1971: 153,159). And to some extent, they put their confidence in the Kabaka, Mutesa II, especially during the critical year of 1953.

The British apparently failed to appreciate the corollary: that after the Second World War the Kabaka could no longer play the mediating role required of a collaborating African ruler. The reported comments of Governor Hall, when he lost patience with Mutesa in the wake of the 1949 disturbances, had shown a significant lack of awareness on the part of the British of the delicacy of Mutesa's position. Thus: 'His Excellency is most dissatisfied with the Kabaka's conduct and gave it as his opinion that the young man was playing a double game by trying to curry favour with the malcontents in his kingdom while, at the same time, pretending to Government that he was in agreement with their views'.[16] But by definition, collaboration had always entailed a 'double game'. The difference now was that it was becoming a game that was impossible to play, especially in the context of a protectorate proceeding unsteadily towards its own eclipse.

Meanwhile, the Lukiiko proved increasingly assertive, as it came to represent more fully the views of the Baganda as a whole. For the Baganda, we must recall, no longer comprised merely peasant producer-consumers, but also included many thousands of the relatively new and aspiring middle class. Mutesa saw that the Lukiiko, now no longer a chief's body, could never again be subdued by local British authority: that 'the more respectably democratic the Lukiiko became, the less the Governor could control or ignore it' (1967: 117). Thus, by the mid 1950s, British overrule was being rejected by all parties to whom the 1900 Agreement had been addressed: the Kabaka, the chiefs, and the people. Governor Hall had earlier admitted, in a report to the military marked Top Secret, that the situation in Buganda 'was for a time out of control'.[17] In 1955, the British effectively abandoned their attempts to control it any more.

Looking again at the protectorate as a whole, why did Britain's strategy for devolving power in Uganda in the 1940s and 1950s fail, in the event, to bequeath to the territory a viable constitution? One reason, as Cranford Pratt has argued, was that British officials assumed that they had more time than was in fact available to them. In the later 1940s, 'it was very far from clear that colonialism was soon to be over' (1982: 258-9). In 1947, East Africa's governors condemned Colonial Office initiatives in London to promote more democratic institutions in their local and central governments. The governors believed that their territories still needed British rule; that western-educated Africans were unrepresentative and were not to be trusted; and that, anyway, there was no significant African nationalist demand for the steps that the Colonial Office was advocating. Despite the Cohen era, comparable assumptions were still being aired among even most senior protectorate officials up to the late 1950s. Meanwhile, also contributing to the acceleration of Britain's departure were African impatience as well as a crude logic: if there was to be independence, why not now? But this 'time' factor, not exclusive to Uganda, may not teach us much. No transition or devolution was ever likely to be smooth; and perhaps it would have been naïve to expect anything other than the prompt revival of historic tensions and divisions, in the case of Uganda, whenever the British left.

A more particular reason for failure was that British preoccupation with reform at the district level not only neglected the urgent need to consolidate authority at the centre but actually fostered centrifugal tendencies. This point was emphasised by Grace Ibingira, himself a player in the drama. Once it was clear that the British would pull out of Uganda, local tribally defined groups sought a place for themselves, if not a prominent then at least a secure place, within the new order. Buganda provides the most spectacular example. From the early 1950s, 'its resistance increased in direct proportion to the preparations for British disengagement' (Ibingira 1982: 288-9).

In the event, the transfer of power at independence embraced a series of unsatisfactory compromises. The hybrid constitutional form which independent Uganda took in 1962 appears to have been shaped more by African political pressures – in what became an age of mass politics, parties and elections by the end of the 1950s – than by British planning and preference. But one can argue that the origins of 1962 should be sought in an earlier past. In a sense, 'the end was contained in the beginning' (Austin 1982: 226). It was not especially surprising that the peculiar constitutional arrangements of 1962, reflecting as they did particularly intractable ingredients of the British colonial state in Uganda from its inception to its demise, were not to last. In particular, the association of Milton Obote (its first prime minister) with the Kabaka, Mutesa II (its first President), appeared doomed from the start. Each enjoyed a form of authority and legitimacy which could hardly have been more distinct from the other. As Mazrui and Tidy have remarked: 'Either the advocate of a strong central government and non-ethnic nationalism would prevail over the federalist/regionalist sub-nationalist; or the latter would prevail over the former' (1984: 103-104). Only four years later, in 1966, Obote's troops attacked the Kabaka's palace and drove Mutesa into exile. A new constitution then ushered in a unitary republic. On the surface at least, this outcome resembled Cohen's goal; but it was post-colonial African political forces, not the British colonial state in its final phase, which (for the time being) achieved it.

Towards a post-colonial economy

The post-war British administration sought once more to be a provider: not only of imported consumer goods but also, this time, of social and economic development on an unprecedented scale. Cautiously at first but then quite lavishly, the Protectorate government spent great sums of money, wealth generated in the main by Uganda's own peasant farmers, to promote the greater social and material well-being of the territory's growing population. They thus set a pattern – an expectation, at least – of the state as a potential source of bounty. Such an expectation of the state was to be inherited, perhaps unfortunately, by the independent African government which replaced the British.

But by then the aftermath of war, and the period of decolonisation leading up to 1962, had further underlined the limited capacity of British rule in Uganda. The fate of several post-war British development initiatives offers examples of continued shortcomings. As D.A. Lury has remarked, with the Funds which we considered in an earlier chapter in mind, 'It was relatively easy for the government to hold back large sums from the grower; it was difficult to use them effectively to develop and diversify' (1976: 235). Big projects struggled to take root. Thus the Jinja textile factory accumulated huge losses by the late 1950s; Kilembe mining was not profitable before the 1960s; above all, the hydro-electric installation at Owen Falls on the Nile near Jinja failed to initiate rapid industrialisation. By 1962, the Uganda Electricity Board – a typical parastatal body of the period – was in serious financial trouble. Meanwhile, the African Housing Programme 'did little to touch the basic problem of creating satisfactory conditions for unskilled workers'; and the Community Development Department 'was unable to create a series of self-sustaining activities', despite an expenditure of £1.5 million between 1952 and 1957 (Lury 1976: 242). Aspiration and initiative on the part of central government were no guarantee of economic success, in colonial times or subsequently.

Not all government spending was in vain. Diversification in the economy, and an expansion of educational provision, brought some new employment opportunities. There was no doubting that the British administration had a positive developmental agenda and, significantly, held out the promise of some future material betterment. On the ground, the new generation of expatriate officers has been described as being 'entirely occupied' in advancing 'the knowledge and abilities' of its protegés (Stone 1979:110). But here was a complex interaction. Not all British policies and projects were fruitful (or even welcome); and when it proved necessary not merely to teach and lead but to 'cajole and perhaps sometimes even to impel', legitimacy was not so much underwritten as undermined. Even with the state now committed to its realisation, there were no simple shortcuts to prosperity for all.

Pressure on African consumers (or at least on those who grew cash crops), and hence on the British Protectorate government, eased from around 1950 onwards. The terms of trade turned sharply in many Ugandans' favour, so that export prices, for cotton and especially for coffee, now far outstripped the increased prices of imported goods. International developments such as these were, as before, beyond the control of the Protectorate government; but on this occasion, for the first time for decades, it was briefly to be a beneficiary. In this more reassuring context, the controversial 'price assistance' from Cotton and Coffee Funds ended in 1952, when monies were transferred to a new African Development Fund. For much of the 1950s – though hardly as a result of their own achievements – the British authorities in Uganda were able to concentrate on constitutional and political issues, freed from anxiety about the protectorate's economy or the basic well-being of its producers and consumers.

The significance of British colonial economic initiatives in the 1950s lies less in what they achieved (or failed to achieve) than in the trend which they confirmed and set for the future: that of the central government assuming responsibility for the prosperity of all. As to actual achievement, the record of the Uganda Development Corporation in its first ten years was not encouraging. Set up in June 1952, its scope was universal. 'Virtually there is no field of development enterprise in which the corporation does not take a potential interest', noted a visitor to Uganda in 1960, by which time the UDC's enterprises included mining, agriculture, building materials, food products, property, textiles, metalware and even hotels (Ingrams 1960: 132-3). But Wrigley's comment of 1959 is a persuasive verdict on the British colonial state's overall incapacity to shape and manage the economy of Uganda by such means during this period:

> In the event, these plans and prognostications have so far not been fulfilled at all. During the past decade wealth on a scale hitherto undreamt of has flowed into Uganda, not from the new forms of large-scale agriculture, which have been an almost total failure, nor yet from mining and manufacturing, which have made but slow headway,

but from the old-established export industries and in the main from the efforts of the African peasant, with his smallholding and his hoe (1959: 68).

Even so, Uganda was evidently an example of a British colonial state which had assumed *central* controls over economic affairs since the Second World War, and had thereby helped set the pattern which post-colonial independent African governments were likely to follow. In the 1950s, the British administration in Uganda established a precedent for heavy government spending, and eventually overspending, of financial reserves which had been built up and guarded cautiously over previous years. Moreover, by 1962, the state in Uganda, whatever its constitutional oddities, was seen to be at the centre of economic management in the country as a whole. The state was the recipient and spender of large sums of government revenue, the regulator of economic affairs, the generator of economic planning and policy and, above all perhaps, the employer of an ever expanding number of the territory's people. It was to become, too, the beneficiary and distributor of external aid.

Political power at the centre in the post-colonial era was to offer easy access to the levers of wealth production and distribution. Before that, however, there were to be several more years of frustration for ambitious Africans. Expatriate Europeans and Indians still blocked access to economic opportunity in the 1950s, and into the 1960s, too. Very high profits were to be made by cotton ginners and coffee curers, in that intermediate level of economic activity between the marketing boards above and the peasant producers below – but the ginners and curers were all non-African in 1945, and substantially so thereafter. This meant that there was still full scope for 'economic conflict aggravated by racial feeling' (Lury 1976: 232). From 1951 there were to be some openings for Africans in such fields, and these became more numerous during that decade. For some time even after independence, however, Africans could be seen as junior partners. In 1964, an African Business Promotion company was born, as a subsidiary of the UDC, to help African traders and businessmen in the field of wholesale buying. It soon became clear that it was not in itself to become a wholesaler but only to be a source of credit for

Africans to obtain goods from Indian wholesalers. When an Indian businessman was appointed to run the organisation, Africans were bemused. In an ironic tone not always to be found in documents of this kind, the 1964 Annual Report commented: 'From a psychological and practical point of view, he as an Asiatic was unacceptable to African traders who simply could not see how an Asian [could be] head of a company which had been established with the sole purpose of helping to promoté African trade' (Annual Report 1964: 84).

In the longer term, of course, both before and after Idi Amin's expulsion of the Indians in 1972, the essential competition for access to economic wealth, at all levels though especially at the centre, was to be intra-African rather than inter-racial. The pursuit of the fruits of independence and of Africanisation came to entail successive struggles between the diverse locally based ethnic interest groups. Their revival of self-consciousness at the district level was, as we have seen, a major element in the political history of the 1950s, and thus in the colonial legacy. Beneficiaries of former regional disparity sought to sustain the pre-eminence they had enjoyed in the colonial period, while those of the marginalised or relatively neglected areas, outside Buganda and the east, sought redress. As Bayart has recently stressed, to be part of the political and hence economic elite was to have access to the whole range of state resources – land regulation, credit, taxation, marketing boards, public investment and negotiations with private capital and importers (1993: 74). The state had always had to sustain itself, since its (colonial) foundation and even in its minimalist form, by diverting surplus wealth 'into its own pockets'. What was transformed latterly was the expansion of its size and scope. In three generations the state had become a far stronger magnet for personal ambition. In Bayart's stark assessment, 'anti-colonial movements sheltered schemes for individual enrichment which anticipated the later pillage of the independent administrations' (1993: 73).

The state was perhaps never more attractive than as a paymaster. Thousands of Africans had experience of being on the state's payroll in colonial times, as participators in the exercise of British rule. To take one single district as an example, in Toro, Western Province, in 1942, there were over 800 local Africans on the government payroll as chiefs, clerks and police.[18] The independent state multiplied opportunities and sharpened competitive opportunism. If no more, a post in government offered income: 'a salary, even if it is modest, paid late and irregularly, is no trivial thing' (Bayart 1993: 75). Then there were to be numerous perks, too, such as access to credit, or access to a telephone. Beyond this, jobs in government could become 'positions of predation' and open up 'bottomless financial reservoirs' for personal advancement (albeit on behalf of district or extended family) (Bayart 1993: 78). It looks as though a great deal changed rapidly from the 1950s, when the government agents of those days, the final generation of British district officers – less needy of personal enrichment or concerned for job security – could be described as a 'collection of almost schoolboy, utopian, theorist-enthusiasts' (Robinson 1979: 180). Such officers provided what Berman has recently termed a 'disinterested competence and fairness' (1998: 341).

The point here is not a moral one, however. Rather, it is to demonstrate that the colonial state, in its last years especially, took on at the centre so much responsibility for the economic affairs of the country that the successor state could only act as a magnet for African involvement – and competition – on a large scale. The shell of the late colonial state, with its innumerable openings for employment in parastatal bodies, in the bureaucracy itself, and of course in the armed forces and security services, was there to be seized and occupied and exploited. It was something worth fighting for.

The legacy
Having visited Uganda in 1893, Gerald Portal said he had seen 'a country which possessed a better climate than England, where fine open country and grassy uplands would afford innumerable playing-fields for such English sports as football, and perfect pitches for cricket'.[19] Football may indeed prove to be among the more durable results of British colonial rule in Uganda. But a less optimistic (and yet perhaps more prophetic) alternative description was offered only a year later. Shortly before the declaration of the British Protectorate in 1894, Uganda was described by a member of the Imperial British East Africa Company as 'a hornets' nest'.[20] What eventually fol-

lowed on from British colonialism was indeed far from Portal's Elysian vision: not cricket fields but killing fields. It is against the sobering backdrop of what occurred in Uganda in the generation after 1962 that we must now seek to summarise the colonial legacy.

We may benefit here from a shrewd and concise historic assessment of a distant European country, in an earlier age, and at a particular stage in its development. E.N.Williams observed, of France at the start of Louis XIV's reign, in the middle of the seventeenth century, that 'the French were not yet a nation, and France hardly a state' (1999: 139). If a nation is a group of people who consider themselves alike, bonded, sharing characteristics and interests which, they feel, distinguish them from others, then in 1962 Ugandans were 'not yet a nation'. And if the concept of a state entails an established instrument of government, capable of both exerting its will uniformly across a given territory and perpetuating itself – and secure and durable borders too, universally recognised – then, at this moment of the transfer of power, Uganda 'was hardly a state'. Frontiers, though inappropriate, were long since deemed immutable by Uganda's colonial rulers. Despite (or because of) this, relations between landlocked Uganda and the five immediate neighbours it inherited in 1962 were destined to range from the fractious to the hostile. There is strength in Basil Davidson's rueful observation that the acceptance by the first generation of African political leaders of 'the nation-state as necessary aim' represented a 'handicap' posing 'perils' for the future (1992: 162-3). Of course, perils lay in acceptance of any alternative 'aim' too.

Within Uganda, the extent of social diversity and the number of separate identities undermined any claims to 'nationhood'. There had scarcely been any re-defining 'nationalist' movement of sustained revolt against British rule. Once British rule ended, long suppressed or containable divisions could, and did, surface or re-surface. The declaration of a state of emergency in Toro, in 1962-63, is evidence of this.[21] Even in the 1890s, the Baganda themselves were already divided; and the protectorate came to contain a great variety of peoples, whose previous relations had tended to be neither close nor cordial. There had been some general acceptance since then of the alien culture: of education and of Christianity, for example, especially when these seemed to open up opportunities for self-advancement in the colonial or post-colonial state. But there was no successor elite as homogeneous and cohesive as the British officialdom which formally stepped aside in 1962. Deep differences between Protestants and Catholics and Muslims co-existed with, but did not correspond with, persistent ethnic divisions reinforced by distinctive language and culture. Indian communities in their entirety were not integrated within the whole: and, no longer part of a three-tier society sanctioned by colonial authority, their social and economic position was both visible and vulnerable. Meanwhile, 'tribalism' represented, in the sombre words of Yoweri Museveni, 'the greatest single tool by which ignorant opportunists destroy the unity and strength of unpoliticised African groups' (1997: 90).

Furthermore, two problematic aspects of the territory's economy in 1962 stand out. First, there was the variability of the colonial economic impact, the uneven regional spread of such advances as had been made. And secondly, there was a degree of overall underdevelopment which left an agricultural sector vulnerable to world crop price fluctuations, as well as an industrial sector far from capable of absorbing Uganda's growing population. These were profound structural weaknesses. The unintended outcome of British rule was that the colonial state had seemingly failed Ugandans in these respects. The protectorate had itself been dependent on exporting a limited range of primary products, in global economic conditions that were seldom helpful, while striving to achieve a degree of self-sufficiency. The outcome of successive attempts at industrialisation was not promising; and the territory did not enjoy the (mixed) blessings of even adolescent capitalism. Perversely, the independent African state was thought capable of remedies. When it proved inadequate as the benefactor for all Ugandans, it was increasingly looked upon – and fought over – to be a provider for only some.

To contain these divisions and structural flaws, there was a new constitution – but no restraining political culture to accompany it. A hurriedly fabricated paper scheme had been introduced which *encapsulated without resolving* the conflict between unitary and federal models of government. The particular position and potential of Buganda remained highly controversial and divisive – as did questions of land tenure within it. Centrifugal tendencies worked against the evolution of a unitary state. Fred Burke wrote of 'the tendency toward continued political and administrative fragmentation' as the 'legacy of tribalism and separatism' (1964: 231). Moreover, the conventional model of territory-wide responsible government through representative institutions had no roots at all in people's experience, which had rather been of the 'one-party state' of British colonial rule. Prophetic African fears were by 1964 already clear to Burke: that 'majority power will be employed primarily to harass and destroy the opposition rather than to pursue policies to which the minority might be opposed' (1964: 231). But then, the colonial state 'was not intended to be a school of democracy', as Berman reminds us (1998: 329). Indeed, it was for the most part not intended to achieve any *long-term* goals: in Crawford Young's words, 'the short run' was always 'the quintessential time frame for the official mind' (1994: 139). Does this make British officials culpable? One might argue that it was, and remains, unfair to charge the last generation of colonial rulers with having failed to achieve goals, within a time-scale – when these particular goals had not been originally formulated, and this particular time-scale was not previously known.

The institutions of the de-colonisation era were untried successors of what had been, under the British, a form of rule more personal than bureaucratic. When Low described government in Uganda before the First World War as 'very largely the work of individual district officers living very often exposed and alone in tiny scattered outposts', he captured the essence of what persisted thereafter (1965: 62)). More recently, Chabal and Daloz have stressed the significance in Africa of district officers who 'paid little heed to procedure and administered their areas of responsibility with a large degree of discretion'. And it is 'questionable' (they continue, in a tone of considerable understatement) whether British indirect rule 'did much to lay the foundations for a properly emancipated state' (1999: 12).

And what of colonial governors? In 1961, Walter Elkan could write that 'in colonial government, the position of the governor is pivotal' (1961: 51)). And Andrew Cohen, himself governor of Uganda between 1952 and 1957, wrote in 1959 that 'governors have continued to take the initiative in putting forward policy proposals; and the sphere of operation over which governments have had virtually complete freedom of action has not diminished, indeed rather the reverse' (1959: 88). It is hard to fully identify with either of these observations. Governors, Cohen among them, seldom achieved what they sought to achieve. Yet they appeared, magnetically to some who sought to replace them, to be 'pivotal'. It is perhaps a key ingredient in the colonial legacy that appearance – that one man could exercise effective, even beneficial, power across the country – disguised the sobering truth that government's 'freedom of action' was more a freedom to aspire than a freedom to accomplish.

In the event, and unexpectedly, the army proved to be a means for achieving a range of goals in the post-colonial era. The Baganda, its first victims in 1966, were not alone in having underestimated the potential of the military once Uganda became independent. This reflected previous experience of the British colonial state, in which armed forces played a generally shadowy, rarely prominent, part. The British certainly did not bequeath either unwieldy armed forces – a mere 700 men – or a huge military budget. By way of partial explanation, a colleague of Andrew Cohen has subsequently written of Cohen's having ignored the army. 'A most unmilitary man', Cohen was not interested in 'an absent army' which was, anyway, responsible to East Africa Command in Nairobi (Griffith 1996: 112). Because Cohen did not see the army as important, it was left out of the general process of Africanisation. In turn, it had little appeal for ambitious Baganda, who had other avenues of advancement which they could follow. Their relative under-representation in the army of 1962 was magnified thereafter in an army which soon became the political instrument of northern interest groups. And the army was the chosen means by which Milton Obote in 1966 imposed the unitary state which had eluded Cohen's more gentle prompting, in an act of arguably unprecedented 'absolutism'.

In short, in the absence of social cohesion and firm political institutions, yet with mastery of the postcolonial state offering access to the country's economic and financial resources, use of the army became the violent means by which one particularist group after another was to seek political ascendancy in Uganda in the first 20 years or more of independence. As we have seen, the British had had no need to create or maintain a large armed force which might have become, over the years, both ethnically balanced and trained in the virtues of political neutrality. And even given more time to work towards decolonisation, there might have been no impulse from any quarter for them to set themselves such a task. If in 1962 Ugandans had been a nation, and Uganda more fully a state, neither the immaturity nor the awful potential of Uganda's as yet marginalised army would have mattered.

The army, then, was scarcely prominent during the independence celebrations in October 1962, except musically in the form of marching bands. Sporting, rather than fighting, prowess was on show: boxing, Kiganda wrestling, athletics, a canoe regatta at Entebbe, and of course, above all, football. Meanwhile, the new flag, designed less than a year earlier, was proudly unfurled, displaying a crested crane against a background of black, gold and red. Black for *negritude*, gold for the sunshine, and red for such blood as had been spilt in fighting for freedom. These were also the colours of Obote's own party, the UPC; and it was to be a postcolonial army, largely of his creation initially, which was to be responsible for the wanton blood spilling that was to come.

It should be repeated, though, that the roots of the violent aftermath of 1962 lie far further back in time. Buganda, in particular, remained host to powerfully divisive influences. There was plenty of evidence of the longevity of sensitive issues: the large-scale boycott of Indian shops in Buganda in 1959/60, the perpetuation of Protestant and Catholic rivalries in Ganda-based political parties of the late 1950s, and the resurrection of the 'lost counties' dispute with Bunyoro in the early 1960s. Each of these issues arose from the dawn of the British era in Uganda: here the end indeed appears to have been contained in the beginning. The colonial period in Africa has been well described as 'the colonial moment' (Roberts 1986: 1). With British authority gone, in Uganda it was to be succeeded by years of political violence, with the destruction of the colonial institutional legacy and incalculable suffering and loss of life. All this was, of course, an unintended outcome, quite unforeseen by the British at any time.

For a final, and contrasting, depiction of British colonial rule we may turn to Elspeth Huxley's portrait of Entebbe, in 1948:

> The seat of Government is a miniature garden city on the margin of an inland sea. By night fat hippos browse beside the reedy edges, by day birds flash their plumage in the trees. There is a sort of dreamlike quality about Entebbe, perhaps because the vulgar shouts of the market-place do not reach here. Senior officials with their wives and retainers are almost the sole inhabitants. Here in Entebbe they formulate policy (Huxley 1948: 293).

They were indeed closer to the hippos and the birds than to the market-place. It comes as no surprise that successive British governors who have been credited with so much by their admirers – or accused of so much by their critics – were far less than all-powerful. Half-hearted in concept, the colonial state remained half-baked in practice. And for most of its life it was subject to and affected by African volition and resource. Like John Hall during and after the Second World War, colonial governors mostly considered themselves to have had 'a good deal of power'. The reality was rather different. The evidence leads us to conclude that they had far less power than they wanted or needed. 'Governing Uganda' proved in practice to be less a matter of direction and compulsion than an exercise in compromise and concession.

---

1. Chamberlain, 16 May 1902, is quoted in Henry Browne, *Joseph Chamberlain, Radical and Imperialist*, 1975, pp 91-92; and, 31 March 1897, he is quoted in Robinson and Gallagher, *Africa and the Victorians*, 1961, p.404.
2. George Hall, quoted in *Uganda Gazette*, 16 August 1945.
3. Ordinance No 1 of 1943, 29 March 1943, PRO CO 684/5.

4. F.J.Gorton, letter, *Uganda Herald*, 2 February 1944.

5. Reported in *Uganda Herald*, 7 August 1946.

6. Reported in *Uganda Herald*, 29 November 1949.

7. Reported in *Uganda Herald*, 20 April 1948. My italics.

8. Introduction to Rita Hinden, (editor), *Fabian Colonial Essays*, 1945, p.17.

9. Uganda Protectorate Secretarial Minute Paper, R 3/82, Uganda National Archive, Entebbe.

10. Provincial Commissioner, E.Province, to Chief Secretary, 13 July 1938, *ibid*.

11. C.A.G.Wallis carried out an inquiry into local government during 1952, reporting the following year; the Wild Committee was set up in 1959 to consider constitutional issues – see Gertzel, *Kingdoms, Districts and the Unitary State: Uganda 1945-1962*, in Low and Smith, *History of East Africa*, volume III, pp.71,79.

12. B.L.Jacobs, Lango District Annual Report, 1958, RH MSS Afr.s.2227/4.

13. O.G.Griffith, Cohen's private secretary. recalls this incident in a Personal Note, RH MSS Afr.s.2027.

14. H.J.B.Allen, letter to friends, 1957, 'Safari Reports', RH MSS Afr.s.1549.

15. Quoted in Low, *Buganda in Modern History*, p.113.

16. Quoted in a military memorandum to Lt General Dowler, 20 November 1950, PRO WO 276/103.

17. Hall to Dowler, 13 June 1949, PRO WO 276/103.

18. Uganda Protectorate Secretarial Minute Paper, R 66/2 (1942), Uganda National Archive, Entebbe.

19. Quoted by the Marquis of Lorne, Royal Colonial Institute, Report of Proceedings, vol.XXV, 1893-4, p.134.

20. Captain W.H.Williams, *ibid.*, p.106.

21. Fred Burke offers 'lengthy comment' on this episode in *Local Government and Politics in Buganda*, 1964, pp. 232-236.

POSTSCRIPT

The 1950s and the 1990s:
In Search of Stability

If we look once more at the policies of the British governor, Andrew Cohen, in the 1950s – the context in which they were formulated, the assumptions on which they were based, and the constitutional initiatives for which he was responsible – we will not only achieve a better understanding of the political dimension of the colonial legacy. We will also uncover some enlightening similarities with the situation President Yoweri Museveni finds himself in, forty or fifty years later, and some of his responses to it.

By the 1950s, the days of the colonial regime were numbered. Whatever the debate, or delusions, about the exact pace of the advance towards Ugandan self-government, it was as clear to the regime as to anyone else that it must prepare, in the short term, for an orderly succession. And it was just as clear that it should try to bequeath a framework for long term political order in the country.

A review of the major characteristics of Cohen's tenure as governor of Uganda from 1952 points towards many parallels. For example, his protectorate was territorially identical to the subsequent independent state. Furthermore, he governed it as sole executive, albeit one subject to an external authority (and the directions and constraints which that imposed on him). The authority of the colonial state was, as always, sustained by the continued availability, should it be required, of a monopoly of legitimate force. Meanwhile, such general legitimacy as the regime enjoyed was based, since a period of conquest, on its having guaranteed order and personal security; having provided opportunities for a materially improved standard of living for many; and having shown itself capable of adaptability and political accommodation. In brief, it worked.

346

This was a political regime without party: or, rather, the political parties that were coming into being in the 1950s were still underdeveloped and limited in competence. Cohen's regime – again like Museveni's – saw itself as enlightened, and also as supreme arbiter. Though instinctively authoritarian or paternalistic, his government accepted limits to its capabilities, and valued persuasion and consensus. This was a country, moreover, in which traditional African kingdoms existed both on the ground and in men's loyalties. At the same time, Indians played a prominent role, in an as yet under-developed economy. And social welfare was slowed by the continued high incidence of disease and limited educational provision – though English had for some time been established as a common language, at least for the elite of all races.

This depiction of the late colonial state looks uncannily familiar. Though the World Bank and IMF have replaced British colonial officials in London as the external monitors of Uganda's economic and financial viability, an observer of Yoweri Museveni's rule at the end of the twentieth century is struck by a strong sense of continuity. 'Governing Uganda' appears in many respects to have changed very little.

The path that Cohen followed, in his pursuit of Britain's short and long term goals, has still more contemporary echoes. Almost at once, Cohen dropped his predecessor Hall's proposal for provincial councils, and recognised the district as the basic unit of local government. He thus reinforced a pattern already established before the Second World War. This favouring of the *district* over the province was a corollary of Cohen's main strategy, which was to see Uganda move towards self-government as a *unitary* state. [One might observe again here an element of contradiction, for if a unitary state might have the merit of breaking down provincial, even Ganda, loyalties, how well would such a move towards an elusive national integration be served by, in effect, reinforcing tribal identity at the district level?] It was moreover the pursuit of his unitary goal that led Cohen into his dramatic confrontation with Buganda. Though it abolished the 1900 Agreement, the so-called Kabaka Crisis served only to reinforce, rather than undermine, enduring Ganda separatist aspirations.

Cohen was committed, also, to the elective principle: for elections to the central Legislative Council, and in the districts, and even in the Buganda Lukiiko. It is interesting in the light of more recent developments in Uganda to recall two characteristics of the involvement of political parties in elections at that time. First, the parties, recent in origin, were ill-suited to effective campaigning. They suffered from shallow roots, internal divisions of policy and leadership, and an inability in many districts to raise consciousness above local issues to those of potentially national concern. Secondly, personalities tended to dominate elections, such as the first direct elections to the Legislative Council in November 1958. Although the Uganda National Congress (UNC), the Progressive Party (PP) and the Democratic Party (DP) all fought as parties, Gertzel writes that on that occasion – less than four years before independence – 'in each district, notwithstanding party affiliation, the election was essentially between individuals' (1976: 92).

So it is clear that when the National Resistance Movement (NRM) advocated district-based democracy within a unitary state in the late 1980s it was returning to a strategy initiated and partly implemented by the late colonial regime. The NRM may not have been conscious that this was indeed a second attempt. For example, Jessica Kisakye has lamented the excessive, exploitative centralisation of the second Obote regime. But she has apparently not recognised that the 'fertile ground for implementing [the NRM's] perspective of *local* government, that emphasized people's participation' had been previously ploughed by the British (1996: 36. My italics).

But *déja vu* does not end here. Faith in constitution-making dramatically links the later 1990s and the 1950s. And at this point the parallels give rise to some concern. After all, constitutions are merely documents – except, famously, in the British case –in their early days at any rate. On them may be written the wisest words. But what matters in practice are not pieces of paper but the springs of power. By what constitutional clause, after all, did the British establish themselves as masters of Uganda in the 1890s? In their relative *power* lay sufficient explanation for their success in the early years. And, one might add, explanation for their eventual departure lay in a widely shared recognition of the erosion, or limits, of that power. Subsequently, how long did the cleverly drafted constitution which was bequeathed by the British in 1962 to independent Uganda last? A handful of years. It could not survive the looming contest for ascendancy which the British had been able only to anticipate – and postpone. The 1966 and 1967 'constitutions' which followed were, in turn, mere window-dressing – lunges at respectability in the wake of the ruthless exercise of coercive power. And if the point needs further elaboration, we need only look at the fate of the 1967 constitution itself. Its utter irrelevance during the 1970s and early 1980s – years marked by coups, foreign intervention and civil war – is confirmed by the fact that no regime bothered to bury it.

Only in the wake of NRM success on the ground, and the coming to power of Yoweri Museveni – without any authority deriving from an existing constitution! – did the conditions exist in which fresh consideration could be given to a future set of fundamental laws for Uganda. The point is not that this renewed search for stability, most thoroughly undertaken, was in any sense mistaken. It is rather that, once the context in which any deliberations have taken place and decisions have been taken has *changed* (as it must change), the future of the state, and its constitution, will be determined by where in fact power lies, and by the extent to which people acquiesce in that allocation of power, rather than in any mystical quality in the text of the 1995, or any subsequent, constitution. As Gingyera-Pinycwa cryptically observes, 'to review or re-write a constitution is one thing; to live by it is quite another' (1991: 224). Few if any written constitutions achieve the iconic status of the American.

What is needed, of course, is not so much a constitution as *constitutionalism*: such respect for constitutional practices that the habit of abiding by the rules becomes permanently engrained. With more than a hint of scepticism, Furley and Katalikawe have asked how far the NRM's constitution-making was a genuine attempt to consult widely, or whether the government 'guidelines' were intended 'to steer the discussion along pre-determined lines, *and at a deliberately slow pace*' (1997: 243. My italics). This question however seems not to articulate the main issue. Naturally, the NRM had its own assumptions about governing Uganda, for which it sought wide acceptance. Certainly, too, a well-drawn up document is more likely to survive than one that is poorly drawn up, whatever the process leading to it. But to the authors' implied criticism of the 'slow pace' of that process, one could reply: the slower the pace the better! Time thus taken could prove a means of achieving not only the relatively accessible goal of a paper constitution in the short term, but also that far more elusive and long-term goal of constitutionalism. The former cannot survive without the latter. Time, accompanied by the experience of a new normality, is possibly the most valuable commodity for the current administration in Uganda; but it is one which, as for former British colonial governors in the 1950s, may be in short supply.

At the turn of the new century, governing Uganda gets no easier. The two main perennial concerns of government, order and finance, continue to pose huge challenges. The current administration has at times struggled to sustain normal government over some of its territory; and though Uganda's colonial borders are still retained, to an extent they appear less secure now than when, in a very different global and East African context, the British ruled. As for revenue, President Museveni's main problem closely resembles that of British governors. Crawford Young had embryonic *colonial* states in mind when he wrote that 'the fiscal capture of subjects was much more difficult than [their] military defeat' but his words apply to some extent also to the experience of the NRM since the mid-1980s (1994: 126).

But perhaps the most fascinating comparison between Uganda in the 1950s and in the late 1990s has been the similar attitude of each regime to politics and especially political parties. What has been said of neighbouring Kenya applies also to Uganda: 'Both the colonial and post-colonial state emphasized that politics were dangerous and that political activity had to be curbed ... to preserve civil order' (Haugerud, quoted in Berman 1998: 335). Participatory democracy *based on political parties* has been no more welcome in the latter period than in the former. At both times political parties have been seen as the tool of individual opportunists, and of interest groups based on ethnicity and/or religion, if not class. First Cohen and colonialism, then Museveni and the 'Movement': each has sought to manage political aspiration and pressure, while inhibiting the growth, exercise and significance of parties. This has been an ambitious enterprise. However, little perhaps has changed since 1962, when an enduring transfer of power proved beyond Britain's competence to engineer, and by which time the longer term stability of the country had proved beyond her ability to ensure. Holland's generalisation applies to both politicians and government in Uganda in the 1950s: 'The late colonial world, in all its diverse parts, was much too complex and mobile a situation to be successfully manipulated as part of an overarching deal' (1985: 220). But when is any political context not 'complex and mobile'?

With such considerations in mind, it has been argued that Museveni's Movement can only be transitional. And yet the colonial precedent suggests that a regime in Africa which places itself *above* politics, as it were, can survive – for as long as it is fair and reasonably open and, above all, for as long as it works. And there are examples elsewhere in the world, at the beginning of the twenty-first century, of attempts at all-inclusive, non-ideological 'politics' (where the focus of attention is on skilful handling of the economy, in order to provide effective health, educational, and welfare policies) which may yet represent a viable alternative to more familiar systems. A lesson of the colonial period is that popular acquiescence in such a government may be forthcoming and may be sustained – but only as long as there is relatively disinterested resolution of conflict, and relatively equitable distribution of wealth and contentment.

Perhaps the starkest contrast between the colonial period and the period since 1962 lies in the size, status and significance of the state. The colonial state was in many respects minimalist: not so its successor. We may agree with what Wrigley wrote, a quarter of a century after independence: that post-colonial Uganda had come to need 'a drastic *reduction* in the power, the cost, and the pretension of the state' (1988: 35. My italics). While this has been acknowledged, an adequate reduction may be possible only when/if alternative opportunities, especially for the legitimate acquisition of private wealth, are so plentiful that the state is no longer seen as the great provider of position and personal advancement. After all, at the heart of this study has been the proposition that the previous, colonial, state was characterised for much of its duration by *limited* power, *minimal* cost, and *modest* pretension.

The colonial model may not in fact prove helpful, let alone practicable – nor, specifically, may the model of the colonial governor. Clearly, no system of government can afford to depend on the life and continued tenure in office of any particular individual, however able. Cohen was replaceable and was indeed replaced. It remains to be seen how President Museveni will one day be succeeded, and whether there can be a smooth transition in the absence of institutions as tested and durable as those at the heart of colonial rule.

Who will inherit the presidential motorcade? By way of further comparison between a ruler of today and one of his predecessors, albeit symbolic, we may observe that Cohen was renowned for visiting peasant households by bicycle – as some other British colonial governors had been, such as Hugh Clifford in the Gold Coast (Wrangham 1999: 165). In this study, we have already described some so-called 'absolutism' as little more than 'government by spectacle'. We should also recall that, for British colonial rulers to remain in touch with reality, it could also at times be a case of 'government by bicycle'.

There was always something idiosyncratic about British colonial rule in Africa. And something enviable, too: no African administration in Uganda can ever enjoy the peculiar *benefit* that attached in so many ways to the British being *alien*. And as the Obote and Amin era becomes more distant there will be fewer who accept current arrangements simply because they have marked such an enormous improvement on what went immediately before. As for what went before *that*, 'Governing Uganda' today remains a challenge which British colonial administrators would find remarkably familiar. For anyone seeking to build the foundations of good government in Uganda for decades to come, it would be unwise not to examine closely, and perhaps learn something from, their experience and their record.

References

Acton E. (1997), ed, *Critical Companion to the Russian Revolution*, London, Sydney, Auckland Arnold.

Apter D.E. (1961), *The Political Kingdom in Uganda*, Princeton. Princeton University Press.

Austin D. 'The British Point of No Return?' in Gifford and Louis, *The Transfer of Power in Africa.**

Bayart J-F. (1993), *The State in Africa. The Politics of the Belly*, London, New York. Longman.

Berman B. 'Ethnicity, patronage and the African state: the politics of uncivil nationalism' *African Affairs* vol. 97 number 388, July 1998. Oxford University Press.

Boahen A.A. (1987), *African Perspectives on Colonialism*, Baltimore, London, Accra. John Hopkins University Press, James Currey, Sankofa.

Boyd L.M. (1949), *Civil Disturbances*, 1949, Colonial Office, London. Colonial Office.

Braudel F. (1974), *Capitalism and Material Life 1400-1800*, Glasgow. Fontana/Collins.

Brett E.A. (1973), *Colonialism and Underdevelopment in East Africa: the Politics of Economic Change, 1919-1939*, London. Heinemann.

Brown D. and Brown M.V. (1996), *Looking Back at the Uganda Protectorate. Recollections of District Officers*, Dalkeith (Western Australia). Douglas Brown.

Bukovsky B. (1978), *To Build a Castle*, London.Andre Deutsch.

Burke F.G., 'Local Government and Politics in Uganda', Syracuse, 1964.

Chabal P. and Daloz J-P. (1999), *Africa Works. Disorder as Political Instrument*, Oxford, Bloomington. International African Institute, with James Currey and Indiana University Press.

Cohen A. (1959), *British Policy in Changing Africa*, London. Routledge and Kegan Paul.

Cowen C. and Westcott N. 'British Imperial Economic Policy during the War' in Killingray and Rathbone, *Africa and the Second World War.**

Crowder M. (1984), ed., *The Cambridge History of Africa*, vol. 8, Cambridge. Cambridge University Press.

Crowder M. 'The White Chiefs of Tropical Africa' in Gann and Duignan, *Colonialism in Africa.**

Davidson B. (1992), *The Black Man's Burden. Africa and the Curse of the Nation-State,* London. James Currey.

Doornbos M. 'The Uganda crisis and the national question' in Hansen and Twaddle, *Uganda Now.**

Dundas C. (1941), *Native Administration in Uganda*, The Protectorate Government Printer, Entebbe.

Dundas C. (1955), *African Crossroads*, London. Macmillan.

Ehrlich C. (1953), *The Uganda Company Limited: the First Fifty Years*, Kampala. Uganda Company.

Ehrlich C. (1958), 'The Marketing of Cotton in Uganda, 1900-1950', PhD thesis, London.

Ehrlich C. 'The Uganda Economy, 1903-1945' in Harlow and Chilver, *History of East Africa.**

Elkan W. (1961), *The Economic Development of Uganda*, London. Oxford University Press.

Engholm G.F. (1968),' Immigrant influences upon the development of policy in the Protectorate of Uganda 1900-1952, with particular reference to the role of the Legislative Council', PhD thesis, London.

Evans R.J. (1997), *In Defence of History*, London. Granta Books.

Fallers L.A. (1964), ed., *The King's Men*, Oxford. Oxford University Press.

Fieldhouse D.K. (1986), *Black Africa 1945-1980*, London. Allen and Unwin.

Flint J. 'Planned Decolonisation and its Failure in British Africa' *African Affairs*, vol. 82, no.328, July 1983. Oxford University Press.

Forward A. (1999), *You Have Been Allocated Uganda*, Yeovil, England. Poyntington Publishing Company.

Furley O. and Katalikawe J. 'Constitutional reform in Uganda: the new approach' *African Affairs* vol. 96 no. 383, April 1997. Oxford University Press.

Furse R. (1962), *Acuparius – Recollections of a Recruiting Officer*, London, New York, Toronto. Oxford University Press.

Gallagher J. (1982), *The Decline, Revival, and Fall of the British Empire*, Oxford. Oxford University Press.

Gann L.H. and Duignan P. (1978), eds., *African Proconsuls – European Governors in Africa*, New York. New York Free Press.

Gann L.H. and Duignan P. (1970), eds., *Colonialism in Africa 1870-1960*, volume ii, Cambridge. Cambridge University Press.

Gariyo Z. (1993), *The Media, Constitutionalism and Democracy in Uganda*, Kampala. Centre for Basic Research.

Gartrell B. (1979), 'The Ruling Ideas of a Ruling Elite: British Colonial Officials in Uganda, 1944-1952', PhD thesis, City University, New York.

Gertzel C. 'East and Central Africa' in Crowder, *The Cambridge History of Africa.**

Gertzel C. 'Kingdoms, Districts and the Unitary State: Uganda 1945-1962' in Low and Smith, *History of East Africa.* *

Gifford P. and Louis W.R. ((1982), eds., *The Transfer of Power in Africa: Decolonisation 1940-1960*, New Haven. Yale University Press.

Gingyera-Pinycwa A.G.G. 'Towards constitutional renovation: some political considerations' in Hansen and Twaddle, *Changing Uganda* *.

Goldsworthy D. (1971), *Colonial Issues in British Politics, 1945-1961*, Oxford. The Clarendon Press.

Griffith O. 'Sir Andrew Cohen at Work' in Brown and Brown, *Looking Back at the Uganda Protectorate.* *

Gunther J. (1955), *Inside Africa*, London. Hamish Hamilton.

Hailey Lord (1944), *Native Administration and Political Development in Tropical Africa,* London. Printed for internal distribution by the Colonial Office.

Hall J.A. and Ikenberry G.J. (1989), *The State*, Buckingham. The Open University Press.

Hansen H.B. and Twaddle M. (1998), eds., *Uganda Now. Between Decay and Development*, London, Athens, Nairobi. James Currey; Uganda Bookshop; Ohio University Press, Athens (Ohio); Heinemann.

Hansen H.B. and Twaddle M. (1991), eds., *Changing Uganda*, London, Kampala, Athens, Nairobi. James Currey; Uganda Bookshop; Ohio University Press, Athens (Ohio); Heinemann.

Hargreaves J.D. (1988), *Decolonisation in Africa*, London. Longman.

Harlow V. and Chilver E.M. (1965), eds., *History of East Africa* volume ii, Oxford. The Clarendon Press.

Harwich C. (1961), *Red Dust*, London. Vincent Stuart.

Henderson K.D.D., *The Making of the Modern Sudan*, London, 1953. Faber and Faber.

Hinden R. (1945), ed., *Fabian Colonial Essays*, London. George Allen and Unwin.

Hoffman J. (1995), *Beyond the State,* Oxford. Polity Press.

Holbrook W.P. 'British Propaganda and the Mobilisation of the Gold Coast War Effort, 1939-1945' *Journal of African History* 26, 1985. Cambridge University Press.

Holland R.F. (1985), *European Decolonisation, 1918-1981*, London. Macmillan.

Huxley E. (1941), *East Africa*, London. Williams Collins.

Huxley E. (1948), *The Sorcerer's Apprentice*, London. Chatto and Windus.

Ibingira G.S.K. (1973), *The Forging of an African Nation*, New York. Viking Press.

Ibingira G.S.K. 'The Impact of Ethnic Demands on British Decolonisation in Africa: The Example of Uganda' in Gifford and Louis, *The Transfer of Power in Africa.* *

Ingham K. (1962) *A History of East Africa*, London. Longmans.

Ingrams H. (1960), *Uganda,* London. HMSO.

Jameson J.D. (1970), ed., *Agriculture in Uganda*, Oxford. Oxford University Press.

Jeffries C. (1938), *The Colonial Empire and its Civil Service,* Cambridge. Cambridge University Press.

Jorgensen J.J. (1981), *Uganda: A Modern History*, London. Croom Helm.

Kabaka of Buganda (1967), *Desecration of My Kingdom*, London. Constable.

Kabwegyere T.B. (1974), *The Politics of State Formation*, Nairobi. East African Literature Bureau.

Kakembo R.H. (1946), *An African Soldier Speaks*, London. Edinburgh House Press.

Katorobo J. (1996), 'Action Planning in Decentralisation' in Villadsen and Lubanga, *Democratic Decentralisation in Uganda.* *

Killingray D. 'Military and Labour Recruitment in the Gold Coast during the Second World War' *Journal of African History* 23, 1982. Cambridge University Press.

Killingray D. and Rathbone R. (1986), eds., *Africa and the Second World War*, Basingstoke. Macmillan.

Kingdon D. (1950), *Report of the Commission of Inquiry into the Disturbances in Buganda during April and May 1949*, The Protectorate Government Printer, Entebbe.

Kirk-Greene A.H.M. (1979), ed., *Africa in the Colonial Period: the Transfer of Power – the Colonial Administrator in the Age of Decolonisation*, Oxford. Published by Oxford University's Inter-Faculty Committee for African Studies.

Kisakye J. 'Political Background to Decentralisation' in Villadsen and Lubanga, *Democratic Decentralisation in Uganda.**

Lee J.M. (1967), *Colonial Development and Good Government*, Oxford. The Clarendon Press.

Leubuscher C. (1956), *Bulk Buying from the Colonies*, Oxford. Oxford University Press.

Lillingston K.M.E. (1934), *Glimpses of Uganda*, London. Church Missionary Society.

Lonsdale J. 'State and Peasantry in Colonial Africa' in Samuel, *Peoples' History and Socialist Theory.* *

Lonsdale J. and Berman B. 'Coping with the Contradictions: the Development of the Colonial State in Kenya, 1895-1914' *Journal of African History* 20, 1979. Cambridge University Press.

Low D.A. (1971), *Buganda in Modern History*, London. Weidenfeld and Nicolson.

Low D.A. (1971), *The Mind of Buganda*, London. Heinemann.

Low D.A. 'Uganda: The Establishment of the Protectorate. 1894-1919' in Harlow and Chilver, *History of East Africa*.*

Low D.A. and Lonsdale J. 'Introduction: Towards the New Order 1945-1963' in Low and Smith, *History of East Africa*.*

Low D.A. and Pratt C.R. (1960), *Buganda and British Overrule 1900-1955: Two Studies*, Oxford. Oxford University Press.

Low D.A. and Smith A (1976), eds., *History of East Africa* volume iii, Oxford. The Clarendon Press.

Lugard F.D. (1923), *The Dual Mandate in British Tropical Africa*, London. Blackwood & Sons.

Lury D.A. 'Dayspring Mishandled? The Uganda Economy 1945-1960' in Low and Smith, *History of East Africa*.*

Mair L.P. (1936) *Native Policies in Africa*, London. George Routledge.

Mair L.P. (1962) *Primitive Government*, London. The Scolar Press.

Mamdani M. (1976), *Politics and Class Formation in Uganda*, London. Heinemann.

Mangat J.S. (1969), *A History of the Asians in East Africa, 1886-1945*, Oxford. Clarendon Press.

Marwick A. (1971), *The Explosion of British Society, 1914-1970*, London. Macmillan.

Mazrui A.A. (1993), ed., *UNESCO General History of Africa: Africa since 1935*, volume 8, London, Berkeley. Heinemann.

Mazrui A.A. and Tidy M. (1984), *Nationalism and New States in Africa*, London. Heinemann.

Mcgregor G.P. (1967), *King's College Budo*, Nairobi. Oxford University Press.

Mitchell P.E. (1939), *Native Administration*, The Protectorate Government Printer, Entebbe.

Mitchell P.E. (1954) *African Afterthoughts*, London. Hutchinson.

Morris H.F. 'Sir Philip Mitchell and 'Protected Rule' in Buganda' *Journal of African History*, XIII, 2, 1972. Cambridge University Press.

Morris H.S. (1968) *The Indians in Uganda*, London. Weidenfield & Nicolson.

Morris-Jones W.H. and Fischer G. (1980), eds., *Decolonisation and After: the British and French Experience*, London. Frank Cass.

Moyse-Bartlett H. (1956) *The King's African Rifles*, London. Gale and Polden.

Mudoola D.M. (1993), *Religion, Ethnicity and Politics in Uganda*, Kampala. Fountain.

Mulira E.M.K. (1950), *Troubled Uganda*, London. Fabian Publications.

Musazi I.K. (1966) 'Strikes and Disturbances in Uganda, Their Origins and Results' in *Labour Problems in Uganda*, Kampala. Milton Obote Foundation.

Museveni Y.K. (1997), *Sowing the Mustard Seed. The Struggle for Freedom and Democracy in Uganda*, London, Basingstoke. Macamillan.

Mutibwa P. (1992), *Uganda since Independence. A Story of Unfulfilled Hopes*, London. Hurst and Company.

Nabudere D.W. 'External and internal factors in Uganda's continuing crisis' in Hansen and Twaddle, *Uganda Now*. *

Oberst T. 'Transport Workers, Strikes and the Imperial Response: Africa and the Post World War II Conjuncture' *African Studies Review*, xxxi, 1988. The African Studies Association.

Oliver R. (1952), *The Missionary Factor in East Africa*, London. Longmans.

Omara-Otunnu A. (1987), *Politics and the Military in Uganda 1890-1985*, Basingstoke. Macmillan in association with St Anthony's College, Oxford.

Orde-Browne, Major Sir G.St.J. (1946), *Report on Labour Conditions in East Africa*, London. HMSO.

Orwell G. (1935), *Burmese Days*, London. Penguin.

Orwell G. (1970), *The Collected Essays, Journalism and Letters,* London. Penguin.

Owen E.R.J. and Sutcliffe R.B. (1972), *Studies in the Theory of Imperialism,* London. Longman.

Parker G. (1988), *The Military Revolution. Military Innovation and the Rise of the West, 1500-1800*, Cambridge. Cambridge University Press.

Pearce R.D. (1982), *The Turning Point in Africa*, London. Frank Cass.

Perham M. (1961), *The Colonial Reckoning*, London. Collins.

Perkins E.R. (1972), 'The Buganda Riots of 1945', MA Thesis, SOAS, London.

Popper K. (1957), *The Poverty of Historicism*, London. Routledge and Kegan Paul.

Porter A.N. and Stockwell A.J. (1987), eds., *British Imperial Policy and Decolonisation, 1938-1964*, volume 1, London. Macmillan.

Powseland P.G. 'History of the Migration in Uganda' in Richards, *Economic Development and Tribal Change.* *

Powseland P.G. (1957), *Economic Policy and Labour*, Kampala. East African Institute of Social Research.

Pratt R.C. 'Colonial Governments and the Transfer of Power in East Africa' in Gifford and Louis, *The Transfer of Power in Africa.**

Pratt R.C. 'Administration and Politics in Uganda, 1919-1945' in Harlow and Chilver, *History of East Africa.**

Pratt R.C. 'The Politics of Indirect Rule in Uganda, 1900-1955' in Low and Pratt, *Buganda and British Overrule.**

Prest A.R. (1948), *War Economics of Primary Producing Countries,* Cambridge. Cambridge University Press.

Richards A.I. (1954), ed., *Economic Development and Tribal Change,* Oxford. Oxford University Press.

Roberts A.D. 'East Africa' in Roberts, (1986), ed., *The Cambridge History of Africa, 7,* Cambridge. Cambridge University Press.

Robinson R. 'Non-European Foundations of European Imperialism' in Owen and Sutcliffe, *Studies in the Theory of Imperialism.**

Robinson R. 'Andrew Cohen and the Transfer of Power in Tropical Africa, 1940-1951' in Morris-Jones and Fischer, *Decolonisation and After.**

Robinson R. 'Conclusion' in Kirk-Greene, *Africa in the Colonial Period.**

Robinson R. and Gallagher J. (1961), *Africa and the Victorians,* London. Macmillan.

Rodney W. (1972), *How Europe Underdeveloped Africa,* London. Bogle-L'ouverture Publications.

Samuel R. (1981), ed., *Peoples' History and Socialist Theory,* London. Routledge and Kegan Paul.

Schleh E.P.A. 'The Postwar careers of ex-Servicemen in Ghana and Uganda' *Journal of Modern African Studies* 6, 2, 1968. Cambridge University Press.

Shuckburgh J. (1948), *Colonial Civil History of the War,* London. Unpublished copy in the Institute of Commonwealth Studies Library, University of London.

Simmons R.J. (c.1942), *A Colonial Veterinary Department in Peace and War,* Rhodes House, Oxford. Unpublished typescript, Rhodes House Library, Oxford.

Sithole N. (1968), *African Nationalism,* London. Oxford University Press.

Southall A.W. and Gutkind P.C.W. (1957), *Townsmen in the Making,* Kampala. East African Institute and Social Research.

Southall A.W. 'The recent political economy of Uganda' in Hansen and Twaddle, *Uganda Now.**

Southam H.J. (1961), *Blind Safari,* London. Robert Hale.

Stone R.E. 'The District Commissioner as the Man in the Middle: East Africa' in Kirk-Greene, *Africa in the Colonial Period.**

Stone N. (1975), *The Eastern Front, 1914-1917*, London. Hodder and Stoughton.

Taylor A.J.P. (1965), *English History 1914-1945*, Oxford. Oxford University Press.

Temple-Perkins E.A. (1946), *Such is the Burden*, Rhodes House, Oxford. Unpublished draft, Rhodes House Library, Oxford.

Thomas H.B. and Scott R. (1935), *Uganda*, Oxford. Oxford University Press.

Tolstoy L.N. (1957), *War and Peace*, London. Penguin.

Tosh J. 'Lango Agriculture During the Early Colonial Period' *Journal of African History* 19, 1978. Cambridge University Press.

Treasure G. (1966), *Seventeenth Century France*, London. John Murray.

Twaddle M. 'The struggle for political sovereignty in Eastern Africa, 1945 to independence' in Mazrui, *UNESCO General History of Africa*, vol. 8.*

Twaddle M. (1975), ed, *Expulsion of a Minority: Essays on Ugandan Asians*, London. Athlone Press, University of London.

Twining E.F. (1939), *Broadcasting Investigations*, The Protectorate Government Printer, Entebbe.

Villadsen S. and Lubanga F. (1996), *Democratic Decentralisation in Uganda*, Kampala. Fountain.

Wallis H.R. (1920), *The Handbook of Uganda*, London. The Crown Agents for the Colonies.

Welbourn F.B. (1961), *East African Rebels*, London. SCM Press.

West H.W. (1972), *Land Policy in Buganda*, Cambridge. Cambridge University Press.

West H.W. (1964), *The Mailo System in Buganda*, The Protectorate Government Printer, Entebbe.

Westcott N. 'The Impact of the Second World War on Tanganyika,1939-1949' in Killingray and Rathbone, *Africa and the Second World War*.

Whitehead E.F. 'A Short History of Uganda Military Units formed during the Second World War'. *Uganda Journal*, vol. 14, no. 1, 1950, Kampala.The Uganda Society.

Whitley N.H.P. (1945), *Report of the Commission of Inquiry into the Disturbances which occurred in Uganda during January 1945*. The Protectorate Government Printer, Entebbe.

Williams E.N. (1999), T*he Ancien Regime in Europe*, London. Pimlico.

Worthington E.B. ((1946) *A Development Plan for Uganda*, Entebbe. The Uganda Protectorate Press.

Wrangham E.M. (1999), 'The Gold Coast and the First World War: The Colonial Economy and Clifford's Administration', PhD thesis, SOAS, London.

Wrigley C.C. (1959), *Crops and Wealth in Uganda*, Kampala. East African Institute of Social Research.

Wrigley C.C. 'Four steps towards disaster' in Hansen and Twaddle, *Uganda Now**

Young C. (1994), *The African Colonial State in Comparative Perspective*, New Haven, London. Yale University Press.

Van Zwanenbury R.M.A. and King A. (1975), *An Economic History of Kenya and Uganda, 1800-1970*, London. Macmillan.

* = Publisher given alongside main source.

PRIMARY SOURCES FOR END-NOTES

At the Public Record Office, Kew.
Colonial Office Records: Series CO 536, 537, Original Correspondence (Uganda), also including Executive Council Minutes; Series CO 684, Acts/Ordinances; Series CO 822, Original Correspondence (East Africa); Series CO 854, Circular Despatches; Series CO 962, East Africa/ Conference of Governors.
War Office Records: Series WO 276, East Africa Command Papers.

Uganda Protectorate Government publications
Annual Report of the Public Relations and Social Welfare Department, 1947-1948
Annual Trade Reports (of Kenya and Uganda).
Annual Report, 1938.
Annual Reports, 1939-1946.
Agricultural Department Annual Report, 1938.
Blue Books, 1938, 1945.
Civil Reabsorption Progress Reports, 1947, 1948.
Labour Reports, 1941, 1942, 1944, 1945, 1964.
Legislative Council Proceedings, 1939-1945.
Official Gazette, 1939-1945.
Organisation of the South-Western Labour Migration Routes, 1943.
Review of Nutrition in Uganda, 1945.
Report on the Labour Situation, 1938.
The War Effort of Uganda, 1 to 7, 1939-1944: Sessional Papers of the Uganda Legislative Council.

Rhodes House Oxford
Fabian Colonial Bureau, Boxes 33,77,111,125,126,127.
Manuscript Collections.
Uganda Civil Defence Board, Minutes.
Uganda Company, Minutes.

The Royal Commonwealth Society (now housed by the University of Cambridge Library)
Entebbe Club, Minutes.

The Institute of Commonwealth Studies
Sir W.K.Hancock, Buganda Papers.

The British Library (Colindale)
The East African Standard.
Uganda Herald, 1939-1951.

Uganda National Archive, Entebbe
Uganda Protectorate Secretariat Minute Papers.
Chief Secretary's Office Papers.
Correspondence.
Uganda Supply Board Minutes.
African Manpower Committee Minutes.

Index